LARAMIE

anding

to FORT COLLINS

1. Old Payne ranch, once the Cross ranch.
2. N. K. Boswell's ranch on the Big Laramie.
3. Payne and Dwinell summer cattle range: West Beaver Creek, Six Mile Basin, etc.
4. Original Moore and Blevins Home ranch.
5. Mendenhall ranch.
6. Dwinell's ranch.
7. Sudduth ranch and Al Marr's place.
8. Case ranch on Alkali Flats.
9. Jack Hunter ranch.
10. The "Neck of the Park" and site of Pinkhamton.
11. Site of Old Camp Teller or Teller City.

WHERE THE ROCKIES RIDE HERD

STEPHEN PAYNE

WHERE
THE ROCKIES
RIDE HERD

SAGE BOOKS, *Denver*

Dedicated to My Wife

and to The North Park Pioneers Association

With a deep sense of gratitude
for help and informaion,
freely given,
the author wishes to thank
Lucretia Payne
Wayne Overholser
Arthur W. Payne
Mamie Leek Hill
Victor Hanson
Archie A. Hunter
Gene M. Gressley
Mary L. Cairns
Agnes Wright Spring and
The State Historical Museum

FOREWORD

The main gateway, or "jumping off place" for North Park, Colorado, in the late seventies, the eighties and the nineties, was Laramie, Wyoming, on the Union Pacific railroad. Today this is still true, so come now and take the paved highway from Laramie to Walden and see this Park for yourself.

Your automobile speeds southwest across the Laramie Plains, along the same route where once rolled treasure seekers' covered wagons and horse-drawn stages, where long freight outfits crawled, and beef herds, market-bound from North Park to the stockyards in Laramie, trampled down the sod.

The valley of the Big Laramie River lies at your left, Jelm Mountain and Sheep Mountain loom ahead, and farther north Wyoming's famous Snowy Range cuts the skyline. Along the base of Sheep Mountain the road swings, first left, then sharply right into Wood's Creek Canyon at old Wood's Landing, once the busiest road ranch of this region.

The highway takes you through lodgepole pines up and over Medicine Bow Range. You cross the Wyoming-Colorado state line and enter the Neck Of the Park. The buildings at John Price's Road Ranch, later Clark's, are gone now; nothing remains except a cow pasture. Nor will you see the site of Pinkhamton Post Office, named for our first settler, Pinkham, who also stamped his name on Pinkham Mountain and Pinkham Creek.

The road now follows Pinkham Creek through a canyon, mis-named King's Canyon, with Pinkham Mountain and Sentinel Peak at your left. It passes the King Ranch, and divides. Its right fork leads westward, on across the North Platte River, and then points northward back into Wyoming. That way lies the famous Big Creek Ranch; Encampment also, once a roaring mining town now a quiet ghost of its early days; Saratoga, where hot springs bubble and warm the waters of the Platte; and finally, either Walcott or Rawlins

7

on the Union Pacific Railroad. The left fork of the road crosses Pinkham Creek, and points toward Cowdrey and Walden.

From the hill above this creek's valley, you now get a comprehensive, breath-taking view of North Park. The vast meadow to the right is the old Jack Hunter ranch, stretching along the wide valley where Pinkham Creek meets the Platte. Then, Independence Mountain, massive and rugged, fills the entire northwest corner of the Park, and far away behind it, though not in sight, is the ghost town of Pearl and beautiful Big Creek Lake, headwaters of Big Creek.

Still looking to the right, your eyes travel southward along the jagged western skyline. These peaks are not fangtoothed, nor are they among the highest in Colorado, but, stretching on for miles and miles, a magnificent mountain chain is etched against a clear blue sky.

This range is part of the Continental Divide. Against its base stands a mighty hogback. Between the hogback and the mountains, lies a wide, deep valley wherein once flourished many ranches. Gradually, however, these were all absorbed by the Big Horn outfit, their identities lost under one name—the Boettcher Ranch.

Farther south Delaney Bute's rugged shoulders and bleak crest greet your eyes, and clearly visible, fifty or sixty miles away, the Rabbit Ears Peaks mark the extreme southwest corner of North Park. From these was named Rabbit Ears Pass, on U. S. Highway 40 to Steamboat Springs and the Yampa Valley.

Extending from west to east, big, forested mountains which are a spur of the Continental Divide block off the south end of North Park and definitely separate it from Middle Park. Yet, today two paved highways lead across this barrier.

Hidden in the shadows of spike-toothed peaks which mark the southeast corner lies all that is left of old Teller City. Slightly farther north are Clark's Peak, Cameron Peak and the Cameron Pass road, connecting Walden and Fort Collins. Here also are the sources of both the Michigan and Canadian Rivers. Then, stretching on northward, the lower and much less rugged Medicine Bow Range hems in the eastern side and northern end of the Park.

Bulwarked against it in two different spots are sand hills; windblown, ever restless sand dunes. Behind the upper set of dunes is Ute Pass, a trail once used by Indians, and later by the whites as a wagon road, but today serving only as a Forest Reserve trail.

Here, surrounded by these mountains, is a vast expanse of sage-brush hills, flats and fertile valleys, each valley watered by its own particular stream. Lone mountains, buttes and hogbacks hunker close to the main ranges; aspen groves dot the hills and small lakes hide among them. This is the floor of the Park, its altitude eight thousand feet and upward.

But it is not the flats and hills, nor the valleys, streams and lakes that grip and thrill and hold your attention. It is the magic spell of these mountains where sunlight and clouds create ever changing lights and shadows. Here, deep in the Rockies, encircling mountains ride herd on the snow-fed fountains of the North Platte River; watchfully and silently ride herd on the Park itself.

TABLE OF CONTENTS

TABLE OF ILLUSTRATIONS

11

EARLY MEMORIES

"His character was big and rugged like the mountains among which he made his home."

This tribute to William Marr, boss of the Big Horn Land and Cattle Company of North Park, Colorado, was written, after his death, by someone I do not know. But these same pertinent words can be truthfully said of other pioneers who also made their homes in the same mountain-ringed land of wood, water and grass deep in the heart of the Rockies.

One of these was my father, Thomas John Payne, who came to North Park in the spring of 1884 and began his long and slow and difficult climb from tenderfoot homesteader to successful cowman. In 1885 he sent for the girl he had left in England and she too entered a world new, strange, primitive and harsh on women.

My brother Arthur was born in 1886 and I came along two years later. In the years that followed, although our mother wanted only boys, the stork was most uncoöperative and delivered not boys, but four girls.

Of the early years of our parents' struggle, I have no personal recollection until I was at least four or five years of age. I do recall, however, meeting "old man" Pinkham, the first white man to settle permanently in the Park.

Dad told us boys that Pinkham was a French-Canadian hunter and trapper, and that he'd go hunting alone with nothing more than his rifle and knife. He'd live on fresh meat, and get his rest at night by building two small fires and sleeping between them. (I at once resolved I'd try that at the first opportunity.) But one cold night Pinkham didn't wake up until his coat had burned off his back; he then almost froze to death while getting home.

As soon as my brother was able to stick on a very gentle horse and guide it, he began to ride to Pinkhamton for the mail. He'd often take me along, sitting behind his saddle, hanging tightly to the saddle strings. At this combination post office, stage station and road ranch, an important place in those days, we met Ralph Coyte and Mrs. Coyte and their son, Joe, who was about my age. But before I really got acquainted with Joe, his family moved away. I did not meet him again for many years.

When the Coytes had moved elsewhere, Jap Munroe and his family took over, and then Arthur and I chummed with the Munroe boys, Jay and Brush. Here at Pinkhamton stood Pinkham's famous block house, said to be the first house built in North Park, and certainly the only one of its type in our small world. The second story projected out over the lower story so it might be used as a fort in case of an Indian attack.

We had never heard of any such attack, but with Jay and Brush Munroe we played settlers and Injuns in this house. We also climbed Pinkham Mountain, an adventure I've never forgotten because two docile, stolid and stubborn burros put one over on us kids.

The four of us saddled and bridled these "Rocky Mountain Canaries" and, two boys on each burro, rode them to the top of Pinkham Mountain. So far all was fine and dandy; a great lark. But when we started back down the mountain, those canny little burros ducked their heads, and the saddles slid right off over their big ears, dumping four kids and two saddles in the rocks and sage.

We liked the Munroes, particularly Mrs. Munroe; but, like the Coytes, they also left Pinkhamton, moving farther up into the Park, and we lost contact with Jay and Brush. Of other neighbors, we knew the Scott "boys" best of all.

For some unknown reason, North Parkers often spoke of grown men as "boys," particularly if they happened to be brothers. For example, there were the Scott boys, the Barnes boys, the Cross boys.

Art and I called George Scott "Mr. Scott" and Charlie, who was younger, "Mr. Charlie." Of the neighborhood women, Mrs. John Coe was the one we just sort of always knew, for "Mother Coe" was the neighborhood midwife.

A neighborhood picnic "up in the Sand Hills" marked my first real acquaintance with Mrs. Montie Blevins, the girl who had been Harriet Mendenhall. It marked too the beginning of my acquaintance with Fanny Barnes, who later became Mrs. Augustus Dwinell. Also at this memorable picnic, my brother Arthur and I got acquainted with the neighborhood kids—especially Montie and Park Blevins—and had a swell time playing with them in the sand.

I also remember Ora Haley's foreman, Ben Lance, possibly because he seemed a wonderfully pleasant man and took me up on his knee while he sat one time by our fireplace, talking with Dad. The Haley beef herd, enroute to the railroad at Laramie from Bear River, as the Yampa was called in those days, had crossed the Continental Divide by way of Rabbit Ears Pass and was in Dad's big field that night.

Earlier Arthur and I had shyly visited with the cowboys, but mostly with the chuck wagon cook, Thornt Biggs, a mulatto, who greeted us with a friendly smile and made us welcome with piping-hot Duch-oven biscuits. This, I believe, was our first chuckwagon meal.

There came a day in late autumn when a party of wealthy English sportsmen—big game hunters—stopped for the night with Dad as they were returning to Laramie from a successful hunting expedition, and we met Cook Rhea, their guide.

At this time we had close neighbors who were great hunters: Pinkham, of course, and the Coes, John, Bob and Joe, each of whom lived on a homestead down the creek from our home.

But Cook Rhea! Ah, he was the mightiest hunter of them all! These Englishmen had wanted bear skins and other trophies. Cook had taken them up into the mountains on the west side of the Park, and how well I remember the elk and Big Horn sheep heads which these men were taking home. There were also bear skins which they hung on our yard fence to air. Black and cinnamon and grizzly; one hide, with wide skull and huge paws still attached, was so large it rubbed the ground on either side of the fence.

"A whopper," we boys thought it. "Big as a cow," we added, completely awed.

Wild and far-fetched stories of the ferocity of bears were the order of that day, but we hadn't yet learned these talks should be taken with large handfuls of salt.

The smell of the bear skins frightened our horses half out of their senses, and we got a big laugh out of the reaction of all our cats. They fuzzed up their backs and tails and then simply vanished, not to show up again until the hunting party had loaded up and was long gone.

Of Dad's milk herd—he always had milk cows—my childhood memory holds a picture of one ugly, high-hip-boned brindle cow with two broken horns. I could not have been over four years old, but I was Dad's little helper as he went out on foot one evening to bring in the milk herd. Feeling important, I was trailing along behind the cows when this brute—Dad had named her XOV for the big brand which ran all across her left side—suddenly whirled around, threw down her head and rushed at me. Terrified, I froze and screamed. But Dad moved. I never saw anyone move so fast. In a twinkling he was up against XOV's shoulder whipping his cap into her eyes, and he turned her back into the herd.

"It's all right now, son," he said. "XOV thought you were either a dog or a coyote."

This explanation called for further enlightenment. I learned that mother cows do not distinguish between friendly dog and a predatory coyote and that instinctively they go all out to protect their offspring.

The first teacher of whom I have any recollection was Miss Hussey, who came to board with the Paynes before my brother began to go to school. But we boys understood that schoolteachers were very special people. Invariably, they came from the big world outside.

First of all, they were perfect ladies, which meant their standards and deportment and habits and—oh, a lot of things—were—well, all they should be. Next, they were really educated. They knew everything, and, because they had culture also, they were models for young girls to imitate. Lastly, teachers were wonderfully well paid.

Teachers actually received fifty dollars a month and worked only five days each week. Fifty dollars a month! Out of this generous salary, they could well afford to pay for room and board, and the family who got to keep the teacher was lucky indeed.

Mother seemed delighted to have Miss Hussey, though it meant some weird doubling up in our cramped home in order to house her properly. I remember she had a small and fussy appetite and was

16

continually asking for hot water. What she did with all that hot water was, to a small boy, a deep mystery.

Dad had made no provision for transporting her the three and one-fourth miles to the schoolhouse. However, she said she was an expert horsewoman. She would ride to school—side saddle of course. The Scott boys supplied the side saddle, and Dad saddled a sorrel named Charlie for her mount. He helped Miss Hussey to get seated, with long skirt covering her pretty ankles all properly, of course, and out she started.

Charlie snorted and shied, Miss Hussey flopped off his back and landed in a sitting position. Dad caught the horse. Once again Miss Hussey began her ride, and again Charlie shied. Luckily, she remained physically unharmed by this flop-from-saddle experience.

Once more Miss Hussey mounted, and this time she rode half a mile before Charlie repeated his act.

Dad had by then gone to work. Arthur and I were watching from the barn roof as Charlie dumped Miss Hussey in the dusty road and then ran away.

The upshot of the matter was that we lost Miss Hussey as our boarder. Neither Arthur nor I was unhappy about that. A school marm who couldn't ride for sour apples wasn't worth bothering about.

Another incident vividly remembered occurred one summer day when Mother and we children were alone. Art and I were stalling on our main job, which was sawing wood, when all at once we boys saw a horseman dashing across Dad's east field (a field we called the Fisher Field) toward our home. Ahead of him came what looked to be a dog, running like the wind.

Mother also was watching this race, and soon all of us saw that the rider was trying to rope this black dog or whatever it was. He made a cast, and missed his quarry by a hair's breadth. Then, as the pursued animal drew near our east line division fence, it suddenly plunged into a large pool of water which was backed up by a small dam in a big slough.

To our utter amazement, the horseman pulled up, leaped from his saddle, jerked a loose pole off the fence and brought it down on the animal's head with a hard whack!

"Who is he, and what's he trying to do?" we asked Mother tensely.

Mother didn't answer. But moments later the rider, leading his panting, sweat-streaked horse, walked to the house, and at last we recognized the tall, fine looking man as Montie Blevins!

He smiled and tipped his hat and greeted, " 'Morning, Mrs. Payne. Hello, boys. I ran across a cub bear up in the sand hills, got it headed this way and took after it, trying to rope it."

"A bear!" Art whistpered to me. "Jiminy! if Mr. Blevins couldn't rope it, that shows how 'most impossible it is to rope a bear."

Mr. Blevins resumed, "It took to the water because it was over-heated, and I managed to kill it. Now, if I may, I'd like to borrow a butcher knife, saw and axe so I can skin it and dress out the carcass."

Mother got the implements for Mr. Blevins, and Arthur and I went along to help him skin the bear, feeling oh, so important and proud. Now at last we were really getting acquainted with Montie and Park Blevins' father.

For several days following this incident the Payne family had bear meat to eat, and for a short time I had a wonderful new play thing—a bear's paw. Trouble was, it got to smelling so strong even a small boy couldn't keep it in his pocket!

My most painful and humiliating experience was the first licking Dad gave me. I had it coming, and he unmercifully blistered my small backside with a broken hair brush and a ruthless hand. Probably, in the long run, this was the best thing that could have happened to me.

Of my very early schooling I strangely hold no memory at all, although I remember vividly my first trip to Laramie, Wyoming. Dad made this trip twice each year, with wagon and team, to bring home groceries and other supplies. The summer of 1895 he gave his two small sons a real treat by taking them with him.

For the very first time Art and I would be getting "outside." Anywhere beyond the boundaries of North Park was spoken of as "outside." "Bill has gone outside." "Jake just got back from outside." However, if a person's destination was Fort Collins, the county seat of our county which was at this early day Larimer County, he was "going down the valley" or "going to the valley."

Most boys whom we knew had either come from "ouside" or had been "outside" at least once, so they were way ahead of us Payne kids. But now at last we could talk about being "ouside."

GOING TO LARAMIE

The first night out from home, we camped beside Pioneer Lake on the Laramie Plains. Art and I watered the tired team at the lake, tied them to wagon wheels and pulled hay out of the wagon box to feed them, while Dad was making a campfire.

By noon tomorrow we would reach Laramie, load the wagon and start back home. Even so, the return trip with a heavy load would require two more full days, making four days in all that we'd be gone from home.

Arthur realized better than I that our father was awfully hard up and that was why we were camping instead of putting up over night at one of the road ranches. People who owned road ranches made a business of accommodating "overnight stoppers," charging money for meals and feed for the horses. Although there were beds, too, it was customary for cowboys, freighters, ranchers and others to carry their own bedrolls.

Dad had our bedroll in the wagon. He also had a box of butter and ten dozen eggs, each egg carefully wrapped in a piece of newspaper torn from either the *Fort Collins Express* or the *Laramie Boomerang*—made famous by Bill Nye. He also had four dry cowhides. The eggs, butter and hides would help to pay his food bill at A. S. Peabody's Grocery Store.

I got a pail of water from the lake. Then Dad made tea for himself while Art opened the grub box and set out the food. It was already cooked, and especially good because Mother had prepared all of it: loaves of fresh bread, homemade butter, hard-boiled eggs, a big chunk of boiled venison, a jar of stewed dried apples which were the standby of those days, and a jar of milk for us kids. To my amazement, a lump of butter rode on top of this milk. This Dad explained by saying the jolting of the wagon had churned the cream in the milk, and then he gave us a dissertation on how the art of making butter had been discovered in this same manner.

Our dad was a solid hunk of man with a heavy black beard which he never shaved. He said he had shaved while he was teaching school in England, but after he came to America in 1883 he threw away his razor and vowed never to use one again. Many years later, when this same Thomas John Payne went courting his second wife, she told him he must shave or she'd not marry him. It seems he promised he would. But when he went back to Michigan for the wedding, he appeared with whiskers as usual, very closely clipped, but untouched by any razor. The bride-to-be gave up then and afterwards even joked about it.

Often to us boys, when at home on the ranch, Dad seemed abrupt and blunt and quite unsympathetic. But now, camping out with us, he was in a genial mood and suddenly, to our great surprise, burst out with a song which must have been popular in the gold rush days:

"Oh, the gold, it lies on top of the land
        'Way out in Id-a-ho,
We're coming, Idaho! Wait, Idaho!
Our four horse team will soon be seen,
'Way out in Idaho!"

Then becoming talkative, as if really wanting to get close to his sons, he said, "I'm glad I came to America. There's a real future to this ranch and cattle business, and you boys are going to have a wonderful opportunity to get ahead which you never would have had back home."

He still spoke of England as "back home," or as "the old country." That was the way it was with all the grown-ups in North Park. Everybody had come from somewhere else and spoke of this somewhere else as "back home," "back East," "back in the states," and "the old country."

At my age I wasn't interested in this "wonderful opportunity." I was wondering, hopefully, if at last in Laramie I could get a pair of overalls so I could be like other kids at school. Art now had overalls, but I was still obliged to wear knee pants and black stockings, and I hated them! I longed for boots, for a real hat, too. But I'd settle for overalls.

"Mark this, you fellows," Dad resumed, "you'll have the advantage over me because I was one of the greenest tenderfeet ever to come West."

I had never thought of Dad's ever being a tenderfoot. Only last winter he'd had trouble with his teeth and had ridden on horseback to Laramie in one day. That night he had seven teeth pulled, and the next day he rode home. After this, I heard neighbors say, "That Jack Payne's one tough, rugged Britisher."

That he was also a "bull-headed Britisher" went without saying. But actually all that Arthur and I knew of his past was that Grandfather Payne had been a blacksmith—all to the good in my opinion, for blacksmiths rated high in my book—and that Dad was one of a big family, four boys and three girls. His oldest brother was a clergyman in faraway England. All the others had emigrated to the United States. Like Dad, my Uncles Dick and Will and my Aunt Mattie had come West, and both Uncle Dick and Uncle Will had proved up on homesteads in North Park.

Then Uncle Dick and Aunt Mattie had gone back East and settled down with my other two aunts in Springfield, Massachusetts. But Uncle Will, youngest of them all, contracted pneumonia and died here in the West.

We knew, Arthur and I, that Dad was a college graduate who had taught school for a short time and that he had also worked as assistant to an English veterinarian, an experience which quickened his interest in livestock.

Now as we sat around the campfire he unfolded more of his life, telling us, "I came to Colorado in 1883 and put in my first winter on a ranch near Colorado Springs. But I didn't like it. The wind blew sand through cracks in the old frame house where I stayed, filling it with dirt every day. I nearly froze to death, too. So when some other young Englishmen, who were going to North Park, gave me the chance to go with them, I took it.

"They had wagons and teams. I had nothing except eighteen yearling heifers I'd bought during the winter. One of the men shared a bed with me and I ate at his wagon and drove those yearlings on foot all the way to North Park.

"That was in May of 1884, the spring of the 'hard winter,'; the winter all the old timers speak of as a stemwinder, the daddy of all hard winters."

"You drove those cattle on foot?" Art asked, full of amazement. "Does that mean you walked all that long way yourself?"

"Yes," Dad laughed. "Of course we didn't travel far any one day. From Fort Collins we followed a stage route past historic Virginia Dale to Tie Siding in Wyoming. There one fork runs on north to Laramie, the other cuts west across the plains to Boswell's Ranch on the Big Laramie. We took this road because it was the shortest. After leaving Boswell's, there was lots of snow across the top of Medicine Bow Range and down into the neck of the Park.

"The 'Neck of the Park' was at that time one continuous mud hole. There were places where the men had to fasten a stout pole so it stuck out on the upper side of a wagon, and ride that pole to prevent the wagon from tipping over. Carcasses of dead cattle all along the trail, too.

"Well, I didn't get very far into the Park, though the other fellows went on. Most of them got far better ranches than I did. I stopped with Pappy Rice on Big Government Creek. He owned forty acres of land which I managed to buy. Then I took up a homestead lower down the creek. All the Pappy Rice buildings burned down, a total loss, and I still don't know how the fire started. However, I had built a house on my homestead and was able to send for your mother to come from England to join me."

Of the background of our mother, Olive Stephens, Arthur and I knew even less than we knew of Dad's — only that she, too, had had the benefit of a college education and, like Dad, had taught school before leaving England.

As a boy it never entered my thoughts that she had done anything remarkable in coming to a remote spot of the frontier West to face a raw, new land and primitive kind of life about which she knew nothing — and it was a life of real hardship for the women of that day.

Art said, "Odd that you didn't get gold fever when most men in the Park are still goofy about . . ."

Dad's eyes flashed. "Yes, I suppose it is odd. I never caught that fever. You boys may not know that out of the thousands who surged West to strike it rich very few succeeded."

He pushed out his lower jaw. "The Teller City boom in our own

North Park is one good example of chasing a bubble that burst. Yet it did more toward settling the Park than any other one thing."

"How?" my brother asked, putting dead grass on the fire to make a smudge against the flies, mosquitoes and gnats which were plaguing us. "We've heard that trappers — some folks call them 'mountain men' — were the first white people to find North Park."

"Yes," Dad said. "Those fellows were after beaver pelts, and they also wanted to find the headwaters of the North Platte River. Which they did, of course. Those old trappers called any remote spot hidden away back in the mountains 'a hole.' To them our North Park was merely 'a hole.'

"Later on," Dad continued, "came the prospectors, almost as self-reliant, self-sufficient, and hardy and tough as the trappers. They, too, could live on a straight meat diet; and no mountain or gulch or canyon was too inaccessible for them to explore and to prospect. But it wasn't until 1879 that someone discovered silver on Jack Creek in the far southeast corner of North Park.

"Mountains made this spot inaccessible for a wagon to get in from the east, or from the south, which is the Grand Lake and Middle Park side of the Continental Divide. But nothing can stop treasure seekers. These men blazed out a road from Boswell's ranch on the Big Laramie River, across Medicine Bow Range, into the neck of the Park from the north, and then all the way across the Park to Teller City, the location of this new strike."

"Sure, we know that," Art said loftily. "That was the old Teller Road."

"Part of it was a horrible road," my father took up. "But people came in droves. In 1880, a stage line was established between Teller City and Laramie, with mail service and a post office at Teller. Other post offices followed, our Pinkhamton being one of the first.

"Then the boom burst, Teller City was abandoned, and a lot of those rainbow chasers, some with families, found themselves broke, except for personal possessions: wagons, teams, household goods and so on. They are the men who really settled North Park. They took up homesteads and built their log cabins in all of the best valleys."

Dad smiled and chuckled. "Almost every early settler built as close to running water as possible. One fellow over on the Michigan even put his house on the bank of the river so he could fish out of his living room window without moving from his chair.

"They call America the melting pot, and we have one right in

23

North Park: Scots, Welshmen, Swedes, French-Canadians, Switzers, English, Irish, rock-ribbed Yankees, Missourians, men from the Midwest and from the deep South, Civil War veterans from both sides, and almost all of these are wonderful people."

" 'Specially the English," said Art slyly.

Dad ignored him, going on, "Men who take up land and stay with it, men who raise cattle and crops are going to be well fixed someday."

This I understood was something he wanted to impress on his sons, and Art nodded gravely.

Art was what the neighbors called "a little old man," and though he did cut loose at school like any normal kid, the Payne ranch and its cattle and horses were his chief interests in life. Already he came near to doing a man's work on the ranch.

Dad was still wound up. "Of course, even before the Teller boom and bust, there were both horse outfits and cow outfits in the Park; some settlers, too, as well as old man Pinkham. The horse men could not make a go of it. No market for their horses, and that spring of '84 the cowmen learned their lesson; learned that they must put up hay, provide winter feed for their cattle. The loss was sickening. Yet thousands of cattle were saved by trailing them out of the Park to these Laramie plains. Here the wind whipped the snow off the ground, and there was in those days planty of open range and grass to spare."

He came to his feet and shook his head. "Putting up hay is the hardest job we have. A man can cut and haul in and stack so little of it in a summer, and he needs so much to get through an ordinary winter. A hard winter is our worst enemy.

"Teller City must have been a real snow hole. Dave Hendrickson, an old Teller man — everybody who once lived in Teller is now called 'an old Teller man' — says that one storm — just one storm — buried the town under six feet of snow and caved in the roofs on more than half of the log cabins." Abruptly changing the subject, he added, "Time for bed, lads."

We fed the team more hay, but left some in the bottom of the wagon box for a soft mattress. Dad had an idea of which neither Art nor I approved. He'd sleep with his head at the front of the box and we'd sleep at his feet. Well, his feet were no worse than the smell of the buffalo robe — an important part of the bedding. (In those days everybody had buffalo robes, and some men even had buffalo skin overcoats.) However, the rich smell of this robe was better than that of the tarpaulin. The latter was Dad's wagon sheet and would cover the load on the return trip, but on the ranch he used it for many purposes, like wrapping it around fresh meat to protect the meat from flies, and it had been stained by dried fat and blood.

The wagon box was snug and warm, and for the first time at night I could look straight up at the stars. Nothing between me and them but space, and I liked it. All went well until, while sound asleep, I bit Dad's big toe, got kicked in the nose and roundly scolded.

When we were rolling again the next morning, Art took notice of many fenced ranches on the plains at our left, each with its cluster of log buildings, and he asked Dad, "Is this country as good for ranching and raising cattle as North Park?"

"No!" Dad snorted. "The Park is so much better that all of us North Parkers thought the Swedes and Dutchmen and Germans who settled on these plains were crazy, they were so far from both wood and water. But they dug wells, and made ditches to bring irrigation water from the river, and do you know what they do for timber?

"They get up at two o'clock in the morning, take teams and wagons and lunches and drive to Wood's Landing. Then up into the forests on the mountains where they chop down fence timber, house logs, or firewood, load up and haul it home, all in one long day. No wonder Swedes win out where others give up. You can't beat men like that, and they are making good."

A moment later he added, "Swedes and Norwegians are the best axemen in the world. Most of these ranchers have well-built log houses, far better than any we have as yet in the Park."

I was more interested in watching the prairie dogs and gophers and jack rabbits, the same kind we had at home. Blackbirds, magpies, hawks and a few meadow larks were the same, too. A small band of antelope was too commonplace to elicit comment.

Soon after sunup, clouds of buffalo gnats appeared and began to bite us and the team.

We'd been told that these tiny gnats drove the buffaloes crazy. In our meadow were many hollows from four to six or seven feet in diameter cupped out in soft clay soil, which Dad said were buffalo wallows. "The buffaloes lay down and rolled in this mud, thus getting all over them a thick coat of it, which the gnats couldn't bite through."

Many years later I told a tenderfoot, who asked me what those hollows were, that they were buffalo wallows. Thereupon he jeered, "Yeah? How green do you think I am?"

I'd never seen a live buffalo. But wallows, bones and skulls, particularly skulls bleached white except for the outer shells of their horns, attested that hundreds of them had at one time grazed in North Park. The horns were so well preserved that people would select good ones and polish them into beautiful ebony-black ornaments, and cowboys sawed pieces off of these horns for neckerchief rings. My brother had one on his bandana neckscarf, or muffler.

Arthur and I escaped the gnats pretty well by spreading out the bedding and getting under it. Dad, however, had to drive the team. He tied a handkerchief around his neck and rigged another one, held in place by his hat, so that it covered his cheeks and the back of his head and neck. But these gnats could crawl through a pinhole. Long before we reached Laramie my father's eyes were swollen almost shut, and lumpy welts decorated his nose, cheeks, ears, neck, wrists and hands.

Eventually we met the inbound Laramie-Walden stage, and I came up like a Jack-in-the-Box to take a look at it when I heard the driver sing out, "Hello, Jack," and stop to pass the time of day.

This stage vehicle was no historical Concord Coach with four, or perhaps six, splendid, high-lifed horses such as you see in pictures. It was merely a strong, three-seated spring wagon with a boot behind and a canvas-covered top supported by uprights. Curtains could be attached to the uprights to enclose the seats and passengers, but, short of blizzard weather, the driver would not go to all that trouble. He had only a two-horse team, which did not zing along at a lope, but plodded at a six-mile-per-hour dogtrot. Yet this stage route served North Park very well.

We also met several North Park ranchmen, homeward bound from Laramie with loaded wagons. There was a good general store a Walden. But, like Dad, a majority of our ranchmen saved themselves the local storekeeper's profit, plus the considerable sum which he had to pay for having all of his merchandise freighted into the Park, by doing the bulk of their trading in Laramie. The fact that Laramie was on the Union Pacific Railroad helped to make all manner of goods available at reasonable prices.

Some of the men we met had two-horse teams, patched-up harnesses, and wagons not much better than ours. Others drove spanking-good four-horse teams hitched to first-class wagons. One such outfit roused my brother's interest and he confided to me:

"When I get big enough to drive to Laramie, I'll have an outfit like that — or better."

"How'll you get it?" I challenged.

He shrugged, and I lost all interest in his idea when we met a real freight outfit — eight horses and two wagons, the lead wagon a high boxed whopper. Small bells, attached to the hame straps at the lower end of the collars on the lead team, made tinkly and pleasant music. Here in this wide-open plains country the bells served no real purpose. But already I knew why freighters belled their lead teams — to warn other travellers, coming toward their outfits along a heavily forested road, that they were about to meet a freight outfit and to find a turnout where they could pass.

We turned off the road for the freighter. He shouted, "Whoa!" then, "Hello, Jack. Like a drink?"

I noticed a shot-loaded blacksnake hung around his corded neck and that he was as dusty and as black as the old saddle he rode on his nigh wheel horse. He handled his long team with a jerk line, and a rope ran back from his saddle horn to the brake lever on his lead wagon. I thought, "Golly! I'll be a freighter! Wouldn't it be great to ride a horse like that big one and be pulling into Laramie every so often."

To the freighter Dad said, "I'll take you up on that. Perhaps the smell of liquor will drive these gnats away." He stepped down from the wagon seat to the ground.

The freighter had dismounted and was reaching into the big jockey box attached to the front end of his lead wagon. He pulled a gallon jug out of it and snorted, "Nine hundred and ninety-nine days out the year the wind howls here. But today the danged gnats b'ile up outa the grass, no breeze a-tall. Can you beat i?

"Speakin' of wind, Jack, it blows hayrack wagons over nigh every day, empty or loaded. Once it took the tarpaulin right offen my lead wagon, sailed it yonderly an' I never did find it . . . You hear the one 'bout the tenderfoot cowboy with the new hat which had set him back twenty bucks?"

"I think I heard it," Dad said, "and I should be rolling —"

"Cowpunchers," the freighter cut in, "has l'arnt to tie down their lids with a leather string like this one I got. See? It comes down around behind my head, anchors my hat on. But this tenderfoot hadn't no string, and right here on these plains the wind lifted his brand-new lid. He took out afer it, chased it seven miles, ridin' lickety-cut. Run his horse plumb down, never did catch up with his hat . . . Doggone!" — shaking his jug — 'Plumb empty."

"Well, never mind," Dad began.

"Hold your hosses, Jack. We'll fill this jug in jus' a jiffy."

The freighter again reached into the huge jockey box and produced a hammer, a large horseshoe nail and a quart tin cup. "Gimme a hand, Jack."

Arthur and I had almost forgotten to fight gnats, watching the freighter, and listening to his talk. The two men now walked to the rear wagon, which was piled high with whiskey kegs. As they climbed up atop this load, the freighter was saying, "Still speakin' of wind, you hear about the chuck wagon cook?"

Dad said, "No."

"Well, this cook stopped on these plains to get dinner for cowboys that was trailin' a herd. Wasn't no wood to burn, so cookie gathers a bunch of tumbleweeds and sets 'em on fire, slices a mess of bacon into his fry pan and starts to cook it. All t'oncet the tumbleweeds turn over. Cook follows after 'em . . . You know, time he got that bacon fried he was plumb to the Missouri River!"

He and Dad had lifted up one whiskey keg and balanced it on another. Then the freighter used his hammer to pound one of the hoops down toward the smaller portion of the keg. Finally, he punctured the keg with his horseshoe nail.

"You hold the cup to catch the stream, Jack, while I handle the keg!" he commanded.

I watched, fascinated, as whiskey squirted into the cup.

Eventually, Dad called, "Full!" Whereupon the freighter pounded the loosened hoop back into its proper place.

Both men jumped to the ground. Dad lifted the cup to his lips and took a "short snort," and strangled and coughed. The freighter took a real "long snort" — and he didn't cough at all. Then he poured what was left into his jug.

At this point I thought, "Maybe I can't ever be a freighter. Dave Hendrickson says they guzzle so much booze it'd kill 'em if it wasn't for the hard work they do. 'Work sweats the poison out of their hides,' Dave says."

Dave had told us how freighters "tapped" whisky kegs. Now we had actually seen it done and I heard Dad ask the man, "You ever get in trouble with the saloon owners when this whiskey you haul for them comes out short?"

"Nope. We take only a li'l bit outa any one keg. Besides, I reckon they kinder expect to be a mite short." He laughed uproariously.

He put jug and hammer, cup and nail back into the jockey box, climbed on his big nigh wheel horse and yelled, "Hit the collars!"

The picture of that man and his outfit, rolling slowly on across the plains in its own small dust cloud, is still clear in my mind. They were tough and hardy men, those freighters of the old days. I'm very glad that once I knew several of their breed.

Art and I crawled back under the bedding. Dad whipped the team along, fighting gnats continually, and eventually we heard him call, "Now you can see Laramie! And a train!"

"Train!" I squealed. At last I would actually be seeing a locomotive and cars!

LARAMIE

Ordinarily you think of the Union Pacific as running almost due west from Omaha to Ogden. The tracks actually follow the line of least resistance, not through, but around the Rocky Mountains, which break off abruptly with the Snowy Range and Elk Mountain in southern Wyoming. Then a vast, open area intervenes before the Rockies uprear themselves once again and resume their northward march. In order to take advantage of this comparatively open area, the Union Pacific tracks turn north at Tie Siding, Wyoming, and follow that direction to a point some twenty miles north of Laramie before again swinging westward.

The train which I saw was approaching Laramie from the south, its engine scarcely smoking as the long string of cars slid snake-like down the grade from Sherman Hill, the steel rails shining like silver threads against the dark earth. Boy, was this something!

Black smoke from other locomotives hung over Laramie, which sprawled upon a wide, open plain. Eastward beyond the town, high hills extending north and south lifted against the skyline. I heard the train's rumblings and clankings, and I heard a whistle so shrill it frightened me. Then the train slid into Laramie and stopped, lost to sight.

Suddenly Arthur called my attention to another amazing and wonderful thing — a big building at our left, part of which had no roof. No roof! Nor was this all that was unusual about it. A man with a rifle was stalking around on top of the walls of this roofless building, looking down into it, holding his weapon as if prepared to shoot.

"Dad! What's that funny place? What's the man with the gun doing?"

"Wyoming Penitentiary," Dad answered. "The law puts horse thieves and killers and other bad citizens in that big place! The man with the rifle is a guard. If you were in there for some crime he'd shoot you if you tried to get out."

"He w-o-u-l-d? Glad I ain't in there."

We croosed a bridge spanning the Big Laramie River. Then our wagon rattled and banged over a series of railroad tracks. Strange sights and smells and noises spooked the team and Dad had trouble controlling them.

Now we were in Laramie! A boy who'd never before seen even one brick, saw big buildings built entirely of bricks! There were also frame buildings; saloons, stores, a hotel, plank sidewalks; streets of packed earth, wide and dusty and, it seemed to me, numberless teams and crowds of people.

Dad stopped at A. S. Peabody's Grocery Store to unload the eggs and butter and to give his order for groceries. Then we went on to a big livery stable and drove right into it. Here was room for several wagons to have shelter for he night. A hostler made cheerful talk as he helped us unhitch. When he watered the team, I saw him turn a tap, and saw water run out of a pipe to fill the trough.

"What is that, Mister?" I asked, awed.

"Water hydrant."

"How'd the water get into that pipe?"

The hostler was still explaining this puzzling matter when Dad called to Art and me, "You fellows grease the wagon. I'm going out to sell these hides I brought, but I'll be back."

Carrying the hides he disappeared, and the hostler told us we might use the stable's wagon jack for the greasing job. Was that jack a wonderful contrivance! Art put it under the hind axle of our wagon, pressed down on a lever, and the jack lifted one hind wheel clear off the floor so we could pull off the wheel, smear grease on the spindle and slip the wheel back on again.

Dad finally reappeared, and was jingling some silver coins while Art and I waited with held breath. We hadn't one cent. Would he . . .?

He did. "Here's twenty-five cents apiece boys. You can walk around town to see things. Don't get lost, and be sure to come to Peabody's store in about two hours. I'll be loading up." And away he went, evidently having forgotten that we kids might be hungry — which we were.

But Art had an idea of what he wanted to see first of all and asked where to find the saddle shop. We soon came to it, went in, sniffing the good smell of leather. A friendly man showed us new saddles and bridles, chaps and spurs, saddle blankets and harnesses. Finally he lifted me up into one fine saddle and allowed me to sit in it, pround as a king.

I had no saddle, and Art's was an old wreck with a broken horn. Today we could look our fill — and dream and yearn. But a good new saddle cost forty dollars! (The same item nowadays little, if any better either in material or workmanship, is priced from two hundred dollars up.)

Leaving this establishment, a blacksmith shop next caught and held out attention. Didn't we both know by heart Longfellow's great poem:

"The smith, a mighty man is he . . ."

This one, however, was not a mighty man, nor did "the muscles of his brawny arms look strong as iron bands." Bare to the waist, and greasy with sweat, he was shoeing horses, using ready-made shoes and nails! We knew our granddad had made his own nails and his own horseshoes, so I was disappointed.

". . . They love to see the flaming forge and hear the bellows roar."

This forge did not flame. It displayed only a glowing bed of coals, and the bellows, when pumped to heat a horseshoe, did not roar.

The smith finally gave us his attention. "Gosh! You're the queerest lookin' rubbernecks I ever seen. Something I can do for you?"

"No. No, thank you sir."

We went on, indignant and stung by "queerest rubbernecks," but looking back at those days now, how right the man was!

I held my quarter gripped in one sweaty palm, thinking, "A stick of licorice and a bag of peanuts and an ice cream soda, 'specially the ice cream soda, would be . . ."

Suddenly I stopped with my face against the window of a dry goods store. Displayed here were men's suits and shoes, boots, hats, shirts, gloves and sweaters.

"Art," I asked, "you s'pose they got overalls for boys?"

"Naw. Come on away. Dad forgot about overalls for you, and they'll cost fifty cents."

"Maybe he didn't forget. Maybe, like always, he can't afford 'em. What's 'afford' mean? I know it ain't like the place where you cross a stream without a bridge."

"Means," explained my big brother patiently, "that when a fella don't have money to buy what he wants to he can't afford it."

"Oh!" That was the way it had always been with us. "But you put your quarter with mine, Art, and we'll have . . ." I stopped. Peanuts, licorice, ice cream soda! All would be sacrificed for overalls. Yet overalls could win over appetite, if . . .

"Nothin' doin', stupid. You know why I'm saving my two-bits? To buy oranges. Oranges for Mama and Mary and Connie and Dot."

"Hello, boys? Anything I can do for you?" The store man had come out and was grinning at us. "I have a complete stock of . . ."

"Overalls that'll fit me?" I squealed.

"Sure. Come in."

In the store, the man selected and held up against me a pair of blue, waist-length overalls strengthened with copper rivets. "A bit long in the legs, but you can turn 'em up."

"You bet I can. And I will. Please, lemme jus' try 'em on."

"Certainly, son. I don't blame you for wanting to cover those ragged knee pants and stockings."

He turned his attention to Art as I wriggled into the overalls.

"You need a new pair, too, big fellow. Those patches are wearing out."

"He don't eiher," I put in. "Mama can patch the patches."

Art let out a deep breath. "Mister, I wish — wish John could get the overalls. But all he's got is one quarter. They do cost fity cents?"

"Yes. Better take them off, son."

"Art," I choked, "you've got 'nother quarter."

"Oranges," he said stubbornly.

I put one fist against an eye and started pulling off the overalls.

The man looked hard at us. "Hold up a minute," he ordered. "Big fellow," addressing Art, "would you swap off that ring you have on your bandana? Polished buffalo horn, isn't it?"

"Uh-huh." Art fingered the ring. He had made it himself, putting in hours polishing it, and I knew how he valued it. "No, I hadn't figured I'd ever swap it off. But . . ." He looked at me. "But I will talk swap, Mister."

When we finally walked out of the store, I was strutting proudly in my new overalls. Art had traded the man his ring for overalls "even up," but Art now had my two bits as well as his own.

"I'm awful hungry," I said. "But what'll we eat?"

"Come on in here." Art had stopped at a saloon. "I've heard men talk and I got an idea."

We went into the saloon, quiet at his hour, with only the bartender on duty. I stared at everything — the bar, the long mirror and the fancy bottles. On the walls was a splendid collection of mounted heads; deer, elk, mountain sheep, and one of a Longhorn Texas steer. There were amazing pictures, too, the like of which I'd never seen. One was a photograph of a prize fighter, "James J. Corbett." He wasn't wearing much clothing. But a colored picture of a fleshy woman was more interesting, for she was wearing no clothes at all. None!

The barkeeper suddenly noticed us, gawped for a moment, then snapped, "No kids allowed. Go on out now."

"We wasn't going to try to get whisky," Art said. "Uh — er, where's your free lunch, Mister?"

Now I knew what he'd had in mind. Men said that in Laramie you could buy one glass of beer for a nickel and then eat all the free lunch you wanted.

"Free lunch? So-o!" the man came out from behind the shiny bar and pulled at each side of his great mustache while he looked us over. "Where you fellows from?"

"The Park," Art informed. "Just got in, all gnat bit and awful dusty and hungry . . . Dry and thirsty, too. But o'course we can't buy beer — or anything."

"Or anything," the man repeated and suddenly laughed. "This way, kids." He led us to a table where all storts of strange, good things were set out, ready to be eaten. "Fill up," he said, smiling all over his wide red face. "On the house."

We began "filling up." I'd never seen such food before, and I don't know now what all we ate. But it tasted salty and rich and lickin' good.

The man went behind his bar and came back with two pint bottles which he had opened. "Soft drinks," he said. "Won't hurt you a bit. Drink up. They're on the house too, though I could get fired for this if the boss finds out."

"And if our Dad finds out I think we'll get blistered for it ourselves," Art told him.

"That so? Why didn't he take his kids to dinner at the hotel? What's his name?"

"He's awful poor," I answered. "All the men he knows call him 'Jack' . . . Wish they'd call me 'Jack' instead of 'Johnnie.' You see my new overalls, Mister Bartender?"

"Stop gobblin', kid, or you'll be darned sick," Art told me. He drained his bottle and said, "Come see us and get a feed when you visit the Park, Mister. We gotta go now, and thanks."

"Don't mention it. I've sure got a bang outa you fellows!" And he shook hands with us just like we were grown-up men.

I wanted to watch the trains, but Art dragged me along to Peabody's store. Dad's wagon and team were in front of it, Dad up in the box, stowing away bags and boxes which the clerk handed up to him.

Art went into the store and when he came back with a package, Dad asked sharply, "What you got there, son?"

"S'prise for Mama and the girls. Our money paid for it, too."

"That's good. That's fine . . . I did get the dress goods and other little necessities your mother wanted so badly. But no luxuries."

"What's luxuries?" I asked.

"Humph! All things you'd like to have but can get along without," Dad explained.

He wired a case of coal oil — two big five-gallon cans in a wooden box — on the outside of the wagon, for, if kerosene should leak, it would spoil the groceries. Then he stretched the wagon sheet over the top of the load and tied it down in several places, put behind the seat the grub box and the bedroll, now wrapped in the buffalo robe, and we were ready to go.

Pulling out of Laramie, we left its wonders behind us, but not my memories of it and of my first trip to the "outside" world. No, not the memories!

THE HOME RANCH

Though our homeward trek from Laramie was slow and tiresome, it was not without interest to a small boy.

The first night we made camp only five or six miles from the town. An irrigation ditch supplied us with water. We picketed the team and then slept on the hard ground out under the stars.

The following day all of us were thankful for a stiff breeze which kept down the wicked gnats. Dad turned off the main road to take a short cut. This led us across one of the largest ranches on the Big Laramie and eventually to Dirty Pete's Road Ranch. Here the trail we were following met the main road from Fort Collins to North Park, and here, our grub box being empty, we stayed over night.

I was eager to meet Dirty Pete whom Dad had often mentioned as a "real old timer and quite a character." But I was much disappointed in him. Pete was not nearly as dirty as I'd expected him to be!

We put our bed in the haymow, but stable room and feed for the team cost fifty cents. Art told me that two-bits, or twenty-five cents, was the standard price for meals, and that this stop would cost Dad two whole dollars!

"Where will he get the money?" we wondered.

Dad, however, promised to bring the road-ranch man a wagon box full of firewood on his next trip "outside," and Pete told him, "Fair enough, Jack. That'll more than even up."

On the fourth and final day of our trip, we passed N. K. Boswell's ranch on the Big Laramie, and Dad told us, "Boswell made quite a reputation as a lawman, and he's now one of Wyoming's most prominent citizens. In the earlier days his ranch here was the best known stopping place on the old Teller Road. It still is for that matter."

Leaving the valley wherein were located the ranch buildings, we crossed the Big Laramie on a good bridge, then climbed a series of abrupt hills to the top of the Medicine Bow Range, which is quite low at this point.

When we reached Howell's road ranch, I remembered that North Park cowboys said they never could get a count on all the Howell kids. "You figger you've tallied 'em all, then outa the brush'll come stringin' another little herd." They also said that Mrs. Howell smoked a pipe, and this I wanted to see for myself.

I saw only four kids, but when Mrs. Howell came to the door of her home and waved to Dad she was sure enough smoking a pipe!

We made a brief stop at Mountain Home Park to let the horses feed and rest, lunching on crackers and one can of tomatoes ourselves. Rolling onward again, we were approaching John Price's road ranch in the neck of the Park when Dad reached down into the wagon box and picked up a short, heavy iron bar, something like a piece cut off of a crowbar.

"If Price stops me, I'll be ready for him," he said grimly.

I went all shivery inside, because I'd heard folks say John Price was a "mean and ornery cuss" who had trouble with everybody. So far as we boys knew, he was the only man definitely unfriendly toward our father. What their quarrel was all about, Dad never would tell us. But he had put this iron bar in the wagon before leaving the ranch and had had it handy on our outbound trip. We had however not seen Mr. Price when we had at that time driven past his ranch. Nor did we now.

Several years later, however, Price started picking on a stage driver named Norv King. Norv, the son of a hot-blooded Kentuckian, warned Price to "lay off" or he'd kill him, and he then started carrying a rifle.

But there came a day when Price stopped the stage and once again began bullying the driver. Thereupon Norv King shot the man dead at point-blank range, and then drove on to Waldon and gave himself up to the deputy sheriff. North Parkers, however, all agreed that Price had it coming, and at Norv's trial in Fort Collins he was acquitted and fully exonerated.

Price's Scotch wife was a fine woman, well liked by everyone. After his death she continued to run the road ranch and eventually married a man named George Clark. Clark was a genial fellow who'd make guests feel at home— and help drink their whiskey—but otherwise was of very little help to his wife. As she herself summed up the siuation: "I've got a good man now, only he won't work."

So Lizzie Clark continued to make the living for herself and her "good" man, while the old Price house slowly settled deeper into the mud; and, between cooking meals and fixing beds for the transients, she fought an endless battle with the mud and a leaking roof and bed bugs.

Our road did not turn sharp to the right at Pinkham Creek as does the modern highway which I have earlier mentioned. We held straight on southward, crossed Pinkham Creek, climbed a long hill and came to Pinkhamton post office, stage station and road ranch. Dad often mentioned George Seifert's store, which had flourished here, but Seifert had by this time moved elsewhere, and I had no memory of it.

But now Jack Payne's kids were back in completely familiar territory! Here the road followed a lane enclosed on either side by strong buck and pole fences. The very narrow gap between the big main house and equally large stable reminded me I had heard that this bottleneck was a hazard to all trail herds.

Range cattle of that day, only one "cross" removed from native Texas stock, were wild, horned critters, suspicious of anything that looked like a trap, and they'd "spook at a whisper."

I recall one story on this subject which featured Andrew Norell, "king of the Swedes" and one of our most successful and prominent cattlemen. Andy had ridden ahead of his beef herd to Pinkhamton, had tied his horse and gone into the ranch house. When his herd drew near, for some reason they promptly stampeded. When Andy heard the racket, he rushed out, shouting:

"Hi, boys! Hi, boys! Scatter dem cattles togeder! Scatter 'em togeder, I tell you!"

Whether the "scattering of 'em togeder" was successful, I don't remember, but Norell's peculiar expression became a byword with all North Park cowboys. For years thereafter, when starting out to round up a herd, one rider would sing out to the others, "Hi, boys! Get busy and scatter dem cattles togeder!"

A certain Englishman, upon hearing this for the first time, exclaimed, "Most extraordinary! You can't scatter anything together, y' know."

On another occasion, one of the Two Bar Two's big herds was approaching Pinkhamton when Georgina Allard, who had come from the Allard ranch to get the mail, stepped out of the main building and, carrying an umbrella, walked down the lane toward the cattle.

A drizzling rain had begun and, to protect herself, Georgina raised her umbrella, whereupon the herd simply "quit the earth." Two miles back along the road the sweating, swearing cowboys managed to stop this stampede, but were obliged to circle far around through fields in order to get that spooked herd past Pinkhamton.

After we had passed Pinkhamton on our homeward journey, Dad pointed to Allard's building at our right and said, "Pinkham persuaded the Allard family to move to North Park. But they weren't too well pleased, judging by what one of the Allard boys said to me, 'Pinkham, he told us he had a fine ranch. Pinkham, he told us he had a lot of cattle. Pinkham, he told us a lie.' "

We drove through a gap in a little hogback. Then I saw the Park spread out, long and wide, ahead of us. Sunset had painted the western mountain skyline red and gold, which helped to give me a deeper appreciation of the great beauty of our homeland than I had entertained before this trip "outside." Somehow I expected great changes to have taken place in the *long* time I'd been gone, and that I saw none was disappointing.

Actually, however, in the eleven years since Dad had come here, there had been many changes of which his sons were now becoming aware.

Our father had known this Park when it had truly been a land "where the deer and the antelope play," and when any settler might, from his front door, replenish his meat supply, taking his choice of deer, antelope or elk.

Not that the deer, antelope and elk had gone from the scene by 1895; they had merely retreated to the foothills and mountains. Trappers had made marked inroads upon all fur bearing animals as well, but these were still plentiful, as were sage hens, grouse, ducks, trout and jack rabbits. Especially jack rabbits!

Too, he had known the Park when fences were few and far between. Now all good valleys were enclosed by fences, leaving only the hills and flats as open range for stock grazing.

Next in the course of change was the turnover in human life. Dad talked glibly of the early comers, the real pioneers: hunters, miners, horsemen, cowmen, settlers, storekeepers, stage drivers, freighters whom Arthur and I hadn't known at all. The big horse outfits and some of the cowmen were gone; mining men had become ranchmen, though a few "die-hards" were still actively prospecting; scores of settlers had drifted away, selling their land if they could, and if not, abandoning it. Father's ranch and the open range adjacent to it were sprinkled with empty cabins. But the "stick-it-out," "stay-and-hang-on-and-rattle" ranchmen, like Dad, were adding to their holdings the homestead, desert and timber claims of these quitters. That is the way both big cow outfits and little fellows built up their ranches.

In these eleven years Dad had acquired quite a respectable block of land. It lay south of Sentinel Peak and along Government, Sand and Spring Creeks, and comprised the Pappy Rice claim, Dad's original homestead which we called the Upper Field, my Uncle Dick's homestead, and the Fisher Field. Included also were Uncle Will's homestead, the Cross Ranch, and the Scott boys' homestead. Dad did not own the Scott Ranch, but no division fence separated it from the Cross Ranch, our home.

More than this, he owned the Lower Cross Ranch, 320 acres lying two miles west and a little north of the home ranch, and Sentinel Mountain—Government land to which he held no title—was his big fenced pasture.

Equally important to securing the land, Dad, with the financial help of a wealthy Englishman named Henry Hadden—of whom more later—had managed to increase his herd of cattle to approximately one hundred and fifty head of she-stock.

In a vague sort of way we boys realized that our father was deeply in debt, yet he at last was beginning to realize his great ambition. He was slowly, surely building up a cow outfit, and that was what Art and I wanted, too!

The open range where he grazed his cattle lay between the ranch and the Medicine Bow Mountains. This was called the Sand Hills, probably because it included the lower set of Sand Dunes on the east side of the Park.

Other ranchmen also summer-grazed cattle in this area. Some of these fellows owned no land bordering on the "Sand Hills," and we did not think they had any right to this range. But it was Government land and there was nothing the Paynes could do about it—except squawk.

Dad owned very few horses at this time; for, although the Cross boys had thrown in twenty good horses when he bought their ranch, he had lost almost all of them through ignorance and neglect. (A lesson learned the hard and costly way.) Apparently, no one told him about loco weed, and the Sand Hills range was a hotbed for this weed, also for wild larkspur (poison weed) each spring and early summer.

No one fed range horses hay during the winter. They stayed on open range and "rustled." Dad's horses, in pawing through the snow to get grass, uncovered loco, ate it and got the "loco habit." When a horse or cow or sheep gets the "loco habit," it hunts the weed and will eat nothing else. Before Dad realized what was happening, most of the horses died, and the remainder were so badly "locoed" they were useless. Several of the few horses we now owned had had a "touch of loco" but had been taken away from it in time. (More on this later, for a locoed horse is a very peculiar creature.)

As we turned off the main road into a short lane which led across Government Creek and directly to our house, I looked at our buildings with a dawning awareness that this Cross Ranch was an impressive place.

The Cross boys, Ben and Will and Dillon (Dill), were not mining men, nor farmers, nor cattlemen. They were horsemen—horsemen to the marrow of their bones. From somewhere "outside" they had come to the Park in the seventies with hundreds of horses to establish a horse ranch. But after a few years, because there was no market for their horses, or prices were so low they could not continue in business, they failed.

For this reason the three brothers sold their ranch to my father and trailed their horses out of North Park all the way to Flagstaff, Arizona. What a trip that must have been in those early days! How did they ever find their way? To my regret, all that I know about that trek are little incidents told by Charlie Scott, who went along as one of the horse punchers.

There had been other big horse outfits in the Park; the Mendenhalls and Benbows for one, the Horse Company for another, and there may have been more. But, like the Crosses, they too failed, and what became of their horses I never learned.

Oddly, I remember hearing about only one man of the Horse Company, not one of the owners but the outfit's bronc buster, Billy Weaver. Why was this? It was because whenever cowboys or others began to talk about bronc busters, Billy Weaver was sure to be mentioned. Some men would claim he was a better rider than even Dill Cross. So although I knew neither Weaver nor Dill at this time, both men were my heroes.

Both the Mendenhalls and the Horse Company left their stamp on our land, for the old Mendenhall place, just south of the lower sand hills along the foot of Medicine Bow Range, is still known by this name. And the Horse Company's headquarters, a few miles from the Mendenhall ranch, was the "Horse Ranch" when I was young, and today is still known as the "Horse Ranch," yet scores of other early day ranches have completely lost their original names.

When the Crosses had established their headquarters, they had built for permanence. They had been the first men in the Park to fence in a full section of land. Their roomy set of pole corrals for the handling and breaking of horses was the best in all North Park. There was a long, high stable, its pole roof heavily covered with clay-like red dirt so it stood out to be seen from a distance. A hay barn large enough to store twenty or thirty tons of hay adjoined the stable. There was also a cow barn for milk stock, one end of it a chicken house; and a small tool house was built around a rocked-up well, for this was one ranch where the buildings were not close to a stream or even a spring.

Unfortunately, the well water was so bad we could not use it, which obliged us to carry water for the house from Government Creek, an eighth of a mile up the lane, and either to lead or haze barn stock to the same water supply.

The original Cross house had burned down before I was born. Because grown men hated the chore of cutting wood as much as Arthur and I hated it, someone of the Cross outfit devised the no-work scheme of poking long poles into the side-door firebox of the cook stove; when one piece of the pole was burned off, it was then shoved farther in. All went well until one day the fire stoker left a couple of small poles projecting from the open firebox and went out to do chores. Not long afterward the burning wood fell out of the stove and onto the dried-out pine board floor. Soon—no more house!

Perhaps the story of this calamity served one good purpose: it warned my father and his boys always to be careful with matches and with fire. Arthur and I handled matches, built fires, and practised shooting, too, months, even years, before most kids would have been permitted to touch either matches or firearms.

The Crosses built another house on the fire-blackened spot, and it had a pretty red dirt roof, but this roof leaked like a sieve in every snow or rain storm. There was a good stone fireplace in the living room, but in cold weather the moment the fire went out all the warm air rushed up the chimney and the house became an icebox, so cold that milk was often frozen in the pans.

But, for our mother's comfort, and also due to necessity of housing the growing family, Dad had built a two bedroom cabin which did have a box stove and could be kept warm in winter.

In those days every ranch had its meat pole, equipped at the top with a pulley and a cord. Someone had discovered that blow flies either do not or cannot get very far above ground, so fresh meat suspended twenty or more feet in the air was safe from the fly menace. But the only way to keep butter and cream in hot weather was to put it in running water or in a cool spring.

All heating of water had to be done either in a tea kettle or a wash boiler atop the cook stove; the washing of clothes, etc., was done by hand in a laundry tub, which was also the bathtub.

This afternoon Mother and the girls, Olive Mary, Connie and Elizabeth Emily, whom we called "Dot," were waiting for us when the team pulled into the yard. I proudly strutted my overalls, feeling I was a big boy now, for hadn't I been "outside"? Arthur presented the oranges, which pleased Mother as much as if they were intrinsically valuable, for any fresh fruit was a rare, rare treat.

Quite naturally it had never occurred to me to wonder how Mother managed to clothe and feed her growing family, and unfortunately I recall very little about our family life prior to her death. Now however I realize that under grim handicaps she must have accomplished wonders, since clothing of any kind was scarce and hard to come by.

But the pioneer settlers of North Park never lacked one item of food — meat. If for any reason a man was unable to kill a deer an antelope or an elk for himself, some of his neighbors would gladly share with him their bountiful supply. Bread, beans and potatoes, plus oatmeal and dried apples, were the other standbys.

"Cap" Fox, the Barneses and Dad all had "green thumbs." Considering the altitude—eight thousand feet—and the short growing season, they raised wonderful gardens. Others who were farmer-minded had quickly discovered that grain crops, with the exception of rye and barley, would not mature, nor would alfalfa do well.

But the strength of the wild native grasses and its quality when cut for hay compensated for the lack of oats, wheat and corn as stock feed. Cattle and horses would stay fat on this grass the year 'round if they had enough of it. Most saddle horses didn't know what grain was and would not eat it if it were given them.

While Arthur and I were small, we took it as a matter of course that Mother should do all of the cooking and baking, washing and ironing, house cleaning, and taking care of all of us kids. Dad did help with making butter, and just as soon as my brother and I were able—I think it was before we were really capable of doing the job—we cut the firewood and carried the water from the creek. We had no enthusiasm for either job, but Dad was a stern taskmaster.

At this time, 1895, we had one hired man, a Spaniard named Rupert Ortiz. I'd remember more about him if he had been a cowboy or a good trapper or hunter. Since he was none of those, all I remember about Rupert is that Dad paid him one dollar per day and that he was the only man I ever knew to smoke Bull Durham cigarette tobacco in a pipe. (That was by far the hottest smoking Art and I ever tried.)

Other hired men who occasionally worked for Jack Payne were John Metcalf and Dave Hendrickson. Metcalf soon rubbed Dad the wrong way — because he was a perfectionist and very particular how he did any job. Dad, on the contrary, was a slipshod workman, a "lick and a promise" workman. "Aw, that's good enough!" was his idea.

This was a matter which griped Arthur quite early in his life. Art believed in doing any job "right" or not at all, and we boys got a whale of a kick one day as we watched Dad and Ortiz throw several logs on a sled to haul them out into the meadow for the purpose of building a hay crib. Dad said to Ortiz, "That fussy Metcalf would never load logs this way. He'd insist it had to be done so and so. Waste of time!"

They started out, and at once the load began falling off the sled.

They stopped and loaded up again. When, for the second time, the logs fell off, my brother was "bustin' himself a-laughing." He told me, "If they'd done it right in the first place they wouldn't have had to do it over again."

Dave Hendrickson and Dad always got along well. Hendrickson was a mining man, first, last and all the time. The Teller City boom had brought him to the Park, and then, probably because he had a family to support and had to work for wages in order to do this, he stayed in the Park. But he never lost hope that someday he'd strike it rich.

Dave could make a hand at any job, and was a splendid axe-man. He did not drink or use tobacco, but he did have a habit of talking to himself. When he was working alone, he'd simply "go it." And the louder he talked, the harder he worked.

Following our Laramie adventure, Art and I went back to school again while Dad and Ortiz started putting up hay. This was, and is, such a big and important job in North Park that the seasons of the year are called "before haying," "during haying" (or merely "haying") "after haying" and "winter."

The earliest cutting of hay had been done with scythes, and we kids often found an old rusted scythe thrown up on a dirt roof. Dad however had gotten quite a lot of ranch equipment with the Cross ranch, and he now had both a mowing machine and a good rake. All the help I could give was to turn the hand-power grindstone while he sharpened a mower sickle, and Art was still too small to make a hay hand. So Dad and Ortiz would mow and rake a patch of hay, then fork it onto the wagon hayrack and haul it and unload it into the hay barn. When the mow was filled, they'd begin piling up the hay into one or more stacks.

Each year this same slow, hard work would begin toward the last of July and go on all through August and into September, or even into October if the job was still unfinished. Other ranchmen, all over the Park, would be doing the same thing. The largest and more prosperous outfits would, however, hire additional help and run more mowers, rakes and wagons.

During this midsummer season cattle on the ranges required very little attention; the spring or calf roundup over, and the fall or beef roundup not yet begun, cowboys were roped in as hay hands. Montie Blevins' crew, for example, with the exception of one or two lucky riders who could do all the range riding necessary, were, for the time being, hay hands.

But you may ask, "Why this all-out drive to harvest hay?"

Well, hay is merely another name for grass. It is grass which has been cut and cured and stacked for winter use as stock feed, and in my North Park of sixty-odd years ago grass was the one commodity which enabled the ranchman, be he settler or established cowman, to make a living.

To be sure, we had one other valuable asset, free timber, and the North Parkers themselves provided a limited market for a sawmill's rough lumber, for building logs, and for fencing timber, poles, bucks and posts.

Building fences was one of the major jobs. Wooden fences were constructed of either posts and poles or bucks and poles. Barbed wire had not come to the Park and the use of it was violently opposed. People who were familiar with barbed wire said that horses got entangled in the nasty stuff and were crippled, often so badly they had to be shot. So the "buck" fence, which is built all above ground —no posts to rot off—was considered the best type.

The big outfit or the prosperous ranchman would gladly pay a man to cut and pile poles and bucks and logs for him. He'd then do his own hauling. A standard fence pole was eighteen feet in length and no less than two and one half inches in diameter at the small end. One cent per pole was the accepted rate to the chopper for cutting down, trimming and piling poles. Two cents was paid for bucks, fourteen feet long, five to six inches in diameter. Rates varied for building logs according to length, size and quality. Chopping down and piling up either two hundred poles or one hundred bucks was a day's work for a good axeman. Thus he'd make two dollars!

Niggardly as this wage now seems, a great many men made their living by working in the timber during the winter months.

But the demand for this material depended upon the prosperity of our settlers and cowmen, none of whom could have made their ranches pay or have made a go of stock raising without grass. So the raising of cattle was a business chained and locked to grass, and when snow covered the mountain world and buried the grass, cattle starved unless they were fed grass in its cured form—hay.

Long before I became aware of things, ranchmen had learned they must irrigate a meadow in order to grow a hay crop; the ambition of every settler was to produce and stack more and yet more hay. If he had no cattle of his own, hay was still his one asset, for our big outfits, also many smaller cowmen, would be glad to buy his crop!

This year of 1895 the routine of our life went on as usual until the greatest loss, the greatest tragedy that could possibly befall the Payne family struck us. It was the death of our mother.

I suppose Arthur pretty well knew what was going on. But the girls and I were too young to realize what it was all about. All we knew was that the doctor had come, and also Mrs. Coe, who was midwife to the whole neighborhood. Then we were told there was a new baby girl. The doctor had gone, and all was supposed to be going well. Then the worst happened.

Afterwards, Art saddled old Billy and rode first to the Scotts' to ask them to get the doctor from Walden again. From there he dashed to Pinkhamton to mail a telegram to Laramie, from where it would be sent by wire to our relatives back East.

In response to this telegram our Aunt Elizabeth came west as speedily as a train and the stage could bring her.

Meanwhile there were strange goings and comings of people, including the doctor, and a beautiful, long black box appeared in the living room. Neighbors came from all around, dozens of people I did not know among the few I did know. Men dug a grave three or four hundred yards from the buildings and everybody congregated around it. But no minister was available, and Dad, with tears rolling down his cheeks—I had never seen him cry and had not believed he could cry—read the Episcopal burial service himself. Then the black box, hidden inside another one of rough pine, was lowered, and men shoveled back dirt to fill the grave.

Then at last, I understood Mother was gone and that I'd never see her any more. I ran away and hid until Mrs. Blevins found me and picked me up and kissed me.

After that I felt better, and I knew, knew for sure, that next to mother, Harriet Blevins was the sweetest, most wonderful woman in the whole world.

THE SCOTT BOYS – MOSTLY CHARLIE

Following Mother's death, our Aunt Elizabeth could not stay on indefinitely to take care of us small Paynes and keep house for Dad, so, taking the baby with her, she returned to Massachusetts, where soon afterward the infant died.

At this period it was almost impossible to find a woman in our country who would cook and keep house on a ranch and also take care of small children. But Dad had sent appeals to relatives and friends in his native England—and there came all the way from England a woman to carry on in this emergency.

Merely to say, however, that this female proved a disappointment is terrific understatement. Her cooking could be eaten if we were ravenously hungry—and for that matter we generally were hungry. But she had no idea of the proper care of little children, and she was so plain stupid that...

Well, this may give you an idea: Dad had provided china nest eggs for the hen house, and one morning a china nest egg appeared among real boiled eggs on the breakfast table.

"Look here." Dad picked up the nest egg. "This an April fool joke, or what's the idea, Miss...?"

She stared at his grim face. "Please don't be angry, Mr. Payne, I thought the cock laid it."

Our little sisters, as well as we boys, were certainly a wild and uncurried bunch of ragamuffins that spring and summer of 1896. Unable to get anyone else, Dad put up with this strange creature through the haying season. That over, however, he lost no time in sending her back to England.

After that we were batching, Dad and Arthur acting as cooks and housekeepers, with three little girls and me on their hands.

Tragedy struck again when all of us kids got the whooping cough. Connie died from it, and this brought Dad to full realization that he simply could not, alone, give his daughters proper care and up-bringing. He decided to take Olive and Elizabeth to our aunts and Uncle Dick in Massachusetts.

While he was gone, a hired man batched on the ranch, did the chores and fed the cattle, and Art and I stayed with the Scott boys.

George Scott was a wonderful cook, and he and Charlie had better and much fancier food than we had at home. Best of all—they never got up early in the morning! George did the indoor work; Charlie the chores, which consisted of feeding eight horses and cutting wood. They had two dogs, but no cats, no chickens or pigs, no cows, so one of us boys would walk the half mile to the Payne ranch every day and bring back milk and cream, and butter when needed.

When Christmas came that year, with Dad gone, Arthur and I told Mr. Scott and Mr. Charlie that we were wise to the Santa Claus myth; we knew Santa did not come down the chimney and leave presents for kids, so we'd not hang up our stockings. But lo! on Christmas morning two heavy paper containers, which were used to protect quart bottles of beer, were hanging at the fireplace!

The sacks were filled with candies, nuts, raisins and other goodies. There were also other packages for us on the floor. More presents and a licking good dinner! George and Charlie celebrated the occasion with strongly spiked egg-nog and gave us our first taste of this delectable concoction.

At this time we accepted their hospitality as a matter of course. Looking back now, however, I know that George and Charlie Scott were true friends and the best neighbors Jack Payne could have had. Yet even we boys knew they were a strange pair, so different from the majority of men in our country that actually they were misfits. In contrast with hard working settlers, who were doing all in their power to make homes for their families, to build up herds and ranches, the Scotts were completely unambitious.

They came from a prominent Ohio family, one of considerable means. When the father died, each of the boys and one daughter had received an inheritance of ten thousand dollars. Instead of going into business or doing anything useful with their money, George and Charlie had "blown it all in." This orgy of spending, plus the fact that they were already heavy drinkers, had impelled their mother to tie up the balance of a big estate in such a manner that the boys would get only a certain amount every three months.

Thus they were in the same category as English "remittance men"; they got money from home—approximately one hundred and fifty dollars apiece four times a year. To us, this seemed a huge sum and we thought they were rich!

It is probable the lure of the goldfields brought the Scott boys West, for that brought all types of kinds of people, but how or why they selected North Park as a home I do not know. I do know, however, they were intelligent, cultured, and extremely well educated men who had been Yale classmates of William Howard Taft.

They had an agreement with Dad whereby he irrigated and put up their hay, of which they withheld a certain amount for their horses and Dad bought the remainder. For some strange reason they did all of their trading at the stores in Walden, except for certain luxuries not obtainable there.

George was definitely a white-color man, and the least outdoor-ish man I have ever known. He liked to fish occasionally but cared nothing about hunting or any other outdoor activity. He could drive a team and ride a horse—after a fashion. ("After a fashion" is a term no longer in use, but at this time it was one of disparagement, almost of contempt.) Never to my knowledge did George take a job which called for manual labor. Yet he could have handled any clerical job, could have made a wonderful doctor or fine lawyer had he possessed any initiative or ambition.

On the other hand, Charlie liked to hunt and fish and was the best trout fisherman I've ever known. He enjoyed camping and was an excellent camp cook. He'd make pack horse trips, hunting with English sportsman Harry Hadden, and would occasionally work for wages and make a "fair to middling" hand.

An example of this was his accompanying the Cross boys on their arduous horse trek to Arizona. He was an excellent teller of stories, and one of his adventures while he was working for the Crosses comes to mind.

Said Charlie, "We were camped somewhere in Utah, letting the horses rest for a few days, and I was fed up on the grub we were eating, mostly pancakes with grease, flour and water gravy to put on

50

them. The stuff gagged me. But in that area there wasn't any game so we might have fresh meat, not even rabbits, so I made up my mind I'd kill a beef.

"I did not tell the Crosses what I had in mind, for they wouldn't have done anything of this sort; wouldn't have let me do it. I took a six-shooter, a butcher knife and big sack with me, rode six or eight miles from camp and located a small herd of cattle, out of which I picked a fat yearling to kill.

"I tried to shoot it in the head, but missed, and then had to chase after it. I finally got up alongside the calf, trying to hit a vital spot with a shot from the six-shooter. Every time a bullet would land in its back it would just hump up and bellow and run faster. Yet at last I did drop it."

(A real cowboy would have roped, thrown and tied the yearling and then cut its throat, but this was something Charlie was incapable of doing.)

"I skinned out one hind quarter," Charlie resumed, "hacked it off, put it in my sack and tied it on my saddle. Then all at once I got scared. I knew what cowmen did to a man caught butchering one of their beeves, and the thought that a starving man was entitled to meat didn't help at all.

"I looked all around, and although I saw no one, I rode to a clump of willows and cut down a long, leafy one, then rode back to the yearling and, from my saddle, tried to brush away all marks of my high-heeled boots. Finally I saw this wasn't going to be of much use, so I detoured a long way 'round on my way back to camp, hoping to hide my horse's tracks.

"As I said," and Charlie laughed, "Ben and Dill Cross would never have done what I'd done, but how they did go for that beef!"

"Did—did you get caught?" I asked tensely.

He shook his head. "No. Yet I didn't sleep well until we were fifty miles from that range."

"Your conscience bother you, Mr. Charlie?"

"My conscience is quite elastic."

Although my father liked both the Scott boys, he told Arthur and me that too much money, plus whiskey and having had things too easy when they were young, had ruined them. They'd never amount to a hill of beans.

"Amounting to something," as we early learned, was all-im-

51

portant to men like Dad. It meant working hard, and having integrity, ambition and purpose.

When I later came to know Dill Cross quite well, he told this story of Charlie Scott. Dill had made a deal with the Scotts whereby in exchange for hay he agreed to settle their grocery bill at the Pinkhamton store, where whiskey as well as other commodities was sold.

Dill asked the storekeeper for a statement of the Scotts' bill, and that evening he presented this statement to Charlie, who was at the time staying with the Crosses, saying, "Look this over and see how much of it is for grub and how much for whiskey. I'll pay for the groceries, but not for whiskey."

Dill then went to bed, but the door to his room was open and he saw Charlie sitting at the table close to the lamp, studying the statement, and heard him say, "Whiskey . . . whiskey . . . whiskey! And ten cents worth of grub," and repeat, "Whiskey . . . whiskey . . . whiskey, and ten cents worth of grub!"

Both the Scotts wore mustaches, but neither ever wore a beard. George always dressed in expensive suits, vest closely buttoned and heavy gold chain attached to a fine gold hunting-case watch hanging across the vest. Charlie was a good deal less particular, but he never did wear overalls, preferring good pants instead.

Charlie was generous to a fault. He liked people and kids, and in turn everyone liked him. Although he was a good hunter and an excellent shot with a rifle, nothing would have induced him to set out traps for any animals—with the exception of badgers and skunks—for, as he told me seriously, "The thing I hate about trapping is it's so darned cruel. Your trap catches a coyote and for perhaps two or three days he stays there suffering, until you come along to put him out of his misery."

At the time this did not register strongly with me, for I was sold on trappers. But later by a few years, a real trapper, Sam Bear, came to Jack Payne's ranch to thin out the coyotes in the neighborhood. As boys, we put coyotes in the same category as skunks and badgers. They must be exterminated. We were "down on" badgers because they dig holes in the ground, and if a rider's horse, while running, happens to plant one or both front feet in a badger hole, he's sure to fall hard or even turn end over end. Often such "spills" cripple both horse and rider. The grownups said coyotes too must be killed because they kill chickens, cats and young calves.

I cannot recall today one instance of the coyotes actually killing any calf of ours, but they did kill cats, and on one occasion, about 1899, I sadly told Mr. Hadden, "The mean ol' coyotes got one of our nicest kitties last winter."

Mr. Hadden had no love for our cats. "Best thing that could possibly have happened to it, I should say," he replied.

Now Sam Bear was a Civil War veteran, and that he was also a great trapper made him a hero in my young eyes; so much of a hero that I could overlook how unclean both he and his clothing and the rest of his outfit were. One morning when he was making his rounds of his traps, both Dad and I happened to be with him, and we came upon a big coyote caught by one foot in a Number Four trap.

Sam jumped out of the rig we were using and, rifle in hand, advanced toward this coyote, laughing and shouting, "Ha-haha, you thunk you could outsmart me, huh: I got you. I got you. Ya! Ya! Ya! Take that!" He threw a rock at the suffering animal.

Next he crouched down on all fours and leered and jeered at the coyote, taunting it and teasing it with a strange gibberish of words, even prodding it with his gun barrel, crowing over having caught it.

Dad looked at me. "Sickening," he said in disgust, and yelled to Sam, "Kill the beast and be done with your fooling 'round."

"Aw, no. I'll play with him awhile first," Sam reurned, and kept on with his torture.

"Sickening," Dad had said, and I felt sick, disillusioned and disgusted. My respect for the trapper did a backwards somersault, and Charlie Scott's remark about trapping came into my mind with full realization of the truth of what he'd said.

As I have mentioned, Charlie liked kids. To be sure, he'd hoorah us unmercifully, but he was genuinely fond of us, and he seemed to like to take me with him when making a short trip.

One of these trips, which took place in the spring of 1896 and thus before the winter when Arhur and I stayed with the Scott boys, turned into a major adventure for me.

Charlie borrowed Dad's sled with a wagon box on it to drive to Walden for the purpose of bringing home a load of supplies. He drove his own team, however, and invited me to go along, planning to return that same day. But the snow was melting so rapidly we had trouble finding enough to get the sled through to Walden, and the trip took not two but five hours.

Consequently, Charlie decided to stay overnight. He got a hotel room for the two of us and told me to get my meals at the hotel. Then he went in search of liquid refreshment. There I was in town on my own. I'd been warned that the town kids would make it tough for country "Jakes," and sure enough, when I tried to make up with a bunch of Walden boys, they had to "initiate" me so I'd belong.

The initiation was no joke. Grabbing their victim by arms and legs, four boys whacked his posterior against a post well greased with black and sticky axle grease. I fought them as best I could, but it was no use. They whanged me, but good, and then were willing to accept me.

But I was scared stiff, so I fled and tried my best to have nothing more to do with Walden boys. That made me a very lonely, homesick eight-year-old boy, just prowling around Walden's hotel and stores and the livery stable owned by Harford Loucks.

Meanwhile, as if the fact that Charlie Scott was in town sent mental telegrams to certain ranchmen, who also liked to imbibe, several other men appeared as if by magic and a "big toot" was on at both saloons—Charlie a ring leader and right in the middle of it.

That first night I went to our room and went to bed. But I woke up when at last Charlie came in, sick at his stomach before at length he began to snore. But this sort of sickness did not stop the spree, which was resumed soon after breakfast. On the third day of this "celebration," Irene Mosman took me under her care, believing that Charlie was neglecting me and that I wasn't getting anything to eat. She took me to the Mosmans' house and gave me a real meal. Then I told her that Dad had said I could buy new shoes, and we went to the Mosmans' big store. But when Mrs. Mosman was fitting me out with some shoes—clodhoppers that fastened with one buckle, the cheapest I could buy—she discovered I hadn't any socks, just pieces of rag sort of wrapped around my itchy chilblained feet. How well I remember her expression and her deep sigh as she fitted me out with a pair of real socks. Nor could she help noticing the condition of my overalls, which had resulted from my earlier humiliating experience and was giving me deep worry for fear Dad would "raise the roof."

"What have you been rubbing yourself into?" she asked. "How'd you get that black, sticky axle grease on your britches?"

I would not tell. But Mrs. Mosman remedied the frightening condition by giving me new overalls, after which I'm sure she burned the old ones and the rags.

This was my introduction to C.E. (Gene) Mosman's wife, whom everyone called "Aunt Irene," and whom I have always considered a wonderfully fine person.

Toward evening of that memorable day, I was once more in the big Mosman store when one of Charlie's friends came in, naked to the waist, with daubs of paint on his chest and face and a few feathers stuck into his hair. He was one of the several men enjoying himself at the big spree, where the roisterers had made him an Indian Chief—Old Sitting Bull.

He told Mrs. Mosman that Jerry, Irene's husband, had said for her to give him an undershirt and a shirt. "He helped tear 'em off me, so it's only right he should make 'em good."

Mrs. Mosman got him the clothing, but her eyes kindled, and I never heard anybody get a sharper tongue lashing than she gave that man, including also all those who were staging this spree. But her contempt slid off him like rain off a saddle — and the spree continued.

The next day, I was so homesick and lonely that I screwed up my courage to knock at the door of one of the two saloons and ask for Mr. Charlie. A jovial ranchman welcomed me, and to him I said, "I think Mr. Charlie and me ought to go home."

"Come in, son, come in," he said, and, remembering the free lunch in Laramie, I went in.

There wasn't any free lunch: nothing but a dozen men, some playing cards, some talking silly, and some doing nothing except to lie back in chairs against the wall. But they ganged up around me and picked me up and set me on the bar and had me shake dice with the bartender. If I won, it would be drinks all around on the house; if I didn't, Charlie or someone else would pay for the drinks.

I was given a botle of some kind of pop, which I found licking good, and I shook the dice in a leather cup just the way Charlie told me to do, and I won and was cheered. I was now beginning to have a big time, but the town marshal pushed his way in and roared to the men, "You can't have that boy in here!" Then he took me out with him and I became miserable again.

Meanwhile, George Scott had somehow sent word to liveryman Loucks that he suspected what Charlie was up to, and he knew Charlie would not come home until he was good and ready, so would Loucks bring George certain articles of food? Loucks immediately looked me up and said I was to ride home with him.

We started out after nightfall in a spring wagon, and due to the mud, the snowbanks and the darkness, Loucks had a hard time finding the way. Toward midnight, however, he reached the Scott place, where George was certainly glad to welcome him. But not half so glad as I was to get home, just bursting to tell Art of my adventures.

A few days later Charlie and his team were back on the Scott ranch, but Dad's sled stayed in Walden until the first autumn snowstorm, when Charlie hired someone to bring it home.

Charlie never offered excuses for having made a fool of himself and never by words or act indicated that he had any intention of reforming. In this connection I recall an event which took place several years later.

In 1898 the Scott boys sold out to my father and left the Park. But in 1903 Charlie came back and made a hand on the Payne ranch, working for Dad all summer. He went "outside" for the winter but returned again in 1904. In 1904 it happened we had a cultured schoolteacher as our cook and housekeeper. She was a wonderfully fine person in every respect, and for a time she and Charlie hit it off nicely. But one day Charlie got real thirsty and drove to Walden, where he stayed for four or five days before he reurned with a hangover and a bad case of alcoholic shakes. When he sat down at the supper table that evening, the lady looked right through him, giving him the full benefit of her frozen and silent disapproval.

"This is going to be awful," I thought. "She never will speak to poor Charlie again."

But by neither look nor word did Charlie indicate that he knew he was in bad and that she was "off him," and in a few days they were conversing as amicably as they had before this incident.

Then, one morning our breakfast talk led to opium smoking. There'd been an article in one of the papers about "dens" in Denver where opium addicts went to "hit the pipe."

The lady mentioned how horrifying this was, and Charlie laughed and said, "So far as I could find out, there's nothing to it."

"What do you mean?"

Charlie grinned. "Oh, I've tried almost everything to see if I'd get a kick out of it. I put in a night in an opium den, but hitting the pipe didn't give me any beautiful dreams or waft me to some far Elysium. The smoke didn't even taste good."

"Do you mean to say, Mr. Scott, that you . . ."

"Yes, of course. What of it?" and Charlie laughed.

"What of it! Indeed!" She left the room in a great huff.

Nobody could stay provoked with Charlie for very long. She didn't, and Dad never did. Dad accepted Charlie for what he was— and liked him anyhow.

To go back to the early part of the winter of 1896 and '97, which Arthur and I spent with the Scott boys, you may ask in wonder, "How did such lazy fellows manage to kill time? And how did two live-wire kids either keep busy or amused?"

Well, the Scotts were great readers, and they had lots of books and several magazines as well as newspapers to which they subscribed. They would sit in front of the fireplace to all hours of the night, burning wood, smoking their pipes and reading by lamp light. I recall one hanging lamp with a big round wick, which burned a quart of coal oil every night, the result being that the Scott boys ran out of kerosene almost as regularly as they ran out of whiskey. This, however, did not disturb them, for the stage would bring them another can of kerosene or gallon jug of whiskey from Walden.

They would send us to bed earlier than they themselves went, however, and we could sleep until nine o'clock in the morning, before George or Charlie would reluctantly roll out and begin to stir around. We boys helped with the chores, both indoors and out, and if Charlie had some major project, such as polishing a buffalo horn or sharpening knives or making a hair rope, we'd help with that, too. Alhough we had neither skis nor skates, there were games to play in the snow, and rustling the firewood took a lot of time, both Charlie and George being quite agreeable to our doing this job.

All through those long, very quiet winter evenings, however, we kids too would read by the smoky old fireplace, and we learned to enjoy it! I concentrated on favorite tales such as *Robinson Crusoe*, *Swiss Family Robinson*, and *The Last of the Mohicans*, reading these over and over again. When I came to a big word or one I didn't understand, I merely jumped over it and went on.

The result was that before our stay with the Scotts was over I had read both *Under The Red Robe* and *Ivanhoe*, and I had strange pronunciations for the names of many of the characters. For example, "Sir Brian de Bois Gilbert" was "Sir Brain De Boy Gilbert."

The six weeks or so during which the Scott boys took good care of us passed quickly and pleasantly. Then Dad came home, and we went back to our own ranch, but happily not to batch, for somehow Dad had found another woman cook.

I was mighty pleased to have a woman in the house again, and I went all out for this one, not knowing that she was really a tough old battle-axe. At first, however, she was all sugar and honey, telling Dad how much she loved children and a nice home. (Could be, she believed he was a wealthy widower and here was her big opportunity!)

She said she liked to eat jack rabbits. So to please the new cook, Art and I borrowed the Scotts' single-shot twenty-two rifle and a box of fifty cartridges and went rabbit hunting.

Two boys on one horse, we hied us to the Upper Field where we could always find rabbits along the willows. This "Upper Field," as we now called it, had been Dad's original homestead; and the cabin, which had been his and our mother's home until they bought the Cross ranch and moved two miles farther down Government Creek, was still standing. Seeing it always reminded me of what we called our "skunk" adventure, which had taken place earlier in our lives.

Accompanied by Charlie Scott, Arthur and I had ridden to this cabin in the late spring and had seen four baby skunks playing in the warm sunshine, exactly like a cat's kittens. Obviously Papa and Mama Skunk were not at home, and the babies were too young to perform as is the habit of all skunks when molested.

"No stinkum yet," Charlie said, and we dismounted to play with the kittens.

"I s'pose we really ought to kill 'em," Art said regretfully, "before they are old enough to catch chickens."

Charlie shook his head. "They're too cute to kill," said Charlie. So we let them live.

But later a grown skunk made its home under the floor of the Scott boys' house, and attempts to dislodge it succeeded only in dislodging George and Charlie. They simply had to move out, and Charlie vowed, "Next time I see any baby skunks, it'll be too bad for them!" Eventually, however, they killed the skunk, and eventually the smell faded away.

No skunks were visible, however, on this day of our great rabbit hunt.

We tied the horse and soon spotted a jack sitting, ears down, in plain sight in his snow-burrow home. We at once opened fire. Art would shoot three or four times, then I'd do the same, and, with the bullets kicking up snow all around him, the rabbit just sat motionless. We were afraid to move in closer for fear he'd jump up and run away. So the bombardment kept on, the supply of cartridges dwindling steadily until at the forty-ninth shot Art killed that rabbit!

Proudly and victoriously we went home and presented our kill to the cook. But when we had skinned it, she found a big, queer sort of boil on its body and would not eat it, so the cats got the jack rabbit and we got hoorahed by Charlie Scott.

"Forty-nine shots to kill one rabbit! Nothing's so safe as what you fellows shoot at!"

Failing to interest Dad, this new cook next tried to "vamp" George Scott. Nor was I so innocent that I didn't catch on either. But George shied off like a horse shying away from a bear, and our nice cook turned ornery; wouldn't get up in the morning, wouldn't give us decent meals, wouldn't keep the house clean. So early that spring Dad fired her.

But Dad had been to Walden the previous day, and quite early on the morning she was to catch the outbound stage, Charlie Scott and the Deputy Sheriff from Walden came to the house. They showed the woman a search warrant which Dad had sworn out and then they opened her trunk.

I was tight-lipped and all eyes, watching this occurrence and also listening to the most shocking language I'd ever heard from a woman. The men, however, paid no attention, but went through the trunk until they found my mother's rings and watch.

"Want to press charges against her, Jack?" the deputy asked. Dad said grimly, "We've found what I wanted to find. Now let her take the stage and good riddance!"

After she had gone, Arthur, Dad and I were batching once again up until haying season when Dad hired a man and wife, which seemed a better idea than trying to get an unattached woman cook.

NEIGHBORS

Other nearby neighbors besides the Scotts included the Barnes boys, and Casper Fox who lived "up creek" from our ranch, between it and Pinkhamton.

New England had put its indelible stamp on George and Will Barnes. They were as Massachusetts as Cape Cod. They'd been farmers back home. Transplanted now, they were still small-time farmers with no gnawing ambitions to become big cattlemen.

Will was a confirmed bachelor; George was a widower with a grown son, Charlie, and a most attractive and much-sought-after daughter, Fanny. An unmarried sister kept house for the family. Charlie had proved up on a homestead but had abandoned it in favor of city life. In 1895 A. E. Dwinell (Gus Dwinell, about whom you'll be hearing a great deal farther on in this narrative) easily outstripped other suitors for Fanny Barnes' hand. He, too, was a rock-ribbed New Englander, with the same deeply ingrained thrift, integrity and moral standards the Barnes family possessed.

Will and George Barnes had one invention of which Arthur and I fully approved—a wood-sawing machine, powered by one horse that walked around and around in a circle. Every autumn, after haying, the Barnes boys took wagons and teams "to the timber" and cut and hauled home load after load of first-class firewood. When this pile was sufficient for a full year's needs, they began sawing this wood and storing it away in a shed-like end of their long, rambling house.

Art's and my hints to Dad about how fine it was to have wood ready-cut by horsepower always elicited a scornful snort, followed by, "Humph! Lots of time in the winter for cutting wood."

Will and George Barnes did all of their own work, irrigating and putting up their hay, and feeding their cattle in winter. They owned only a small herd, plus their milk stock, and kept it all in a fenced pasture—most of it government land—during the summer. Each fall they fattened up their herd bull and butchered him for their winter beef.

Dad would comment regularly, "They must like tough beef!" Actually, however, it was a thrifty idea, for this saved feeding a bull through the winter, and, come spring again, they'd buy a new one.

Although these brothers were both intelligent and well educated, the Barnes boys had unlimited faith in the weather predictions depicted on calendars put out by certain patent medicine concerns of those days.

"Lot of bosh!" Dad always said. "The forecaster is bound to hit it right once in a while. When he does, George and Will forget how many times he's been wrong—which is most of the time."

Our father also scoffed at the "water witch" method of locating underground water, a method in which George and Will firmly believed. Their buildings stood on a low hill, and here George had located the spot to dig a well for the house; a good well supplying plenty of water.

Later, when they decided to dig another well for their barnyard stock, Arthur and I happened to be present and we actually saw George Barnes use his "water witch." It was merely a piece of forked willow. Holding it firmly in both hands, he walked slowly around the area where they wanted the well to be located, and presently, to our open mouthed amazement, the stick curved downward.

"We'll dig here and get water," George said.

We boys hurried home to report to our sceptical father, who hooted at the idea, but when we again visited the Barneses, there was a brand new, good well in the barnyard!

The Barneses were the only people I knew who had a homemade cheese press, and if you did something neighborly for them, they might give you one of their cheeses. Yummie! Each brother had his own wagon and team, and each owned a saddle, bridle and blanket. But they did not keep any saddle horses in addition to their two teams. Oh, no. A horse from a team could pinchhit as a saddler whenever they had to do any riding. Although both George and Will smoked pipes, they were so thrifty that they made great stacks of paper matches which they'd light either at the fireplace or over a kerosene lamp when it was necessary to fire up their pipes. (Even the less thrifty Scott boys did this too, matches were so very precious in those days.)

Another of their thrifty ideas was a big vegetable garden, which helped much with both summer and winter food supplies.

Looking back down the years now, I believe these two men were happier and more contented than any I have ever known. Certainly they could not have made much more than a living, and certainly they worked hard, but, as they often said, life had been much harder in Massachusetts than here in this new country which they loved.

"Cap," as everyone called Casper Fox, a native of Switzerland, was at this time a bachelor, living all alone. Dad spoke of him and two or three other men of the same origin as "Switzers." His house and barn were all under one roof, with a partition between the stable and dwelling unit. For myself, I would even have dispensed with the partition. Then a fellow could live right with his horses!

In earlier days this same Cap Fox had captured two young elk and had broken them to drive a sleigh—a regular Santa Claus outfit. But to my regret he had sold the elk, and I'd never seen that wonderful team. In addition to his all-in-one house and stable, Cap Fox had another place most interesting to a small boy—a side-hill, double-doored cellar, in which he stored potatoes and other vegetables, where a hungry fellow might grab up a carrot or turnip to munch on.

One autumn night, so Cap reported, he stepped out of his house and saw an animal on top of the cellar. Believing it was a skim-milk calf that had gotten out of his corral, he called, "Come, bossy; come, bossy!" But when "bossy" did not come, Cap went to bed. In the morning, he took a close look at his cellar and saw bear tracks all over the dirt roof.

"B'jabbers," he told us, "if I'd tried to drive what I though was a calf to the corral, I might not be here to tell about it!"

Like the Barnes boys, Cap owned a small herd of cattle which he grazed on open range, a few chickens and cats, and a team, one of which was also his saddle horse. Occasionally Cap would acquire one or more pigs, and I shall not forget the day when our father, accompanied by us two small boys, helped Cap Fox butcher a hog.

Everything had been made ready for scalding this pig, and Dad was about to knock the victim on its head with an axe and then "stick it" wih a long, sharp knife when Cap cried, "Wait, Jack! I got to feed him first."

"Feed him!" Dad repeated, completely astounded. "Waste grain feeding a pig we're going to kill?"

"Sure t'ing," said Cap. "My mother always said, 'Feed a hog before you kill it; then the meat won't shrink in the pot.'"

Apparently the unsuspecting porker enjoyed his last meal, and we got a piece of the pork, but I don't remember whether or not the meat shrank in the pot.

Off and on through the years, another Switzer, Matt Rust, made his home with Cap Fox and earned his living either by working for wages or cutting timber. Matt was a favorite with us boys because he'd been gifted with a terrific imagination and with the ability to tell "tall" stories.

Here's one example: "When I was in Leadville, chopping cord wood up above timberline . . ."

Matt would pause and look over his audience, and if no one challenged his statement, he would then resume, "I tell you it was cold."

If, however, someone sceptically challenged, "Now how can you chop cordwood above timberline?" Matt would be delighted. "Haho-haw!" he'd chortle, "I got you bested. Full length logs had been hauled up above timberline and I was chopping 'em up for cordwood."

Or this story: "Aw, you fellers never seen a real freight outfit. Now when I was freighting down in Texas, we had fifty spans of mules. One hundred mules. It took two men half a day to hook them up and half a day to unhook them. I had a whip with a lash one hundred feet long and every time I'd miss a mule I'd cut a tug in two."

"Now hold up a minute, Matt," someone was sure to put in. "If it took half a day to hitch up these mules and half a day to unhitch them, when did you get time to do any freighting?"

Squelching the sceptic with a frosty stare, Matt would say, "Young fella, there's a whole lot about this freighting business you don't know . . . I rec'lect one night we was crossing a deep swale with that one hundred mule team. The wagons was still on high ground one side this swale, and the lead teams on high ground t'other side, an' b'gosh, as the chains tightened up, we hung four spans of mules right in the center of that hollow."

At this point the sceptic was sure to say, "But I suppose you swung that one-hundred-foot whip lash and cut the harness, or whatever was holding up the hung mules, and saved their lives."

"Young fella, you took the words right outa my mouth."

I'd never seen Matt riding a horse, so one day I asked him, "Mr. Rust, did you ever ride, or punch cows?"

"Did I ever ride? Did I ever ride! Young fella, I wore out four brand new cowboy saddles in yust one summer. Yust one summer!"

Next to the Scotts, the Coes were our nearest "down creek" neighbors. All three of the Coe brothers had been hunters before they settled in the Park, and for a short time they made their living by killing elk and selling the meat in Laramie. They were interested in mining, also, but by the time I came to know them they had become ranchmen, on a small scale.

John Coe, a rawboned, spare and bearded man, was so hidebound British that he never became Americanized. In talking with Dad—who often agreed with him, to Art's and my disgust—John would rip the "Yankees" up one side and down the other. But he wasn't entirely consistent, for he held a deep respect for the Cross boys and liked the Scotts and the Barneses, all of whom were as American as anyone could be.

John owned a few milk cows and an uncounted number of range horses, which, being more of a liability than an asset, made him "horse poor."

His family consisted of Mother Coe, her daughter Carrie by an earlier marriage, Carrie's husband, Albert Patton, and a very young adopted daughter, Mabel.

John complained a great deal about his wife's son-in-law living off him, "sponging" as he called it, but scathing—even insulting—words had no visible effect on Al Patton. So long as he had smoking tobacco and was sure of a place at the table for meals, Patton was contented.

Dave Hendrickson, speaking of Patton, said, "That moocher's too lazy to say 'Sooie!' if the hogs were about to eat him."

During the winters, however, he took excellent care of his team of horses, which he stabled in John Coe's barn and fed with John Coe's hay.

But about 1899, a miracle happened! To the neighbors' amazement, to Mr. Coe's great sorrow and to John Coe's delight, Albert Patton loaded his wagon, and taking Carrie with him, he moved to

Walden and went to work for John Riggen on Riggen's ranch at the south edge of the town!

Yet it seemed as if John Coe was destined to be plagued forever with worthless boarders. From Iowa now came another distant relative. This man held decided opinions about many subjects, including food, and once told Mother Coe, who was in the habit of baking pancakes before breakfast and stacking them up, "I like my cakes hot, right off the griddle."

Whereupon she replied, with a snap of her lips, "I won't stand over a hot stove and bake pancakes for any bum," a remark which failed to squelch or influence the boarder, who presently sent for a friend to come and share the Coe's hospitality.

Soon a big-framed, hulking, very slow fellow, Albert Bush, appeared on the scene and proved to be both a fiddler and a carpenter. Very shortly he was in demand to play his violin at the neighborhood dances. Since this service called for passing the hat for the musicians, Mr. Bush was able to keep himself—and possibly his friend as well— in tobacco.

Eventually there came a day when Bush surprisingly came to life and bestirred himself to build a new frame house for John Coe. And his pal helped him do it! So, all in all, John fared not too badly at the hands of these two spongers!

Mother Coe openly smoked her pipe—a red clay pipe, but her daughter Carrie smoked on the sly, not wanting the neighbors to know that she too was addicted to the pipe.

Their first squatty old log shack sat in the mud of the meadow, so low to the earth that every spring water oozed up through the flooring or seeped in at the doors. To this original cabin the two women were forever adding new rooms, every one of which leaked. When we visited the John Coes on a rainy or snowy day, we could hear the drip-drip of water spilling into pans set here, there, everywhere through the house.

Mother Coe made soap and tallow candles with wicks of common string. A lima bean hung from the ceiling would give as much light as one of those candles! She also manufactured rag rugs, both small and large, weaving them on a huge loom which occupied all of one side of the kitchen. Watching her or her daughter run this loom fascinated me as a small boy, and the process of dying the strips of rags which they used proved even more fascinating. But much as

I would have liked to do so, I was never permitted to dye any of my clothing like those rags.

The two women must have used every cent they made from the sale of candles and rugs to pay for cure-all nostrums, both pills and liquids, which they bought by the case. They were never happier than when they found and tried out some new "miracle medicine."

"A lot of bosh," my father would snort to his sons when we brought home news of some new medicine. "Nothing's the matter with those women unless it is that they're poisoning themselves with that humbug stuff."

John Coe firmly believed it was bad luck to kill a cat; hence the cat population on the Coe ranch was never checked or restricted. In summer they found plenty of food, but in winter one had to run a gauntlet of yowling, starving cats in order to get in through the kichen door.

The Paynes always had too many cats, also, and often, to my dismay and sorrow, Dad would find a new-born litter of kittens before I'd even seen the precious little mites and would ruthlessly "knock 'em all in the head."

We often visited the John Coes, exchanging Thanksgiving and Christmas dinners, and when John wasn't busy cutting wood or carrying it in, he'd sit close by the kitchen stove over which Mrs. Coe would be working. Every few minutes she'd call out impatiently, "Johnnie, put some wood in the stove."

John would obediently fill the stove's firebox. Then a few minutes later would again come Mother Coe's, "Johnnie, put some wood in the stove."

There was no rest for John Coe. When he wasn't cutting wood, he was putting it in the stove!

Bob Coe batched at his home, one-half mile down creek from John. He owned a small herd of high-grade Shorthorn cattle and a small bunch of horses. He had been married and had one grown son, Lindsey, who was at this time roaming about the West as a cowboy. Bob kept his small ranch in tiptop shape and thought the world of his work horses and his fine saddle horse, Snip. Snip would come to the house every morning and nicker for a biscuit—and get it. An excellent hunter, Bob was rarely wihout fresh meat. He was the cleanest bachelor—not even excepting George Scott—I've ever known, and his immaculate house was open to anyone who cared to stop for a meal or for overnight.

Joe, the third brother, died when I was quite young, and for several years thereafter the Coe boys' sister, Mrs. Leek, made her home on the Joe Coe ranch. She was a widow with one grown son, Eber, whom she called Ebe, and a daughter Mamie. Mamie was Arthur's age and naturally we boys came to know her very well and to admire her as a girl who was "plumb all right."

While other women and girls still stayed chained to side saddles and the awful skirts that made up feminine riding habits, Mamie rebelled. She wore a "divided skirt" and rode astride; she could break horses to ride; in handling cattle she could hold up her end with any of the young cowboys—older ones too, for that matter. Nor was this all, Mamie was the first girl in North Park to wear overalls!

With all of these people Dad had much in common because they too were trying to adjust themselves to a new environment and to make a living in a new country.

But at this early day our father knew almost everyone in North Park and numbered among his friends a great many different ranchmen who lived "farther up in the Park"—ranchers and cattlemen who made a practice of stopping overnight with Dad either on their way to Laramie for supplies or when bound for the same destination with their beef herds.

Jack Payne's big field was a handy place to hold a herd of cattle overnight. For this privilege Dad would charge the stockmen two cents per head for cattle, five cents for horses. But he never charged the men with wagons and teams, quite often accompanied by their wives, who stopped with us. For example, we often saw the three Marr brothers; Bill of the Big Horn outfit, Jim and Alec. Alec K. Marr at this time experimented in "growing out" his steers for beef, rather than selling the animals as "feeders" as most North Parkers did. This meant that Alec would hold the steers until they were three and four years of age before shipping them. Accordingly, the steers were big and fat, weighing eleven hundred pounds up and simply thrilling for a boy to look at. Strangely, however, Jim Marr was content to remain a small rancher and cattleman, but all three of these rugged, lanky Scotchmen were ever-welcome visitors on the Payne ranch.

Naturally, Dad had more in common with the Scotch and the English fellows, which included some of the men with whom he had come to the Park. Of these I have a clear recollection only of the Winscoms, Will and Charlie. But Dad hit it off well indeed with the Swedes and our native Americans, too.

Thus, as small boys, Art and I came to know many of these splendid men from all over the Park. Quite early, we knew Jack Hunter and his large family, who lived on the Platte only four miles from our home. (Later I'll have more to tell about "Uncle Jack," as everyone called him, because he was a "real character.")

Quite early, too, we knew the Blevins family and, with the possible exception of the Scotts, counted them as our best friends. This came about largely because we boys went to school with Montie and Park Blevins and because the Moore and Blevins ranch, their home, was situated on the Michigan only a mile and a half from the schoolhouse.

This big cow outfit was the one of three big outfits in the Park with which we were completely familiar. The other two were the Big Horn Land and Cattle Company, managed by Bill Marr, and Swift and Company's Two Bar Two. None were really *big* in comparison with Texas ranches and the "open range" cattle outfits of the '70's and '80's.

However, each was running approximately five thousand cattle, mostly she-stock. This made them "cow" outfits as distinguished from "steer" outfits. A steer outfit is one which handles no she-stock, but buys young steers, either as calves, yearlings or two-year-olds, and "grows them out" for "feeders" or as "grass beef." "Feeders" go to the "corn belt," the great Mississippi Valley, and the Midwest area of our United States, to be fattened and "finished" on corn or other grain before being marketed as "corn-fed beef." "Grass beef" goes directly to the packing houses.

Moore and Blevins was a partnership outfit, and it is probable that Col. D. L. Moore, who owned a distillery in Kentucky, had put up the money for this ranch and cattle enterprise. I remember him as a rather fat, jolly man with short black chin whiskers, very much the Southerner, who occasionally visited the ranch in midsummer, bringing with him a bountiful supply of his distillery's produce—something which endeared him to the Scott boys. But even on these visits Moore took no active part either in the work or management of the business. Montie Blevins shouldered the full responsibility of running the Moore and Blevins outfit. Its brand was V V, one above the other.

Right at this time, the 1890's, practically everyone agreed with my father that Montie was the top cowman of North Park. He owned, personally, a small herd of purebred Hereford cattle. Although the registration papers on them had been allowed to lapse, they were nonetheless "purebreds," and, by selling the male increase from this herd to other ranchmen, Blevins was one of the first men to improve and build up the quality of North Park cattle. Among the first bulls I can remember on Dad's ranch were two Blevins' Herefords.

Due to the man's personal charm and magnetism, everybody liked Montie Blevins. His striking appearance also helped, for he was unusually tall, slender, and very erect, with jet black hair and trimmed black moustache under a rather prominent nose—a man who stood out in any company, a man who knew the cattle business forwards and backwards. I am sure he had learned this while working as a cowboy with big open range outfits, for once he told the four of us boys, young Montie, Park, Art and myself, "By the time I was twenty-one, I was drawing a hundred dollars a month as foreman."

On one occasion, when he was discussing with Dad the many problems of raising cattle in North Park, I heard him say, with nostalgic yearning, "It was so much easier in the old days of the open range, Jack. No fences, free grass and water, no hay to put up. All a cowman had to pay out was for horses, 'herders' (as they first called cowboys), grub, and a small amount of taxes. The cattle grazed and increased unmolested. We rounded them up to brand the calves and then ran a second roundup to gather the beef steers and ship them to market.

"But now we must feed 'em during the winter—or lose most of 'em; we must build ditches to irrigate the hay land, fences to protect the meadows, and sheds to protect the cattle; we must harvest hay. Already the open range for spring and summer grazing is getting short. The answer is, Jack, we must raise cattle worth far more money per head than the native Texas open range stock was ever worth. But there's nothing either cheap or easy about this cattle business now."

Montie was already an "old timer" in the Park when my father came, and he had been foreman of the Two Bar Two for Swift and Company before he went into business with Colonel D. L. Moore. Two incidents of his early day adventures which he told Dad come to mind:

"Got word by the grapevine that—(we won't name the man

here) was shipping his beef, and knowing him, I made a forced ride to overtake his herd. Took seven head of Two Bar Two steers out of his herd and brought 'em home."

Dad asked, "Have any trouble with the fellow?"

"No. But I told him not to do it again or there'd be real trouble." His second story runs:

"About daylight one morning I was riding close to Blank's fence and I heard cows bawling. I came upon five of them bunched against the fence, minus their calves, and with udders swollen. Listening hard, I heard calves bawling down among the thick willows. So I opened the fence and let the five cows lead me to where the calves were penned in a little corral deep among the willows.

"I opened the corral bars and let the calves out. The mother cows claimed them and they went back to the range. Then I wrote a note and fastened it to a post for Mr. Blank."

"You—you didn't have him arrested, or do anything to him?" Dad asked curiously.

"No. He was a pretty good fellow—if he'd stop his petty thieving."

"And did he stop?"

"So far as I know, yes," said Montie. "My note read, 'Don't ever do this again, or . . . ' I left it like that so he'd think about that 'or'."

Thus, very simply, without anger or malice, Montie gave both of these would-be cattle thieves another chance.

Good cattlemen rated high in my book—only bronc busters rated higher—and, although Montie Blevins did not break broncs, he could certainly handle cattle. And how the man could throw a rope! As small kids we had watched him, pop-eyed, roping horses out of a bunched cavvy, a performance done on foot, the roper standing at the edge of the herd. Mr. Blevins, without swinging his loop, would toss it out across a sea of horses' backs, rumps and heads, and land the noose true around the neck of the particular horse he wished to catch. Other men often missed or caught the wrong horse! Montie never missed, "never spilled a loop." It was the same when he was mounted and roping cattle for branding.

One great day from the safety of the corral fence we had watched Montie Blevins, with three other cowboys, including Harry Green, Blevins' foreman (he, too was a cracker-jack roper), "heading and heeling" the brutes to throw them down. The other ropers "spilled" many loops; Montie caught his animal the first throw.

"Heading" is to rope a cow brute around its neck or to catch its horns; "heeling" is to noose both of its hind legs, although one leg will suffice. Then the critter, when stretched out between two horses, falls down and both head and heel ropes are held taut by the ropers' horses until the brand has been applied.

Meanwhile another cowboy has gotten the "tail-hold." He runs the tail between the fallen animal's hind legs and brings it up toward its backbone. Then he plants his own knees in the small of the animal's back and pulls hard on its tail. For as long as a man retains this hold properly, no cow brute can get to its feet. It is "tailed down."

The branding done, the ropers slacken their ropes, and someone removes the nooses from head and legs while the "tail hold" man holds the animal down. Ropes off, and all clear, this cowboy releases his hold and jumps for the fence, for the cow is sure to be "on the prod."

Ah, yes, even before that day when I enjoyed my first trip to Laramie, I had thrilled to adventures with the Blevins boys!

SPRING WORK

After our being more or less isolated and shut in during the winter months, the coming of spring was an event we looked forward to eagerly. To see the snow begin to turn to water, to see the dark earth come into sight, to hear and to see our first meadow lark, and then to find the first shoots of new, green grass and the tiny yellow buttercups and small, many-blossomed blue flowers!

Once again the mother cats would have kittens and the hens would start "settin'," and we'd hear the odd song of the kildeer by day and the croaking of frogs by night—all of which made a fellow long to get out and hunt frogs, hoping to get enough big ones for a mess of frog legs.

The horses would now begin to shed their shaggy coats, and their loose hair would be sticking to our clothes and to everything else. Now perhaps we might stop wearing overshoes or, if we had no real overshoes, stop bundling our feet in gunny sacks. (Gunny sacks! How many hundreds, how many thousands of feet have they saved from frost bite.) Now we could get out and travel afoot or on horseback or by rig without sticking to a snow-packed trail. Soon there'd be green grass which meant we would no longer be obliged to feed the cattle.

Soon, too, Skinner, the persistent vegetable peddler, would again show up. Then we would know for certain that spring had really come. Skinner had become an institution in the Park. He spent his winters "down the valley," in either Fort Collins or LaPorte. But as surely as snow melted in the spring, as surely as the song bird returned, as surely as the gophers and other hibernating animals came out of their snug winter quarters, we could depend upon Skinner's returning to the Park.

A spare, wiry, and spry old greybeard, he drove one grey horse and one grey mule to a covered wagon. Directly behind his vehicle, there always came another grey team and another covered wagon, driven by his wife. She was a shapeless woman, wearing a shapeless, colored dress, her head hidden under an enormous sunbonnet. Their mutual bed took up much of the space in her wagon, but they were expert in burrowing under it to get at vegetables and other items stored underneath it.

Boots at the rear end of each wagon afforded places upon which to store camping equipment and food, grain for the teams, nose bags, hobbles, picket ropes, water buckets, and, of course, axle grease and a wagon jack. They often camped out on their long, long trek from La Porte to the south end of North Park and back again. But when they came to the Payne ranch, they stopped at my Uncle Will's empty cabin and made use of its stove and empty bunk for that night, turning their teams loose in the pasture to graze.

This was a "good deal" for us boys, because Skinner would pay with vegetables for the privilege of stopping over night and for pasturing his three horses and one mule. So, when we saw Skinner's wagons at the cabin, Art and I would run the eighth of a mile from our house to the cabin to greet the "old coot" and his pleasant-spoken wife—and to get some goodies not included in our regular bill of fare.

None of this produce was very fresh, but we thought it was. Later in the summer, Dad's garden would provide some vegetables but no fruit. So we'd still patronize Skinner for, in season, he'd have apples, peaches, watermelons, and I haven't yet forgotten my first muskmelon!

The next morning Skinner would drive away, visiting ranches convenient of access, and, when all of his goods were sold, he'd head back to La Porte and Fort Collins—one grey team with its white-covered wagon right behind the other. In due course, he'd return to the Park with another load, these visits continuing until autumn storms stopped him.

All at once he began adding other lines to his merchandise, and

73

it took my old friend Charlie Scott to make a big joke out of this. Said Charlie, "I met Skinner today on his way out of the Park. He stopped and called in his high, squeaky voice, 'Hello, Charlie? Want any fresh vegetables today?'

"I thought, 'Some good fresh vegetables'd go well,' so I said, 'Why, yes. What have you got?'

"And Skinner said, 'Baloney, head cheese, mouth organs and other musical instruments.' "

Skinner—I never learned his first name—and his wife were not our only itinerant peddlers. Mrs. Leek, accompanied either by her daughter Mamie or her son Eber, ran a vegetable wagon for two or three seasons, freighting produce from "down the valley," the same as Skinner, and selling it in the Park. She supplied a far better and fresher grade of vegetables and fruits than Skinner, and somehow we always contrived to purchase a few goodies from her too.

But the peddler who appeared on the scene in 1897, and really caught and held a small boy's amazed and longing-filled interest, was William Dryer. This man sold dry goods, clothing for the entire family, blankets, sheets, pillow cases, towels and many other items. Moreover, Dryer drove a three-horse team to a made-to-order wagon, a great, heavy, van-like wagon with a flat space on top rimmed by iron rods where he piled all sorts of things—mostly hides when he was bound out of the Park.

Dryer's wagon was covered by canvas curtains which fastened onto buttons. He'd remove a section of this sheathing and unlock and open either a drawer or a cupboard filled with ... Well, one drawer would contain gloves, another pants or entire suits of clothes, another shirts, and so on. When Dryer stopped at the Payne ranch, two boys were all eyes and all eagerness and curiosity. But Dad bought very sparingly, not being able to afford things. So all we boys did was look and smell and touch and yearn, and, after he had gone, remember all the wonderful items Dryer had shown us.

At this time I considered Dryer and his wonder wagon only from my own little, personal angle; looking back now, this man's coming must have been a shot in the arm, a real morale booster to lonely ranch women. Chained to the jobs of cooking and of raising children, they got out and around very little, seldom saw visitors, and most certainly enjoyed no "shopping splurges."

But Dryer's big wagon brought a complete dry goods store right to their homes. Imagine the average ranchwoman with four or five small kiddies, some hanging back, yet all eyes, others clinging to her dress, while Mr. Dryer opens drawers and cupboards. Starved for something new in the line of dresses or hats or shoes or "unmentionables," this woman can look at and touch beautiful new articles of clothing. Dryer also carried ribbons, needles, thread, buttons and so on, and materials for making clothes for the family, as well as curtains and drapes. All in all, there is no weighing how much he did for the morale of our women. For kids, too.

Unlike Skinner, however, Dryer did not stay with us year after year. Perhaps he found greener pastures closer to his source of supplies, for he, too, stocked up at Fort Collins and it was a hard, hundred-and-ten-mile pull to North Park. The merchants both in Walden and Laramie resented Dryer's intrusion of their territory and they were not unhappy when he faded out of the picture.

But while there were many pleasant things about the coming of spring—the "before haying" season—spring also brought the realistic, all important, problem of saving the calf crop. In those early days North Park cattlemen, with a few notable exceptions, never had a sufficient amount of hay. They believed in "roughing" their stock through the winter. In the summer and fall let 'em get fat—on grass. Consequently, my father's cattle, and particularly the cows and heifers "heavy with calf" were thin (we used the word "poor" a good deal) and weak. In extreme cases animals might be so emaciated they could not get up on their feet without being helped. To give this help, one grasped bossy's tail and, as she struggled to rise, you lifted and boosted—"tailing 'er up."

Some men were much better at this job than others, but Dad, Gus Dwinell and Dave Hendrickson could qualify as experts. The expert, in some manner known only to himself, after assisting bossy to her feet would prevent her from whirling around and attacking him, the first thought of the outraged cow and a move which generally resulted in her falling down and becoming helpless once again.

Too, the very weak critters seemed to have an obsession to wander into the nearest bog hole or slough, where, lacking the strength to extricate themselves, they'd mire down and die unless rescued.

Spring brought both tailing up and bog riding, but it was also calving time. The she-stock was bred so this would occur in April and May because spring calves make the best growth in the summer and fall and, come winter, are old enough to be weaned.

In warmer climes, on the contrary, particularly in Texas, bulls ran with the she-stock the year round and calves were born each month of the year. But in our high mountain land, and for that matter on all the Northern ranges, the early day cowman had soon learned—the hard way, though, by experiencing heavy losses—that winter-born calves froze to death.

To overcome that loss some ranchmen attempted to shelter their expectant cows in sheds or barns, which did not work out too well. First of all the range cows were so wild and so suspicious of anything that looked like a trap that it was almost impossible to drive them into a barn. On the slightest provocation the range cow would go "on the prod"; she would "fight a buzz saw."

Next, a large per cent of these winter calves, after getting off to a good start, would contract "sniffles," which was probably a cold or pneumonia, or else get the "scours" (a veterinarian's term for diarrhoea). Both these diseases would be approximately eighty per cent fatal.

As the cattlemen of North Park had learned in the winter of 1884, they must provide hay for winter feed for their herds, and they must so conrol the breeding of cows that the bulk of the calves would be born in April.

Shortly after this period of the 1890's, some of the outfits pushed the calving season one month farther along. They wanted no calves born before the month of May. "Ye-es, an April calf will be heavier in the fall," they'd admit. "But the April loss will be so much greater than the May loss that the increase in numbers will far more than make up for less growth and lighter weight."

They were experimenting, these cattlemen, learning through trial and error. Later on, when ranchmen learned they must feed thir stock better in winter (Andrew Norell was one of the first North Park cowmen to practise feeding—"All dey can eat," he'd say—and to show with results that this paid off big), the tragic conditions which I am now telling no longer existed; for, with few exceptions, cows and heifers that were healthy, fat and strong in the sping had no difficulty in delivering their calves.

Over the years we learned, too, that all cattle when turned out to graze on the range in prime condition put on far more fat and weight than animals so skinny that they "had to stand twice in the same place to cast a shadow."

But along in the 1890's, young heifers, bred at one year of age and calving as "two's" were so thin and so weak that many of them simply could not deliver their calves. Dad, however, was a wonderful cow midwife, and working with him, Arthur and I understood all about it before I was eight.

To save the life of the heifer or cow was always more important than to save the calf. We did not always succeed in saving either one. Moreover, due to the death of a mother cow after she had calved, for one of half a dozen reasons, we often had orphan calves on hand. No young calf can live on grass alone, so we'd raise some of these "dogies" on skim milk, or we'd "put them on another cow" which already was nursing her own calf.

Gentle milk cows would "take on" additional calves without much fuss; range cows on the contrary wanted no part of such an unnatural deal. So we would shut the calf we wanted adopted and the cow's own calf in a pen; then, morning and night, we'd rope this cow, snub her to the corral fence, bring out both calves, and stand over the cow with a club until the calves had "pumped her dry." In a week or so—if this cow wasn't too scrappy and too ornery—she'd consent to the adoption, and then the calves could be turned out with her.

Now you're going to ask, "What about saving young colts? Did mares experience the same difficulties as the cows and heifers?" The answer is a definite "no." In all the years when Art and I worked with our father I recall only one instance of a mare's being in difficulty.

This particular mare was one of our winter feed team and was due to foal toward spring. Dad kept a close eye on her and there came a day when, from the manner in which she was acting, he became sure something was badly out of kilter. "Boys," he told us, worried, "she's trying to foal and for some reason it won't come."

He got a bucket of hot water, rolled up his sleeves, greased his right arm with lard and made an examination. Result: "I'm sure the colt's already dead. Head's twisted down under its body. Knees doubled back . . . Unless we help her get rid of it, she'll die."

We had a thick veterinary book. Dad spent a few precious minutes looking at it and then went to work by the light of three dim lanterns. We boys held the mare's head and consoled her as much as we could. She was on her feet, which was the way Dad wanted her to be. How the sweat rolled off him! How tense and worried all of us were in this matter of life and death as important—so it seemed then—as if our mare were a human being.

Dad, with a tiny penknife, cut the colt's legs off at the knee, disjointing them, and took out the lower parts of legs and feet. Then he tied a cotton clothes line to a small harness snap, from which Arthur broke out the spring so the snap was actually an open hook. Using this crude implement Dad contrived to hook the snap under the colt's upper jaw and pulled the head up . . . up . . . up . . . to where it should be for a normal birth. Lastly he got a cord around the abbreviated legs and finally a dead colt was delivered.

Was that a victory!

We fed the mare a bran mash, hoping she'd live. Our hopes were fulfilled, for within a week she seemed to have recovered completely!

Dad was not so lucky with a cow upon which he performed a Caesarean operation. With his two boys his only helpers, he tied that cow down, cut her open and took out a dead calf. But the cow died.

During the spring calving season, bad storms created the greatest menace. On the Moore and Blevins ranch one or more of the cowboys would be ordered to look after calving cows, and these men were dubbed "calf boys." I have seen the main room of the old bunkhouse there literally alive with baby calves, packed in by the "calf boys" to get them warmed up, to feed them warm milk, to get them up on their feet and able to join their anxious mothers. Once a calf got up on its feet and got its stomach filled with the mother's milk, the "calf boy" would chuckle, "You're doin' fine, feller. Now you'll make out jus' dandy!"

As soon as most of the calves had been born, usually any time from May first to fifteenth, we'd brand 'em, and then shove all the cattle out of the meadows onto the range. Dad'd ask some neighbors to help with this job, and in turn he'd help them with their cattle. His method was to corral his herd, then cut all the grown stock out of the corral, leaving only the unbranded calves penned up.

This was a big day for us boys. I'd get to help round up the fields, although this meant riding double behind Art. Then I'd "make a hand" in the corral, for, with the exception of a few late fall calves and a few winter ones, these to be branded were so young and so small that even a small boy could "rastle 'em."

Except on the big ones we never used a rope. All would be

crowding against one corner of the corral, bawling their heads off, and a fellow would slip up to the bunch, grab one calf by a hind leg, and drag it up to the branding fire. A helper would then throw it, and either one man and a boy or two men would hold it down while another burned Dad's brand—U Lazy Three (U ᴗ) on its left side. Dad himself would earmark and castrate the bull calves. "Cutting 'em," it was called, and I am reminded that the word "cut" certainly had a lot of different meanings in range terminology. (In his book, *Western Words*, Ramon Adams has tallied twenty-four different uses of this word "cut," including "cutter" and also "cutting.")

The big cow outfits turned their young calves out on the range unbranded and later ran a calf roundup. But even though Art and I were all for the way Blevins' outfit did things, we'd admit that Dad's method, branding the calves while they were very young and easy to handle, was faster, easier and far more humane.

When at last the herd was out on the open range, the work was not ended, not until all dangers from bog holes and from poison weed (wild Larkspur) were pretty well over.

Our big job with the cattle each spring was only one part of the work that piled up at this season. One ranchman, meeting another, might begin, "Heard you got your calves branded, but you got your water on yet? . . . Got your fences fixed up? . . . Manure hauled outa your corrals and sheds? . . . Got your meadow drug?"

"Got your water on?" This meant putting dams in the creeks and filling ditches with water, and then by means of laterals (plowed furrows) and small dams scattering this water all across the meadow. This was irrigating. In North Park, once water was turned on it was not turned off, but ran over the meadows continually until it was time to permit the land to dry out for haying; or until the supply was exhausted; or until someone who had a prior water right forced you to shut off your ditch—or at least limit its flow.

Since water was the life blood of the hay crop, stealing it was not uncommon, and ranchmen got into more trouble and fights with their neighbors over water than over any other one thing. Although I was very young at the time, I still remember the day when my father, as a Justice of the Peace, settled one violent dispute between two of our Pinkham Creek neighbors.

On this midsummer occasion, I was in the bedroom taking an after-school nap when loud voices woke me. Peeking out from behind a curtain, I recognized Williams, a Kentuckian, and Hertzog, a Dutchman, in the living room with Dad, and I quickly caught on that they had come to him, as an officer of the law, to settle their irrigation dispute.

Hertzog had shut down Williams' headgate so that he could get some water for his ditch farther down stream. Thereupon Williams had warned Hertzog to let his headgate alone; yet early this very morning Williams had caught Hertzog tampering with the headgate and had used his shotgun on his neighbor.

Hertzog stripped down his pants and pulled up his shirt and his underwear to show Dad what had happened.

Gee-whiz and golly! Had he been peppered with bird shot right in the rear end!

The two men began jawing at each other, but Dad didn't let them get out of hand. "Shut up," he ordered. "You came to me to settle this business, and I'll settle it."

Hertzog sputtered, "Villiams has got to pay me damages and pay toctor bill."

"Yeah?" Williams derided. "I'm entitled to damages for his shutting off my water."

"Be quiet!" Dad snapped and went on, "Williams, you took the law into your own hands and it's only fair you pay Hertzog's doctor bill. How much do you think 'll be right, Hertzog?"

The Dutchman thought fifty dollars would be not too much.

Williams screamed, "Robber! Hertzog's wife can pick the shot out of him. I'm the one to get paid. Fifty dollars for loss of hay crop due to this coyote's shutting down my headgate."

"That's fair," Dad said. "Hertzog, pay Williams fifty dollars."

"I got no money a-tall. I von't pay dot shot-gun skunk von cent."

"Williams, I know you have money," Dad said. "Pay Hertzog fifty dollars for damages to his person and for his doctor bill."

Williams blustered he'd do nothing of the kind.

"You'll prefer to have this case go to court at the county seat in Fort Collins?" Dad demanded.

No, Williams didn't want that. After more bluster and hard words, he dug out of a pocket two twenty and one ten dollar gold pieces which he gave to Dad.

Dad handed them to Hertzog. "Here you are," he said. "Williams has now paid you. But you are fined fifty dollars for the damage you did Williams. I order you to pay this fine!"

There was more argument, but finally Hertzog gave the money back to Dad. "All right. I pay my fine."

"Right," Dad agreed, and he handed the two twenties and the ten back to Williams, stating, "Both of you have paid your fines. Are you satisfied?"

Both men stared at him. Then Williams looked at the money in his hand and nodded. "Something darned queer about the deal. But yeah, I'm satisfied."

Hertzog scratched his head, looking puzzled. "Yes," he agreed finally. "Yas. Me too."

"Case closed!" Dad said. "Go home and don't ever let me hear of any more trouble between you."

They went out. I was still standing behind a curtain at the bedroom entrance and all at once I saw Dad smack his hands together and begin to laugh.

This was my one big scoop to relate to the boys in school the very next morning! "Fellers, you should ha' seen what I saw. Ol' man Williams caught Hertzog a-monkeyin' with his headgate and he give that Dutchman a load of bird shot right in his back and tail-end. I saw where the shot hit 'im. Boy! Williams sure peppered him!"

Just as "getting the water on" was a must, for otherwise you'd not get a good hay crop, so too was "fixin' up the fences." For if you did not get them repaired, range stock would break into the fields and eat up the hay crop.

The very first buck fences in the Park had been put together with wooden pegs. Holes had been bored in the bucks at the point where they were notched together, and a peg driven in to hold the buck together; then the poles were pegged to the bucks in the same manner. I often thought what a lot of holes the men had bored and what a lot of pegs they whittled out! The chinking between the cracks in log houses was held in place by wooden pegs, too.

Soon, however, the square nail replaced pegs. It was made of a very low grade of iron, and, if one were bent, it could not be straigtened without breaking it. Finally came the round, steel-wire nail, which proved completely satisfactory.

We had miles and miles of buck fences and we were never, never fully caught up with repairing it or rebuilding portions of it.

Hauling manure, cleaning out sheds, corrals and the barnyard, was something which should be done, but a job that could be delayed—and oh, how often it was delayed!

"Got your meadow drug?" the neighbor means, "Have you run a drag over it?" We hitched a team to a drag made of several poles or planks and rode on this contraption in order to weight it down while we drove the team back and forth across a meadow. The purpose was to break up all cow chips and scatter the fertilizer evenly; also to pick up rocks and rubbish, thus clearing the meadow of trash.

As well as getting the most important tasks done, Dad tried to do this job also, but not until Art and I were old enough to drive these drags was this job ever finished.

In the spring of 1897, Dad resigned himself to the necessity of batching, so the three of us were obliged to do all the indoor work as well as the outdoor jobs. Somebody had to take care of the milk and cream, make the butter, wash the clothes, cook the meals, tidy up the home—at least a little bit—and wash the dishes.

Dad hated fried food, including fried meat, so he was strictly a "boil" cook. He boiled spuds, onions, carrots, rutabagas, meat, oatmeal and eggs. We ate soft-boiled eggs, hard-boiled eggs—eggs, eggs, eggs every spring. He had no use for the standard and most common food item of both cowboys and miners—beans; nor did he approve of the great American dish, corn meal mush, but he out-Scotched the Scotch when it came to oatmeal. Oatmeal was THE STUFF for growing kids!

He also abhorred the standard bread item of all North Park bachelors, biscuits. Sour dough and soda, sour milk and soda, or baking powder biscuits, he condemned all of them regardless of their quality. So, driven by necessity for bread, he quickly learned to make yeast bread—called, "light bread"—and eventually, after many failures, he managed to produce a fair-to-middling product.

Although there were several definitely British dishes, as prepared by both our mother and Aunt Elizabeth—roast beef and Yorkshire pudding, suet dumplings, deep-dish pork pies—which Art and I liked, Dad had three oher favorites which met with no approval from us boys. One of these was stewed kidneys. To me kidneys were sickening and horrible, and I said so.

"You kids don't know what's good ... All the more for me."

Blood pudding was another. You caught all of the fresh blood as it gushed from the slaughtered beef's cut throat, and just what you did to and with this blood afterwards, I don't recall. But the final result was a thick, rich and luscious (according to your taste) blood pudding.

But neither Art nor I would have any part of this dish. "Finicks!" said Dad.

We'd have gobbled up this mess, however, rather than go for Dad's fresh milk pudding. When a cow comes fresh, you do not ordinarily use her milk until the ninth milking. (That's standard). For this milk is a thick, yellow, sticky, rich and gooey fluid, quite unlike milk as you know it, and it is considered unfit for humans.

But whenever a milk cow would give birth to a new calf Dad was indeed delighted. He'd strip her dry and save the sticky yellow mess. I do not know the recipe for making the pudding, but soon he'd have a milk pudding. Ugh!

In later years he sort of forgot all about both blood and milk puddings, however, and Arhur and I were very, very careful not to remind him of either one.

Naturally, it fell on us boys to set the table, clear the table, wash dishes and sweep the house in addiion to our rustling wood and water, and in a remarkably short time after we really began to batch, Art was taking on most of the cooking. This when he was only eleven years old.

But although pure necessity drove Art to cooking, he was eager to do it right. He had learned much by watching George Scott, and by asking questions. He also studied cook books, and, considering the limitations of our larder, he managed to "rustle up" pretty good chuck including pancakes for breakfast each morning, or—if Dad happened to be gone—some golden, light, fluffy, melt-in-your-mouth biscuits. He quickly learned too that there are other ways of cooking eggs than merely to boil them.

There were occasions when I too would try my hand at cooking, even though I'd be obliged to stand on a box or chair in order to stir a bubbling pot on the stove or to turn over frying meat. But, strangely, the results were seldom satisfactory even to me. Later on, learning most of my how-to-do-it from Art, I became a passable cook, too.

Ah, yes, from 1897 on there were many springs when he had no woman cook, so throwing a bait of grub together three times each day was an important part of the work; and, if there ever came a time we got caught up with he cattle jobs, the irrigating and the fencing, there was always manure to haul and scatter. Always!

Those springs Dad was lucky if able to hire just one man. Yet, regardless of how far he was behind on urgent work, when summer school opened the middle of May his two boys *must* attend.

SCHOOL: "PARDS" AND PRANKS!

Although all of the neighborhood boys, including Arthur and myself, stoutly insisted they hated school—an idea fostered by hired men, we actually experienced some of the happiest, best remembered and most adventurous days of our lives, particularly in the summers of 1896, 1897 and 1898.

If we were batching when school opened, about the middle of May, we must put up a lunch for ourselves, and our lunches were really something. No cake, no pie, no fruit, no jam or jelly. Spring was the season when fresh meat was scarce indeed, and we had no bacon or ham nor any of the tinned preparations of meat so plentiful nowadays. So lunch consisted of bread and butter and hard boiled eggs.

If we were out of bread, Arthur and I would wad up a batch of cold pancakes for our lunch. A soggy, unpalatable mess they were, a mess we could not swap off to other kids for something better. Occasionally we might swap an egg for a piece of cake or a few bites of ham.

"Swapping" was one of the first things we learned at school.

First boy: "Swap you my jackknife — and it's a jim-dandy — for your sling-shot. Even up."

Second boy: "Even up? Nawthin' doin'. Gimme two bits t'boot."

First boy: "Boot? Heck,no. D'you take me for a sucker?"

So it would go.

To school we rode one horse, double, Art always the boy in the saddle. I was not permitted to have this honor; I rode behind the saddle, hanging onto its long strings. Most cowboys used these strings to tie slickers behind their saddles. We had no slicker, so whenever it rained we simply got wet, often sopping wet.

I do not recall much of anything about our first horse, Billy. But our second mount was Arthur's very own horse, a heavy-bodied bay which he had proudly named General Grant. We believed General was tops as a mount. In reality he was a stupid jug-head as lazy as a lazy burro. But he had his good points, being gentle enough to allow kids to do all the silly things kids do with and around a horse, such as sliding off his rump over his tail, and crawling underneath his belly; carrying strange and frightening items while riding him; and by means of a rope dragging all manner of articles behind him.

Unless the horse was close to a fence or near a rock or a box from which I could swing aboard, I was quite unable to mount properly. But pulling myself up into the saddle, or to my place behind it, from the ground by means of the saddle strings and other handholds was not impossible, provided the horse stood still.

School took up promptly at nine A.M. So with lunch and picket rope tied to the fork of Art's saddle, we'd mount General and head for the schoolhouse as near eight o'clock as possible.

Probably Ovid Allard and his younger sisters, Anne and Jessie, would be ahead of us on the road, or they'd catch up with us. Ovid boasted a horse and saddle of his own; Anne and Jessie rode astride on another pony, bareback. Dad Allard was not a cattleman, but Art and I had two things in common with the Allard kids: they were every bit as hard up as we were, and they also had no mother.

Following the main road, we turned left at the northwest corner of Joe Coe's ranch into a lane bordered on our right by the Canadian field, owned by Moore and Blevins. Half a mile farther along, the lane ended and we came to a good bridge over the Canadian River. Here the valley land, dubbed "the Canadian bottom," was still open range, and the road across this "bottom," lying between the bridge and the high hill upon which stood the schoolhouse, was always a bog hole in the spring.

Here each year through April, May and part of June, the freighters' wagons mired down without fail, until at last a road overseer named Pleasant Bain — yes, "Pleasant" was his real name — got hold of three new-fangled wheel scrapers with which a load of dirt or rocks could be hoisted up and hauled wherever needed. Across this bottom land Bain built a turnpike which stood up to the test of freight wagons and was, at that time, considered a marvel of road building.

At the period of which I am writing, however, General and the Allards' horses slogged through the mud until at last we climbed the steep hill to the schoolhouse.

Hundreds of brown gophers were the only permanent inhabitants of this sagebrush hill. They came in for a rough time from us kids. Lots of fun to throw rocks at them, scoring a hit possibly once in fifty throws; more fun to drown them out of their holes. But drowning out a gopher required five or six bucketfuls of water, which must be carried from the Canadian River. So, after one splurge of drowning out gophers each year, the sport became unpopular.

The most ambitious gopher project, as promoted by some of the boys, was to trap gophers, brand them and turn them loose. Then each boy would own his herd of gophers carrying his brand, the same as men owned herds of cattle. Although this great project died a-borning, rumore concerning it leaked out with the result that girls and women and some men were horrified.

"What'll those little monsters think of next!"

By the time Art and I reached the schoolhouse, other pupils would be showing up, too. As the cowboys phrased this: "The kids come stringin' in from all directions, like cattle to a roundup bunch-ground."

From the north came Harry and Joe Hunter on horseback, and from a slightly different angle, four of the McCaslands, on foot. From almost due west came the teacher and Montie and Park Blevins in a one-horse buggy, and out of the south — the direction of Walden — more kids from the Michigan River ranches. Cora Davis, the oldest girl in school, wore a divided skirt and rode astride with the reckless ease of a cowboy, which had won her the nickname "Bill Cody." Charlie Fletcher, the oldest boy in school; the Cowdreys and the Fishers — all one family — with Walter (Sonny) Cowdrey on horseback, because although only my age, he was sure he was already a real bronc buster. But Ida Cowdrey, Walter Fisher and Beatrice Fisher arrived in a small buggy drawn by one sad horse.

Then, coming across the Canadian bottom, but not on the same route Art and I had taken, was Clara Murray, a squatter's gal — the family had moved into the buildings on the abandoned Charlie

Barnes place — astride a stumble-footed plug, with her long skirts wadded and bunched high and her small sister hanging on behind Clara much as if it was a squaw with her papoose.

Finally, out of the south from "way up" on the Michigan, appeared the Brownlee boys, Fordice and William — "Dice" and "Bill." (Later Forest Brownlee, who was younger, also attended our school.) At this time Dice and Bill were trying hard to live up to their reputation as the toughest kids of our neighborhood. Their father, Sam Brownlee, rated high with all of us boys because Sam had once on a time come up the trail from Texas with a herd of Longhorn cattle. So he qualified both as a real cowpuncher and cowman.

Dice and Bill didn't make out too well as the toughest in school. On one occasion, which I vividly remember, Ovid Allard, a small-framed, wiry and very quick in his movements, boiling mad over something they had done to him, took both of them on at the same time and licked them. Then our teacher, Miss Best, walloped Dice, but good, and followed this by laying Bill low. That tamed Dice.

Bill however was still "plenty ornery" a year or two later when we had an Irish girl for the teacher. I was all jitters when she really laid it on Bill with a heavy stick across his shoulders and back. When he broke free, he rushed out of the room, picked up two rocks and came back prepared to throw them. Quite undaunted, that spunky little teacher faced him and made him back down — in front of all the pupils.

The first one of my teachers I remember distinctly was jolly Miss Best. In a land where eligible males outnumbered eligible girls at least four to one, she had many admirers, but Alec K. Marr, one of our most prominent cattlemen, "beat the others' time" and made her Mrs. Marr.

The months she was teaching, Miss Best boarded with Mrs. Blevins and drove a one-horse buggy. At first Park and Montie rode with her. But that was sissy stuff for young cowboys and they soon started riding horseback, Park behind Montie on "old Mex," always accompanied by their black and white dog, Punch.

By 1896, or maybe earlier, a wonderful, white-painted frame building replaced the old log schoolhouse, which however was left standing for use as a stable. Dad was a member of the school board, so I know this building cost *five hundred dollars*. Although there were some frame houses going up in Walden, they were almost unknown on ranches, and Dad held them all in contempt, snorting,

"Cold in winter, hot in summer, while log buildings with dirt roofs are warm in winter and cool in summer."

The summer term of school would get off to a grand start in the spring. Soon, however, some dad would need his oldest son to help with the cattle or with irrigating, and that boy'd be out of school for a few days.

The same was true for the bigger girls when Mama needed her daughter's help. Two of Uncle Jack Hunter's boys, Harry and Joe — and later on, Ed — would attend school for a few short weeks, then drop out. Uncle Jack didn't care. He often announced publicly, "I don't want my boys to be any smarter than I am."

As soon as "haying" began, all boys who were able to make hands in the hay field stopped school for the duration of the hay harvest. Our father was more determined that his sons get an education than most of the dads, but he too was often hard pressed for help, and Arthur could ride after cattle or drive a hay rake as well as a man.

How well I remember the year we had a man teacher. This "he-schoolmarm" was hired by the school board in the mistaken belief that a man was better qualified than a woman and much better able to handle the big, tough boys. But this fellow had no understanding of kids, no ability to win their confidence, and apparently no desire to do so.

The big boys (I was not yet one of these) were soon onto him and openly and derisively flouted his disciplinary measures. His method of whipping them was to use a light willow and switch them low on the legs, during which they'd grin at the schoolroom, and afterwards chuckle and joke about getting a licking.

He introduced "setting-up" exercises. One of these drills called for all pupils to stand in line and raise their legs at his orders: "Right, left! Right, left! Up! Higher! Down!"

This was most embarrassing to our girls, and when the parents were told of what the teacher was demanding, whole families dropped out of school. During the haying season I was the one and only pupil — much against my will. The he-schoolmarm was not asked to return, nor did the school board ever again hire a man teacher.

But for at least the three summers of 1896, '97 and '98, Art and I roamed around with Montie and Park Blevins. We four were "pards," and pards meant something pretty special. Occasionally we might visit the Jack Hunter ranch and play with Harry and Joe and experience the thrill of staying overnight with them. Sometimes, too, we'd stay overnight with "Sonny" Cowdrey or he'd return our visits. But most of our overnight visiting back and forth and our roaming around was done with the Blevins kids. Montie, one year older than Art, was the leader, naturally; Park was just one year older than I; Dean, several years younger, was not included in our adventures. But the Blevins boys' dog, Punch, was one of our gang!

Mrs. Blevins never failed to make us welcome and always had something good for us to eat, even though we made extra work for a ranchwoman who had her hands more than full. In addition to raising her family and making a home, she, at this time, cooked for all of the hired help. But I can still hear her either whistling or singing as she worked! A bit later on, however, Montie Senior installed his round-up cook in the bunkhouse as cook for the entire crew.

It wasn' long before Park was given both a saddle and a horse of his own, a sort of mouse-colored pony named Blue, after which I had a wonderful choice of riding behind any one of the other three boys. With Mr. Blevins' permission, all the pupils picketed their horses with long ropes inside the Moore and Blevins Canadian field during school hours. After school we four pards would ride down on the Canadian bottom — at this time open range land — and put our picket ropes on old buffalo skulls or old cattle carcasses and drag them around, or perhaps rope clumps of sagebrush and try to pull them up. Or — this was the most fun — we would chase cattle and practice our roping skill on them.

Art was, however, hardly capable of roping a wild range cow, and Montie knew better than to try to do it. His small pony, Old Mex, could not hold such a brute, even if Montie managed to "take his dallies." (Most cowboys we knew preferred to take dallies — turn around the saddle horn which can be easily released — rather than to "tie hard and fast.") Moreover, the cow was sure to "go on the prod instanter," which might result in a badly gored horse or badly injured kid, and neither Art nor Park could "heel" the cow and thus throw her. So Montie realized that if he roped a wild cow she would probably go over a distant hill with a lost rope trailing behind her.

But if a fellow noosed a gentle milk cow it would stop and stand quietly so he other young cowboy could practice trying to noose its hind legs. Best of all, the roper could be sure of getting his rope safely off a tame animal without danger of losing it.

Right at his time Mrs. Leek, with Eber and Mamie, were living on the nearby Joe Coe ranch and were grazing their milk herd on the Canadian bottom, Mamie rounding the cattle up each evening to take them home. This milk herd was a temptation to mischievous boys, and we four pards — for a short time only — got a big kick out of chasing and roping the Leeks' cattle.

Then came one evening when Mamie, on horseback, carrying a heavy quirt, came flying out to where Montie had noosed a cow by the horns and Art was vainly trying to "heel it." Reining her horse to a sharp halt, she confronted the four of us with sparks in her eyes and all storm signals flying.

"You kids let our sock alone or I'll lick all of you," Mamie told us. "One at a time, or all four at once. And don't believe I can't do it!"

Park and I had nothing to say; Montie tried to kid Mamie. She wasn't in a mood for kidding and the upshot of the clash was that four shamed and humiliated boys "sort of tucked in their tails and snuk away," defeated by one spunky girl. Thereafter the Leek milk cows grazed in peace.

As soon as the weather became warm enough, the school boys all went swimming each noon in the Canadian, a sluggish stream with a sandy bottom and consequently not dangerous. We'd hike downstream for about a half mile, thus getting out of sight of the schoolhouse, peel off our clothes and plunge in. The "swimming hole," about six feet long, was not deep enough for real swimming, but that is what we called plunging across this hole. No soap, no towels, so after we came out of the water, we put on our hats — hats of course came first — then quickly pulled our clothes over our wet bodies or the mosquitoes would "eat us alive."

But Saturdays were days for real fun. During these summers either Art and I would go on Friday evening to stay overnight with the Blevins, or Park and Montie would go home with us for the night, where Dad always had a welcome for the Blevins boys.

Saturday adventures at the Moore and Blevins ranch often took the form of a fishing trip on the Michigan, or we just might get in on helping the cowpunchers. This was the biggest and best cow outfit in the world so far as we were concerned, and we knew and liked all the Blevins cowhands; the other hired men, too. They loved to hoorah us, and "put us up to mischief." Yet we enjoyed being with them, helping out with their work if possible.

Adventures when Park and Montie stayed overnight with us

would be a climb up Sentinel Peak (Round Mountain), or a trip to the Sand Hills, where it was always fun to play in the sand and roll down the dunes. We might also find raspberries or gooseberries or chokecherries and gorge ourselves. This Sand Hills trip would include a stop at the old Indian teepees on Governmen Creek, where three teepees were still standing, made of dry quaking aspen poles piled up in regulation teepee shape. In these we could play we were real Injuns or look for arrowheads, of which we found a good many, but rarely a perfect one.

One bright and sunny day we went swimming in Sand Creek which flowed through Dad's big field about three-quarters of a mile south of our buildings. Here the stream's channel was approximately thirty feet wide, but the water was scarcely one inch deep and so loaded with sand as to clog, or dam, the flow of water. Then, as water backed up behind this "clog," exerting pressure, the current would carry the sand along downstream in waves.

All of this made it interesting to small boys. Stripped bare, we lay down on the soft sand and let the waves roll over us. We also romped about in the warm sand and sat in the sun, thoroughly enjoying ourselves for the greater part of that Saturday.

But that night I woke up on fire and screaming with pain. I wasn't merely sunburned. I was blistered! The other boys, being older and maybe tougher than I, stood it better. Moreover, the Blevins boys had the kind of skin that tans; Art and I had skin that never tans, but only burns and blisters and peels. All of us suffered plenty, but it nearly killed me. Dad didn't know what to do. He had heard that soda was good for sunburn and tried to rub plain soda on my skin. Just the touch made me howl and hurt me so that he gave up that treatment, and I had to endure the pain until at last new skin replaced that which had been burned. None of us even again went "swimming" in Sand Creek!

The humiliation of having no horn on our saddle troubled both Arthur and me to a point where something had to be done. So, in studying Mongomery Ward's catalogue, Art discovered that we could buy a steel saddle horn with four prongs which could be screwed to a saddle tree, and by saving our money for months we at last were able to send for this saddle horn. What a great day it was when big brother stripped the leather off the saddle fork and put the new horn in place, drilled holes in the tree and screwed it down, then put the leather back. Now we could ride proudly and show off that horn to the other kids!

Conquering this problem prompted Art to embark on new ventures. In a certain magazine he saw an advertisement:

"Win a stem-wind, stem-set, nickel-plated watch by selling only eighteen packages of bluing for ten cents per package."

Without consulting Dad (he'd have been sure to snort, "Trash! Where you ever going to sell it? The watch'll be nothing but a piece of junk!") Arthur became a salesman. Thereafter our Saturday, and even Sunday, trips about the neighborhood were business visits to the neighbors, selling bluing.

This bluing was in the form of blued paper which, when put in water, was excellent for rinsing clothes, and, if a larger quantity were used, it also made wonderful blue ink. Eventually Art sold all of it!

Park and Montie invested ten cents in a package and supplied the whole school with ink; not to mention the pint or so we used to doctor the saddle of a certain boy we didn't like.

In due course the watch arrived. It was bright and shiny, but otherwise a terrible disappointment, for it was as thick through as an alarm clock and we had to pry off the back to get at the knobs to wind it and set it. Not our idea of "stem-wind and stem-set."

Even so, Art swapped off that watch to good advantage, and then — aha! Then he branched out as a real salesman. This time he sent for a cure-all salve in small tin boxes, and the premium was a *camera* with some films and materials for developing the films!

Our neighbors, however, were "kinda sold on bar grease and skunk grease" as salves for humans, and on plain axle grease for sore spots on horses or cattle. Highly regarded and popular disinfectants were turpentine and carbolic acid. Selling the ointment was a slow, long drawn out ordeal. But eventually we got the camera!

Arthur fixed up a dark room, took pictures, and developed and printed them. They were bad enough to make even a kid shudder, but I wish I had them now!

Finally we embarked upon the biggest salesmanship venture of all, and I was in on this with both feet. The enticing offer this time was, "Sell so-and-so-many packages of chewing gum for only five cents per package and win a pair of ice skates."

Skates and a tricycle were two of the things which I wanted so badly it hurt. I'd look at them in the big mail order catalogue and fairly drool, knowing that Dad would certainly never buy anything he considered so utterly useless as those two items. So when Art sent for chewing gum to sell, I sent for some myself. But it seemed as if the grown-up neighbors just weren't gum chewers. Moreover, this was winter, so it was hard to reach the kids, most of whom, like us, never had money anyhow.

Art somehow managed to sell his consignment of chewing gum, but I was my own best and only customer. Boy, what fine chewing I enjoyed — when Dad wasn't watching. If he did catch me, I would hear, "Spit that stuff out of your mouth into the stove!"

One trouble was that after the goodie-good flavor was gone I'd went fresh gum — and it was there to be had. So the days and the weeks ran along, the gum supply ran short, and little Johnnie hadn't raked in any cash in sales. Not one darned cent! Letters from the company began to arrive, each more demanding, each nastier than its predecessor.

How, where, was I going to get the money? My good friend Charlie Scott was no help. He laughed at me, thought it a good joke and finally said, "You got yourself into this mess. Now get yourself out."

"Mr. Charlie, will — will they put me in jail if I don't pay?"

"You bet they will. You'll wear a striped suit and all you'll get to eat will be bread and water."

I thought, "I'll trap muskrats or a coyote." But I couldn't trap either. I'd skin a dead calf. That was no good, for Dad skinned any critter that died, and he took the money its hide brought.

I suppose it would be gratifying to say I worked my way out of the dilemma myself. But I didn't. Art told Dad all about it. Dad gave me a talking to and then did something which, in spite of his snorting and roughness, made me realize he was a pretty good dad after all. He sent the gum people the money — and I got the skates!

With all the roaming around we boys did, we seldom got as far from home as Walden. Park and Montie had more money than Art and I, but even so they were never flush, and there was no fun in going to town unless we had money to spend.

At first none of us had cowboy boots. They were not as yet manufactured in kid sizes, but oh! how we wanted the real high-heeled boots! I recall one occasion on the Blevins ranch when the punchers had all gone to Walden for some "doings" which would conclude with a dance. Now, contrary to both fiction and the movies, cowboys of those days much preferred shoes for dancing, so these fellows had donned their "going to town duds" and dress shoes, leaving their boots at home. The four of us thereupon invaded the bunkhouse and each kid became the puncher whose boots he appropriated.

The boots of that era had high tops reaching up to a man's knee — even after they sort of wrinkled down at the ankles. So our legs were well encased from feet to hips, making it difficult to go clumping around in footwear several sizes too large. But what fun making believe we were the real thing! Really, truly cowboys.

Most of the lads as well as the girls wore high-buttoned shoes. To fasten these properly a buttonhook was a must. Who, today, seeing a buttonhook, would know what it was for?

Eventually all of us "regular fellows" acquired boots. My first pair was made of split cowhide with flat heels and wooden-pegged soles. And, oh boy, they had brass toes!

How badly Arthur and I wanted real cowboy hats too! Dad believed that dinky little caps — I remember Art's wearing the same old winter cap into the summer — were the thing for boys. We boys did not agree with him.

Eventually big brother acquired a hat which answered the purpose, and then he hustled for me a discarded, low-crowned, wide-brimmed and very floppy relic. Stuffing paper inside the sweat band made it almost fit my head, but it still flopped down into my eyes and all the way around my head as if it were a piece of rag.

Someone told Art of a method to remedy this defect. Forthwith he heated a flatiron, mixed up a strong solution of plain sugar and water, doused this mixture liberally on the hat brim and then carefully ironed it. Result, success! The brim of that hat was as firm and hard as a pine board. Its color was a sort of streaky brindle and yellow. But at last little Johnnie had a cowboy hat. (Maybe.)

The games at school we liked best were first, marbles; then, Steal Sticks and Pum-pum-pullaway and Ante-over. Ante-over was the only game we played using a ball, for we knew nothing of baseball, football or basketball. So we never missed them. Wrestling was popular and, like all normal kids, we were always getting into fights to settle who was the best man. The only kid I could lick was Walter Cowdrey — and he'd then lick me. So we took turns.

It was customary for the school day to open with the singing of two or three hymns, always followed by "America." The grades ran from first to eighth; and, when there was a full attendance, there would be a pupil or two in each grade for the teacher to struggle with. Subjects: reading, writing, 'rithmetic, spelling, geography, grammar, history, physiology.

History was good stuff, for it told about the early colonists who settled America, and with them we had something in common. However, life was even rougher and tougher for them: cooking in front of an open fireplace, making their own clothing, putting up with sand for flooring material. We at least had stoves, we could buy our clothes, we had floors of rough pine boards.

Physiology was interesting, but plumb scary to little girls and little boys. The reason for this was that someone had sold the school board a big chart supported by an easel. Its highly colored pages showed the human anatomy. The skeleton was frightening enough, but those internals — stomach, liver and other organs pictured in garish red and other equally vivid lines to show the horrible, destructive effects of nicotine and alcohol — made me shiver.

I wanted to talk to Charlie Scott about it, but somehow I couldn't make myself say, "Mr. Charlie, all your insides must look like our forest fires look at night."

Every autumn forest fires raged unchecked in the mountains and no one did anything to stop them. Winter snow extinguished them, however.

I went for our Barnes school readers in a big way; I liked their stories and their poems, and at one time I could reel off almost every poem in the old Barnes Fifth Reader. But my memory was not that good the first time I was called on to recite in the presence of the school and Teacher and the parents.

"Johnny Payne will now recite 'Excelsior.' "

Johnny marched up to the front of the room and put his hands in his pockets. He saw Teacher frown, so he pulled them out and put them behind his back and took his stance and spouted:

"Theshadesofnightwerefallingfastwhenthroughpinevillage rode a boy of snow and ice. He bore — He bore — bore — Uh? Banner! Boy bore banner. EXCELSIOR!"

Johnny stopped with his mouth open, turned red, and fidgeted and squirmed in a silence that was terrible — at least for him. Then Teacher came and took his hand and led him back to his seat, and the pupils came alive, snickering.

Later on in my school years however I took active part in several dialogues (trivial little plays), remembered my parts and was loudly

The correct and proper dress for cowgirls of yesterday is shown here: Full length divided skirts. (Girls' names unknown to the author.)

A chuck wagon of the type used in North Park, 1903. Walter Zipful, back to camera, cook: Oliver Allard, flunkey. Breakfast is over and they are loading up to pull out.

Lucretia and John Stephens Payne taken several years before she became Mrs. Payne. Jack Payne ranch background.

The Laramie, Wyoming, to Walden, Colorado stage. Taken 1901.

The author, John Stephens Payne, at thirteen, saddling his horse at the Payne-Dwinell range camp. Photo taken 1901.

John Payne making Dutch oven biscuits — for a picnic party.

This is the author, mounted and dressed for winter, taken many years ago. Johnie Payne.

Haying or harvesting hay at Jack Payne's ranch in North Park.

The mowing machines.

The rakes, three in all.

Two "sweeps" or "buck rakes" bringing hay to the stacker.

Haying. Rancher, Jack Payne, making a hand in the hay field — and his "pusher" team.

Here the team will back up and deposit load of hay at foot of slide stacker

A sweep load of hay being pushed up the slide stacker.

102

Cattle, North Park, Colorado

Taken 1901. Winter hay feeding scene at Dwinell's ranch, North Park, Colorado.

Taken 1903. North Park cattle on the way to the shipping pens at Laramie. John Kimmons foreground.

Corralled cattle. Jack Payne's ranch, 1908.

Texas Longhorns like these were common in early day North Park.

Cows on a winter feed-ground. Dwinell's Horse ranch, North Park.

104

applauded. Proudly I once said to Charlie Scott, "Would you like me to recite my school dialogues for you, Mr. Charlie?"

"God forbid!" he said.

The old schoolhouse now served as a playhouse for the boys, no girls allowed. When we had a teacher whom we could "work," it served another purpose.

First one boy would get excused because he had a killing stomachache and must go lie down for a little while. With the first boy excused and safely out of sight in the old log building, a second boy would quite suddenly develop a frightful headache, and he'd join Number One. Soon One and Two were followed by Number Three; possibly even by Numbers Four and Five.

Now for a game of mumblety-peg or marbles or something equally unrelated to our studies — with an eye out to see if Teacher were coming. If she was, how quickly the marbles got back into pockets and how quickly the boys would stretch out, holding hands over stomachs or to heads, groaning with misery and pain.

Getting a pail of water was another method of killing time and avoiding studying. Water was carried from the Canadian, one-quarter of a mile distant and this job always required *two* pupils, boys generally, nor could it be done at recess or at the noon hour. It must be done on school time!

Accordingly, two boys would receive permission to go after water. They'd dawdle down the hill and poke along the road to the bridge, stopping along the way to throw rocks at gophers or blackbirds.

Underneath the bridge, when the stream was low, was a nice sandy, shady spot on which to rest for a few minutes. Or the boys might walk upstream or downstream to see if they could catch a few minnows or kill a big sucker. Or if a traveller were coming along the road, the boys might hail him and possibly carry on a lengthy conversation.

They mustn't kill too much time, though, or Teacher would get nasty and refuse this particular pair of boys permission to go after water again.

So eventually the pail would be filled, and the slow trek back to the schoolhouse began. Lugging water at home was an imposition, an ordeal, a darned tough job, but going after water at school was quite something else!

Incidentally, farther upstream, this Canadian River water had previously been used over and over again for irrigating meadows.

Range stock watering at the stream in the open range areas had polluted it further. It was, in short, vile stuff. Yet at this time there was a theory, firmly believed by people, including my father, that water purifies itself every half-mile!

During these summers there were many home seekers with teams and covered wagons passing along the road; most of them, I think, pointing for the Steamboat Springs country or beyond. All such outfits were legitimate prey for pupils of our school. We got a big kick out of one silly trick. This was for a boy to rush out toward the teamster as if frightened and shout, "Hey, Mister! Hey, Mister! Your horse has got a bone in his hind leg."

Or, "Hey, Mister. Your wheels are turnin'!"

Most times the driver would either grin or glower and go right on. But if he should stop and look alarmed and sing out, "Which one?" we'd be laughing for hours aferwards.

Occasionally the boys would carry this joke beyond the line of good clean fun. For example:

Montie, Park, Arthur and I were still at the schoolhouse one day after all others had gone home when we saw a covered wagon outfit pulling across the Canadian bottom with a bearded man driving. Montie, as the oldest kid and consequently the leader, was good at keeping in the clear himself while putting Park and Arthur up to something, and this time he told Park and Art what to say to this bearded man — all of it words for the saying of which little boys get their mouths washed out with soap!

"Do it yourself, Montie?" Park suggested.

"You're scairt to, huh?" Montie retorted. "You're both scairt. Well, if you're too yellow . . ."

That settled it. Park and Arthur rushed out to intercept the covered wagon and they spoke their insult.

The man cupped a hand around one ear and yelled, "How? Come again."

Again Park and Art parroted the words, and again the man pretended he didn't hear.

"Now just what did you boys say?"

I was peeking through a crack in the little schoolhouse barn and could see the two boys getting uneasy, mighty fidgety. But they stuck it out, and for the third time loudly repeated the words.

This time the man straightened up on his seat and said in a mild tone, "Well, well, you are certainly a pair of nice little boys. My

106

wife and daughters are in the back of this wagon and have heard every word you said."

Then he clucked to his team and drove on, leaving behind him the two most subdued, sheepish, hang-dog boys I have ever seen. Nor did Montie ever again suggest that sort of stunt.

A major event for the entire school took place during the summer of 1897. Mr. Blevins had brought to the Park a big herd of Oregon cattle. The animals were shipped by rail from Oregon to Rawlins, Wyoming. From that point the Moore and Blevins outfit trailed the herd on into the Park and put the cattle in the Canadian field.

In this same field on the sagebrush hill close to the schoolhouse, the outfit's chuck wagon made camp for the purpose of feeding the cowboys while they were engaged in branding the herd. Each day the punchers would cut out approximately one hundred and fifty cattle from the main bunch, drive them to the corrals at the home ranch and rebrand them with Moore and Blevins' $\underset{\vee}{\vee}$. Afterwards, they'd move the cattle so branded out to open range.

One day while this work was going on, Montie and Park told all of us at school that the chuck wagon cook, Bill Brennan, was going to Walden for the day. Before leaving, however, this cook was to make dinner for the cowboys and leave it ready to be eaten.

"If Bill goes away before first recess," Montie said mischievously, "we can get a real feed before the punchers'll show up at noon. And all of you are invited!"

Before first recess, there were many eyes peering anxiously out at the windows to see what Mr. Brennan was doing. Ten o'clock came and he was still at camp working over the fire. Then, lo! he swung to saddle on an old plug and whipped it to a lope heading townward.

The moment we were dismissed for recess, Montie said, "Come on, everybody." Fifteen or more boys and girls trooped across the sage to the fence, crawled through it and came to the now deserted camp. There was no tent, but the cowboys' beds were either rolled or scattered about here and there; a great pile of old fence timber had been dragged up for firewood, and a large barrel sat on a sled like a "stone-boat" which the horse wrangler dragged to the river each day and, after filling the barrel with water, dragged it back again to camp. But all of us lost interest in mere water when we saw in big pots and Dutch ovens, carefully banked with ashes and coals to keep the food hot, that dinner was indeed all cooked and ready to be eaten.

"Let's eat!" Montie whooped and he led the procession to the chuck box at the rear end of the wagon. Every kid grabbed a plate, cup, knife, fork and spoon and then we raided the pots and Dutch ovens. There was delicious boiled meat, with onions and potatoes in the same liquor, baked beans, stewed canned corn, golden brown biscuits, light and hot with plenty of butter, black coffee, and, to round out the meal, dessert of cold canned tomatoes.

Each and every kid filled cup and plate, and then sat on rolled-up beds or on the ground, gobbled up the food, and went back for more!

All at once the school bell rang. The little kids began to squirm, but the larger girls laughed and said, "Teacher can't lick all of us. Let the bell ring."

Presently the bell stopped ringing and Teacher came striding purposefully across the sage. At the fence she called, "Whatever are you children doing? Come to school this minute."

"Come and join us," invited Montie. "We're having a swell meal."

This teacher, a plucky Irish girl with a good sense of humor, joined us and laughingly said she'd like to be hiding close by when the cowboys came back for dinner!

Oddly, however, although all of us were sure there would be violent repercussions, we never heard anything about the raid, either from the cowboys or the cook.

But from the entire neighborhood we pards heard planty of outspoken words, none of them complimentary, after we hanged the billy goat. We were little monsters, we were "little fiends," we were sure to come to a bad end. (Aw, shucks, we were only getting even with the dratted goat for pickin' on us.)

As for how this came about, all of us would often visit the Cowdreys, and Charlie Cowdrey owned a small band of Angora goats, one of them a billy goat, who quite soon "got it in" for us four pards. Could this have been because Billy resented our teasing him and his lady goats, wrestling with them, attempting to rope them, and offering the insult of pulling Billy's beard and daring him to fight? Well, could be!

Billy'd sneak up on any one of us he could find, and attack from the rear in true goat fashion. Once, in butting me down, Billy nearly knocked me silly and skinned up my face in the gravel as well as making it painful for me to sit down.

He had all of us buffaloed. But we were fair itching to get even with him when there came a day that Walter Cowdrey just happened to mention at school that there'd be no one at home on the Cowdrey ranch the next day, Saturday.

This announcement gave Montie and Art a brilliant idea, so on Saturday morning, four determined boys, gleefully excited in anticipation of "besting" Billy, rode to the Cowdrey ranch. None of the Cowdreys were at home, but Billy and his harem were very much present, Billy waggling his beard and stamping his feet and glowering at us.

Adjoining the main Cowdrey house was a woodshed in which was a curbed-up well with an overhead frame which supported a pulley. The pulley was equipped with a strong well rope, and to each end of this was tied a big bucket.

"The bottom of the well is just the place for that doggoned goat," said Montie.

"Sure," Art agreed. "But a goat in the water'll spoil the water. Maybe it'd make Mrs. Cowdrey and Ida and Bee and little Frances awful sick."

Park came through with a solution to this problem. "We'll just hang him part way down the well."

We were safe from Billy's attacks as long as we were on horseback, so Montie roped Billy around the neck and dragged him close to the well curb, where Park and Art wooled him down and tied all four of his legs togeher, making him helpless. Next, Art cut both buckets free of the pulley rope, took Montie's loop off the goat's neck, and tied one end of the pulley rope around Billy's horns.

All four of us now began to tug and heave to lift Billy up over the well curb. Seemed as if four sturdy kids weren't going to win, but tugging on the pulley rope helped a lot and at last Billy was actually in the well! Montie and Art tied the free end of the pulley rope so it held him right where he was — partway down the shaft.

We had hanged the goat!

But unnoticed by us, Mr. Cowdrey had returned and his unexpected voice did more than startle us. It petrified us. "What the blank-blank do you kids think you're doing!"

Receiving no answer, Mr. Cowdrey charged up to the well and looked down into it.

"Quick, John," ordered Montie in a whisper to me. "Get up behind me on Mex!" and he threw me aboard his horse. Park and Art were already running to reach their horses, and a minute later we were gone.

But although Mr. Cowdrey had arrived in the nick of time to save Billy's life, he was not content to let the matter drop.

For a week thereafter all of us felt the effects of what we got at home. And we heard about the event for months afterward. Even so, after giving the hanging of Billy a cold second thought, none of us were really displeased because Billy came out the victor!

Just as the raid-on-the-chuck-wagon-dinner was our most enjoyable adventure, the most unpleasant was our skunk adventure!

Art and I, riding to school one summer morning, discovered a full grown skunk under the Canadian River bridge. Since everyone agreed that skunks must be killed, and it was plainly our duty to dispatch this one, we had the big news to report to Montie and Park.

It so happened that we four were at this time the only boys at school, although a full quota of girls were present. So at the noon hour, the four of us, accompanied of course by Punch and armed with rocks and sticks, gobbled our lunches as we marched to the bridge.

Mr. Skunk was in a shallow hole in the river bank underneath the bridge. We hurled rocks at what could be seen of his lovely striped coat, to which he retaliated by firing much, much stronger ammunition than we possessed!

Then Punch, who certainly should have known better, went into the hole after the skunk and dragged him out onto the small sand bar. After a long battle four undaunted boys, plus Punch, came out victorious.

But Punch, smelling even worse than we did, became the sickest dog I've ever seen. Nevertheless, thrilled by our victory, we returned to the schoolhouse, where the girls took one look and one sniff and stampeded. Teacher refused to be routed, however, and said severely, "All of you deserve a whipping."

She got her switch, but when she came close to Montie, her nose and her face knotted. She shuddered and choked. "Go home," she snapped. "All of you go home. At once."

As we scurried to get our horses, Park remarked with a chuckle, "Skunk killing is one sure way to get out of school. With Teacher's permission, too."

"Yeah," Art conceded. "But there's worse things than school. This stink is one of 'em."

Trusty old Mex and Blue and General didn't like us any better than the girls and the teacher!

The following day Montie and Park were wearing a complete change of clothing! Art and I had no other clothes, so Dad made us boil ours in the wash boiler and put half a can of lye in the water.

Ah yes, those school days of '96. '97 and '98 were wonderfully pleasant and adventurous. But in 1899 Moore and Blevins dissolved their partnership by selling the ranch and the cattle.

Blevins apparently found no local buyer for the five-thousand-odd cattle, for all summer and fall he was busy rounding up herds, trailing them to Laramie and shipping them either to market or to distant buyers.

To help with this tremendous job, both Park and Montie quit school. The Payne-Blevins boys' days as "pards" were almost ended, and new faces were replacing the old, familiar faces at our school. Life was no longer quite the same.

MY FIRST HORSE: WRINGTAIL!

Often to me it seemed as if I never would get a horse I could call my own, and my yearning in this matter was something which only another kid, either boy or girl, can fully understand. He wants something so much that it hurts way deep down inside. Fulfillment of this desire will lift a kid to heights almost beyond comprehension.

There came at last for me the great day when I experienced such a lift. This was in June of 1897 when Mel Miller came to the ranch to break three colts (we called green, unbroken horses "colts") to ride for Dad. One of these was to be mine!

But not Dandy, a beautiful dark bay so spirited and high-lifed that he jumped every fence on the ranch — except those of the corral — as easily as most horses flick their tails; not Sandy, a chunky and mettlesome sorrel with a white stripe in his face and one white hoof. Sandy was to be Art's new horse, although he already had General. No, I could have neither of those first-class ponies. I was to have Snip, an ill-shaped, toothpick-hipped and fiddle-headed bay which was a natural pacer.

Cowboys call this gait (pacing) "sop and tater," and a horse which paces or singlefoots is also a "sop and tater," as "Oh, ho! He's a 'sop and tater.'"

Mel Miller, who was related to Dave Hendrickson and highly recommended by Dave as a buster, could not have surmised how supercritically we two boys sized him up when he rode into the ranch while we compared him with the Blevins' bronc busters. Would he rate? Would he measure up?

What we saw was a slender young fellow, scarcely more than a kid himself, with a big nose, little blond mustache and a pleasant grin. We wore the finest made-to-measure boots we'd seen, boots with extremely high heels; his spurs had Mexican rowels about two and one half inches in diameter. No chaps, but his saddle and blanket and bridle, hackamore and rope, had seen plenty of service and looked all right.

The man himself just had to be a "passable" hand since he had worked for Haley's outfit as a horse wrangler. But he couldn't be in the same class with Montie Blevins' top busters, Alec Dunbar and Wash Alderdice. Wash Alderdice had come direct from Haley's outfit to take a job with Blevins about a year ago. Park and Montie had proudly reported at school, "We got a new bronc buster. Name's 'War Shoulder Dice.' Must be an Injun."

None of us had ever seen a live Indian, and for a few days we were keyed high, hopeful that "War Shoulder Dice" would prove to be such an interesting character. What a letdown when we learned that the correct pronunciation of "War Shoulder Dice" was Wash Alderdice — short for George Washington Alderdice — and that Wash was the son of an Irishman who had a small ranch farther up in the Park.

But as a bronc rider Wash had never let us down. He was also the biggest "josher" and player of practical jokes ever to work for Blevins. But if Mel proved himself, we'd be able to brag at school, "We've got a real bronc buster right on the Payne ranch."

Mel went to work as if he knew his business. Helped by both Dad and Dave Hendrickson, he cut Sandy away from the other horses and into the round corral where the Cross boys had once broken horses to ride. While Sandy circled the corral, snorting, and leaping at the fence in his frantic attempts to escape, Mel told Dave and Dad just what they were to do. Then he shook out a big loop in his rope, and, with us two boys watching, all critical eyes, he noosed Sandy's front legs. Instantly Dave and Dad gave Mel a hand with the rope and they "busted Sandy wide open."

As he went down in a cloud of dust, Dave ran up close and held the foot rope so Sandy could not get his front foot in contact with the ground; Dad jumped on the fallen horse's neck, grabbed one ear and the lower jaw, and turned Sandy's muzzle up toward the sky.

Of course, the horse was kicking, but his flailing hind hoofs could not quite reach Dad. Mel put his hackamore on Sandy's head; next, using a long, soft rope, he tied a rope collar about Sandy's neck, close against his shoulders. He then placed the loose end of the rope around one of Sandy's rear fetlocks, ran the rope back through the collar, pulled this leg up fairly close to Sandy's belly and tied the rope.

"Let him up," Mel said.

Dave let go of his rope; Dad jumped clear. Sandy fought the hobble and squealed as he lunged around the corral on three feet, for he could not touch the fourth foot to the ground.

"That's the same sort of hobble a blacksmith uses to shoe a bad kicker," Dad remarked. "What do you call it, Mel?"

"The only name I know for it is a 'Scotch Hobble,'" Mel said. "Best thing I've found to control a bronc and take the fight out of him. Lots better than just snubbing both front feet together."

Outside the corral, and well out of danger, Art looked at me and nodded. Mel was beginning to measure up.

He now picked up the trailing hackamore rope and tried to approach Sandy. The horse wheeled away, and Mel jerked his head so hard he forced the bronc to face him. This game went on, Sandy falling down often, until Mel won his way, while Sandy sniffed at him and snorted as if the man was a bear.

This was the first step in halter breaking, or breaking a horse to lead. Afer Mel taught Sandy that he could not pull away and must allow a man to approach him, he began getting the bronc used to a saddle blanket. He let the horse smell of it, flipped it all over his body and, when at length Sandy submitted to the blanket, Mel gently eased his saddle into place.

Sandy looked suspiciously around at the saddle, but remained quiet until Mel tightened the cinches. Thereupon Sandy had a spasm. He'd get rid of that thing; he'd show that human critter. But after he had exhausted himself, the saddle was still on his back, and, further to humiliate the horse, Mel stepped up into it. The hobble was still in place, so Sandy was quite unable to kick when Mel slid off his rump. Then, using his knife, Mel trimmed Sandy's long tail. (This was important, for no cowboy would ride a horse with a long and flowing tail!)

Finally Mel fixed reins for his hackamore, took off the hobble and, mounting, started Sandy moving around the corral.

Art and I were hoping Sandy would buck real hard. But he didn't

114

buck, and Mel, using the hackamore reins, turned him to the right and the left, getting him "bridlewise." Eventually the bronc buster stepped down, removed the saddle, and then resumed teaching the horse to lead.

Dave and Dad had long since gone to do chores, and supper was very late that night. But one of the three colts had been halter broken and corral ridden, and we boys reckoned that Mel "stacked up pretty doggoned good" as the right kind of a buster!

In that day there were two distinct types of bronc riders. One was the man who handled a bronc as humanely as possible, attempting to win its confidence, teaching and training it in a gentle and kindly manner. The second type was the rough, tough and brutal horseman who believed in beating the "ornery" out of a bronc, deliberately making it fear him and thus conquering it. He is a "bronc fighter."

Had such a buster been working on Sandy, he would have thrown the bronc and put his hackamore on him as Mel had done. Then, while Sandy was still down, he'd have cinched his saddle in place as cruelly tight as he could pull the cinches. Finally, he'd tell his helpers, "Turn 'im loose," and settle into the sadlle before the horse could bound to its feet.

"Man on you! Go high!" he'd have yelled, ripping Sandy's tender belly, shoulders and flanks with his spurs, and slashing him with his quirt.

Believing that an enemy even more greatly feared than a mountain lion had landed upon him, Sandy, or any horse would have bucked and fought until completely exhausted. Whereupon the bronc fighter might boast, "That's showin' 'im who's boss!"

Our North Park cow outfits had no use for the "bronc fighter" type of busters, who, nevertheless, had a following and were heroes to many men and boys. One might well ask why. Because a great many of us admire traits in another person which we do not possess ourselves: toughness, brutality, ruthlessness and absolute fearlessness; so we say, "Like him or not, he's got guts!"

The first night Mel Miller was on Dad's ranch I went to bed so excited I couldn't sleep, but a mighty happy boy. Tomorrow he'd work on Snip, and maybe by the day after I'd be riding my own horse!

But a pony for a nine-year-old boy must be thoroughly broken, must be gentle, and must be taught to stand still to be mounted. Although Snip proved by far the easiest of the three colts to break, I did not win permission to ride him until late autumn of 1897.

Mel Miller stayed with us only long enough to handle all three of the broncs, getting them halter broken, bridlewise, and used to being ridden. Then he went to work for Montie Blevins. But he took Dandy, Snip and Sandy with him as mounts for himself or some other cowboys, to use on the calf roundup. This work was to finish breaking them.

While Mel was available on Dad's ranch, however, I was his shadow; and, since he cottoned to kids, we got along fine. He taught us how to make a McCarty, meaning a hair rope, to use as a tie or lead rope for a hackamore. The word comes from the Spanish "mecate" and has been Americanized to "McCarty." Not that we as yet owned a hackamore — an absolute must if you acquired a full cowboy outfit.

He also showed us how to make a horse-hair saddle blanket, such a blanket when properly made being very desirable because it is a thick and soft hair mat which allows air to get between the horse's back and the saddle, thus tending to keep the horse a little bit cooler and to prevent sore backs.

Best of all, Mel taught us to make saddle cinches of soft cotton clothes line. Most front cinches were then made of hair, woven tight. They were hard and brittle and harsh on a horse, tending to cause cinch galls. Art's old front cinch was worn out. With a twenty-five-cent bundle of cotton clothes line, and making use of the old cinch rings, Mel made for us a jim-dandy cotton cinch. Later we had no difficulty in making them for ourselves!

(The hind or flank cinches, most saddles being double rigs, were made of either canvas or leather. But there was no real reason why the flank cinch should not be a cotton cinch, too.)

Mel told us many stories of his life while working for Haley's outfit on the Bear — later Yampa — River. But already we had been around cowboys long enough to take many of these stories with large doses of salt. When this Haley outfit had stopped with Dad the previous autumn, trailing a beef herd to Laramie, there had been the same good old cook, Thornt Biggs. But a new foreman named Hi Bernard had replaced Ben Lance.

I was very curious about the big six-shooter in an ornate holster attached to a cartridge belt which Hi Bernard carried, for he was the only cowboy or cowman so armed I'd seen up to this time. None of his crew had guns — at least in sight.

So I questioned Mel, "You worked under Hi Bernard?"

That was right.

"Well, he carries a six-shooter. Can he hit anything with it? Why's he lug it around?"

"Can he hit anything with that hog-leg!" Mel grinned and chuckled. "One day we'd bunched a big herd on roundup and Hi was still working this herd, cutting out cows and calves, when along came a farmer who rode into the bunch insisting that he chop his cattle out right now.

"Hi told him to wait until he was through. Nope. No doggoned roundup foreman could tell this bird what he was to do.

" 'Get out of the herd until I tell you it's your turn,' Hi said.

"But the man went right ahead, and then old Hi pulled his gun and started shooting. First bullet went through that farmer's hat, singeing his hair, and he started moving, but fast. Hi emptied his gun, putting four shots through the man's clothes — real close to his hide."

"Golly! I bet that farmer never stopped going."

"So far as I know, he didn't stop," Mel laughed. "He was just a streak of dust going over a hill. Likely the main reason Hi goes around heeled is because some mighty tough hands work for the Haley outfit."

"Tough hands? None of 'em, when last they camped here on the ranch, had any guns — and they didn't look any meaner or tougher'n any other cowpunchers."

"They had the six-shooters rolled up in their beds, you can bet," Mel said. "There're always two or three men on every drive to Laramie with a herd that turn back as soon as they get in sight of town."

"Why do they do that, Mel?"

"They're outlaws. Won't go near a railroad town where the sheriff might have dodgers describing them."

Art and I didn't use salt with that story, for we'd heard the same thing from other cowboys. Some real "tough hombres" occasionally worked for Haley, men who rode far around towns unless they were reasonably sure they'd be safe in the town.

Returning now to Hi Bernard, I saw him three or four different autumns when the outfit trailed cattle through the Park, and then the last thing I heard about him was a word-of-mouth story which ran: "Hi Bernard rode to Brown's Park (one of the stops, or hide-out station, on the old Wild Bunch and horse thief trail in the far northwest corner of Colorado) to check up on Queen Ann, who was reputed to be queen of a rustling gang actively stealing cattle.

"However, instead of arresting Queen Ann or any others of the outfit Hi Bernard fell in love with the woman and married her."

That was the end of this word-of-mouth story and is all I ever heard about it.

Although Mel Miller soon quit his job with the Moore and Blevins outfits, Mr. Blevins was glad to have our three broncs, Dandy, Sandy and Snip, and kept them in his cavvy all summer and fall. But when he returned them to Dad, they were still not thoroughly broken. The prevailing idea in fiction, and among folks who don't know too much about breaking horses, is that once a wild horse has been halter broken and ridden he is tamed, or broken. On the contrary, during the process of being gentled and trained, at least fifty per cent of these horses acquire mean and tricky habits in order to outwit and defeat man.

As a boy—and I believe this holds true for most lads—I was sure horses and other animals could think and reason almost the same as human beings, and I still believe they learn bad habits in some manner from other horses.

In any event, Sandy and Dandy had each learned a tricky habit. Although Sandy never bucked, he was a "salty" bronc and he became "hard to crawl to," which means "hard to mount." He'd do his best to lose his would-be rider before the man could get into the saddle. The hard-to-mount horse will pretend he's not even watching his would-be rider, but the instant the man puts his toe in the stirrup and reaches for the saddle horn the horse leaps right or left, backwards or ahead, or wheels away from the rider. Unless the cowboy is sharper and quicker than the horse, he's left sitting in the sagebrush, or he lands behind the saddle, or he is thrown clear across the horse.

This trick does not bother the professional bronc buster, one able to make a "Wild West mount." He'll come up into his saddle no matter which way, nor how high, wide and crooked the horse goes, and laugh about it. But the only way the amateur can counteract this sneaky trick is have another man either snub his mount to the saddle horn or "ear down" the critter until the amateur gets set.

Although my brother was itching to ride Sandy, he knew he

118

wasn't up to "getting a-straddle of 'im.'" But it so happened we were given a chance to turn this bronc over to Wash Alderdice. I can still see both the man and the horse the day Wash saddled Sandy and led him out in front of the big barn on Dad's ranch. Sandy was cocking one ear slightly and smiling to himself and just waiting to "bust this fellow wide open." Wash took a short grip on the reins, grabbed the check strap of Sandy's bridle with his left hand, and, standing very close to the bronc's left shoulder, reached with his right for the stirrup, turned it, lifted his foot, put just the toe of his boot in the stirrup, and then reached for the saddle horn with his right hand.

At this instant Sandy moved like a shot from a gun, bounding high and away from Wash and slamming his body against the barn wall.

Had Wash been in the saddle, his leg would have been broken against the wall. But he wasn't in the saddle. One hand on the bridle, the other gripping the saddle horn, foot in the stirrup, he was hanging on the side of the horse as unconcerned as if Sandy hadn't moved.

Now the horse lunged ahead fast. After he had gotten past the corner of the barn, Wash calmly, even slowly, threw his leg across the saddle and settled down into it. Then Wash reined Sandy sharply around and rode back to us Paynes, while Sandy cocked one ear back at the rider and rolled an eye as if to say, "How come I didn't lose you?"

"Can you break him of that trick?" Art asked anxiously.

"I'll straighten him out, Art," Wash promised and rode away. The following spring, when my brother began riding Sandy, the pony had forgotten all about his tricky habit.

Dandy, the mettlesome bay, had become a "stampeder." Dad wanted this splendid horse for his mount, so after Mr. Blevins had returned the three broncs, Dad saddled Dandy and mounted without any trouble. But only a few minutes later, Dandy was running like a scared jackrabbit, Dad completely unable either to control or to stop the horse.

In circling around the big field, he came close to us boys and shouted, "I'll fix him. I'll make him keep running after he's ready to quit!"

But Dad was tuckered out long before Dandy was ready to quit, and later, when the use of a severe bit failed to control the horse,

Dad gave up trying to break him of his bad habit and finally traded him off.

I was burning with impatience to ride my horse, Snip, and at last Dad permitted me to do so.

Somewhere and somehow, Arthur acquired another and a better saddle for himself and gave me the old one. It would not have brought two dollars in a second hand store, but I was as happy to have it as if it were a good rig. For one thing, it was so light that a small boy could lift it up to a horse's back.

I was as proud of Snip as if he was a good horse. I shut my eyes and mind to the fact that he was a "knot-head," a stupid jug-head, and locoed to boot. Loco acts in a different manner on individual horses. Snip would not lead. No matter how hard I tugged on the bridle reins or halter rope he'd mope along with halting steps as if each was to be his last. And it was almost impossible to persuade or force him to step across a bar pole or other small object. He'd stop and back up and snort and his eyes would bug out, and then — if savagely gouged with spurs or quirted from behind — he'd jump this pole, leaping as high and as far as he could.

It was the same with a creek. There were very few fords on the creeks which flowed through the ranch, and all our horses either stepped over them or jumped them as a matter of habit. Not Snip. At the creek bank he'd halt even if going full speed, look at the narrow opening, snort, rear back, eyes bugging and nostrils distended with fear and alarm — and he'd not cross the creek unless his rider or someone behind him simply made him do it. Then he'd make the most terrific leap of which he was capable.

Although dopey and lazy most of the time, Snip seemed to enjoy putting on a bucking exhibition every morning when first saddled, and also at unpredictable intervals during the day's ride. This had been laughable to Mel Miller, who said, "He can't get six inches off the ground; couldn't throw off a saddle blanket even in a high wind." Actually, all he was capable of doing was a "limber-jointed crow hop."

But I believed he was really "turning it on." And when I got so I could ride him without pulling leather, I knew I was a rip-tooting good rider.

Now, as this creature "turned on his buck," he'd switch and wring his tail. How he did wring it! Too, whenever I spurred him — and that was often, for he'd never go any faster than he could help — he'd switch his tail as if fighting flies and also wring it, so it wasn't very long before the teasing school kids dubbed him "Switchtail" and "Wringtail." Although burned up and resentful at first, I gradually came to accept these derogatory and contemptuous names for my great horse.

In spite of the fun made of Wringtail, in spite of how boiling mad I'd get at him sometimes, I had a real affection for this strange, locoed critter. He was easy gaited and easy to mount; he never kicked me, was never sore-footed, yet never wore a shoe in his life; and he'd stand a lot of hard work. It was fun indeed to "touch him off," spurring him as hard as I could and waving my hat while he wrung his tail and crow-hopped. It was a wonder I did not break my spurs, for they were fragile little things which cost me thirty-five cents — That's right! Thirty-five cents at Montgomery Ward's!

Once only did my horse shame and humiliate me — frightfully. Art and I had ridden to J. S. King's ranch, to which the Pinkhamton post office had been moved, for the mail. A pair of dehorning clippers which Dad had sent for had arrived, so we must take them home. They made a heavy package about eight inches wide and three feet long, which Art handed up to me to carry across the fork of my saddle. The rustling of paper, or something else about this heavy package, irritated Wringtail, and the next thing I knew both the clippers and little Johnnie hit the *hard*-frozen ground, *hard*.

I was badly shaken up, but I was more surprised and mad than hurt — fighting mad. I got on Wringtail again and gouged him. But now he wouldn't crow-hop.

Art said, "I'll hand 'em to you again."

I thought that over for about two-tenths of a second and growled, "Oh, no. You carry 'em!"

Art didn't like that idea. "We'll come get 'em with a team," he decided.

On another much later occasion, however, Wringtail almost killed me. A man named Bill Rosebrook and I had picked up five horses somewhere on the far side of the Canadian and were driving them home. We had crossed the Canadian bridge when two of these loose horses bolted to the right, following along a fence, while the others took the lane road, which was the route we wanted them to follow. Rosebrook stayed with the latter, while I raced to head off the runaways.

To do this I simply had to outrun them, and I had forged up

alongside them when my mount's front feet hit a badger hole. I sensed that he was falling, but that was all before I blacked out completely.

Four or five hours later I came awake, discovering that I was lying on a bed in a strange room. Dad and several other people were there, all looking grave and anxious.

"Rosebrook found you and carried you here," Dad said. "Do you remember what happened?"

"Only that I felt Wringtail going down. Nothing more."

OUR RELENTLESS FOES

The year 1897 marked a revolutionary improvement in the method of stacking hay. Everyone interested in ranching realized that something must be done to accomplish this big job in a cheaper, easier, faster manner, and many ranchmen had already experimented with various manufactured stackers and sweeps or buck rakes.

Admittedly, these were a vast improvement over the hand-power pitchfork, but both the patented stackers and the patented three-wheel sweeps were forever breaking down. Then a North Parker named Jack Greene — I believe full credit for this belongs to him — came through with an idea so simple, so practical, that everyone else wondered, "Why didn't I think of that?"

The idea was to shove or pull the hay up a slanting framework constructed of poles and let it fall straight down from the top of this "slide" onto the stack.

Jack Greene, the son of an itinerant preacher, Ike Greene, who'll be long and fondly remembered in North Park, built the first slide stacker and then experimented with various block-and-tackle methods of pulling the hay up the incline. These methods, however, proved so slow, cumbersome and unsatisfactory that it was not until another North Parker, Joe Lawrence, invented the "pusher" that ranchmen began to realize that the slide stacker, plus the pusher, plus home-made two-wheel sweeps, was the answer to their hay-stacking problem. Moreover, anybody who was handy wih tools could, using pine timber, make all three of these implements. Wheels of old mowing machines were just the thing for sweeps. The only items a ranchman had to buy were spikes and bolts!

What a great day it was for us Paynes when Dad hitched George and Ben to his new slide stacker, dragged it to the spot where he wanted a hay stack, and then hitched the team to his pusher and dragged it into place. John Metcalf meanwhile brought in several sweep loads of hay, shoved each load in behind the stacker to hold it in place and to start the hay stack, and finally put a load on the teeth apron of the slide stacker.

Now Dad spoke to George and Ben, hitched at the farther end of the long, long pusher tongue. The pusher rattled forward, its head contacted the load of hay and moved it up, up along the sloping stacker, all the way to the top. Oh! but it was wonderful and beautiful to see the bright green hay tip over the top and cascade downward!

As Dad backed up the team, the pusher descended by force of gravity until its head touched he ground, whereupon Dad turned the team around and dragged the pusher out of the way. Metcalf was already coming in with another load of hay on his sweep, while Dave Hendrickson, the only man now using a pitchfork, shaped up the hay stack.

Another sweep load, another and another, went up the stacker and fell over the top, and the stack grew as if by magic, so much more quickly and easily than the old hand-power, pitchfork method of hay stacking.

A few short years later, hay stackers (men who worked on the stacks) like Louis, the Swede, began to boast, "I can stack von hundred tons of hay a day."

This was fifty tons more than any human being could possibly have handled, but a full stacking crew, consisting of two sweeps, a pusher driver, one or two men on the stack, plus at least two rakes getting the hay ready for the sweeps and raking up the scatterings, could and usually did put up from thirty to forty tons of hay in one day.

During those early years Dad could not afford to hire a full haying crew, nor did he have the horses and machinery. He would get a woman cook, or if possible a man and wife, and hire one or two extra men. Then, after mowing a patch of hay, the men who ran the mowers would become the stacking crew, using the same teams. Arthur could not have been over eleven when he began making a hand on a rake, and I yearned for the day when I might do the same.

Turning the spotlight on willing worker, Louis the Swede, for a moment I must quote a remark made by him to bystanders when he overhead a "green" Swede attempting to express himself in the English language. Said Louis, grinning smugly, "I shoost to talk like dot ven I foorst come to dis country. But now I bane yere so long you could not hadly detect dot I bane a Swede."

As this event-crowded year of 1897 marked a tremendous advance in harvesting our hay, it also marked what we hoped and believed would be a big upward step in the cattle business for the Paynes.

Somehow Dad was able to buy from Mr. Blevins fifty Oregon heifers picked out of the big herd which the Moore and Blevins outfit trailed into the Park that spring of 1897.

Oregon cattle were bigger-boned, heavier-bodied and of better quality than Texas stock, and these heifers were far better cattle than the scrubs which Dad already owned. Best of all, they were due to calve during the summer and fall, so they were sure both to improve and to increase Dad's herd.

But it did not work out that way. Disaster hit us like a thunderclap out of a blue sky when the heifers began "slinking" their calves — giving birth to premature, hairless, lifeless calves.

At first Dad tried to convince himself that there was nothing radically wrong because we always had a few "slinkers" due to accidents befalling cows. But within a few days he realized that the heifers were afflicted with one of the most dreaded diseases of our day, contagious abortion.

Many years later a vaccine was perfected to control this scourge. At that time, however, there was nothing we could do, except helplessly watch abortion run through this new herd like measles running through a large family. Out of the fifty heifers, forty lost their calves. Fortunately they had been put in Dad's Sentinel Mountain pasture, and our other cattle did not come into direct contact with these diseased animals.

Moreover, although this was a terrific setback, the heifers fattened quickly, so, without suffering a heavy money loss, Dad was able to market them as grass beef. But the dream of a bigger and far better herd had vanished.

This was merely one of the many setbacks which befell early day cowmen. We lived in dread of calamity overtaking our stock, the greatest dread being that of a hard winter when, if you ran out of feed (hay), starvation would gut your herd. In our high mountain country there was little fear of drought. Dry years, yes, but the real thing in the way of drought, no.

Next to a hard winter, livestock diseases were the greatest menace. Those common to horses were colic and distemper, neither necessarily fatal, although distemper would run through an entire head of horses. Ofter horses also had bad cases of worms, and occasionally one would develop a nasty fistula which, unless treated, would stay with the unfortunate horse all the rest of its life. Water-foundered horses were quite common, this condition being brought on when an overheated horse drank its fill of cold water. As kids we were warned never to let our ponies drink more than a frew sips of water when they were "all a-lather."

Water foundering — I do not know the technical name — resulted in an intense stiffening of the horse's shoulders and front legs and contraction of his front feet. One horse I remember well was "stiff as a poker" early in the morning, but after an hour's work, he'd limber up somewhat.

The worst disease of horses, and one which took a very heavy toll, did not hit the Park until about 1905. Because ranchmen believed this disease was brought on through the animal's eating swamp grass, it was called merely Swamp Fever.

Diseases which struck our cattle included plain dropsy, wherein a watery substance gradually replaced the normal tissues. Fortunitely, it was not contagious and rarely hit more than one or two cattle in a season.

Calf diphtheria, a germ disease and highly contagious, began with a strange sore spot in a calf's mouth or on its tongue. Other sores quickly developed, and all would keep growing, eating away live tissue and even bone. But this disease could be cured by scraping off the hard crust of the sore spots and painting them with carbolic acid, repeating this until the sores healed.

Meanwhile, inducing the victim to eat enough to keep it alive was a problem, for its mouth would be as sore as that of a person suffering from an infected tooth. We actually spoon-fed some calves with oil meal or cottonseed meal and bran mashes, and poured warm milk down their throats until they'd begin licking up such soft feed themselves.

Big jaw was quite common. Germs attacked the jaw bones of a cow brute and caused an unhealthy, honeycombed and abnormal growth. Unless checked by use of corrosive sublimate, the cow's jaw bones — usually the lower jaw — would continue to enlarge and remain raw and sore for the balance of the animal's life.

If this disease strikes the tongue instead of the bony structure, or the tongue as well as the bones, it is called "woody tongue," is much harder to treat and usually fatal. Worse still, human beings are not immune, and a person who got big jaw, or "woody tongue" was in for a nasty illness.

On one occasion in later years, the scab or "scabbies" got into the Park, forcing a few ranchmen to dip their herds. But, fortunately, we never had a case of anthrax or of the most dreaded of all cattle scourges, hoof-and-mouth disease. The prevalence of blackleg however was quite enough by itself.

During the 1890's, the government was going all out to perfect a vaccine against blackleg, and about 1900 this vaccine came into general use, though it was still far from being a certain preventative. In North Park alone blackleg took a terrific annual toll of fat calves between six months and one year old. Grown cattle seemed immune, although occasionally blackleg would pick off yearlings and two-year-olds.

In desperation the stockmen tried a crude method of vaccination. This was to cut a slit in the side on the animal's left shoulder in which a mixture of gunpowder and sulphur was inserted. This created a running sore which might stop the blackleg. Another method was to take a big sacking needle, thread it with heavy cord, run the needle through the calf's tail and leave a piece of string dangling from this wound. It is very doubtful if this had any beneficial effect.

The best thing ranchmen could think to do — and this often worked out well — was to drive immediately all the other calves out of a corral, in which a calf had died, trail them around and warm them up to get their blood circulating, and then, making as sure as possible there was in the herd no other calf which had already contracted the disease, move these calves to some fresh spot. Also, the owner must burn the dead calf — without skinning it since the skin would carry the germs — and bury the remains deep in the ground.

This blackleg was extremely contagious, and often only one epidemic of it would almost break a cowman. I remember our father's buying two registered Shorthorn bulls, both under two years of age.

One of these was a first-class animal and Dad was mighty happy to get him.

Suddenly this bull was taken sick. Dad put him in a barn and had Art and me and the hired man help him doctor the animal. We boys knew darned well what was wrong, for there was a patch of skin on Mr. Bull's left shoulder that made a rustling, crinkly sound like paper when we rubbed our fingers over it. It felt exactly as it sounded. The shoulder was swelling, too.

Not until the bull died would Dad admit he'd had blackleg, and then for the first time I saw our dad lose his grit. Usually he could take any setback in stride, shrug it off and go on looking ahead. This jolt, however, got him down. What was the use of trying to improve a herd of cattle? What was the use of going on with this grim, cruel business?

Somehow, it was a shocking thing for a boy to witness — Dad blue, down, ready to quit.

Yet, a week or ten days later that characteristic trait of the true Britisher was once again on top — stubborn determination to fight on, steadfast belief that nothing, nothing at all can lick an Englishman.

Nevertheless, our continual and grim fight against dreaded diseases of livestock was not without its humorous incidents. One day a ranchman visiting with Dad reported how his stock was getting along: "All fine and dandy so far, except that one of my cows lost her cud."

"Lost her cud?" Dad stopped what he was doing and looked hard at this neighbor. I knew he was wondering if the man was trying to "stuff" him or if he really meant it.

"Yes, lost her cud," the neighbor returned. "But I fixed her up with a piece of greasy rag wrapped tight around a bit of wood. Put that in her mouth and now she's doing all right."

Dad offered no comment, but after the neighbor had gone, he laughed uproariously and said, "That fellow really believes a cow loses her cud and that a man can supply her with a substitute? . . . Or did he think he was stringing a greenhorn?"

"Oh, he believes it all right," I said, and then, showing off my knowledge, "but anybody ought to know that a cow — or any cud-chewing animal — swallows her grass unchewed. These wads go into one of her four stomachs and later, when she's got lots of time, she lies down and coughs up a wad of this grass, chews it fine and re-swallows it. That's 'chewing her cud.' You've told us all that. Have I got it right?"

"Right, Johnnie," Dad said and added, "when a cow doesn't chew her cud in a normal manner it's a symptom that something's seriously the matter with her. She's sick."

Another *terrible* ailment of cattle on a par with "Loss of Cud" was "Hollow Horn." Just how hollow horn affected the brutes I never did learn. But there were people in North Park who firmly believed that hollow horn was a virulent disease which might take a whole herd.

One such man came to Dad with desperation in his bearded face and a pitiful story: "My cattle are dropping on me. They got hollow horn. Anything you can do for it?"

Dad held a straight face and said, "I'll take a look at them."

He took me with him to this neighbor's ranch where one look was enough for even a little boy to tell what was wrong. Those cattle were just skin and bones, dying of starvation. By "dropping on me," the man meant they'd either lie down or fall down and were too weak to get up again.

Dad had his look, and then he glared at the neighbor. "Hollow horn? Bunk! Hollow guts!"

"Hollow guts?" the man repeated blankly.

"Yes. Feed 'em and they'll be all right. There's no such thing as hollow horn."

We went away, leaving the neighbor unconvinced about hollow horn. But he did promise to buy hay and feed his starving herd.

Other disastrous forces which menaced cattle and horses included predatory animals. But losses from these were minor until the winter when the grey wolves came to North Park (of which I shall tell later). I have mentioned that coyotes — we always had a lot of them — were not nearly the enemies of ranchmen that fiction and some people will try to make you believe. Mountain lions would occasionally kill a colt, but such losses were infrequent because deer and antelope were so plentiful that a mountain lion was never close to starvation.

On the other hand, the nonbelligerent and noncarniverous porcupine was nevertheless a menace to both horses and cattle, as well as dogs, all because of livestock's curiosity to "sniff" the prickly porcupine, whereupon the horse or cow would get a "snootful" of quills. These quills would continue to penetrate, so eventually the porcupine-hit animal would become unable to eat and death would follow. Only pulling of the quills would save the critter's life.

Two-legged predators were, of course, always with us. But these confined their activities to butchering a beef now and then or to petty mavericking of young, unbranded calves. Such calves the mavericker could "put on" a cow which already had a calf of her own, and thus she would raise a pair of "twins," or — being very prolific — she might have triplets or even quadruplets, though seldom identical!

Rustling on a big scale was practically unknown, it being entirely too difficult to get a herd out of the Park without being caught with it. Shipping strays to market and collecting the money for them was the easiest form of cattle stealing and the one most practiced until we got a good system of stock inspection for brands. Stock inspection also checked both mavericking and stealing of horses.

With us, poisonous plants also took an annual toll. Loco weed was a continual menace to our horses, and along about June each year wild larkspur or poison week would knock off a few cattle. This weed was, however, really dangerous only when wet from rain or snow or when a cow ate too much of it and then filled up on water. Thereupon death from bloating would result. But if found in time, there would be a fifty-fifty chance of saving her by "sticking her" to let the gas out of her stomach.

Cows and sheep as well as horses will eat loco, so once in a while we'd have a cow "go loco." Once having acquired the habit, a cow scorns any other food. Her eyes become glittery, with a crazy light in them. She gets thin and shrivels up; her hair looks dry and undernourished, and she finally goes crazy. Shaking her head and trembling all over, she will froth at the mouth and fight any animal that comes near her; she loses her sense of balance; her gait becoming sort of wild, her front feet striking at the stars and her hind legs jerking and twitching like those of a "string-halted" horse. Soon she'll forget all about going to water and stay in her loco patch until she dies of poison and starvation.

But if this cow is taken off the weed in time and put in a feed lot or pasture where there is no loco, she will recover and put on flesh once again. Then the ranchman can ship her to market and get a fair price for her. As a result we did not actually lose any cows from loco poisoning. But we always, always had to watch our horses to make sure they did not start to eat the weed; also we had to see that those which had already been affected, but were still useful, did not get any more of it.

Now you are going to ask, "Wasn't there a still greater and more powerful force than any that you have mentioned for the small rancher and small cowman, such as your father, to combat?"

Ah, you mean the big cowman? The range-hog cowman. The answer is no. To the best of my knowledge, there was no conflict between the big man and the little man in North Park. Undoubtedly, one reason for this happy situation was that, compared to the vast Western plains and other easily accessibly areas, the Park had been settled so late in point of time that already the great transition from open range to fenced ranches had taken place. The heyday of the big, open-range cowman had ended; the day of the small, individual owner of land and stock had dawned.

Moreover, the set-up in North Park did not lend itself to the open-range method of handling cattle because it was impossible to graze a herd the year round. Winter feeding was an absolute must.

The nearest some of our North Parkers came to an open range war was an incident which took place in Middle Park somewhere about 1907. Quite early North Park ranchmen began finding themselves short of summer range, and in 1893 several men pooled their young steers into one big herd and drove them to Middle Park, where they found splendid summer range.

Year after year this summering of steers in neighboring Middle Park continued, the stockmen establishing right to the open range there through their prior use of it. Eventually the Two Bar outfit leased from the state all of a vast hunk of range called Lookout Mountain and fenced it with barbed wire. Scarcely was this fence finished when, in one night, somebody cut the wires between each two posts around the entire pasture.

But, rather strangely, the whole matter died away; no court battle, no range war. Apparently whoever had cut the fence preferred to remain unknown. When the Two Bar rebuilt the fence, it was not again molested.

MY FIRST HARD WINTER

I was nine years of age before I was destined to experience my first real hard winter, the winter of 1897 and 1898.

Quoting Mr. Longfellow:

"Ever thicker, thicker, thicker,
Froze the ice on lake and river;
Ever deeper, deeper, deeper
Fell the snow o'er all the landscape."

How true! Snow, driven by cruel winds, filled the lane through which ran the highway. The stage and the freighters forged out a new trail right past our home and, taking advantage of Dad's feed trail, travelled down the meadow past the Scott boys' ranch and thence onward toward Walden.

Fences on either side of the lane disappeared completely and quite soon all of our fences were buried under snow drifts. How strange it seemed to look across the vast white expanse to blue-green pines on the slopes of our mountains, an expanse broken only by the dark blobs of sets of buildings.

Often the evening sun was flanked on either side by sundogs a more vivid red than the sun itself. The appearance of sundogs, Dad said, always meant cold weather or storm or both, and what happened after we did see them certainly proved he was right.

132

Dad, Arthur and I were batching. During the years since Dad had bought the Cross ranch he had been busy at every odd time, building a big, square cattle shed. This shed opened to the east and hooked onto both stable and hay barn, their walls making its south side. Its west and north walls were of logs, and we boys daubed its cracks with fresh cow manure. Cow manure, you see, comes ready mixed for daubing mud, and at nine years of age I could not understand why ranch women objected to its use in daubing houses!

This cattle shed had a flat, hay-covered roof, stringers supporting the roof propped up by dozens of posts scattered throughout the space. Whenever it rained, or when the snow melted, this roof turned water as effectively as if it were mosquito netting. All of the corrals were soon filled with snow and the shed was buried, only a small tunnel-like hole through the snowbanks remaining open on the east side. Often we had to shovel that out.

With fences rendered useless, there was no way of keeping weaned calves apart from the main herd of cattle, so all of the cattle were soon in one bunch. Through the tunnel they would slowly emerge from the shed each morning, plastered with their own muck and steaming as the cold air struck them. (Dad credited this shed with saving his herd that winter, but as I now look back, I think it's a wonder all of he brutes did not get pneumonia and die. But they didn't.)

Unless a blizzard was raging to drive the cattle back to their hole, they'd mosey along down the meadow to the hard snow-packed feed ground, and eventually Dad and his kids would dig out hay from a snow-covered stock to feed them. Dad almost counted the straws, giving them just enough hay to "keep 'em up" and not one spear more.

We kept the work team in the stable, but in with the cattle were an extra team and one saddle horse. Those horses fared badly, for cows eat as fast as if they are hay balers, and the cow which can gobble the most the fastest, at the same time hooking other cattle away from her pile of hay, is the one that stays fat. But the unfortunate horse must chew his feed, so all the hay is gone down the cattle's throats long before Mr. Horse is satisfied.

Dad would rail at the darned horses when they kicked the cattle, trying to protect some feed for themselves, while Art and I, loving horses, were all for 'em. But the cows always won this battle. Yearlings and calves even sneaked in under the horse's belly, gobbled up hay; and, while the horse was chasing one cow away, others'd push in, grabbing great bites of the precious feed.

The meal over, the cows would string off on a well-packed trail to Spring Creek to drink. Here was a first class water hole, and it was one major factor in helping the herd to survive that winter. Sheep and horses do all right licking snow for their drink, but cattle fail to thrive on it.

We made no attempt to keep a water hole open on Government Creek where we usually watered the barnyard stock and also got water for the house. But here at Spring Creek, Dad watered the feed team just once each day, and — this was good break for us boys — we hauled home on the hayrack, in three five-gallon kerosene cans converted into pails, water for domestic use!

What a boon was the five-gallon kerosene can to the ranchmen, first as a kerosene container until emptied; then, with its top cut out and fitted with a bail, as slop pail or water pail; or as a vessel to heat water atop a stove and serve for a wash boiler. It could be easily cut into several small or one large sheet of tin for repair jobs. With a hole of the right size cut in each end of the can, it made a good roof outlet for a stove pipe; and, finally, a can, cut in half, was useful for boiling beans or meat and vegetables.

Having drunk their fill, the cattle might stand around on the feed ground, chewing their cuds until toward evening. But if it was storming, they'd hurry back to the shed, and I wondered a great deal as to what they were thinking about. How, how do they stand just doing nothing? Cattle are sure funny . . . Maybe they — if they think at all — think we are funny critters, too.

This was the daily routine for the cattle — except when the storms were so savage it was impossible to feed them. In addition to digging out the hay, we three had all the chores and the cooking, which kept us busy most of the daylight hours.

As long as the road stayed open, we would see people going by, and they'd stop to talk. But of the neighbors, also struggling with the winter conditions, the Scotts were the only ones we saw with any regularity. Then, along about the middle of February, the road simply snowed completely shut.

For six weeks not even the stage got through from Boswell's ranch to ours. No mail, no anything from the outside world, except that once three men on snow shoes came past the ranch from "outside."

George Post, who was holding down the old Pinkhamton ranch at this time, put a notice in the *North Park Union* which read:

"I want people to know that I still live upon a public road and am still running a road ranch. Stoppers welcome. Meals twenty-five cents."

Since there was no mail service, I do not recall how we got that copy of the paper. But we did.

This was the winter when the Scott boys made skis for themselves, so, in order to get around when we could neither ride nor drive anywhere beyond the Scott place, Art and I made skis, too.

It was impossible to find any boards really fit for this purpose, yet Art contrived to make two pair of skis out of one-inch lumber. We were told to soak or boil he tips until the wood became soft and pliable enough to bend. So for several days we had one end of those skies sticking into the wash boiler on the stove, with the opposite ends tied up to a ridge log.

Big brother made a passable job of bending his skis, but the ends of mine snapped off. This was tragically disappointing until Art solved the problem by nailing barrel staves to the points of my skis. Dad's attitude was one of tolerant amusement.

Soon thereafter, on a bright day, here came George and Charlie Scott and Mamie and Eber Leek, eager to do some coasting. They believed that one of the hills in Dad's Upper Field was the place for this sport, and Art and I were delighted to join them. Six of us then skied a full mile and a half to the field and the fun began. Mamie and Eber rode their skis standing up all properly as they zoomed down the slope. After several spills Art, too, managed this stunt, but neither Mr. Scott, Mr. Charlie nor I could cut it. We rode our skis sitting down on them, but our zest for the sport was soon dissipated because climbing back up the hill was simply too darned much hard work. Just the same, this was a most welcome break in the monotony of our snowbound lives.

Skiing, Art and I found out, was harder than walking, yet we grandually began venturing farther and farther from home until at last we made a trip to the lower field where all our extra horses were grazing. My Snip (Wringtail) was one of these, and I was most anxious about his well-being.

Because there was no loco weed in this 320-acre field, Dad reserved it for the horses during the winter. There was no running water in it, but there was plenty of grass which the horses uncovered — "got at" — by pawing holes in the snow. As a usual thing they "wintered well," coming through to spring both fat and strong.

On this particular day my worry disappeared, and I burst out laughing when we drew close to the horses, busy getting their feed. Their heads, front legs and shoulders were deep in the snow, out of sight — their tails, hind legs and hips sticking up out of the holes they had dug.

"Art," I shouted, "we've read about ostriches burying their heads in sand. Look! Our horses are burying their heads in snow. Ain't it the funniest thing you ever saw?"

"Don't know if it's the funniest," he rturned chuckling. "But it is the darndest thing I ever saw. They're standing on their heads."

The horses had now heard us, and they all at once emerged full-bodied from their snow pits. They were terribly shaggy, but all of them, including my Snip, were "doing all right," and I had learned that horses — if there is plenty of grass after they uncover it — can survive in deep snow. Nor do they require the shelter which cattle must have. Horses merely hump up, turn tails to a storm, and take it in stride.

Skiing back home, and most awfully tired by this time, we stopped to see the John Coes and to hear Mother Coe and Carrie Patton wail about the bad winter. Shucks! they were snug and warm. It was John Coe who was having his work cut out for him.

Like Dad, John Coe had learned the hard way about what loco does to horses, and realizing this danger, he had brought in his horses off the Sand Hills range. Because he could not stop them from breaking into his hay stacks, he had this bunch shut up in a corral — a corral which he continually built higher and higher as the snow got deeper and deeper.

Once a day John let the horses out to go to water and then herded them into the corral again. To feed them, he hauled hay to the corral and pitched it over the fence. Knowing he must bring them through the winter on the amount of hay he had, Joe Coe had these poor horses on a just short-of-starvation ration.

But the thing which amazed me was to see how the horses had gnawed the tough pine poles of the corral. They had eaten and were eating wood. Dry wood!

A short time later Art and I attempted to ski to the Blevins ranch to see our pards, Park and Montie. We made it; stayed over night, too! The boys said they had tried to come to see us, getting as far as the Canadian Bottom where Mex and Blue floundered in snow "plumb to their ears," and they had to turn back.

Mr. Blevins was at home, and when we told him about John Coe's horses eating pine poles, he said:

"A horse will get hungry enough to eat anything. In very early days, when I was working for the Mendenhalls, we missed a small bunch of horses one fall, and it was just by chance I found their skeletons the next summer. They'd gone up on top of the Medicine Bow Range and hadn't sense enough to come down when winter began.

"I counted nineteen skeletons; I saw that the dead horses had eaten not only the branches of quaking aspens but also tree trunks six inches in diameter, and they had eaten all of each other's manes and tails!"

Well, John Coe's horses pulled through the winter without ever eating manes and tails.

One other trip we made on our skis was to visit Cap Fox and bring home from his snug cellar all the potatoes we could carry. All of ours had been frozen. Some people had told us that if you do not thaw out potatoes until you cook them, they are edible; we, however, found them most unsatisfactory — a sweetish, watery mess which would gag a fellow.

This was the winter when Art learned a lot more about cooking with what we had. I helped, too. I ground the coffee. We had one mill nailed to the wall, and we stood up to turn its crank; the other mill, which I liked better, was a small, box-like item I held between my knees. The wonderfully good-smelling ground coffee fell into a small drawer which I emptied into the pot.

The economical method of making coffee, of which Dad did not approve but condoned because coffee was precious, was to boil it, then leave the grounds in the pot, adding only a small quantity of coffee for the next pot full. When the pot was eventually so filled with grounds that there was no room for water, we'd empty it.

I had also become an experienced wiper of dishes, and I made toast, using a long-handled fork to toast slices of bread over glowing coals in the fireplace. To my notion, no modern method of making toast equals this old method. Possibly it was the quick crisping, plus the tase of the wood smoke, which made it really "good stuff."

When some article of food ran out, that was that. We got along without it. It's surprising the things you can get along without when you have to!

This also was the winter when, in our spare time — we had much spare time in the long evenings — my brother was always making something or other. Someone had left an old shoe last on the place, so Art half-soled all of our shoes, using old pieces of tough and dried-out saddle and harness leather. Having no real cobbler's nails he used carpet tacks. They served the purpose.

He had learned to braid and to tie knots, so he was always puttering with rawhide and leather, making hat bands and bridle reins.

He had collected all the old boots and shoes he could find to cut into leather strings. To get a long string out of a small piece of leather, he cut it around and around somewhat as one would peel an orange. He soaked this string in water, stretched it and had a nice, long, leather string. His most ambitious job was a rawhide rope. This did not turn out well, being too small and light and lacking strength, so he cut it up into bridle reins.

More than this, he learned to sew. He made a pair of mittens for Dad out of some tough cloth, facing the mittens with some goat skin which happened to be available. Then he made cloth mittens for himself and me. We had several deer hides but had not learned to tan them. So — no buckskin.

When weary of reading or of playing some game with Art, I put in my spare time studying Montgomery Ward's catalog — a fascinating book! I'd make long penciled lists of all those items I wanted most for myself, and jot down the prices. Then I'd make up an order for all different pieces of machinery we could use on the ranch if we had them, and for the house furnishings and kitchen articles we needed. It was fun, even if I could buy none of the things I wanted.

Included in the games we boys played were poker and other card games, checkers, dominoes, and a cattle game we and the Blevins boys had invented, in which we used beans as cattle. Red beans were Shorthorn cattle; navy beans, Herefords; spotted beans, Texas cattle and other scrubs, including milk stock. Because no herd of cattle was complete without its quota of bulls, we sprinkled in a few lima beans to represent those dominant males.

I'm reminded that many men, when forced to speak of a bull in front of women and kids, referred to it as a "he-cow," as, "The Barnes boys just butchered their he-cow for winter meat." This "nicety" also held for horses. A stallion or stud was a "male horse."

But the rule did not apply to tomcats. A tomcat was always —
well, just a tomcat. All quite puzzling to a small boy.

Several years later, when Gus Dwinell's boys began growing up,
their parents substituted the word "duke" for bull in young Gus'
and Frank's vocabularies. Then I'd hear one of the boys say, "Two
of our big dukes got in an awful fight!" or, "Dad just bought four
new dukes," all of which was either amusing or highly irritating to
my father. With him a bull was a bull and a stud was a stud.

Each player in this bean-cattle game pretended he was a big, important cattleman, and if the four of us were playing, one would always be Montie Blevins, another Swift and Company, another Bill
Marr. This left the fourth boy in doubt as to who he might be, but
he'd likely go outside our Park and choose Ora Haley or one of the
many Hunters of the Big Creek outfit, all of whom were real cowmen, Barney, Lem, Jeff or Granny Bill. Each player counted out fifty
red beans, fifty white, fifty spotted and eight or ten limas, placing all
of these in one pile which was his herd, and the player — an expert
cowman mounted on his top cutting horse — who "cut" his herd into
three bunches the fastest won the game.

All the Shorthorns must go into one bunch, Herefords into another, the scrubs, which remained in the main bunch, into the third.
Three bulls went in with the Shorthorns, three with the Herefords
and the rest were left scrubs.

But if the player who made his cut in the best time inadvertently
put some white beans (Herefords) in the red (Shorthorn) herd, or
failed to get all white and red beans out of the spotted bean herd
(the scrubs), he'd still lose to a slower player who did a clean and
correct job of cutting.

That we four boys figured out this trivial game shows how bound-
up were our thoughts, our actions, our lives, with cowboys and cattlemen and the raising and handling of cattle.

All in all, I was neither unhappy, bored nor disappointed during
this, my first hard winter.

My greatest miseries came from common cold and chilblains, and
from cramps in my legs which Dad said were "growing pains."

"Don't pay any attention to 'em," he'd say gruffly. "You'll out-
grow 'em."

Pretty hard for a little kid "to pay no attention" when the pain
of knotted muscles would fairly make him howl.

As for colds, Mother Coe recommended at least sixteen different remedies. "Even if it don't do any good, it won't do any harm." With one exception, a cure for sore throat, none of these cure-alls ever seemed to do me any good—and I'm not sure they "didn't do any harm."

Wrapping a wet rag around my throat at night and covering it with a dry one did, however, help many times to relieve a sore throat. Some men advised tying one of his own stocks around the sufferer's neck. When my Aunt Elizabeth was with us, I had told her of this supposed cure, and she had thrown up her hands in horror. "The very smell of it would be more apt to strangle you than to cure you!"

Every winter both of us boys had the reddest, most swollen, itchiest chilblains of any of the kids we knew. This was probably because we suffered so much from cold feet, and to warm them we really "toasted" them in front of the fireplace. Neither salves nor kerosene nor turpentine did any good. So Mrs. Coe advised, "Peel a raw onion, dip it in salt and rub the chilblains good and hard."

I let Art try out this remedy — and was glad I hadn't — for it made his feet more sore and more itchy than ever.

Charlie Scott's medicine for any ailment was, quite naturally, whiskey. Dad's small stock of home remedies included, first of all, castor oil. If a boy was "off his feed," a dose of castor oil was all he needed. The horrible idea of being forced to swallow the stuff was enough to make me say, right quick, that I was all well. The other items were laudanum for pain, Jamaica Ginger for upset stomach — "belly-ache," turpentine for a liniment and disinfectant, and carbolic acid.

"The less dope of any kind you take the better off you'll be," Dad would say, and yet, like almost everyone else, he did believe one should take a "spring tonic."

Since the standard tonics were unavailable, he substituted sage tea. I always hoped fervently there would be a shortage of sagebrush leaves for this purpose, but alas! sagebrush was one of North Park's heaviest and most dependable crops! So, for several years, I never could escape that spring dose of sage tea. It had its good points, however, for one cupful of the bitter brew would make a small boy forget all his other miseries!

But spring was still far off, and sage tea was not in my mind on that day during the winter of 1897 and '98 when Art and I resolved to break the Payne cats to work. The underlying thought behind this major project had doubtless developed from reading and hearing stories about the wonderful dog teams of the Arctic.

At this time news of the Alaska gold stampede had penetrated even our remote land. Lots of our men, still miners at heart, had gotten that certain itchiness, that certain treasure-seeker's gleam in their eyes, and were "fair bustin' " to hit out for the new diggings. But they were now well-tied at home, and the tremendous distance, plus the extreme difficulty of getting to the Klondike, stopped them.

Anyway, I thought, "Why not use a cat team hitched to a small sled to take me dashing around over the snow?" Art approved of the idea. Forthwith he made collars out of pieces torn from worn-out overalls, to be slipped over the cats' heads. To these he sewed tugs of the same material. The vehicle he chose to start the breaking was a little iron fire truck, a gift of George Scott, which was equipped with a tongue and a driver, but no horses.

Our half-dozen cats sneaked or bolted into the house at every opportunity; their favorite spot and sanctuary was under the kitchen stove, a stove supported by four legs which raised it six or eight inches above the floor. Only the broom would dislodge them and send them out at the door, and for this the broom was often used!

Patiently we waited for a day when Dad was out doing the feeding alone. Then each of us picked up a couple of cats, carried them into the living room and planted them in front of the truck. Here I managed to hold all four cats while Art slipped on their collars and fastened the tugs.

"All set. Let 'em go," he said. Then, "Yippee! What a stampede!"

Rattle and bang of the iron vehicle! "Wrouw! Spit! Grrrr!" of cats as they scooted out of the living room, across the kitchen and under the stove. Here occurred a calamity as they and the harness and the truck tangled up around one of the stove's legs, resulting in a yowling, snarling, scratching and biting mess of fuzzy-tailed cats which we dared not try to untangle.

Cats, for their size, are very strong. Tugging and yanking, they pulled the stove leg loose and tipped the stove halfway over! This disconnected the stove pipe. Down it crashed, its joints breaking apart and sending thick black soot cascading all over the room. To worsen matters still more, there was a fire in the stove from which wood smoke immediately began to fill the kitchen.

"B'lieve I can get the cats free now," I said. "They've quieted down."

"To heck with the cats!" Art retorted. "Help me get the stove straightened up and the pipe back in place, afore we set the house on fire. Gosh, what a mess!"

What a mess was right. And would Dad raise the roof!

I opened the door to let out the smoke, and out charged the terrified cats, truck and all. Later, we found the vehicle and parts of the harness out of which the cats had managed to wriggle.

Now to get the stove fixed. Art was so excited and scared he was able to lift it and hold it while I put the leg in place. Then, choked with smoke and black with soot, we finally got the pipe jointed together and back where it belonged. Casting anxious glances down the field to see if Dad was still out there, we went to work to clean up. But that darned soot had gotten over everything, stove, chairs, tables, cupboards, and floor. Brooming only smudged it and smeared it; rags the same.

"Got to heat water and scrub — everything," Art panted. "And hurry up, kid. If Dad finds out — " He left that hanging.

I grabbed the wash boiler and shoveled it full of snow and put it on the stove. But it seemed the snow'd never melt, the water never get warm, so we began using snow and cold water for the scrubbing.

Eventually the kitchen got the most thorough cleaning it had all winter!

Eventually, too, Dad came in and took a sharp look at the kitchen and at two tired and uneasy kids.

"Boys," he said, "this is the nicest surprise you could have given me. Glad to see you've got enough gumption to clean the house without being told."

"Oh, we do lots of things without being told," Art said enigmatically, and we grinned at each other.

For a full week thereafter those cats would start to leap in through the open kitchen door and suddenly stop and back-track, fuzzing their tails. I began to fear my pets were off me for good. But I needn't have worried.

Toward April, someone — there must have been several men — broke out the road from the Laramie River to Walden, and travel was resumed. Now we saw the stage driver, freighters and other people every day. Often we had stoppers overnight once again, one of whom was Bill Marr.

142

This I remember because he was trailing a carload of twenty-five pure-bred Shorthorn bulls into the Park. Bill himself was driving a four-horse team to a loaded sled, while two young men, just over from Scotland, on foot, drove the bulls behind this vehicle. They were the Simpson brothers, John and William, both of whom worked for Marr on the Bighorn Ranch for many years and became prominent ranchmen themselves.

But on this occasion the thing that hit Arthur and me hard was that those two green Scottish boys were not merely sunbrned but were blistered as badly as I'd been when I went swimming in Sand Creek. Had they not worn dark glasses, they would have been snowblind — as were several of the bulls.

Later on I was to experience the same sort of thing many times myself. But this was my first clear-cut realization of the glare and the terrific searing heat thrown back at man or beast as sun rays strike white snow. At this time I also learned that cattle often go snow blind, but that horses do not.

Spring was well advanced when I made a discovery about our hay-roofed cattle shed which alarmed me tremendously. All during the winter this shed had been a most interesting place. I could prowl around inside it and mingle with the cattle without frightening them or being in turn frightened by them.

But it was a low building, the walls no higher than six or seven feet to begin with, and since it had not been cleaned out all winter, the floor had been constanly building up; slowly, surely getting closer to the roof, until at last there was barely room for grown cattle to stand upright.

Dad was entertaining a visitor in the house one certain afternoon and our cattle were out on the feed ground, when I noticed twenty or thirty of them hurry back to the shed. Curious as to why they'd do this on a bright day, I followed them in through the shed's tunnel-like opening.

Then I fair legged it to the house and burst in on Dad and his visitor, exploding,

"Dad, Dad! The cattle are eating the roof right off over their heads!"

To my astonishment the visitor howled with laughter, and said, "I've heard of a man being eaten out of house and home, but never before of cattle eating the roof over their heads. Just what do you mean, boy?"

"Mean what I said, Mister. They — the cows — are reachin' up between the poles — the poles that hold up the hay — and gobblin' up the hay roof. We got to stop 'em, Dad. But how can we?"

Dad laughed unconcernedly. "Well, winter is over, and if they're eating that rotten old stuff, it'll save me a few loads of good hay."

And the cattle went on eating the roof over their heads!

UNCLE JACK HUNTER

News of the sinking of the battleship *Maine* penetrated even remote North Park, and the patriotic hysteria which immediately swept across our nation gripped North Parkers, too!

Wars with us school boys had been a matter of reading in history books. But this one was right now, here, in the present, and all of us wished we could help whip the Spaniards and free poor Cuba.

But we heard that Teddy Roosevelt (he'd been a cattleman, so he was absolutely all right) was organizing his Rough Riders and we could trust Teddy to fix the enemy. News reached us, too, about Richard Hobson who became a hero and a whole swarm of girls kissed him. Golly, to a boy that was "worser" than just fighting and becoming the hero.

This was more than three score years ago, but today I still remember two very sentimental songs which everyone — even John Coe — was singing: "Just As The Sun Went Down" and its companion, "Just Break The News To Mother."

Of all the Norh Parkers who tried to enlist in the Rough Riders I recall only one who succeeded, saw action, and came home a hero. Known as "Post Hole Bill" when he worked for Moore and Blevins, this man's right name was William Slee. The war changed the pattern of his life. He, the erstwhile "Post Hole Bill," married one of Walden's social leaders (who is quoted as saying, "It will take me five years to make a gentleman of William"), engaged in business for himself and soon became one of Walden's best-liked and most influential citizens.

Meanwhile, Art and I were back in school, and the adventures of the "four pards" reached their highest peak during that summer of 1898.

This was the year Dad bought the Scott boys' ranch. With the ranch they threw in their household goods, but they kept their horses and some of their vehicles, and, after summering in the Park, they went "outside."

Late that autumn we Paynes moved to the Scott place, the main reason for this move being easy access to water, for Government Creek flowed through the Scott boys' yard. In fact, an additional room which they had hired built onto their main house was propped up on wooden blocks which were set into the south bank of the creek. Anyone sleeping in this room could certainly wake up to the music of the gurgling stream.

Other than that the fireplace smoked, the main house was an exceptionally good one. Its red dirt roof never, never leaked, and the bunkhouse — the Scotts' sleeping quarters — was a first-class log building.

The two small stables with an improvised hay mow between them were, however, mere hovels. Dad made a cow barn and chicken house of one; the other had room for four horses — If you squeezed them in. There were no corrals, just a big fenced yard which enclosed both the stables and the houses.

But this nearness to water was enough to outweigh other unsatisfactory considerations, especially since, in addition to the creek, there were three good springs approximately one hundred yards south of the house.

Quite soon Dad built a log shed and an additional stable, both as makeshift as the old barns. No Swedish ranchman would have put up with such a mess, but Dad quite agreed with his close friend, Uncle Jack Hunter, that good buildings were unnecessary and did not increase the value of a ranch.

In this connection, J. S. King, who lived on Pinkham Creek, east of and thus above Jack Hunter's wide-spreading acres, introduced some "new-fangled" ideas which griped Uncle Jack, my father and many other "sot-in-their-ways" North Parkers.

Mr. King, a native of old Kentucky, didn't exactly fit in, largely because he believed in supervising work rather than putting callouses on his own hands. He was dubbed a "gentleman rancher." Instead of being content merely to raise hay and cattle, King promoted the first hunting and fishing lodge in our area. He offered to paying guests both fishing and hunting trips complete with all necessary accoutrements, guides, cooks, and horses.

It may be truthfully said that King's and other such lodges were the forerunners of the modern dude ranches. To accommodate his guests, King built a huge, three-story, squared-log house with plumbing and a *bath room*. Whereupon, Uncle Jack Hunter, who confidently expected to acquire the King ranch in the not distant future and at his own price, remarked to my father: "Fools build big houses and wise me live in 'em."

"King's nutty," Dad agreed.

I do not know if this business of King's paid or not, but after a few years he abandoned it and went in for Registered Hereford cattle. But Mr. King still wasn't exactly accepted as a North Park cowman. Soehow he didn't fit the mould, and Uncle Jack Hunter predicted he'd sure go broke with "them fancy, hothouse cattle."

Mr. King did not go broke, however, and as time ran along, my father stopped making fun of him, admitting that the Kentuckian had progressive ideas.

Since I have temporarily placed Uncle Jack Hunter in the spotlight, let's take a closer look at this rugged individualist. In appearance he reminded me of old man Pinkham, lean, spare, tough and wiry, sharp-nosed, hollow-cheeked and straggly grey-bearded.

Right at this time, 1898, Uncle Jack and his large family were the only North Parkers of this great Hunter clan, all of whom had come from Illinois, all of whom were cowmen. But prior to Uncle Jack's coming to North Park, one of his brothers, Tom Hunter, had in 1880 established a ranch on the Platte.

I believe this is still known as "the Tom Hunter Ranch." Just below it the northbound Platte flows into a canyon. The present day highway out of the Park toward Saratoga and Rawlins runs northwesterly across the Tom Hunter ranch, climbs a sagebrush hill, and leads on into what is called the Platte Valley, though this valley does not actually touch the canyon-locked river. It is a huge basin lying between the Sierra Madre Mountains on the west (part of the Continental Divide) and the North Platte River on the east, and extending northward to Saratoga.

Dad had known Tom Hunter, who took an active part in the Teller City mining boom and was one of the real old timers; also his sons, Hank and "White-haired" Tommy. They were men of about Dad's age. Eventually I met both of them and developed a great admiration for White-haired Tommy. He was an expert cowhand and he'd tell me stories of the early days.

In 1887 Uncle Jack Hunter bought Tom Hunter's ranch and his cattle, an excellent herd of high grade Shorthorns. But he also acquired a great deal more land and established his home some three miles farther up the Platte from the original Tom Hunter ranch. His summer range comprised the north side of Independence Mountain and on northward, along the Platte Valley into Wyoming, a vast area which was not as yet crowded by the herds of other ranchmen.

Uncle Jack and my father had become good friends, a friendship cemented by Dad's respect for the older man's opinions and his success as a cowman. Whenever those two got together, they'd chinwag far into the night, thoroughly enjoying themselves.

His good wife was one of those patient, uncomplaining women who, except for the help Jack gave her (he always pitched right in to help her), did all of her own work, even when they had a hay crew. In the regular family were plenty of mouths to feed, clothes to wash and mend, beds to make; for although Tom, the oldest son, was gone somewhere, and two daughters were married, there were at home "Antelope Bill" (he'd have sure roped an antelope—if he'd had a rope), Charlie, Harry, Joe and Ed.

Ed was the baby, five or six years old, in the autumn of 1898 when Dad and Art and I rode to the Hunter ranch to help Uncle Jack brand his summer and fall calves. But four boys and Uncle Jack were saddled up and waiting for us. Three fierce-looking stag hounds, which Uncle Jack kept to kill coyotes, were leaping and yelping, eager to be off.

Antelope Bill was the "Master of Hounds." He took them on trips about the neighborhood to kill coyotes, and I recall how the Sand Hills range proved a bad place for these dogs. Patches of sand-burs dotted this area. These thorn-spiked burs, which were shaped much like a peanut, were easily knocked loose by any moving animal, whereupon they flew upward and lodged somewhere in the animal's body. Horses, not used to them, went crazy, ran away and bucked when the sand-burs hit them. Our horses paid no attention to them, except that it was always a touchy job to remove sand-burs.

Naturally, Uncle Jack's stag hounds, in addition to getting burs in their bodies, hit them with their feet, which really gave both Antelope Bill and the lamed dogs plenty of grief.

The Two Bar Two outfit also had a pack of hounds, some of which developed the habit of straying far from home. Consequently, in order to discourage theft of these valuable dogs, and also to let ranchmen know to whom they belonged, the outfit branded them with their horse brand, Two Bar on the left shoulder. This was the only instance of dog branding with which I am familiar.

On this day when we Paynes rode to help Uncle Jack, I was a proud young cowboy of ten, proud because I was at last riding my own horse, Snip, later known as Wingtail; and Art was forking just as proudly Sandy. We inspected the Hunter boys' and their dad's personal outfits with mighty critical eyes. Nothing wrong with the horses. But somehow and somewhere Uncle Jack had adopted the California type of riding gear. All of the saddles were single cinch (center-fire rigs) and because of this they rode too far forward on a horse's withers. (The center-fire saddle invariably creeps forward.)

Unbelievable though it seemed—even unthinkable to a real cowboy—there was not a rope on any of the saddles. Uncle Jack did not permit his boys to carry ropes, never carried one himself—and never roped a critter from a horse's back. Instead of ropes each rider had an Australian stock whip, and Uncle Jack could handle one of these expertly. He and the boys wore flat-heeled boots, but none had spurs, for spurs, too, were nonpermissible. No chaps today, though the boys did later win permission to wear chaps.

The saddles and whips were sufficiently "goofy," but the bridles were the craziest of all. Uncle Jack would not tolerate the use of curb bits. If he had a hired man, that man too must use a big-ringed snaffle bit, the same type as a harness bridle bit. Real cowboys would have gone over the hill talking to themselves rather than use such bits. But this was Uncle Jack's outfit, so all the bridles were equipped with snaffle bits.

From the moment of our arrival, greeting and talk had been going on. As Uncle Jack swung to saddle, Dad noticed a big lump in his right hip pocket.

"What you got there?" thus Dad. "Looks like a flask."

Uncle Jack reached to his hip pocket and pulled out a .38 caliber, snub-nosed pistol. "I always carry this," he said. "Three different times I've caught rustlers at work on my herd. Each time I had those *plaque-taked* thieves brought to trial according to law. They were guilty as Hannah's pup and I offered proof of it, yet every one of those galoots was found not guilty and acquitted.

"I told the court what I thought in plain words and said that hereafter I'd carry justice in my hip pocket. I haven't caught a thief at work since the last court case, but when I do, I'll kill him just as sure as my name's Jack Hunter."

From the flash in his eyes and the snap of his jaw, we boys reckoned Uncle Jack would kill the thief, too.

As all of us rode out across the big field, the hounds sighted a coyote. Instantly the crazy dogs were bounding after the grey-brown scavanger, and all four Hunter boys, yelping louder than the hounds, were instantly racing after the dogs.

The excitement of the chase nipped me, too. I belted Wringtail and tore out behind the boys. Now the coyote crossed a wide and muddy slough. This didn't trouble the hounds, but our horses went in up to their bellies and wallowed across it, then gained again when they struck solid ground.

Cattle fled right and left, and the coyote dipped under a buck fence, with the hounds closing in. Bill set his horse to jump the fence, cleared it, and went ripping on, acing as crazy as the hounds. Charlie leaped off and yanked loose the top pole. Then his horse and Harry's and Joe's bumbled over the fence. This left me with Snip, who would not jump over even one pole, on the opposite side of the fence from the wild chase.

However, the coyote swerved and came back. Possibly believing the fence would protect him, he followed it, sailing along underneath the bucks. But the biggest dog shot up alongside the coyote, forcing him out into the open—and in another second this same dog, the other two right on his tail, ducked his head and threw his body directly underneath the flying coyote.

Boy, was that something! I hadn't known how these hounds worked. But now I had a close-up of the action. Hurled upward by the big dog's weight and height, the coyote simply bounced high into the air. As it touched earth again, off balance, the other two dogs grabbed it, one by the throat, the other by a hind leg, and the third big dog rushed in to help with the kill.

Suddenly the wild excitement died in me. This, the torture kill, was horrible. But it didn't faze any of the Hunter boys. They were somewhat more than excited and hilarious.

My brother and Uncle Jack and Dad were excited, too, Dad telling Uncle Jack about " 'Unting to 'ounds" in England, or fox chasing, which, as a sport, was on a par with steeplechasing and horse racing. Not that Jack Payne had ever been rich enough to engage in any of these, but he had run countless miles on foot trying to keep up with a fox chase and to be in at the kill, the kill being when the fox's brush (tail) is presented to the most distinguished lady taking part in the hunt.

But I could not see this as great sport. Probably something the matter with me. Like the coyote I had just seen killed, I felt the poor fox hadn't a ghost of a chance.

The excitement ended, all of us started rounding up the cattle in the field. Now, Art and I were extremely biased in favor of the Blevins' cowboys method of handling cattle. But Dad said cowboys were too rough on stock, always eager to rope a critter and "bust it wide open." Maybe it was all right to use horses for roping and throwing grown stock, but certainly not for calves.

Today, he had told us, we'd see how Uncle Jack did it—and his method would be just right. "Uncle Jack and his boys aren't cowpunchers, mind you," a statement with which we agreed. They certainly were not cowboys.

Nevertheless, this crew, with our help, rounded up more than one thousand cattle—the entire 66 Bar herd—and then corralled the critters. Then on foot, armed with stock whips, pitchfork handles and other clubs, Uncle Jack, his boys and Dad chased all of the cattle except the unbranded calves out of the corrals.

Neither Montie Blevins nor his foreman, Harry Green, would have corralled all these cattle. Harry Green would have rounded up and bunched about half of the herd, and then, holding it very quietly and very loosely, he would have cut out the cows with unbranded calves and corralled only this part of the herd. Nor would he have separated the cows from the calves after they were corralled. One mounted cowboy would have roped each calf by its hind legs, dragged it up to the fire and turned it over to the "rastlers." If this roper's horse tired, he'd get another mount, or another roper would spell him.

Eventually the Uncle Jack crew, sweating from the hard, fast footwork and from clubbing the frightened, half-crazy cattle, did finish this big job. It was then apparent that Uncle Jack had missed branding a lot of winter and spring calves, for fifty per cent of those calves were big, fat and husky.

Dinner was a welcome interlude, after which Art and I helped as much as small boys could by tending fire and handling irons. The small calves were easy to handle, but the big ones forced the Hunter boys to use ropes. And such roping you never saw in a real cow outfit.

Bill goes into the herd and puts the noose around a big calf's neck. This rope is then snubbed to a post on one side of the corral, one man holding it to take up the slack as the calf struggles. Another rope is now put—not thrown—around the calf's hind legs, or at least one hind leg, and snubbed to a post on the opposite side of the corral. Both rope holders, taking up the slack, eventually stretch out the calf. The other boys rush in and "wool it down," mostly by main strength and weight of numbers. Uncle Jack runs his 66 Bar on its right side. Most outfits brand cattle on the left side or hip, but Uncle Jack likes to be different. He has no ear mark or wattle. But if this calf is a bull, he looks it over carefully before using his knife.

Like the old-time Texas cowman, Uncle Jack raised all his own bulls. It was said of this Texas cowman that if a calf would not make a good steer he'd save it for a bull, but Uncle Jack did not go quite that far. He picked the best of his calves to save for bulls.

Another big calf got the same "on-foot-roping" treatment, and another and another, until at long last the job ended. Then the bawling calves were turned out of the corral to rejoin their bawling mothers.

Dad had worked like a beaver. He was tired and silent as we rode homeward. Eventually Art prodded, "You still say Uncle Jack's way of handling cattle beats the cowboys' way?"

"Yes," briefly and not too emphatically.

But there came another day when we again helped Uncle Jack. This time the job was to "sort" his cattle, which was to cut the steers and dry cows for shipping into one bunch and also to separate the strays belonging to other people from his main herd.

Half a dozen other ranchmen besides Dad were present to get their cattle and take them home. So we had lots of help to round up all of the stock and shove the big herd into a lane with buck-and-pole fences on either side. Two men were stationed behind the cattle to hold them; all the rest worked up front—on foot of course! There was a gate in the fence to the right and another to the left. One man handled each gate.

The cattle were to be cut into three bunches, steers and fat cows through the left gate, strays through the right, main herd straight ahead along the lane. Accordingly Uncle Jack and his helpers would slash one or more critters from the main bunch, haze them along the lane and shout, "By!" or "In right" or "In left."

Incidentally, this is supposed to be a speedy way of sorting a herd and it does work well—in stockyards. Here in the lane, however, the wild cattle were packed like sheep in a car and individual animals were hard to separate from the main bunch.

Quite soon this packed and crowded herd broke down the fences both right and left and poured out at these gaps. Horses were put to use to chase down the runways while other men repaired the fences. The runaway cattle had no desire to get back into that lane (trap) again and it took hours of sharp riding to bring them back. I was one of the riders attempting to do this job.

Eventually, however, we got the cattle jammed into the lane once again and the sorting job was resumed—with extra men now stationed along each side of the lane to forestall another such break. They failed to do this, and there followed more wild chasing to bring back the escapees. Then nightfall put an end to the work, and how Uncle Jack finally got his cattle sorted, I do not know.

Dad, Art and I headed homeward and we did not return on the following day—nor did Dad have anything further to say about the superiority of Uncle Jack's method of handling cattle compared with the cowboys' method.

In this case the cowboy's, or cattleman's, method would have been to bunch the herd either against a fence with riders stationed around the other sides of the herd, or out in the open; then one or two men on good "cut horses" would cut out the steers and dry cows into one herd, the strays into another—each cut held together by one or more cowboys. As soon as both jobs were finished, the main herd would be turned loose.

In some other respects Uncle Jack was an eccentric cowman as compared with men we considered tops in the business. He built no sheds for winter shelter, depending entirely on willows—which are excellent natural shelter for cattle. He never separated his bulls from his cows and made practically no effort to save winter calves, accepting this loss as a part of the business. He never sorted his herd

153

into two or more bunches for handy winter feeding and thus he took a loss of weak animals which could not survive in a big herd.

He refused either to vaccinate against blackleg or to dehorn until long after other ranchmen had been doing both for several years. He'd always be putting up hay long after everyone else had finished, and, so far as I know, he never spent a dollar for a purebred or even a grade bull to improve his herd.

With Uncle Jack almost anyone was a "galoot." A person he did not like was a "plague-taked galoot." He broke his own horses both to drive and to ride, but I never heard any stories of his ability as a bronc rider. Perhaps they just didn't buck with him.

He was progressive in building ditches and grubbing sagebrush to get more hay, and he had to keep up old fences and build new ones, but he never improved his house or his stable. The stable, with hay mow adjoining it behind the manger, had no stalls, just a long manger. Therefore, horses could be crowded in as thick as they could stand—and this seemed to work out all right.

But eccentric or not, he was certainly a good neighbor, a wonderful fellow this Uncle Jack Hunter, an individualist.

HORSE ROUNDUP

In addition to buying the Scott ranch, my father made one other upward step in 1898. Heretofore he had sold his marketable cattle—young steers and fat dry cows—to local buyers. This year he threw his herd in with Uncle Jack Hunter's drive, helped trail the cattle to Laramie and then went on to the Omaha stock market.

Arthur and I, however, were not all alone for the short time he was gone. He had a young man named Vincent Janski, who had worked for Dad during haying, to stay with us. A native of Austria, Janski was known throughout the Park as "The Coffee Count."

He was one of those unfortunate fellows who never quite made the grade as either a good ranch hand or a cowboy. But oh! how the Count would have loved to be rated a cowpuncher. As nearly as he ever came to it was a job on one big roundup as the cook's flunky. As the story goes, the punchers were eating dinner when someone sang out, "Coffee, Count. Bring me coffee."

When Janski ran out with the coffeepot to fill this puncher's cup, from all hands came the call, "Coffee, Count . . . Coffee, Count!"

I shudder to think what might happen to a cowboy who'd dare ask a real roundup cook to come fill his coffee cup, but Janski was delighted to wait on cowboys—and forever after he was known not merely as "The Count," but as "The Coffee Count."

His unsatisfied yen to be a cowboy took the form of investing his wages in the best quality of cowboy equipment and clothing. He never failed to send for any saddle catalog he'd find advertised, so before spring his collection of catalogs numbered about fifty. But after getting together a "swelligant outfit," I believe he rather enjoyed letting some real puncher have choice items for less than cost.

On one occasion the Count threw away a brand new pair of buckskin gauntlets simply because, while we were branding calves, he got blood on these gloves. My thrifty brother retrieved them at once and then had for himself a fine pair of gloves—if slightly too large.

The Count was a good cook, so both Dad and Art were happy to let him take over that job. He had a habit of twirling the ends of his neat mustache, most annoying to Dad, and another of sticking out his tongue, of which Dad tried unsuccessfully to break him. One day, however, the Count inadvertently stepped through a hole in the bottom of the hayrack and almost bit off the tip of his tongue. Dad had to rush him to Walden to see the doctor and have stitches put in it.

At this time the Western and cowboy songs, which are now familiar to everyone, had not as yet been collected and published. But they were circulated by fellows who could sing one or more. Naturally, all of us boys, the girls too, went for these songs in a big way. Art and I soon learned that the Coffee Count did not need much coaxing to burst forth with

> Dig my grave six feet by three,
> But bury me not on the lone prairie
> Where the coyotes howl and . . .

Or,

> First took to drinking and then
> to card playing,
> Got shot in the body. I'm dying today.

He also knew "The Cowboy's Dream":

> Last night as I lay on the prairie,
> And looked at the stars in the sky . . .

So, with Dad absent, we'd get the Count wound up and he'd go through his entire repertoire, enjoying himself as much as we enjoyed the songs.

One evening I said, "Now sing 'The Chisholm Trail.' "

"I don't know that one, and your father wouldn't want you fellows to hear it, even if I did."

"Humph," Art said. "I reckon he knows we've heard it a good many times, and others just as bad."

Yes, indeed, we had heard it. Passed along by word of mouth, the same as off-color stories are passed along, every verse of "The Chisholm Trail" was unprintable. Many years later I was flabbergasted when a young woman mentioned having heard this song at a school rally.

"Oh, no!" I gulped. "You didn't hear 'The Chisholm Trail.' "

"Yes we did. Goes like this:

> I woke up one morning on the
> old Chisholm Trail,
> Rope in my hand and a cow by the
> tail.
>
> Come ti yi youpy, youpy ya,
> Come ti yi youpy, youpy ya.

"Oh," I said and then, "That ain't the way I heard it."

In this connection, a good many of the cowboy songs as they now appear in print are quite different from the originals as sung around campfires. Or, for that matter, as they were sung by the Coffee Count.

It was the spring of 1899 before I at last saw and—to a limited extent—took part in a real horse roundup. It was the last big and important horse roundup to take place in North Park, and Ralph Coyte, foreman of the Two Bar Two, was running it. He was making use of the Two Bar Two's chuck wagon and a few of its punchers, but all the other riders were individual horse owners or reps for these owners. Clint Riggen was representing not only his father, John Riggen, but also John Coe. This Riggen family was one of the very old-time families and they and the Coes were great friends.

Fortunately for Art and me, this horse roundup was to hit the Moore and Blevins ranch, where it would use the extensive corrals, on a Saturday. Otherwise we'd have been in school.

So, bright and early Dad and his kids, accompanied by John Coe and "Babe" Detro, headed for the roundup. Excitement and anticipation were a burning fire in me, and perhaps also in this Babe Detro, a young buck who had come to the Park from the upper Laramie

River and hired out to break horses for John Coe. The stirrups on his saddle were perfect circle steel rings very similar to the center ring on a neckyoke, the first we had seen of this type. Babe explained that they eliminated the danger of a "turned" stirrup.

We were still withholding judgment on Detro. Perhaps he knew his business, perhaps not. Later, however, Babe won our full approval, and in addition to breaking Coe horses he broke one for Dad, a good horse named Charlie which later on became one of "my string." I rode him for many years.

We kids took no active hand in the rounding up, but the punchers swept all the vast range lying between the Michigan and Canadian Rivers clean, as well as other big flats and Independence Mountain. The half-wild horses came pouring into the Blevins ranch from three directions at once, more horses than I'd ever seen before, more than I have ever seen in one bunch since. There must have been a thousand head, too many for the corrals, so at least half of them were left in a pasture while the men "worked" those that were corralled.

To digress for a moment: you cannot "work" wild range horses on the open range or in a field as you can cattle by bunching them and cutting out certain animals. A solid wall of riders would be unable to hold such a herd together in a compact unit, and a horse "cut out" of such a bunch would not stand quietly in the "cut" to one side. He'd take to the "tall timber," as the saying goes, or "make a streak of himself" going back to his range.

Here I was amazed to see the great number of men who had come to see that their colts got branded and that nobody put anything over on the owners of such colts. Charlie Cowdrey was very much present, and whenever there was any question of the ownership of a colt, Cowdrey was positive it was "Old Madge's colt." Old Madge had at least eight colts that one day! Manley Capron from Walden, who owned a lot of horses, was there, looking completely out of place in white collar and tie, suit coat and town hat. In fact, there were men from all parts of the Park, at least fifty or sixty of them. But neither Montie Blevins nor any one of his cowboys was present, being busy handling cattle elsewhere.

Park and Montie were at home, however, and at once Art and I joined them. We four perched on the corral fence along with men lining the fences. Only a few actually did the hard work, supervised by Ralph Coyte.

These fellows would cut a bunch of horses away from the main bunch and whoop them into a small corral, then rope, throw and brand the colts. But, unlike calves, horses are not altered until they are at least eighteen months of age, so the young studs, in most cases, had already been branded and must now be roped and thrown again for this sharp knife operation. Handling these big fellows was fast, rough, hard work. But mounted men roped them by the front feet, "busted them wide open," whereupon one or more men pounced on them to hold them down.

Being an expert with the knife, Dad was in the thick of this. In fact, neighbors from twenty miles away often sent for Dad to come and fix their young studs. Anybody at all could castrate a calf, a pig or a cat, but only an experienced man could perform the same operation on a horse. This day, Ralph Coyte was mighty glad Dad had shown up.

Downing or throwing the mere colts for the hot iron was accomplished in two ways. Either the colt was roped by its front feet and thrown down hard—"busted"—or it was caught by the neck. Then stout men held it while one man ran down the rope up to the fighting animal's head and, grabbing it by one ear and by its lower jaw, wrestled it down. After this, by planting a knee on the colt's neck and pointing its nose skyward, the same wrestler would hold the colt until the brand was run on shoulder, jaw or hip. Horses are never branded on the ribs, nor have I ever heard of them being either ear-marked or wattled.

All horses which owners wished to take home, either to break or for some other purpose, were thrown into a corral by themselves, and when work on one small bunch was finished, it was turned out, another "cut" from the main bunch replacing it.

Quite soon it was dinner time and we boys got a big kick in finding the cook "right on the fight." "What the Sam Hill?" he roared. "Expect me to feed all this blankety-blanked mob?'

He was "up to his neck" throwing biscuits into two huge Dutch ovens, frying ham in two others and keeping two coffee pots going. So, regardless of his profane sputterings, the men did get fed on biscuits, ham and coffee. Utensils for eating being insufficient, as many as four persons shared one coffee cup and sandwiched their ham in hot biscuits.

Harassed Ralph Coyte had scarcely got the men who would work back on the job when someone raised a cry, "Beer! Let's send to Walden for beer."

To my amazement, all those grown men immediately acted like small kids with a promise of ice cream coming up. "Beer! Beer! We want beer. Let's take up a collection and send for a keg."

"Make it two kegs!"

Now, there was a hard and fast rule against liquor of any kind being brought to the chuck wagon on roundup or trail, and it is probable that Ralph Coyte, experienced foreman that he was, didn't like this new development. But realizing he was helpless, he did not crack down.

All work stopped and two hats were passed for contributions. Then, mere moments later, someone's buckboard was appropriated and away sped a man to Walden—for beer. It was fully ten miles, yet he made the round trip in less than two hours. Two kegs of beer, fitted with spigots and well flanked by cakes of melting ice, held down the back of his rig. At once work stopped while all hands swarmed to the vehicle. Several men even drew beer into their hat brims and drank from them.

We four kids had slipped up to the house and provided ourselves with cups. But we relinquished three of them to three of our favorite men, and one cupful for four of us was all the beer we got. Both kegs were empty before we could get to them for a refill.

Meanwhile Ralph Coyte was pleading with the men to go back to work. I suspect that as boss he very much wished beer had never been mentioned! But nobody except Coyte and perhaps Dad wanted to work. The men were eager for more fun and excitement. Did anybody own an outlaw horse they wanted to see ridden? And who'd ride it?

Things were picking right up, getting interesting for a little would-be cowboy named Johnnie Payne!

Clarence Webb and his younger brother, Clyde, were both present, and Clarence offered to supply the horse. At this time I was not well acquainted with these Webb boys, but had heard a lot about them and their parents. The family lived on the Canadian River at the point where the old Teller road crossed this stream, where in earlier days a settlement had sprung up with a road ranch, stage station and post office, named Canadian. But there was no longer even a post office at Canadian. It was now the "Webb Ranch." I knew the Webbs ran their cattle in the Sand Hills, Dad's range, and some of their horses, too. Other horses in their brand were scattered all over the Park. Both Clarence and Clyde were recognized as top cowhands and top bronco busters, and today at this horse roundup I was getting to see them for myself and to size them up.

Again the hats were passed and five dollars was taken up for the man who'd ride the outlaw.

Tex Jurgis was either prodded into doing so, or he volunteered. He was a stranger to me and I do not know for whom he was working. But the nickname "Tex" was not a misnomer, for here was the genuine old-time Texas trail-herd and range cowhand; genuine from run-over heels of his high-legged boots which crowded his knees, soiled corduroy britches, brown flannel shirt, ragged, unbuttoned vest, gaudy silk neckerchief loosely tied to reveal a sun-browned, corded neck. Above this, a wrinkled, saddle-leather-hued face, a small brown mustache, deeply socketed eyes and black hair under the conventional hat of that period. This was a rather narrow-brimmed Stetson, brim down-tilted over the wearer's eyes, low crown creased precisely with either three or four dents and equipped with a leather thong to come down around the back of the head.

Unlike ninety-nine per cent of cowboys, to whom gloves and silk neckerchiefs (mufflers) were as important as boots and spurs those days, Tex wore no gloves. No holstered gun rode at his hip either. Among the men present at this horse roundup in the year 1899, there was not a single gun—at least, not in sight.

We four pards, Montie, Park, Art, and I were now asking, "Who's he? What's he done? Does he stack up?" reserving our judgment of the man until we saw him ride. We sensed, however, that there was a definite hostility toward this "outsider" without understanding any reason for this feeling on the part of many of the "regulars."

Now a tall bay horse, a splendid creature of about eleven hundred pounds, was roped and led out to the rocky ridge, a hard, gravelly area strewn with small boulders. Men swarmed to tie his front feet together, blindfold him and hold his head down by its ears while Tex himself saddled the brute, fitting hackamore reins to suit himself. Two mounted men, one of them Clarence Webb, were to act as hazers, and Tex was told that to win the five dollars he must ride the horse clean—not pull leather at any time.

There were no such hard and tight rules as are enforced on to-day's rodeo contestants. The rider could use his spurs as he pleased; even "ride on his spurs." Quirts, which were to be barred at all rodeos later on, were at this time required equipment, and a top bronc rider would swing his quirt at every jump the horse made.

Tex spat, hitched up his britches, hung his quirt on his right wrist, and "stepped across," ordering, "Turn 'im loose, boys."

The crowd backed away to give the horse room. I was wedged in by men but managed to squirm through to the front line where I'd be sure to see everything. Men released the big bay, jerking off the blindfold as they did so, and the act was one.

This horse bucked high—away, away up—thudded back to earth, landing stiff-legged and hard, the rider taking a terrific jolt and wrench. Left hand on hackamore reins, and solid in his saddle, taking the punishment, Tex Jurgis used his quirt with his right hand. Oh, it was beautiful to see! But his spurs were pretty well set just behind the front cinch, and men howled, "Scratch 'im! Scratch 'im," Clyde Webb's voice louder than anyone else's.

Now the horse swapped ends, thudding back to earth and landing crookedly. Under Tex daylight showed. He reached for his saddle horn and seized it. Releasing his hold in a mere instant, however, he had his quirt waving again, but the hostile crowd was yelling, "Pulled leather! Pulled leather!"

I was mad at them, furious. To my notion Tex was putting up a ride.

Suddenly the big bay lost its feet and landed flat on its left side, Tex firm in the saddle, his leg underneath the horse. The pick-up men swept in close.

"Broken leg!" someone gasped and others shouted. "You hurt?"

"Naw!" snorted the bronc rider, and as the bay bounded to its feet, Tex rode on, quirt swinging, until the horse quit cold and threw up its head.

As the hazers took charge of the bronc, Tex limped to a shady spot and sat down, his breath coming and going in great gasps. Ralph Coyte gave him the five dollars and then shouted, "Come on, fellows! Come on! Fun's over. Let's go back to work."

But nobody paid attention to the roundup boss. All were talking of famous bucking horses and famous riders, and a hassle developed, for, while Tex had sold himself to a large number of those present, Clyde Webb was hotly and vociferously shouting his dissatisfaction. "Tex pulled leather. He didn't win the money."

"He stayed with the horse when it went down and rode him to a finish," someone countered. "Tex won it."

Clarence Webb kept out of the argument, but Clyde stormed, "I'll bet five, ten, even twenty dollars I can outride that Texas rannie."

Clyde's round face, one big freckle, was now as hotly red as his hair, which was bristling with anger and challenge. When no one took his bet, he snapped, "I'll ride any horse you fellows pick out and show you how it should be done. That is, for five bucks. Not for free."

"All right, have it your way, Clyde," said Ralph Coyte in desperation. "Perhaps when we get through with this monkey business we can do some work."

Another purse was collected and another horse brought out, a snaky little roan, and like the bay, a Webb horse. For his ride Clyde donned a pair of white angora chaps.

The roan pitched straight ahead, Clyde raking him from shoulders to flanks and quirting him at every jump. When it was over, all those backing Clyde patted him on the back.

"You made a clean ride! A right pretty ride."

Even we boys knew the roan had not been nearly as hard to stay with as the bay. But now that Clyde had at last won five dollars and shown up Tex, he was satisfied, and Coyte persuaded some of the men to go to work.

Darkness put a stop to the work which would be resumed the next day. Babe Detro stayed to help with it, but John Coe, Dad, Art and I rode home, me with my head filled not so much with my first horse roundup as with bronc riders and bucking horses. Someday I'd be able to ride like ... Which one of those fellows was my present hero? I decided it was Tex.

Since we were not permitted to go back the next day, thus ended the adventure of my first roundup. But later I was destined to know both Tex Jurgis and the Webb boys very well, and Clarence Webb merits special attention.

North Parkers spoke of Clarence as "clean and steady," meaning he neither gambled nor went on big toots with the boys and was steady on a job. Big-framed, stalwart and muscular, with calves to stretch a pair of boots, and thighs to match, he was as strong and virile as the wild horses he rode and tamed.

He had irregular features, a prominent and slightly hooked nose, light colored eyes which I thought held steel glints, and blond hair which he always let grow out long in the back, for either typhoid or scarlet fever had left him with a peculiar hairless scar just at the base of his skull, and long hair hid the scar.

But the fever had not harmed him otherwise. He was a man, big, dominant and aggressive, who stood out in any company. As I've said, he was both a cowhand and bronc buster, and Clarence never let a bad horse whip him. If he were thrown, he'd try that horse again and again until he did ride him. If we had had movies in those days, what a Western movie hero this man would have made! And if we had had the modern rodeos, what a professional rodeo hand Clarence would have been. That was the sort of sport for which he was cut out and ideally suited—and the lure of it would have appealed to him. Roper, bulldogger and bronc rider, Clarence would have been hard to beat. Unfortunately, he was born too early.

Some two or three years after this horse roundup, I was privileged to see Clarence Webb make what I call the greatest and most thrilling ride I have ever seen in all my life.

Dad had gotten two green horses from John Coe to break for their use in the hayfield. Both of these horses had had a liberal dose of loco, so they were most unpredictable. We had Eber Leek using them for his team on a sweep or buck rake. When a sweeper brings a load of hay up to the stacker, it is necessary for the horses to back up and release the load. Neither of these horses would back up. All of Eber's stratagems failed to persuade them to take one backward step. So, in desperation, Dad hitched his pusher team behind one of these locoed horses and dragged the horse backwards.

It was all this strong team could do to move that horse, for it simply dug its hoofs pulling ahead. Eventually, Eber did get them both to back up enough to unload his sweep. However, when they got warmed up and sweating, it seemed as if the loco would start to work and make them crazy. All at once one or the other or both of them would start running and kicking and bucking, Eber hanging to the board at the back of his sweep and riding out the storm. Every two or three days, haying would be delayed for several hours to mend the sweep.

There came a night when both horses jumped out of the pasture and vanished.

Thereupon Dad sent us boys out into the Sand Hills to find the horses and bring them home. Eventually we found them in with a big bunch of Webb's horses, but we were unable to turn this bunch toward home and our corrals. Instead, the herd stampeded down along Webb's fence, and finding a gap in it, plunged into Webb's upper field.

By this time Art and I were licked. Our ponies weren't fast enough to head off these horses or to do anything with them. So we rode to the Webbs' house. Clarence was running the ranch at this time and was busy putting up hay. He and his crew were at dinner when we came in and told him our sad tale.

"We brought halters with us," Art said. "What we really want is to get just those two horses and lead 'em home."

"Sit up and eat," Clarence said. "I'll corral your horses."

He went to the stable and led out a tall white horse, with a light hackamore on its head and a long lead rope attached to the hackamore. He opened the gate in this upper field fence which led right into his set of corrals, sprang on his horse and went after the horses.

We'd just finished eating when we saw him coming back. Oh, boy! Was that a sight. Those horses, about thirty of them, were running like scared jack rabbits, behind them on a snow-white horse, Clarence bareback and hatless, his long black hair flying in the wind, face close to his mount's ears, his eyes shining with enjoyment. I could not have stuck on that flying horse for a second, but he was piece and part of the animal, and he was flogging those horses with the loose end of his hackamore rope.

Closer they came, thundering down along the fence. Then—how perfect was his timing—suddenly Clarence and the white horse were alongside the bunch. How that splendid horse was running! How the man was riding! Just as the leaders of the bunch reached the gate, Clarence was there in front of them to turn them through the opening.

Regardless of rides on bucking horses—and I've seen some splendid rides—this was the most magnificent exhibition or horsemanship I have ever seen, the picture still vivid in my memory today.

VACCINATING AND DEHORNING

During the summer of 1899 we had a jolly woman cook whom all of us liked. She and her husband and a grown nephew came from Denver in a covered wagon to work through the haying season, and Dad was lucky to get them.

The nephew had with him a great stack of paper-bound magazines with garish covers, which introduced us boys to a type of literature not found in the best homes. *Young Wild West, Do and Dare, Work and Win, Buffalo Bill,* were some titles I recall. This young man slept in his uncle's wagon and read these tales by lantern light.

Art and I realized that they were the sort of stories a boy reads in the haymow when he's sure his parents are somewhere else. Nevertheless, we did not try to hide them, and Dad said merely, "I hope you'll see the difference between this trash and good stories and learn to appreciate worthwhile stuff."

Perhaps he was a good psychologist and knew if he'd forbidden us to read these magazines we'd have done it behind his back. As it was, we soon found the stories, particularly the Westerns, unbelievably ridiculous.

That autumn, Dad again shipped his stock to the Omaha market. This time with John Kimmons, a newcomer who had come from Fort Collins and brought his cattle and horses with him to a ranch which he had purchased on The Michigan, twelve miles southeast of

Walden. Kimmons and Dad had become close friends. Art and I liked him because he was a jolly man who understood kids, and also because, in addition to being a real cattleman, he was a top-hand cowpuncher. Many first class cowmen are not good cowboys, so this rated very high in his favor.

Late in December, Dad and we boys rode to the Blevins family's new home, the J R ranch one mile east of Walden on the Michigan. It was thirty below zero, so Dad wanted me to stay at home, but I'd have gone had it been fifty below zero. Wouldn't I see Park and Montie and Dean, Mrs. Blevins and her small daughters? And, even more enjoyable, I'd be a cowboy helping to trail a herd of cattle home.

Dad was buying from Mr. Blevins approximately one hundred cows with calves, dry cows, steers and heifers. The cattle were part of a big herd which had been trailed to the Park from the Chugwater country near Cheyenne. Thereafter we called the bunch which Dad bought, "the Chugwater cattle."

In spite of the intense cold the visit was a pleasant one, but we missed the crew of men which had been on the old ranch. Harry Green and Wash Alderdice were now working for someone else, and only Alec Dunbar was on hand. Although Alec was a bronc buster, he was doing chores and pitching hay!

There was nothing of the roughneck about Alec, a pleasant man with a shy smile, a quiet modest man, but every inch a cowhand. He also loved music and occasionally played the violin for dances.

Yet, with all his *good* qualities, Alec Dunbar often lost jobs because of his great love for horses. He would hire out to break a string of colts and he'd make pets of the broncs. The foreman or owner of the outfit would then expect to dole out these horses among his other riders. To this Alec would object, hating to see anyone else riding his pets. Since he owned none of them, however, he had no recourse other than to accept the situation or quit or be fired.

Another friend of ours was at the new Blevins home, "Granny Bill" Hunter. All of us boys liked and respected him but thought of him as a funny old codger. Granny Bill often visited Dad, and whenever he came, Arthur and I would sidle up to him and look expectant, and Bill would fish around in his coat pocket. "B'lieve I've got some stick candy here some place. Yes, here it is." Or— "B'lieve I've got a couple of oranges left. Or did I eat 'em? Nope. Here they are, sure enough."

Granny Bill was one of the owners of the Big Creek outfit, actively working to improve its cattle and build up the outfit. Yet his major interest seemed to be in purebred bulls. He'd talk about bulls by the hour, and his watch fob, suspended from a gold chain which hung loosely across his vest, was unique—a solid gold replica of a bull's head!

We heard immediately that Mr. Blevins was having serious losses from blackleg among his purebred Herefords—losses which continued over the years following and at one time almost broke him. But the Chugwater scrubs, perhaps because they were thin and scrawny, seemed immune, and by noon of the following day, Montie had the herd Dad was buying cut out and counted, and in the bitter cold we headed for home.

Since the days were short and it was already past noon, Mr. Blevins told Dad to cut across the sagebrush flat, lying between the Michigan and Canadian Rivers, to Gus Dwinell's ranch and there stay over night, which we did.

Up until now Dwinell had been a man whom Dad saw once in a while, but none of us had really known him except as "the New Englander who married Fanny Barnes." She was now the mother of two small sons and was helping her husband in a thousand ways, doing all those things my own mother had done.

But on this occasion, by that strange meeting of minds or something which you cannot pin down, Jack Payne and Gus Dwinell cottoned to one another as if they were twins. Only a few years later North Parkers were saying, "Payne and Dwinell are married."

Dwinnel at once put us boys at ease when he said in his friendly way, "Call me 'Gus.' Everybody else does." So 'Gus' he was from then on.

This was really the Sanborn and Dwinell ranch, which they had named "Sunset Ranch," but nobody ever remembered this poetic name. It was always "Dwinell's."

The buildings and corrals sat on a bluff above the Canadian River valley, about two miles below the Webb ranch, the fences on either side of the river enclosing much government land as well as the acreage owned by the partners. They also owned the old Horse Ranch which lies right against the Medicine Bow Range—like the Mendenhall ranch—between the lower and upper sets of sand dunes.

Sanborn, an Easterner, and a high class fellow in every way, visited the ranch almost every summer and "made a hand" although he never rode horseback. The Sanborn and Dwinell herd had been "bred up" by crossing purebred Shorthorn bulls on native Texas cows. Many of the original cows were still in the herd when I first became acquainted with it, big-framed, long-legged and sharp-horned brutes, largely brindles and pale reds. They were almost as wild as elk and as quick as antelope, and they'd fight a buzz-saw. But already, in 1899, the young stock were first-class beef cattle, their predominant color all red.

Dwinell was at this date very much sold on Shorthorns, and Dad went right along with him. But a few years later both men switched over to Herefords. Why? Because in our country of hard winters there was ample proof that Herefords were "better rustlers" and "easier keepers" than Shorthorns. "Better rustlers" means Herefords would get out and root for grass in the snow where Shorthorns would stand around, awaiting to be fed; easier keepers, because, under exactly the same conditions, a Hereford would hold its flesh far better through a winter than a Shorthorn.

Dad found Dwinell up on his toes to grow the best cattle he could, attempting to learn all possible about the business through stockmen's papers, and that very evening he persuaded Dad to subscribe for *The Breeders' Gazette*. The *Gazette* fascinated Arthur and me, the advertisements alone enough to keep a fellow ga-ga, and pictures of wonder cattle of all breeds such as we'd never seen. These were raised on farms of the great Midwest, the Corn Belt area. There were horses, too, great, fat draft horses, Percherons, Shires, Clydesdales, and lighter weight, hot-blooded breeds. A fellow could learn all about hogs, sheep and poultry, too—if he was interested.

Getting acquainted with this splendid farm-and-livestock periodical was only one of the helpful and progressive steps our contact with Gus Dwinell brought about. He had already taken advantage of the Federal Government's campaign against blackleg. If a cattleman applied for vaccine, the government would supply it free of charge. Gus had tried the vaccine and was sure his losses had been reduced.

"Here's an application form, Jack," he said. "If you send for as many doses of vaccine as you'll need, I'll come and vaccinate your calves."

Of course Dad took up this offer, and along in January first vaccination of our calves took place in the old log stable on the Cross ranch. Gus had us boys put a rope around a calf's neck and snub it close to a post. He then put his body against the calf to hold it against the wall while he inserted the syringe needle just behind the left shoulder. Meanwhile one of us bobbed the tassel of this calf's tail to show it had been vaccinated. This was, indeed, a major event with us boys.

Right at this time, too, there was lively agitation about dehorning cattle. Old timers were loath to do anything of the kind. Some men even declared emphatically that dehorning made cattle crazy. Plumb crazy. "B'gosh, you can't drive 'em or do anything else with 'em after they're dehorned." Also, they'd be unable to fight off predatory animals, and the operation was brutally cruel.

I'll go along with that—cruel. Dehorning cattle over two years of age is the most brutal thing cowmen ever did to livestock, and for a short time after the operation animals are, indeed, nearly crazy from shock and pain. But either sawing or clipping off yearlings' horns did not hurt very badly.

Also, there were already on the market caustic potash and various pastes which, if properly applied to the small horn nubbin on a young calf—before the horn actually appeared—stopped the horn's growth. The drawback to this treatment was that the horns would be well started before a ranchman got around to using the paste.

Dad had come back from his trip to the Omaha market with full knowledge that the Corn Belt cattle feeders were now demanding that all steers they put into their feed lots be dehorned. Dad's commission man had said, "Why don't you dehorn 'em, Payne? Dehorned feeders bring from fifty cents to a dollar more per hundred pounds."

The reason for this? First of all, dehorned steers were quieter, more tractable, and easier to handle in the feed lots, so they put on more weight than horned steers. There was less fighting and, therefore, fewer injuries, more cattle could crowd up to a grain feed trough, and, lastly, they *looked* better.

Naturally, Gus and Dad were interested in getting the best possible price for their young steers, and at this time when we stayed overnight with him, Gus was intending to dehorn all of his steers in the coming spring. He had a chute, but for the dehorning job he'd have to have a special door made for it. He'd have this done if Dad'd buy a pair of dehorning clippers. To dehorn Dad's cattle we would bring them to Dwinell's chute.

(I have already mentioned these clippers in connection with my first horse, Wringtail)

Accordingly, the following April we Paynes helped Dwinell and his crew dehorn his young steers. Then, early one morning, we drove our small herd to Dwinell's—about five miles—to use his corrals and chute. Gus, with his sleeves rolled up—the only ranchman I knew who rolled up his sleeves for a job—handled the clippers, and one man splashed a gob of pine tar on each raw wound. Tar was supposed to ward off blow flies and to help heal the wound.

This first dehorning was a big occasion for me. Before the next spring, however, my brother had built a set of corrals and a chute on the Scott place, where we were living, and we dehorned at home. But Gus was there to do the job, and by this time he had learned that a saw was far better than clippers.

Quite soon nearly everyone in the Park began dehorning heifers as well as steers. Uncle Jack Hunter was one of the very last—if not the last—to yield to this new order.

In 1900 Gus found himself very short of feed for his cattle on the range. He was running them on the great flats lying between the Canadian and Michigan Rivers. So many others also used this range that it was badly overstocked. So were our Sand Hills. No room for Gus there, although his ranch bordered this area on the south, and we too were getting pretty badly squeezed.

Gus began scouting around and learned there was a large area of unused range land lying just north of the Colorado-Wyoming state line and west of the main highway extending from Mountain Home Park westward along West Beaver Creek. Beaver Creek is a tributary of the Douglas which flows into the North Platte.

Gus talked it over with Dad. "The thing to do is grab that range now. Right now. Throw in with me, Jack. There's enough for both of us."

Dad wasn't ready to go to all the work and trouble of making such a move. He'd wait until next year. Gus, however, rounded up his herd of she-stock, trailed them across the Sand Hills, up through the neck of the Park and thence to West Beaver Creek.

That summer of 1900 Arthur was a full-fledged cowboy and got in on all of the work. But I, with a longing inside me fit to bust me wide open, got in on none of it, except for one evening after school when I flogged Wringtail homeward and then on to the Sand Hills to meet Dwinell's herd on its march to a new range.

He had a grub-and-bed-carrying wagon along—not a chuck wagon by any standard—and behind it the driver led a couple of extra saddle horses. This was Dwinell's cavvy. The punchers were

Gus and Art, Bill Caudle, whom not even a greenhorn could make the mistake of calling a cowhand, and a Pennsylvania Dutchman named John Schultz.

Schultz was a personable young fellow, willing and eager to learn, but he didn't know much more about cattle work than Bill Caudle. Nevertheless, Schultz was Gus's cowboy and he was to batch at a certain cabin on Beaver Creek and ride herd on the cattle at this cowcamp.

Now a real cowboy—I—rode up to the herd, fair itching to help trail it onward. This lasted only until nightfall, for Dad would not let me miss school the next day or the next. Yet, riding back home that night, I had, to cherish and to console me, Gus' saying, "Next year, when your dad puts in with me, you can stay at the camp with John Schultz and ride range!"

Next year I'd ride range! And it did work out that way.

Meanwhile in 1900 I was having a heartbreaking time trying to gain recognition as a cowboy. My pards were all gone, but I must go to school. New faces were there now, Fred and Bessie Baker, Ed Hunter, Forest (Speck) Brownlee, Henry and Bella Seymore, some of the many McCaslands, Frances Fisher of the Cowdrey family, among them. Although I was now one of the big kids, school was a prison while Art was having the time of his life, right in his glory as a cowboy!

This came about largely through Montie Blevins. The Chugwater cattle did not produce many calves that spring, and Mr. Blevins found a good buyer, Charlie Hardin, for the dry, fat cows—in fact, for all our fat cows. Hardin and his partner, Hartman, had a butcher shop at Laramie, and must have had big contracts for dressed beef, for Hardin bought more cattle in North Park than Laramie City could possibly have eaten. (In fact, I wonder how any humans ate some of the beef Dad sold; mighty "shelly old pelters.")

When Hardin bought Dad's cows, it developed that he liked to have kids trail cattle for him, saying they were often more reliable than men. So Hardin hired Art and his horse Sandy for one of his cowboys to drive cattle to Laramie. But he did not think I'd had quite enough experience, nor would Dad let me out of school.

How well I remember Art's first trip with a herd! He got one dollar and a half per day for horse and man and pay for one more day to return home. One other boy, slightly older, accompanied him. I was in a fever of expectation looking for my big brother the night he was due home, six days after he'd left with the herd. I saw him and the other fellow as soon as they came in sight, just at dusk. Both horses were limping, but that hadn't stopped the boys from riding all the way from Laramie in one day.

I met Art as he pulled up at the stable. "How'd you make out?"

"Fine and dandy, except that Sandy went lame. Got to have him shod. Got some things for you, kid."

That wonderful big brother had spent his wages, nine dollars, for clothing for Dad and himself and me. Gloves, a shirt, and a silk neckerchief for me!

M. C. Ward—everyone called him "Mac"—had taken over the old Pinkhamton ranch, and, as I remember, he shod Sandy for Art, who made many more trips to Laramie that summer and fall. Hardin made arrangements along the road for pasture for his cattle each night and for his riders to put up at road ranches. Art helped Dwinell, too, with his roundup and big move, and late in the fall got to go along with a big herd of cattle belonging to four or five different outfits.

The nearest I came to my goal was once during the summer when Jimmy Taylor and Joe Coyte stopped overnight at the ranch with a bunch of Hardin's cattle. They were to make Boswell's on the Laramie the next night, and Hardin had told Art they might need the help of another man through the timber, though only as far as Boswell's.

The next day being Saturday, I cut myself in on it. I rode with Art and Jimmy Taylor and Joe Coyte, who was reputed to be the best kid cowboy in all North Park. I'm sure he was, too, though only thirteen at this time.

Trailing up along the neck of the Park, we four kids began practising roping on Hardin's beef cows. Jim, the oldest boy, showed us how to tie the loops of our ropes so the nooses could not close. With such a loop one could hold a cow for a second or two before she would slip out of it, and we had a high old time, whooping the cattle along as we roped them.

It's not to be wondered at if I didn't catch very many cows. But Joe and Jim and Art were pretty good, and often they'd "bust a critter" before it fought free of the noose, all of which was hard on the cattle. They were simply steaming with tongues out. Would Mr. Hardin have thought highly of kids as cowboys had he known about this?

I got as far as Boswell's where all of us stayed the night. Then Art and I turned back. He got three bucks for his work; I got nothing except the thrill, yet felt well paid.

My longing to trail cattle to Laramie increased all summer, and, when the big herd I have already mentioned stopped overnight and Art got a job with one of the owners, I was simply on fire to go along. One of the riders was Billy Hill, well remembered by us from the days when he worked for Moore and Blevins.

While we were rounding up the field to start the herd, I ventured to ask Billy, "You s'pose any of these men'd give me a job?"

Billy started to laugh, looked hard at me and stopped and said gravely, "You might just ask Captain John Ish."

John Ish, a Southerner who had served during the war, was a tall, very dignified red-bearded gentleman, who sat a horse like a cavalryman. But I didn't let his dignity stand in my way.

Riding up to him, I took a deep breath and said, "Captain Ish, don't you need another man?"

If he had laughed, I'd have sunk into the sod. But he held a perfectly straight face and answered sympathetically, "Sorry, but we're full-handed."

The story must have been too good to keep. Anyhow, it got out and I'd hear someone say, "That little bit a kid asked Captain Ish, 'Don't you need another *man?*'"

A HOODOOED CATTLE DEAL

However, late in October, this same shamed and embarrassed "little bit a kid" was given another chance to prove he was a cowboy — "good as a man." Earlier in the year, Dad had agreed to buy from Charlie De Weiss one hundred spring calves at weaning time. But we must go to De Weiss' ranch to brand and wean the calves and then bring them home. This part of the deal developed into the worst botched-up and badly handled mess of my entire experience in the cattle business.

Mr. De Weiss was closing out his herd. Bill Jones, a genial Welshman who often stopped overnight with Dad, was to get the "wet cows" (the mothers of the calves), and our old friend, John Coe, was buying ten head of cows with calves by their side from De Weiss. Thus it came about that John Coe and Jack Payne joined forces to go to De Weiss' ranch to get their new cattle.

Naturally, De Weiss would feed all of us, but he had told Dad that he had insufficient bedding for a crew of men, so John Coe provided a team and a bed wagon. Right at this time Mr. Coe had two strong men boarding with him, Al Bush, carpenter and fiddler, and Fred Boudalier, jack-of-all-trades — if he was of a mind to make use of his abilities.

One thing at which Fred was expert was rolling cigarettes. He could whip together a neater and tighter cigarette than any cowboy

175

I ever saw roll one, so perfect it might have been "tailor made," as the manufactured cigarettes just coming into use were called.

These two fellows, who knew as much about horses and cattle as a pig knows about Sunday, were John Coe's cowboys.

Dad's cowboys were himself, Arthur and I. But Dad rode with John Coe in the wagon and led his mount behind it when this cow-punching crew started out for the De Weiss ranch.

Since we had no hired man, we turned the skim-milk calves out with their mothers, which took care of the milking problem, and we put out a big, flat box filled with wheat enough to last the chickens for several days. Otherwise, we left the ranch to take care of itself.

According to plans already made, it would take one day to get to De Weiss' ranch, another day to round up his cattle, separate cows from calves and brand calves. These would be left corralled over-night, and on the third day we'd drive them with John Coe's cows twenty miles or so home. Later by a few days, so we understood, Bill Jones would come and get his part of the herd.

But the best-laid plans of mice and men . . .

Art and I were not thrilled over the prospect of working with Bush and Boudalier as fellow cowpunchers but accepted it as something to be endured.

The trip took us across the sage flats bordering the south side of Independence Mountain to the Big Horn outfit's Boettcher Ranch, and thence up along the North Fork to De Weiss' place, which snuggled against mountains of the massive Continental Divide.

De Weiss was batching alone, and well I recall that he would not let anybody help him with the cooking, about which he was a fusspot and granny. He'd make soda and sour milk biscuits for each meal, moulding them oh! so carefully and packing them close into a pie tin to bake. They were licking good, too.

The moon was bright that night when we spread beds on the floor, and Art and I went right to sleep in spite of John Coe's real fear we'd get "moonstruck." The next morning, however, a chill wind was blowing and clouds hid the sun. Was this perhaps because we'd defied the moon?

Led by De Weiss, the cowboys went to work, and now I learned about trying to gather, or round up, cattle in willows. This ranch was, except for small, open patches of meadow, all willows, with dense masses just north of the corral into which we must drive the herd. The cattle, very suspicious of that corral, "took to the brush."

Good dogs might have chased them out of this jungle, but men on horseback or on foot were almost helpless. Somehow we finally managed to corral about twenty cows and calves; all the rest got away. This was followed by a two-hour-long stop for dinner. It appeared that Charlie De Weiss must be present when each calf was branded, but now he must get dinner, so the rest of the crew sat around and talked while Charlie did the cooking.

Snow was falling by the time we started branding calves, handling these husky young brutes in the same manner that Uncle Jack Hunter advocated with no horses allowed inside the corral. I was to tend fire and hand the branding irons to Dad. But John Coe tried to take my job, and he and I clashed. He didn't know how to build a branding fire, and I told him I did. He was remaking the fire according to his ideas and I was changing it to mine all afternoon. Night and the storm put an end to the branding, and to the argument.

By the next morning—morning of our third day—there was a good foot of the white stuff bending the willows half-double. Both cattle buyers and cattle seller were in a quandary.

But it looked as if it might clear up so work could be resumed, and neither Dad nor John Coe wanted to go home and make the long trip again, so it was decided to stay with De Weiss. Dad, however, was worried about our cattle breaking into haystacks and also about things freezing in the house, so he sent Art home.

This was the first time my brother had held down the ranch entirely alone. But he took care of everything in first-class shape, started to milk the cows again, made butter, and saved a haystack which cattle had broken into.

To my way of thinking, we had now lost the only fellow who qualified as a cowhand. Well, of course I was pretty darned good— yet completely stumped when it came to "chousing" those stupid cattle out of the brush.

The storm did stop and the work was resumed on our fifth day away from home. Every effort was made to hold the cattle out of the brush once we got them rounded up. I believe cowboys would have succeeded in corralling the herd, but our outfit did not. Bunches broke away from us and took to the willows like quail. No cattle went into the corral.

One more attempt was made before the Payne-Coe-De Weiss crew gave up. De Weiss, however, had a solution for our problem. It was for Bill Jones to take all of the cattle to his ranch. There in Jones' corral the Payne outfit would wean the calves and take them home.

Somehow we did get John Coe's ten cows and calves separated from the main De Weiss herd, and Mr. Bush, Mr. Boudalier and I took them home. I recall it was not necessary that I help with this job, but I was a mite leary those two greenhorns wouldn't get the cows home unless I stayed with the herd.

A week later we got word that Bill Jones now had the De Weiss cattle at his ranch on the Michigan about two miles above the Blevins' new home.

Once again Dad, Art and I started out to get those calves, and we found that, except for his wife, Jones had no help. She was a pleasant and altogether wonderful person, and a good cook, so staying overnight on Jones' ranch quite met with my approval.

Bill Jones was the best farmer in all North Park. He could always raise good potatoes, other vegetables, barley and oats, where others failed. But this deal with De Weiss marked his first venture into the cattle business. He had a good ranch and wintering this herd was no problem. But he had left one figure out of his calculations. He had no summer pasture and his only available open range was the sage flats between the Michigan and Canadian rivers.

As has been mentioned earlier, this area was overstocked, and that following summer Jones' cows almost starved to death. He sold them at a loss and was glad once again to resume selling hay to more fortunate cowmen.

With Bill's help we Paynes succeeded in corralling the cows and calves. But the rickety old corral proved neither high enough nor strong enough to hold those ornery critters. When they broke out of it, scattering in all directions, we were a mite discouraged. But not licked.

Mr. Jones, Dad and we boys put in a couple of days rebuilding the corral, and then we succeeded in weaning the calves! We left them corralled overnight, let them out at daybreak and stampeded them for about three miles to get them going and to make them forget their bawling mothers. (This is the only way to drive freshly weaned calves away from the cows—whip them into a run, giving them no opportunity to scatter or turn back.)

Safely home, we found Charlie De Weiss on hand to tally the calves and help us finish the branding job. As planned, the entire job was to have taken three days. We had used up a total of eleven. But perhaps the hard work and grief we went through to get this herd was worth it, for we had learned never to get into such a mess again!

RANGE RIDER

At last came the spring when, as Gus Dwinell had promised, I was to make a cowhand. Art would have been the logical choice, but he was much more valuable at home than I, and Dad needed him, so I got my chance.

Early in May, before we turned the cattle out of the fields, Dad and Dwinell moved their joint herd of she-stock to Beaver Creek. John Schultz, with whom I was to batch and ride range, was Gus's top man; Gus, John, Art and I were the cowboys.

For the riders who'd stay at the cow camp, Dad drove the wagon loaded with beds, grub and supplies, including a cook stove, table and cupboard Schultz had made, a sack of oats, six bales of hay, and several lumps of rock salt.

As the herd of approximately six hundred cows and heifers, plus at least two hundred young calves, moved out of our field, I was busy nearly all the time chasing runaway calves back into it. Those runaway calves! Mother cows and their offspring were sure to get separated, and the bawling of cows for calves and calves for mothers dinned against your ears all day long.

The calves become obsessed with the idea that their mothers are somewhere behind the herd and away they go. Back! Always back!

Gus was working on "point," but Art, Schultz and I nearly ran our horses down. Sometimes Art and Schultz, if unable to head off a calf, roped it and brought it back a-whooping. I wasn't quite up to that—yet.

Trailing cows and calves is really a hateful, gosh-awful job, but at this time I thought it wonderful!

Soon another trouble developed. The Payne cattle, accustomed only to the ranch and the Sand Hills range, objected to being driven away from home, and dozens of those homesick brutes were forever attempting to break back.

Yet, slowly, no faster than a mile an hour, this herd crawled up the neck of the Park until at last the drag end passed the Clark Road Ranch (which had once been John Price's). In a lane opposite the buildings we made camp for the night.

There was no real night herding, for here in a narrow lane we could stop the cattle from going back home. But Gus and Dad got no sleep at all. I'd wake out of a fitful doze to hear them yelling and see them waving a coat or blanket at cows trying to sneak past the camp.

By the next afternoon the cattle were on their new summer range. It was, I found, a heavily forested country spotted with open parks, both large and small, and open areas along stream valleys. We had arrived much too early, for the new grass had barely started and in shady spots lingered snow banks. This vast range included, in addition to Beaver Creek, a tributary of Douglas Creek which joined the Platte far to the west and north of our camp; Elkhorn Creek; and other small streams flowing directly into the Platte. Most of this mountainous country lay north of the Colorado-Wyoming state line, and all of it was a part of the Medicine Bow Range.

There were two old cabins situated on a sagebrush bluff above Beaver Creek at a point where the hills closed in and the valley was narrow. This bottleneck, I soon learned, was a good setup for range riders because both cattle and horses always try to back trail along the same route by which they enter a certain area. Dwinell's herd had become settled the previous year, but fifty percent of the Payne cattle wanted no part of this new land and were determined to go home. Schultz and I could both see and hear them coming, and we'd get out and whoop them far back down the creek once again. Holding the cattle on the range was our biggest job.

The other work consisted merely of rescuing animals from bog holes, giving help to calving cows if absolutely necessary, scattering rock salt at various "licks," and, in general, looking after the herd's well-being. Fortunately, there were no poisonous plants, not even loco. Occasionally a critter would get a "snootful of porcupine quills" and we'd have to pull them out.

Upstream from the cabins lay a large park-like area which, as soon as the baled hay was gone, we used for a horse pasture. A fence, extending across the draw along which ran the wagon road—no more than a trail—effectively stopped our horses from going home. At first we had only one horse each and fed them oats to keep up their strength. Later we acquired two horses apiece and turned all of them loose at night. Early in the morning we'd go out on foot with bridles and a pan of oats. Usually the ponies would be close to the fence and a slight rattling of the oats in the pan would induce them to come up to us, whereupon we slipped bridles on the two we wanted and rode them back to the cabins.

The smaller of these cabins we used as a stable. The other boasted two rooms, each with only a hole for a window, and doorless doorway. The dirt-covered roof leaked only in a few spots; the floor was hard packed earth. In other words, our quarters were a doorless, windowless, floorless shanty, which I thought simply wonderful.

We slept in Schultz's tarp-covered bed on a bunk made of small poles covered with pine boughs which served as both springs and mattress. I loved their redolent smell. Lifting my sleepy head early in the morning I'd see dozens of chipmunks, striped gophers and plain brown gophers, all busy at the sack of oats. With teeth and paws they'd shell the oats, stuffing their cheeks to bursting. When those pouches would hold no more, they'd "high-tail it" and soon return for another load. I wondered how they managed to unload but never found out.

We had to hang that sack of grain from the roof by a wire, or they'd have carried off all of it. Other pestiverous small critters were magpies, and Canada jays commonly known as "camp robbers." Much smaller than a crow, they are grey-white in color, and, where-ever one pitches camp in a wooded area, they are always on hand to filch anything they can carry off. Rather strangely, at this camp we were not bothered by pack rats.

Schultz, who was a clean and particular cook, did the cooking. I rustled firewood, carried water and washed dishes. For the first two weeks we were mighty busy fighting the homesick cattle. Every day and often at night a bunch would come marching up the trail, determined to get away. At night we'd merely scare them back for a short distance, but in daylight we'd "chouse" those trouble makers away off down country until at last they gave up and decided to make the best of their new range.

Now the work became easier—in fact, a soft snap—and we rode around exploring far parts of the range. Schultz made me familiar with trails he already knew, and we ferreted out many others. To pack rock salt to out-of-the-way spots, we'd put a chunk in a gunnysack on each side of our saddles and then walk and lead the horses wherever we had to go. When we ran out of necessities, one of us rode to the stage road to waylay the stage driver and ask him to get word to Dad that we needed such and such. A few days later, we'd again meet the stage and the driver would have the items.

Schultz was forever taking photographs, and, having brought equipment with him, in his spare time, preferably on a bright, sunny day, he'd develop and print films. I had little patience with this hobby and would remind him we should be doing something useful, though just what I didn't know when we were quite sure the cattle were doing okay.

There came a day when Schultz decided he must go to the home ranch (Dwinell's). "You'll be all right, John, if I leave you alone overnight?"

"Sure thing," I assured him, never giving it a thought at the time, but I suppose the man felt considerable responsibility in having a thirteen-year-old kid under his wing.

I spoke boldly enough, but after he'd gone and after darkness closed in, I began to get mighty lonesome and kinda spooky. The only wild animals we'd seen were coyotes, one red fox, deer, and a bob cat's tracks. But there just might be a mountain lion or a fierce bear prowling around.

I suddenly wished we had a door, a stout one I could bar on the inside. Since there was none, I built up quite a barricade, using the table and benches and tin pans. Then I put the axe close beside the bed so I could be sure to grab it quickly if a bear did come. More than all this, I put the butcher knife under my pillow before I ventured to go to bed.

The next thing I knew I awoke to broad daylight and wondered what was all that stuff at the door. Oh, it was my barricade. I began to laugh at myself. "Gee whiz, you 'fraidy cat, never tell anybody about this." So far as I recall, I never did—until now.

Schultz did not own a gun. He was odd that way and never gave either fishing or hunting a thought. Our meat had to come from the ranches, for we never shot a deer, nor even a grouse or a snowshoe rabbit although both were plentiful. It wasn't long before the job began to wear thin; same routine day after day, never seeing anybody unless we went out to the road to meet the stage. I was right happy when, about July first, we were called home to bring up the bull herd. Sure was good to see Art and loosen up the flow of gab to him once again.

Gus helped with the bulls. He had twelve of them, mostly Shorthorns but one big Hereford that was boss of the herd. Dad had ten, and we made the mistake of putting the two bunches together to trail them to the range, for this resulted in several savage bull fights. Like stallions, bulls have got to see who's boss; then the boss bull gathers to himself a herd of cows and runs all other bulls out of his harem.

Quite early in life I learned to keep far away from bulls when they were fighting. When one whips the other, the whipped bull breaks away at a dead run and, running blind, is apt to hit anything in his path.

On this occasion Dwinell's big Hereford whipped all challengers, but, in spite of all the fighting, we managed to get the scrappy herd to the range where Schultz and I "scattered 'em out" among all the bunches of cattle.

With the coming of haying, Gus decided the stock was safe without a rider always on the job. He needed Schultz in the hay field but would have him ride range once every week or two. I was not going to school that summer, so I also made a hay hand.

But at last I had climbed one big step up the cowboy ladder—I had ridden range! The next summer, John Schultz dropped out of the picture and I was the lone range rider. But we did not establish quarters at the old cow camp, and I boarded at Clark's road ranch for a couple of weeks, until sure the cattle were well settled. Then, after going home, I'd strike out all alone about once a week to ride range. I carried a lunch, and when I stopped to eat it, I unsaddled and unbridled my horse to give him the best opportunity to graze and rest—if fighting flies, mosquitoes and gnats would permit the poor horse any rest.

During the last of June, all of July, and well into August, those pests were really terrible. Cattle bunched up at salting grounds (another name for which became "fly grounds"), crowding together and stirring up dust to fight off the flies. There were two or three kinds of gnats as well as mosquitoes, deer flies, and the big, green-headed

184

There was one large gnat much the shape of a small fly that dug into horses' breasts, under their jaws and around their flanks all night long. horse flies. The coolness of night quieted some of these, but not all.

Cooler weather put an end to these, but not to house flies, which swarmed during September and October. No matter where one stopped to make camp, house flies immediately put in their appearance. They preferred houses, however, and drove ranch women half-crazy, but at least they did not bite humans or livestock.

Dad said that almost anything might happen to a fellow riding all alone, but we had to take chances that no serious accident would overtake me, and, outside of having a horse fall down once in a while or getting lost temporarily, nothing happened to me, not in all the years I rode this range.

In prowling around in heavy timber in unfamiliar country, I got turned around very easily. But I knew that if I followed a water course downstream I was sure to come to a larger stream, probably one with which I was familiar. As very small boys we had been told that a horse would take a lost man home if the rider let it pick its own route. On more than one occasion, when confused, I tried this out, and although I'd be dead sure the horse was going in the wrong direction, he invariably knew exactly what he was doing and where he was going.

My most serious mishap took place in 1902 when we were just starting to move cattle to the range. Gus and Bill Caudel, Art and I had pushed a herd of Dwinell's out of one of his fields and were starting them across the Sand Hills. As always, cows and calves had become separated and, singly and in bunches, calves were stampeding back.

I was riding a good horse named Charlie, and when I was unable to turn a husky calf back into the herd, I roped Mr. Calf around the neck. Charlie, the calf and I had already gone over a hill, out of sight of the other riders, and I was mightly careless with my rope.

(As early as 1897 Mr. Blevins had jumped all over young Montie and Park and Art for the sloppy manner in which they coiled their ropes and strapped them to their saddles. "Coil them neatly," he'd said. "Don't ever let me see coils hanging down almost to your stirrups. Should your horse fall and you happened to put a foot through that coil, you'd be dragged to death." More than this, Montie had told us to weaken our rope straps, cutting niches in them at the place where the straps are fastened to the saddles. Then, if a

185

rider should get hung up in his rope, the rope strap would break and let him free.)

My rope, a limber dishrag of a picket rope, was coiled sloppily, nor did I re-coil it before building a loop and catching the calf. Both calf and horse were running full tilt, and I had only to bend down and almost place the loop on the calf's neck.

Fine and dandy so far. I started to rein Charlie to the left and to take my dallies (turns around the saddle horn) but this rope had frightened Charlie. He was now running away, and a runaway horse pays no attention to the bridle. With a burst of speed he shot on past the calf. I lost my handhold on the rope and then I felt coils tighten around my ankle and the stirrup leather. Worse still, as the full weight of the calf came against the rope, my spur-shod foot was dragged back into Charlie's flank. With the spur gouging him, he started to buck. I hung onto the bridle reins for dear life, believing it was sure enough for dear life. But down I keeled over Charlie's shoulder, right foot trapped in the stirrup by the rope, which, because the stirrup leather did not break, was dragging the calf.

For a hectic instant I still clung to the reins, Charlie wheeling away from me, before I lost my grip on them. My head, shoulders and back hit the ground, and I bounced and whacked against Charlie's flying feet.

They say that when a man believes he's a goner all his past mistakes will flash through his mind and he'll suddenly regret all of his sins. Strangely, my only thought was, "What'll I look like when they find me?"

Had Charlie kicked me with one or both feet, it certainly would have been the end of me. But he did not, perhaps because he was running too fast. I whacked against his heels two or three times more, and then my foot came free. The rope had slipped!

Presently I picked myself up out of the sage, hatless, covered with dust, bruised, but otherwise unhurt and all in one piece. Charlie was flying over a hill yonderly, and as I looked around, I saw the calf that had caused all this trouble. He was plastered with dust and flat against the earth, so beaten out he had not yet moved. Triumphantly, I grabbed the rope and tied it to a sagebrush.

Soon thereafter Bill Caudel materialized and loped to where I was standing. "Wondered why you hadn't come back," he said. "Wh ... what happened?"

"Aw," disgustedly, "guess I'll have to admit I got bucked off and drug. You'll go get my horse?"

While Caudel was gone after Charlie, I looked for and found my precious hat. When he returned, although I climbed right on Charlie, I let Mr. Caudel lead the calf back to the herd! Never, never again in all my life did I handle a rope in such a careless manner as to permit coils to snare and trap my foot.

The move to Beaver Creek proved to be, for both Gus and Dad, one of the best they ever made, for it enabled them to stay in the cattle business and assured them of future summer grass for their herds, not that Dad relinquished our Sand Hills range entirely to the many, many ranchmen who were using it. After the experience of 1901 when we trailed to Beaver Creek much too early, we continued to graze cattle in the Sand Hills every spring until mid-June or so.

Rounding up in the fall was a simple matter. Following the first big snowstorm, and often this was too early, the cattle would string down the neck of the Park, small bunches and big bunches, all heading for home. Most of our cattle would stop outside our fences in the Sand Hills and wait to be let into the fields; most of Dwinell's would go on to his ranch. Hunting for stragglers in out-of-the-way pockets was the biggest job of this fall rounding up on Beaver Creek range.

In about 1904 all of the land we were using as range came under the supervision of the Federal Forest Reserve. This was no hardship on us, because, due to prior use of this area, we were entitled to continue using it. All we had to do was apply for a permit for so-and-so many cattle and pay the required fees. For many years after the Forest Reserve started, we never saw even a ranger, much less a supervisor.

My father was in favor of the Forest Reserve, but he was an exception. Most of our stockmen were bitterly opposed—opposed to restrictions and regulations, opposed to any change for that matter. They had settled and made this country. The timber and the grazing areas now enclosed by National Forest boundaries belonged to them— without any Government interference and management.

For quite some time game laws had been in effect, but most ranchmen winked at them and the game wardens made only token efforts to enforce the rules. For example, if a game warden was eating a meal at some rancher's home, he would very carefully follow his host's example and say, "Please pass the steak," when he darned well knew it wasn't beef steak he was eating!

Like it or not, however, all were compelled to accept the new order of controlled Forest Reserves, also to accept the Government's edict to pull down fences on government land and move such fences to the correct section lines of their own deeded land. Our friend Gus, although complaining loudly that it worked a terrific hardship on him, was obliged to hire additional men to move and rebuild miles and miles of fence. The Barnes boys were obliged to tear down their stock pasture fence on Sentinel Mountain, and, rather than let their herd mingle with other stock on open range, they then sold their cattle, depending thereafter on sale of their hay to make a living—Dad becoming their steady hay customer.

But neither of these restrictive measures took place as early as 1901, when I was taking my long step up the cowboy ladder and when Dad, in addition to making the good move of securing better range, made another advance forward and upward.

At this time Swift and Company, owners of the Two Bar Two, apparently decided that their experiment in raising their own cattle for the packing plant was not working out profitably, so they put their North Park ranches up for sale. Actually, several years elapsed before they were able to close out all of their properties, and meanwhile they continued to raise cattle. But the Mendenhall place was up for sale, and once again Montie Blevins did us a good turn, making a special trip to see Dad and tell him, "That ranch fits right in with your outfit. If you can possibly swing such a deal, buy it."

This original Mendenhall Ranch snuggles against the foot of the Medicine Bow Range and lies between Dwinell's Horse Ranch on the south and the lower Sand Hills to the north. Two small streams water it, one of these remarkable in that it flows out in full volume from a mere hole or tunnel at the foot of the mountain — not exactly a spring, but, rather, the outlet of an underground stream.

The ranch was fenced only on the outside, the Park side, the mountains forming the rear barrier. All of this area the Two Bar Two had used merely for pasture. But Montie pointed out that here was a good meadow with priority water rights, which would produce one hundred tons of hay, and that on top of the mountains, behind the ranch, lay open parks and valleys, sure to become valuable for grazing later on. (This area was later on incorporated in a National

Forest, for which we took out a stock grazing permit and obtained exclusive use of it.)

Mr. Hadden, who happened to be summering on the Payne ranch, financed Dad to make the deal, and this Mendenhall Ranch immediately proved a valuable asset. Once there had been a great many buildings and corrals on the property, most of which had been moved away, but two good cabins and a small stable remained. In 1902 we fenced off the meadow land from the pasture land and harvested a hay crop. Feeding this hay, six miles from home, posed a problem which we solved by leaving a hay rack at the place and a team turned loose in the corral adjoining the stable. Someone would then ride to the ranch, do the feeding and return home.

Another event which was to affect the future of the Park, at least so far as schooling for its ever-growing population of children was concerned, also took place in 1901. Charlie Cowdrey homesteaded a part of the land where our schoolhouse had until then stood all alone, and established his new home quite near the school. Within a short time he opened a road ranch and store, and established a post office named Cowdrey.

This encouraged other families to build homes in the new settlement in order to send their children to the school; not to summer school but to *winter* school. Dave Hendrickson and his wife, who'd had great difficulty in getting their boys to school, immediately put up a house. One year later, the Dwinells followed suit, Mrs. Dwinell and her two boys moving to Cowdrey for that winter while Gus and a hired man batched on the ranch. I was still attending school, so Gus made a deal with me whereby I'd get a hot lunch (dinner) in return for rustling both wood and water for Mrs. Dwinell and their small boys. Daytimes I stabled my horse in Cowdrey's barn and the arrangement worked out satisfactorily.

Naturally, I came to know the Dwinell boys well. My brother attempted to tie two nicknames on these up-and-coming youngsters. That for Frank, the youngest, was "Kit Carson," for Augustus, "Bill Cody." 'Kit Carson" never stuck. "Cody" did.

I once heard young Gus complain to his father, "That doggoned Art Payne always calls me 'Cody' and I don't like it."

Now Gus had a pet name for his oldest son, so his reply tickled my funny bone. He said very greviously, "I don't like it either, *Dustin.*"

CAMP BREAD AND THE DIAMOND HITCH

To me as a small boy, Mr. Hadden was a mystery man. I knew that he had helped Dad to get a bunch of cattle and that he came from England, stayed with the Scott boys for a couple of months in midsummer, and then returned to England. But they told Art and me he was a woman hater and that he did not like little kids. Certainly, he ignored us as completely as if we didn't exist, so he was more than a mystery man; he was sort of a bogie man.

He was well-known around Laramie and often visited English ranchmen on the Little Laramie River. But apparently he had come West too late to play a part in the big cattle boom of the late seventies and early eighties which attracted so many wealthy English and Scots. He did put some money into the glassworks at Laramie, which was probably the only foolish investment Mr. Hadden ever made! It was said in Laramie that he was a millionaire. I never learned for sure whether he actually was or not. Certainly, no one acquainted with Mr. Hadden would have suspected that he was well-to-do. Occasionally he was mistaken for a tramp and more often for a working man. Nothing pleased him more than to be asked, "Hey, fellow, you want a job?"

He did not belong to the nobility and, strangely, no one ever called him "Lord" or "Duke" or "Earl" as Americans were wont to call all Britishers, including remittance men. But on the other hand no one addressed him as "Henry"; always it was "Mr. Hadden."

My good friend Charlie Scott liked and respected the man, took hunting and fishing trips with him, yet poked lots of fun at him.

"He's so doggoned stingy that if he bought some food that made him sick, he'd eat it rather than throw it away," Charlie told me, and went on, "Once when I happened to be in Laramie, several fellows thought they'd put up a job on Hadden and get a good laugh at his expense. They knew he was going to hire a horse at the livery stable to ride out into the country, so they fixed it with the liveryman to give him a bucker.

"Hadden mounted the horse and away it went, bucking up the street for about four blocks before he managed to pull up its head. Then, kicking the horse in the ribs with his big shoes, he rode back to the barn and we heard him say to the liveryman,

" 'I wish you'd give me another 'orse. This one's a bloody 'ard galloper.' "

According to Mr. Hadden, American newspapers were hopeless, oh, quite! The *London Times* was the only thing fit to read, you know. In connection with the *Times* and Mr. Hadden's perusal of it, Charlie told this story:

"He once owned a wagon and team with which he prowled around the country. On the Laramie plains, he'd tie up the lines, let the team follow the road and walk behind his wagon reading the *London Times*.

"One day the team turned off into a lane, and Hadden, head buried in the *Times*, walked on for a mile or so before discovering he had lost his outfit."

This wagon was out of the picture before I came to know him, but he owned two horses, which Dad fed for the use of them, two saddles, and camping, hunting and fishing equipment. These articles, when not in use, were stored by the Scott boys. One of the horses got so badly locoed that Dad finally shot it; the other died of old age.

Dad said that Mr. Hadden had been all over the world. An exaggeration, yet he had been in many parts of it, seeking adventure and sport — And in Old Mexico, he got into mountains where the natives had never before seen a white man. But after he discovered the North American West, it seemed to hold his interest and he returned to it again and again.

In England, so Dad told us boys, he was classed as a "gentleman," and "gentlemen" do not work, or at least did not in those days. In this connection Mr. Hadden was called as a witness in a certain court case which took place at Walden. When summoned to the witness chair, he was asked, "Your name?"

"Henry Hadden."

"Occupation?"

"Nothing!"

There followed a startled and definite pause before the questioning was resumed!

Now Art and I knew a great many men who did nothing — North Park was filled with them. That is, they never worked if they could possibly avoid it. But Mr. Hadden didn't fit into that category. On the contrary, he was a bundle of energy. I never knew anyone who worked so hard at his hobby of hunting and fishing. At home in England, he engaged in many other sports, among them, steeplechasing. One of his rare stories ran:

"My blooming horse wouldn't take the fence, you know. I began to talk to him in vigorous Western language, and the other chaps all stopped on the other side of the fence with their mouths open. They wanted to know what I was saying."

Prior to the day when Dad bought the Scott ranch, Mr. Hadden had suffered a bad fall while steeplechasing. Hospitalized for a long time, he eventually recovered, but it left him almost stone deaf in one ear.

He reappeared in North Park in 1899, and since the Scotts were then gone, he could no longer put up with a completely bachelor outfit but was more or less obliged to stay with Jack Payne.

At this time, although he was to me still an enigma, he began to emerge as a fellow human, and little boys were not so utterly repulsive to him as we had been led to believe. Oh, he was a "queer duck." To North Parkers, all Englishmen were "queer"; queer ranging in meaning from being definitely locoed to being just mildly eccentric; their queerness was likely to be transmitted to their offspring, too, as I learned to my complete amazement some years later. One of my good friends, a schoolteacher, confided to me that another pupil had said to her, "Oh, I like Johnnie Payne all right. But don't you think he's a little queer?"

When teacher offered no comment, the pupil resumed, "That's probably because his father's an Englishman."

Soon after Mr. Hadden arrived at the ranch, via stage, I discovered he always brought with him old clothes to be worn out. Suits and shirts, underwear and woolen socks, all of wonderfully fine material. He also brought along from three to six pairs of "boots" as he called them. We called them shoes — and were they something! The uppers were of fine leather as heavy as harness leather, soles and heels a good inch thick.

The morning after his arrival at our home, I was watching Mr. Hadden pounding hobnails into the soles of some of these "boots," when he took notice of his wide-eyed and shy audience.

"The nails are to keep a fellow from slipping while walking, you know."

"Can you walk in those shoes, Mr. Hadden?"

"Ah, yes. American shoes aren't fit to walk in. Terrible things, American shoes."

But two items of Western American attire he had adopted, overalls and a hat of the type in use at this time. He also used a Western saddle equipped with wide, flat-bottomed stirrups. It looked as if it might have come up the trail from Texas with the very first herd of Longhorns!

When I helped him to find a harness strap for a belt for his new pair of overalls, he said, "Useful things, overalls. So handy to wipe your hands on after cleaning fish."

Most fishermen use hip rubber boots. Mr. Hadden scorned them, stating truthfully, "First thing you know, the boots are full of water, so what's the good of them?"

He protected his feet with an old pair of shoes and his legs with his overalls as he waded the cold streams. Consequently, his overalls were soon bleached a pale blue at the bottom and farther up were a very darkly stained, indefinable color.

A small-framed man, wiry and lean, he was as tough as rawhide and as tireless as a bird dog. He had thin, light blond hair, a high and bulging forehead, grey eyes and sharp features. Although always clean-shaven, he had the least growth of beard of anyone I have ever seen.

Dressed for fishing and hunting, he should have sent a portrait home captioned, "What the English sportsman should wear and how he should look in the American West." But if he realized that he looked odd to our natives, he didn't give a hoot. He was here to fish and hunt and thoroughly enjoy himself. If we had cattle work on the fire, he was always happy to make a hand, and occasionally he liked to work in the hay field.

For his initial fishing trips, before he really got lined out, he merely rode to one of the ranches on the Michigan or Platte, fished until midafternoon, and came home — always with a good catch of trout. Since he never carried a lunch, he'd drink about a panful of cold milk, change his clothes, don pants, a clean shirt and tie, and other "boots," then read the *London Times* or merely relax until supper time. After supper he would read again.

He varied the fishing trips by hunting sage hens, ducks or grouse, with a double-barrelled shotgun of English make which Dad said cost two hundred dollars, a splendid gun for that day. I always watched in fascination when he reloaded shells for it. Once he came home from a sage hen hunting trip empty-handed, and reported, "All I saw was a brace of old cocks, you know." For a couple of weeks our hired men howled over this as if it was the richest joke ever told.

Before long Mr. Hadden would be restless for a trip "down the Platte" with saddle horse and pack horse.

I'm sure he believed he had discovered the Platte and owned that portion of it extending northward from North Park for twenty-odd miles. Here the stream, ripping its way through the mountains, is canyon-bound, but small streams entering the river from both east and west afford places where a horseman or, in some cases, a rig can get to the river.

"Three Mile" and "Six Mile" were the best-known of these places. But Mr. Hadden discovered others he named "Five Mile" and also "Nine Mile." (I've never heard a satisfactory explanation for these names, but obviously "Three Mile" must have meant three miles from some definite place farther up stream, and so on.)

Anyway, entirely alone, with his rifle and shotgun, fishing gear, grub, bed, tent and camping equipment tied on a pack horse, he'd meander off down the Platte to be gone three, four or five days. On his return he'd be loaded with trout packed in leaves and grass, and probably with ducks, grouse and sage hens as well. One summer, I recall, he kept the haying crew so well stocked with fresh meat that we never had to buy or butcher any beef.

He held a deep aversion to our ranch cats, but to quiet their yowling for food — not because he sympathized with them — he began to waste a few shotgun shells on jack rabbits. One evening, following his return from "down the Platte," he and Dad carefully placed a dozen big rainbow trout on a board which they put up under the eaves of the house, the purpose being to allow the fish to air and also to keep them out of the cats' reach.

All in vain! During the night the cats knocked down the board and gorged themselves. Mr. Hadden, angrily surveying the wreckage, stormed, "Blasted cats! Here I take pains to feed them and this is the way they act."

Mr. Hadden was keenly interested in Dad's and Dwinell's new cattle range on West Beaver Creek. He stayed a few days with Schultz and me at the range camp and later took it on himself to do some exploring of the vicinity with his pack horse outfit. Since a large area of this range bordered the Platte on the east, it was definitely in *his* country. He scouted some of the little streams — one, the Elkhorn, the others nameless — and reported,

"If it's any advantage you can ride on the west side of the Platte to Three Mile, Five Mile or Six Mile, cross the river, and be on your range without going around by way of the neck of the Park."

This was the route Mr. Hadden and I took one autumn when he initiated me into the mysteries of camping out with a pack horse outfit.

I'd taken a great shine to this "queer duck." He was not a bronc buster, cowboy, cattleman, or even a great hunter and trapper. But he was an outdoors man, an adventurer, a man from whom I could learn a great many things of keen interest to me.

Although he was cold fish where most people were concerned — not unfriendly or the least bit high hat, merely politely indifferent — Mr. Hadden had warmed up toward me, had become sympathetic with my weighty problems, and he'd actually talk to me!

Not all of our cattle had as yet come home from the range, and the purpose of our trip was to hunt for stragglers, for:

"You can do more with a pack horse outfit in two days than you can in a week working from a permanent camp," said Mr. Hadden.

I was all a-twitter the day we got ready to pull out. While we were waiting for Dad to get a batch of bread baked so we might take along two or three loaves, Mr. Hadden assembled the rest of the grub supply.

"The necessities of life only, you know. Meat? We'll take a bit of bacon and this piece of ham since I shan't be fishing. But of course I shall have my shotgun and may knock off a few grouse . . . Meat and bread and a bit of flour, with baking powder and salt added.

Some dried fruit. These apricots are quite good. Butter I shall put in this can so when it melts it shan't run over everything . . . Treacle? This black strap molasses answers the purpose quite well, for if the cork comes out of the bottle, it is so thick it won't run out anyway. Coffee? Grind about one pound, John. No more. Don't want to bring anything home, you know. Tea, sugar, salt. I believe that is all."

"No spuds, onions, beans, canned goods?" I asked.

"No. I said the necessities of life. Keep the pack light. My word, you Americans live out of cans. Most canned stuff is very nasty."

"All right. I sure want to live on the wild game you kill. Salt's a necessity for that?"

"Quite. On a hunting trip with a party in Canada we ran out of everything and were obliged to live on meat alone. I got along famously until we also ran out of salt. Without it, the meat made me desperately ill."

His camping equipment was as meager as the grub supply. Two long-handled frying pans, one small coffeepot, one granite-ware pan for stewing dried fruit, two tin plates, two cups, two knives, forks and spoons. A pocketknife would serve as a butcher knife, but we must have an axe, or at least a hatchet.

My best horse, Charlie, and a knot-headed, undersized pony we called Champ, which was Mr. Hadden's mount for this trip, were saddled and waiting, and now we were at last ready to put the pack on Tom. A stolid bay plug which Dad had bought from John Coe, Tom was well broken to the saddle, but it was possible he might object to carrying a pack.

Mr. Hadden's A-shaped, seven-by-seven tent, carefully folded, served as the blanket for his old pack saddle. He owned no panniers, so a roll of bedding was placed on either side of the pack saddle. One of these was his bed, the other mine, for although it was customary for two men (sometimes three) to occupy one bed, Mr. Hadden would have none of it. He preferred to sleep alone and vociferously resented it if, compelled to stay overnight at some ranch, he was "doubled up" with someone — sure to be the case on most ranches.

The grub, including the three loaves of hot bread, and the utensils, all crowded into a gunnysack, were placed on top of the pack saddle, as were Mr. Hadden's extra coats. He scorned slickers, and made use of an English raincoat. I had neither. The axe was tied on one side of the pack saddle under the bedroll, rifle on the other, and now Mr. Hadden was ready to throw the diamond hitch.

In packing merely a bed on a bareback horse, one uses the squaw or the N hitch, and I could manage either of those. But when using a pack saddle, the diamond hitch was the proper way to lash a pack so it would "stay put" even on a bucking horse. Mr. Hadden was quite delighted, I'm sure, that he was able to show me how to tie — or throw — this hitch.

Ready to go, I climbed on Charlie and Mr. Hadden mounted Champ, holding in his right hand the coils of a picket rope, which was knotted around Tom's neck, and also his shotgun — in case we should come upon a flock of sage hens. But before we were two miles from the house, a disaster which might easily have been very serious overtook us.

Tom suddenly spooked at some shadow and gave a violent leap. This made pans in the gunnysack rattle and really "touched him off." Away went Tom at full gallop, running right past Mr. Hadden and me. Had I been as much of a cowboy as I believed I was, I would have leaped my horse up alongside the runaway and caught him.

As it was, I merely sat, watching the show like a bump on a log while the lead rope somehow entangled itself around Mr. Hadden's right hand, already burdened with his shotgun. As the rope tightened, off Champ's back and into the sage and dust keeled Mr. Hadden, big hobnailed shoes, shotgun and all. Fortunately, the rope came free of his hand and he escaped being dragged.

Tom was scooting away with rope a-trail, but I came alive at last and caught Champ and turned back to Mr. Hadden.

"Are you hurt? Are you hurt?"

"A bit shook up is all," examining his shotgun critically. "Ah, it's unharmed. The gun, I mean." And then, "My word, I wish Jack had seen this. He always seems to believe I can use any half-wild beast for a pack horse. Never seems to realize the necessity of having a gentle pack horse . . . I'm afraid the bread will be a complete loss."

We got going again. Tom had stopped against the fence of Dad's lower field, and it was no trouble to catch him. But I built a rope hackamore on his head in order to have better control over him other than with the rope merely knotted around his neck and snubbed the rope to my saddle horn to lead this "half-wild beast."

Tom gave us no further trouble, however. We crossed Jack

Hunter's ranch and, after fording the Platte, took the road in the great valley on the west side of it. Eventually we turned off this road to the right, and heading down a gulch, struck the Platte at Mr. Hadden's Five Mile Gap.

Here, in an open area affording room to pitch a camp and to picket several horses, my friend discovered evidence that disturbed him, empty tin cans and bottles and rocks piled up to form a sort of fireplace.

"Someone's been poaching on my campground. I never leave that sort of thing, you know. This fellow has spoiled it for me. We shall go along and camp up on the Elkhorn. But we have time for a bath."

"Water's too cold," I objected.

"You soft Americans! Afraid as cats of the water."

We forded the river and tied the horses, and, thus taunted, I too took a cold bath — an every-day necessity with Mr. Hadden if it could possibly be arranged. He also always washed all his clothes, underwear, handkerchiefs, shirts and socks.

Mounted again, we rode a few hundred yards downstream, then turned east up the pinched valley of Elkhorn Creek, flushing three grouse which flew into a grove of aspens.

"Grouse for supper!" I cried, suddenly realizing how empty I was.

We had started out about eleven o'clock, not waiting for dinner, and I'd have carried a lunch, but Mr. Hadden would not have condoned this. It would have been yielding to a weakness.

"Easy matter," he said, "to train yourself to go without eating in the middle of the day. Nor should you be always stopping at every stream to drink water as you do, John. Bad habit to get into."

Dismounting now, he approved, "Ah, yes, grouse for supper. Tie the horses, John."

"Uh — er? I can hold them while you shoot —"

"But I can't shoot them sitting, you know. It simply isn't done. You must flush them out of the trees, then I shall — "

I was open-mouthed. "I'd shoot 'em off the limbs. Why isn't it done, Mr. Hadden?"

"Not cricket. No sportsman — unless he's a Frenchman — will fire at a bird walking or sitting. Tie the horses, then go ahead and flush the grouse. You needn' be afraid I shall hit you."

I flushed the grouse and "Bang-bang!" Mr. Hadden brought down the two young ones. He had immediately identified the mother hen, which he intentionally let escape.

He was carrying the grouse when we returned to the horses. Either the smell of burned powder or the grouse, or both, frightened Champ, who snorted and tried to pull away.

"Come around here and stand still, you silly little fool," commanded Mr. Hadden and then growled like an angry dog. He always growled when provoked, and his profanity was a weird mixture of English oaths and the Western mule skinner's best efforts.

But the pony continued to cut up, and Mr. Hadden remarked, "My word, you boys say this beast is a good horse. I say he's fit only for boiling."

I took the grouse and tied them to my saddle, and at length Mr. Hadden was able to mount.

"For boiling?" I asked blankly. " 'Fit only for boiling?' "

"Quite! In England, when a horse is of no further use, we boil it and feed the meat to the dogs."

"How horrible!" I gasped, having a shocked vision of a pack of dogs devouring my old Wringtail.

"Horrible? Not at all. Best thing that could possibly happen to them." Then his sharp grey eyes noticed my expression and he amplified, "All old animals should be relieved of their suffering; put out of their misery. Don't you agree with that?"

"Well ... er-umm ... People too?"

He smiled and chuckled. "We have become much too civilized to consider performing the same merciful act for hopelessly ill or hopelessly crippled human beings."

Our walking horses moved into an open and comparatively level area where big hills rolled back to form a little basin beside the stream. Here we made camp for the night, Mr. Hadden doing most of the work and directing me from time to time.

Immediately we had unsaddled and unpacked, he said, "I'll cut picket stakes. You hold all the horses until we get them safely picketed. On many hunting trips I have spent far more time and energy looking for lost horses than I have in hunting game. The silly beasts dearly love to skip out and leave a man afoot."

He went to a grove of small quaking aspens, cut stakes three feet long and we drove them deep. But although I should have learned something important, I was foolish enough in later years to let horses get away from me several times before at last I learned you never can trust them to stay around a camp.

The next step was to gather firewood—"Plenty to cook supper,

199

for the evening fire, and to cook breakfast"—for which we pulled down dead quaking aspens and carried hem to the camp site. Now my instructor cut small green aspens for tent poles, chopped and pointed tent stakes, and we put up the tent. Sweat from the horse had soaked into the canvas, but this rich smell was not at all unpleasing to me.

"Fix your bed before dark, John. I'll take one side of the tent, you the other. First, spread out your saddle blanket. Not a great help toward softening the bed, but it will be warm in the morning."

"Why," I asked, toting both of our saddle blankets into the tent, "should a saddle blanket be warm in the morning?"

"I once made a hand on one of the big roundups in Wyoming," he replied. "Each morning was bitterly cold, and there'd be from four to a dozen bucking horses. Many of the riders couldn't stick on, either. It was frozen saddle blankets that made these horses buck so savagely. After getting badly shaken up myself, I learned to put my saddle blanket underneath my bed."

He made up his bed, and, noticing what I was doing wrong, he told me, "Don't make a double bed for one person. Great waste. I could sleep on a plank a foot wide. Let me show you how: spread out the tarpaulin full width, your two quilts on top of it, and the blankets on top of the quilts. Now fold all of this bedding over once, exactly in the middle . . . There you have it. Next thing to a sleeping bag."

Neither of us had a pillow. Our pants or other clothing had to answer that purpose. But this lesson in making a single bed I never forgot.

"How soon do we eat?" I asked hungrily. "What can I do? Build a fire?"

"Yes. Make a very small fire right there," indicating the correct spot. "Tenderfeet, and a great many others who should know better, build a roaring big fire. Then they can't get near it to do their cooking . . . Another thing, John, don't ever leave a camp with a fire still burning. Be sure that it is jolly well out."

"Oh, I knew that rule, Mr. Hadden."

"Very well." He emptied food and utensils out of the gunny sack. "Here, take the coffeepot and this stew pan, fetch water from the creek. Might wash your hands and face while you're there, too."

I got the water and made the fire while he expertly skinned and cleaned and cut up the two grouse with his pocketknife. "Now make

200

Weaned calves. Payne ranch.

Yearling steers. Jack Payne's ranch, 1908.

Purebred Herefords, Jack Payne Ranch

Payne's Herefords in fields.

The Payne and Dwinell range camp on West Beaver creek, Wyoming. The author's range home when, at thirteen, he began herding cattle.

Jack Payne's home, North Park. Stables, sheds and corrals not shown.

James Pinkham's block house, the first permanent settler's home to be built in North Park, about 1875. It is said that Pinkham hoped to trade with the Utes.

Ute tepees, made of aspens, north end of North Park near the King ranch. Photo 1903. Doubtful if any trace of them remains today.

Mendenhall ranch. One of the first to be established in North Park.

Another view of the Mendenhall ranch.

38 Walden Colo.

Walden, North Park, Colorado, in the early days.

the coffee and fry the grouse. You should be able to manage both . . . The fresh bread, thanks to that silly Tom, is badly mashed. We'll give it a go in the morning but I shall make camp bread tonight."

Charlie Scott had told me that camp, or frying-pan, bread was "licking good," and now, while keeping an eye on the coffeepot and frying the grouse, I also watched Mr. Hadden prepare this delicacy. First, he washed his hands; then, using a tin plate for a bowl, he mixed a portion of our flour, previously spiked with both baking powder and salt, with cold water, making a not-too-soft and not-to-stiff dugh. He used no shortening.

Next, he took up our second frying pan— now I saw why he had brought two of these— and warmed it over the fire but did not grease it. Then, dividing the dough into two equal parts, he placed one portion in the pan and flattened it down until it filled the pan. This he held over the flames for a few minutes, saying:

"The object is to make the loaf stick just a bit to the pan . . . Ah, that does it," and with a willow stick he propped the frying pan up on edge close to the fire. Thus the frying pan became a reflector baker.

I watched the loaf puff up and turn crisp and brown, and I'm sure the ashes it gathered and the wood smoke added much to its good taste. Mr. Hadden used a knife to loosen this loaf, turned it over, crisped the other side, then propped this loaf up with a twig and prepared the second loaf exactly like the first.

I'd done a good job with the grouse and the coffee. We filled our plates and cups, squatted cross-legged and ate. We had butter for the bread and black strap molasses to top it off, and oh, how good it was! Nothing left but the grouse bones for a pair of camp robbers (Canada jays) which had materialized as soon as we'd stopped to make camp.

"Are you filled up—quite?" Mr. Hadden inquired abruptly.

"Well, yes, but if only we had gooseberry pie, I could . . ."

"Pie!" he snorted. "I've always claimed the American pie was an invention of the devil . . . Must have been invented when flour was very cheap and plentiful and fruit was very scarce and dear. You get a great mass of most indigestible pastry with a thin layer of fruit you can scarcely taste."

Thus squelched and also taken aback, I made no comment, but, taking notice of the dried apricots which my companion now had simmering in the one stew kettle, I thought, "They'll be lickin' good for breakfast, yet even better made into an 'invention of the devil,' the American pie."

"How can I heat water to wash the dishes?" I asked.

"Wipe all the grease out of both frying pans with a bunch of grass or weeds or sagebrush, go to the creek, bring back water in each and heat it. Wash these few dishes and wipe them. Here's a rag for that purpose. Finally, swab out the fry pans with grass and dry them over the fire."

"Yes, sir."

He watched me for a few minutes, then arranged the camp supplies to his own satisfaction, stepped into the tent and brought out a copy of the *London Times!* He threw light wood on the fire to make a good blaze, settled himself and became lost in his paper—and here I'd been hoping he'd tell me stories of his adventures!

I finished my chore and, thinking how Charlie Scott had enjoyed his pipe, remarked, "Seems as if smoking around a camp fire would add the final touch. Didn't you ever take it up, Mr. Hadden?"

The reply was a grunt, followed by, "As an Indian I once knew said, 'Me heap lazy. Smoking heap great help to laziness.' Most people are plenty lazy enough without smoking." He again gave his full attention to the *Times*.

I lay back and patted my well-filled stomach, looked up at the seemingly close, friendly stars, and listened to the slight noises of small nocturnal animals rustling the grass and brush, to the sounds of our horses crunching grass and the occasional stomp of a hoof, to the murmur of the little stream making its music in the quiet night. I thought, "I can't pin it down, but there's something awful nice about camping out with a pack horse outfit. I wish it'd last forever."

The rest of our trip after this first night was pretty much anti-climax. We camped out two more nights, and we did find and take home thirty-odd cattle. But the highest point of all came the morning when Mr. Hadden said, "Let me see if you can tie on the pack properly—with the diamond hitch." And I did it—properly!

HOMEMADE CHAPS

The year of 1901 ended without my having reached the goal of cowboy on a trip to Iaramie with cattle. As in the past, autumn saw ranchmen, with their teams and wagons and with their beef herds, stopping overnight with Dad, and Ora Haley's big steers ate Jack Payne's grass for one night on their march to the railroad. Thus, we kept up our friendship with these many men of the Park, and with Thornt Biggs, Haley's roundup-and-trail-herd cook.

Also, as in the past, come winter we Paynes were batching, and now at Cowdrey I attended a winter term of school. Not Art however. He had passed the eighth grade, and the school had no higher grade to offer.

This winter's monotony, however, was relieved by a perfect rash of neighborhood dances. Bob Coe started it off with "open house" at his ranch, and other neighbors took it up. The Cowdreys, the McCaslands, Mr. and Mrs. Frank Lyons, the Bakers, who were now living on the old Moore and Blevins ranch, were some of these dance hosts. Occasionally Dave and Mrs. Hendrickson could be roped in to play for a dance, but mostly Al Bush provided the violin music, sawing away on his fiddle the whole night long.

Dad never attended. He wouldn't have gotten within gun shot of one of these "hops." But Art and I were on hand for every dance. Nor did it trouble us that we were unable to reciprocate, and neither by look, word nor act did any of these good neighbors make us feel unwelcome or that we weren't doing our part. Jack Hunter did not entertain the neighborhood either, but two of his boys, Harry and Joe, were always Johnny-on-the-spots.

Men outnumbered women at least two to one, so the current schoolteacher, the unattached girls, the ranch women, all the small girls too, were simply danced off their feet. But they ate it up. So did all of us kids. We'd get a rest for the midnight supper when sandwiches, hot coffee, cake and ice cream (homemade ice cream brought along by the guests) were served.

Then again it was:

> Honor your partners. Lady on the left.
> First couple out to the couple on the right,
> Cage the birdie and three hands 'round,
> Bird hop out and the crow hop in,
> Three hands 'round and go again.

And so on and on until dawn when at last the sleepy merrymakers would put on their wraps, wake babies, and by sleigh or horseback hurry home to do chores and feed stock.

Ah, yes, when we came home from a dance there was no going to bed or any other rest until the day's work was done and the supper dishes washed.

Our friend Gus Dwinell disapproved of this form of entertainment, just as he disapproved of many things the neighbors did—swearing, card playing, gambling, horse racing, drinking. To many North Parkers this make Gus a "queer duck." Someone told me that when Gus was in Laramie with other cowmen he did not want to desert, he would wait outside while they went into a saloon.

But the Dwinells would open their home to the only other form of winter entertainment of this time, the Church Social, dubbed "Sociable." At a sociable the ladies brought baskets of food to be auctioned off to the highest bidder who would thereby obtain for his supper partner the lady whose basket he bought. Money thus raised went to the local church, so this was a good cause. Games of many kinds took the place of dancing, and everybody, including Art and me, seemed to have a good time.

I'm reminded, however, that everyone who has written about the early-day West has told all about country dances, so with, "Honor your partner and don't be afraid to swing corner lady with waltz promenade," I'll waltz on to the next subject.

In the spring of 1902 I was range-riding once again, and I made a full-time hand in the hay field. I raked every spear of hay we harvested, and as I had learned about locoed horses, I now also learned much about balky horses.

Dad was a good horse trader. He was always either swapping off or selling a horse or two, and if he had a chance to buy one or a bunch worth the money he'd buy them. He had bought a dozen or more from M. C. (Mac) Ward after Mac had taken over the Pinkhamton ranch. Most of these were old stage horses, and all old stage horses are balky. Old saddle horses when broken to work (and many were broken to pull hay rakes) are likewise balky. The old cliché runs: "Won't pull the hat off your head."

My team was a pair of these old stage horses, and for the first week or so I had a dreadful time getting them started to work. But I did not try any of the cures advised by older men: one, to put a grasshopper in the balky horse's ear; another, to light a fire under him. A man we knew did try this. He was moving a hayrack loaded with furniture when his team balked, so he made a sagebrush fire underneath them. Oh, yes, he got action all right! The team pulled the load just far enough so the fire was under the load of furniture, and continued to balk.

I was leery of the grasshopper-in-ear treatment. It might make my team crazy enough to run away, and I'd been told over and over how dangerous is a runaway with a hay rake. The driver may be thrown off in front of the rake, get caught by its teeth and dragged to death.

Two or three summers later one horse of my team kicked over the tongue and started running. I was just getting the horses under control, hanging to the seat with one hand, when the bit in the other horse's mouth broke.

Having no control of the team, I tried to make a backward leap, landed on my head and stood on it for what seemed a long time. But I got up unhurt and watched the team jump a small creek. As the wheels of the rake hit the creek, the vehicle bounced ten feet into the air. Then the doubletree snapped, and the team ran on into the yard at home before they stopped.

My old friend Charlie Scott was working for us, but did he sympathize with me? Not a bit. "You looked so darned funny," he remarked, "boring a hole in the ground with your head. What are you? A new kind of post-hole digger?"

That spring and summer of 1902 Arthur began driving a four-horse team to haul posts and other timber, finally driving to Laramie to bring back a load of grub.

There was something big and wonderful about being a real teamster handling the "ribbons" over a four-or-six-horse team. It was one of the goals sought by all the boys, for it rated almost as highly as being a cowpuncher. (In this connection we held a deep respect for stage drivers and regular freighters, one and all. They were men.)

Accordingly, making the grade as a teamster was one high triumph for my brother. Another triumph came about when he made a pair of chaps.

The first chaps I remember were of the plain leather "shotgun" type, one seam only, laced down the outside and with an ornamental leather fringe. Saddle catalogs and Montgomery Ward's catalog called them Chaparejos or Cowboys' Riding Pants. Mr. Hadden called them "leather pants with the seat out"; Texans called them merely leggins.

When as a little boy I first began to take notice of people and clothing, many cowboys did not have chaps! But quite soon more and more "shotgun" chaps appeared, and then the "hair" or "woolly" chaps began to come in.

Mr. Blevins wore a pair of "hair" chaps, the front part, or outside, made of black Galloway cowhide tanned with the hair on. Other hair chaps appeared, made of dog skins, colt skins, bear skins. Wild stories were told about bear skin chaps. They were all right so long as the weather was dry, but when the chaps got wet the cowboy better look out. His horse would go crazy. Either he could not get near it, or if he did get mounted, the horse'd buck or run away.

Why was this? When the skin got wet the bear smell would come out strong and pungent. Since most horses are deathly afraid of a bear, some of the tales were true.

Finally someone introduced Angora goat skins for chaps. This caught on, and the true "woolly" chap was born. Since Angora goats have silky white hair, three to six inches in length, their skins made beautiful, warm chaps. More than this, the skins could be dyed almost any color.

As far as I remember, a type of chap very popular today—the Bat Wing—did not appear until several years later. But Angora chaps were common in the Park long before the day when my brother and

I were ruefully inspecting a pair of leather chaps which John Kimmons had given him. They were hard lookers, and the neighborhood kids and cowboys had poked lots of fun at them while Art was wearing them.

He scratched his head and said, "That's still a good belt, and the front part of this leather in the legs is good enough so I can make the backs of a pair of chaps out of it. Now, if I can just get an Angora goat skin to make the fronts."

"What you muttering about?" I demanded.

"I'm going to make a pair of chaps."

"Aw, go 'way back and sit down. You can't..."

"Who says I can't? Darned right I can."

"But," I protested, "even if you can get a goat skin, we can't tan it."

"Can too. Sam Bear told us how to tan hides with the hair on. You use powdered alum, and the Scott boys left a big package of it here, so I'll use it."

The Webb boys had Angora goats, so did Charlie Cowdrey. Art went to see Mr. Cowdrey and somehow—I don't remember what he traded—he acquired a fine white goat skin, and thus the neighborhood learned of Art's intention. The boys were even more sceptical than I was. "That goofy Art Payne says he'll make a pair of chaps. Durned fool can't do it. They'll be hot things."

This was the sort of stimulation my brother needed at this period in his life. Tell him he couldn't do a thing and he'd be sure to do it—to show the sceptics he could.

He went to work on the goat skin, mostly in his spare time at night. I became enthused and helped, but oh! that tanning and cleaning was a job. At last we had it done, not a well-tanned skin by any means, but good enough. Art decided how much goat skin and how much leather to use, made patterns of cardboard, carefully pulled all the stitches out of the chap belt to save it, then cut the old chaps and the goat skin to fit his patterns.

Then he sewed with leather strings, punching holes with an awl, the two seams for each leg—a slow, tedious job. Finally, he sewed each leg into the old chap belt. Chap belts are made in two pieces laced together in the center, and the belt is buckled behind, not in front.

But all cowboys, when they get new chaps, rip out the lacing and substitute for it one or two light, easily broken leather thongs.

Why? Because if a rider gets his solidly laced chap belt hooked over his saddle horn, as he well may when a horse falls or when it is bucking, he'd then get his stomach frightfully bruised, or even ripped open. Therefore, an experienced cowboy makes sure the belt lacing will break in case he gets snagged on his saddle horn.

At last the new chaps were finished, and were we proud! Beautiful white goatskin face and leather backed chaps, but no lining in them, no binding at the bottoms, no pockets.

Everyone who had scoffed at Art had to back down. "B'golly he done it! Purty good chaps, too. Fit lots better 'n them boughten ones."

This success opened for my brother a new field of endeavor. But he did not have money to buy leather, goatskins and other items, including tools, so the next pair of chaps he made were really something. He attempted to tan one calf skin with the hair on and another with the hair off for leather for the backs of the chaps. We had used all of the alum. But certain baking powder advertisements proclaimed that such-and-such baking powder put out by a competitor was nothing more than alum. So we got a couple of cans of this cheap baking powder and tried it to tan the "hair-left-on" hide.

The experiment was a flat failure. Nevertheless, we scraped and rubbed and pulled both hides until they were a little bit softer than rawhide, and then Art sewed them into a pair of chaps. He had by this time swapped off the white ones and now tried to wear his new calfskin chaps. This, however, was torture; they were as stiff as boards, and when they got wet—what a smell!

Eventually he made a gift of these chaps. I was most grateful! I said I wouldn't be caught dead wearing those gosh-awful things. But come cold weather, I put them on and was mighty glad to have them. Constant wear helped to soften and tan the hides until they fitted more comfortably, though they still sank like a dead cow when they got wet. Strangely, neither kids nor grownups made as much fun of me and the chaps as I had feared.

Art's next venture in the chap-making field came about when he returned in the spring from a trip to Springfield, Massachusetts, bringing with him six "woolly" goat skin mats, each twelve inches by two feet. Three were dyed green, the others a glaring red.

"Just see what I found in a store back East," he told me, pleased as could be. "I'm going to make chaps of these mats. I managed to buy some nice, soft calfskin, too, and a piece of saddle leather for the belts. Now, which will you like, red chaps or green ones?"

Oddly, the green skins fascinated me. White or black were the standard colors for chaps, although bright golden ones were now being seen.

"Sure I'd like green chaps," I said. "But you'll have to splice those mats to make the legs long enough even for me."

"I know it. That's why I had to buy three mats of each color."

Now, two of the green hides were a very dark, alfalfa green, the third light green. Art put the light green at the bottoms of the chap legs, so my chaps were two tone! But they were the best-fitting and the warmest chaps I ever owned, and people did not make much fun of them although I was the only *green*-chapped kid in the country.

The red chaps caught the immediate attention of Newton Bellairs. Without any quibbling Newt bought them for twenty dollars, and this launched Art on a spare-time hobby which soon became a real business venture.

As time ran along, my brother learned where to buy leather and Angora skins, tanned and dyed, if he wanted them dyed. Chaps were his specialty. He made them to order and to measure, so they fitted the customer. His pleased customers were his only advertisement, but for many years he always had many more orders than he could possibly fill.

He also branched out, making bridles, belts, cuffs, quirts, hackamores, and finally a saddle. For this task he bought only the tree ready-made; all the rest was his own handwork. The first saddle was not perfect, but the next was the work of a master craftsman. He loved working with leather, and, being a perfectionist, every job he turned out had to be the best article of its kind obtainable.

Though he no longer lives there, my brother, who had been born and reared as a cowman and rancher, is today best remembered in North Park not as cowman or rancher, but for the superb workmanship and excellence of the chaps he made.

TO LARAMIE – WITH A BEEF HERD

But back in 1902 both of us kids were the eager young cowboys, and for me at last came the lifting to the heights . . . the long anticipated experience of being a cowhand with a herd bound for Laramie.

This was a "pool" drive. Dad, Gus, Bill Kerr, John Kimmons and Andy Swanson (I do not remember if Andy had his own cattle or was representing some outfit, but he was one of the pool) threw their herds into one bunch of approximately five hundred cattle—feeder steers, fat cows, old bulls, canner cows—to be trailed to the railroad.

Dad was the chuck wagon driver and cook. Not that his wagon was a real chuck wagon, nor that he drove four spanking good horses, for he drove only two, but his wagon hauled beds and grub and utensils. Nor was there a horse wrangler and a cavvy, the riders having only one mount each. The big outfits still used cavvies, for real cowboys abhor the idea of riding one horse all day long or day after day. But these ranchmen had learned that one horse would suffice one rider on this short trip. After all, the horses would merely be poking along behind a slow herd, and there was no night herding since the cattle were pastured in fields each night. There was no grass, anywhere close to the road, even where the country was still unfenced, so even the big outfits, excepting Haley's, no longer attempted to graze their herds and night herd them.

Gus, John Kimmons, Andy Swanson, Bill Kerr, Art and myself were the cowboys. My mount being old Wringtail, Mr. Kimmons advised me to throw away my spurs and use only a quirt to stop his tail-switching and wringing. Throw away my spurs! What an unthinkable idea!

Before daybreak of a late September morning, when the horses' hoofs left trails in the frosty meadow stubble, we were out and rounding up the big field. Kimmons and Swanson counted the herd through the gate into the lane, and then we were off with a beef herd, bound for Laramie! Kimmons and Gus rode point, Swanson and Bill Kerr worked in he "swing," Art and I brought up the drags. Naturally, I'd be put on "drag," bringing up the slow critters and eating dust. But that was okay with me.

Both Kimmons and Gus warned us not to belt the cattle with ropes or quirts. Let them take it easy. Easy. John Kimmons quoted an old range adage about how to graze a herd: "Never let 'em know they're being driven, yet never let 'em take one step back."

But, of course, we were not merely grazing this herd. We had to drive them to make the twenty-four miles between Dad's ranch and Boswell's, and these fat, well-filled and frisky cattle stepped out at a three-mile-per-hour gait. We had no trouble passing Pinkhamton, nor did any stray into the timber, and by five o'clock the herd was watering at the Laramie River and eating grass in Boswell's lower field.

Gus had ridden ahead to see whoever was managing the Boswell Ranch and find out where we could hold the cattle. Returning, he piloted us across country to this lower field, so I did not see Boswell's buildings at all.

Dad was there ahead of us, team turned loose, campfire made in the willows and aspens close by the river, and supper ready. None of us had had dinner, or even a lunch this long day, so the grub disappeared as fast as if the Payne cats, plus John Coe's, had found it. But before they ate, two of the men, with spikes and hammers "rode fence." When putting a herd into a field, cattlemen invariably rode all the way around its fences to assure themselves there were in it no open bars or gates or other holes.

Some of the horses were picketed, others hobbled, others, which could be trusted not to leave the picketed animals, turned loose. Supper over, dishes washed, there came one of those wonderful interludes around the campfire, the men making talk and me listening; listening and tucking away stories they told, or scraps of information from which I might be learning something important.

Before long they were selecting spots to spread their beds, and were turning in. We had no tent and only three bedrolls. Kimmons and Gus had one; Swanson and Bill Kerr shared another; Dad, Art and I slept three in a bed, and Dad's tarpaulin was the same old wagon sheet of many uses which I have mentioned early in this story.

When a heavy rainstorm came up during this night, the other men, who had good heavy tarps, suffered not at all. But Dad, Art and I and our bedding got an unpleasant, cold bath. Oh, well, this was all in the day's work when a fellow was a cowboy!

Come daybreak, both the cattle and the horses were safe in the field and, breakfast over, we were again hitting the trail. Down the Laramie, with Jelm Mountain on our right, past the old mining camp of Jelm where now was only a post office, past Wood's Landing, where Jim Pollock, Mrs. Pollock and their daughter Maude ran a road ranch.

This ranch was now the main overnight stop for freighters, for Park ranchers hauling supplies, for men hauling lumber to Laramie. A stage station, too, it simply boomed every autumn, teams pulling in, teams pulling out, at almost any hour of day or night.

Pollock's women folks set a good table and made a good living for themselves and Mr. Pollock. But Pollock's customers cleaned the stable and even hauled in from his field the hay they used, Pollock never lifting a hand to help. The man often went fishing; at all other times he was, as the freighters expressed it, "The best chair warmer in all Wyoming."

I was learning already that the laziest man often had the "workingest" wives—wives who often ran road ranches, boarding houses, hotels, restaurants.

However, we did not stop with the Pollocks, but went on down the river to Lund's ranch. The Lunds were Swedes and Lund himself, his wife and his grown daughter furnished the sharpest contrast to Pollock. They not only worked all day but all night as well.

Lund had the first apple orchard I'd ever seen. Dad said the man was crazy to try to raise apples at this high altitude, as cold as it was, and that the apples were no good. John Kimmons, who got far better apples at his old home, Fort Collins, agreed they were no good. But they seemed wonderful to us boys! They were still better when Dad stewed a kettleful of them for breakfast.

Rain again on this second night, and Dad had been unable to dry out the blankets and quilts from the previous night's storm.

All day long on our third day we were creeping slowly, slowly across the wide Laramie Plains; level, monotonous, seemingly endless, with wire fences to right and left, the hills beyond Laramie in the far distance, and the nagging thought, "Will we ever, ever get any closer? Ever get to Laramie?"

This night the men were going to make Pahlow's ranch, only ten miles from Laramie, but it was a long drive from Lund's, so we stopped at noon to let the cattle rest. The herd was bedded quietly when Mr. Kimmons saw an automobile coming toward us and shouted, "If that thing runs into our herd we'll have a rip-snorting stampede."

It seems strange to say now, in the present day when horses pay no more attention to automobiles than if they were people, that when cars first appeared, both cattle and horses were as terrified by them as if they were cougars or grizzly bears.

Wild tales which ranchers told of runaways due to meeting automobiles, owned by "rich bugs" in town, on these plains were suddenly in my mind, and all of the men of our party were worried and alarmed.

"That contraption is sure to touch off the herd," Bill Kerr agreed. "We might do what Montie Blevins did when one of the prominent business men of Laramie, on a bicycle, approached his beef cattle."

"What did Montie do?" Gus demanded.

"He loped out to meet this fellow and politely asked him to walk on the off-side of Montie's horse, far around the herd. He'd keep his horse between the man and the cattle so they'd not see him.

"This big businessman blew up and said the road was a public road. He had as much right to use it as any doggoned cowman and he intended to keep riding regardless of cattle or anything else.

"Montie quietly unstrapped his rope, started to open a loop and said, 'All right. Go ahead.'

"The fellow looked at the rope and at Montie's face and changed his mind."

"Al Marr tells an even better story than that," I piped up, feeling important. "Al said they'd had trouble with one big steer which had tried to break away, and when they got it back into the herd, it was right on the fight. Well, this bicycle man came along, rode right into Al's herd, and this wild steer took after him. Al said you never saw a man peddle so hard and so fast as that fellow!"

While this talk was going on, the automobile was coming along very fast, or so it seemed to all of us, and now Andy Swanson said, "You go and meet it, Gus. Ask the driver to pull off the road and shut off his engine until we can get past him."

"I doubt if I can get George (Gus' horse) anywhere near it. But I'll try," said Gus and rode toward the oncoming chug-chugging, smoking demon.

Tension held Art and me as well as all the others. We were mounted and ready to try to control the cattle if . . .

But—what a relief!—before Gus met the vehicle—which would never be of any real use except as a rich man's plaything—it turned off the main road on a trail leading to the river's valley, and vanished.

At twilight we turned the herd into one of Pahlow's big fields. Dad's wagon was encamped in the yard, our bedding spread and hung out to dry. Tonight, happy thought, maybe we could put our bed in the bunkhouse.

Pahlow and his hard-working wife and family were Germans. They had built up a real ranch on the plains, raised several hundred tons of hay, although a great deal of it was foxtail, and raised fine barley and oats as well as vegetables, including splendid potatoes. The older Pahlows and Dad seemed to have something in common and got along famously.

Following our noon stop, Kimmons had ridden ahead to Laramie to order the stock cars. At some time during the night, he returned and at breakfast we learned he had been unsuccessful. There was a shortage of stock cars, and the railroad agent could promise only that he would have them on hand as soon as possible.

"How soon?" Gus asked.

"Maybe a week. Maybe longer."

Gloom settled over the cowmen. This sort of situation was not unprecedented. So-and-so had once waited three days for cars; so-and-so had waited ten days. But Gus and Kimmons and Bill Kerr, Swanson and Dad, hadn't believed they would face such a calamity. What could they do? What would they do?

Taking the cattle home was not out of the question but was unthinkable after trailing them this far. We were only ten miles from Laramie, a short day's drive—and I had counted on getting into Laramie, that wonder place—this very day.

Dad went and talked to Pahlow, came back to the breakfast fire and said, "Men, we can hold 'em in Pahlow's field, but it will cost us five cents per head per day."

All seemed to think this was terribly expensive. But there was no open range and no grass in the road lane, so they'd have to make the best of it. The point settled, some of the men decided to visit Laramie.

"Me, too!" I cried. "Count me in," and held my breath, wondering would Dad let me go.

He said, "All right, you kids," and hitched up the team, but did not load the camp equipment and beds into the wagon.

Swanson and Kimmons said they'd stay at Pahlow's and look after the catle. Gus, Bill Kerr, Art and I climbed into the wagon with Dad, and away we went—for a day in Laramie!

Toward six o'clock that evening, Dad was getting his team hitched up at the livery stable where all of us had gathered when a messenger boy from the railroad freight offices appeared.

"I was told you stockmen were in town," he said, consulting a slip of paper. "You are Payne, Dwinell, Kerr, Kimmons and Swanson?"

"Yes, and I'm Dwinell," Gus replied quickly. "What . . . ?"

"We'll have cars for your shipment sometime tonight. If you can be ready to load out at daybreak tomorrow, you can have them. If not, someone else will . . . "

"But— but our cattle are ten miles out of town," Gus cut in, and oh! how worried he looked. "It will take us until noon tomorrow to . . . "

"That's your worry," the messenger said. "I was told to tell you to begin loading at six o'clock, or . . . " He started away.

Dad and Bill Kerr were staring round-eyed at Gus, and he was staring back at them while Art and I fidgeted. The cars were coming, but we'd lose 'em unless . . . "This is awful," I thought.

"Wait!" Gus called. "Cattle have been yarded at night before this. I believe . . . "

"You fellows will be here then and make use of those cars? I must have a positive answer."

"We'll be ready to load at six o'clock," Bill Kerr snapped, and Gus added:

"Gorry! Yes! That's your answer. Don't let anybody else have those cars."

223

"We won't, and we'll be banking on you!"

Gus ran over to the liveryman, saying tensely, "Hook the fastest team you've got to a light rig and drive four of us out to Pahlow's ranch. Hurry man, hurry!"

"But here's my team," Dad protested. "I must go to Pahlow's too, to bring in our beds and other stuff."

"I know it, Jack," Gus said. "But the best time your team can make to Pahlow's is two hours. This livery outfit will make it in one hour."

"I know. Every minute counts now," Dad replied. "But I'll drive out and come back and have our beds here by the time you cowboys need them tonight."

He pulled out immediately, but our livery rig overtook him before he was clear of the town. Then we were streaking across the plains at the fastest trot a pair of lightweight, trotting-bred horses could travel.

All of us felt a terrific urgency as we raced against time. By Gus's watch we made Pahlow's ranch in just fifty minutes. Even so, darkness and cold drizzling rain had overtaken us. All the sky was cloud-banked, not one star visible, lightning flashed and thunder rolled across the plains in reverberating echoes.

As soon as Swanson and Kimmons heard our big news, they had their horses saddled and were out in the field in a matter of moments, but it took Art and me, Bill Kerr and Gus longer to get going. Gus stopped to ask Pahlow whether he would haul a big load of hay to the stockyards for the cattle. Pahlow promised he would.

I stuck close to my big brother as we rode out into the dark, rain-drenched field where seasoned hands and expert cowmen John Kimmons and Andy Swanson were going about rounding up the herd.

"Golly, but this is spooky and scary," I confided to Art.

"Aw, shut up," growling, probably to hide how uneasy he was himself. "If you're going to be a cowpuncher you got to learn to take whatever comes up and say you like it."

"Oh, I like it all right! I like anything about cowboying," I asserted stoutly, resolved I'd not let anybody know I was plain scared.

Slowly the herd poured out of the field, and then we were on the road, which we had all to ourselves, except that Dad with his wagon bound back to Laramie and Pahlow with the load of hay overtook and passed us. Occasionally I'd see the lights of a ranch, mere pinpoints of light in the dark night.

The rain, scarcely enough to wet a fellow, was intermittent, but the thunderstorm continued; vivid streaks of lightning cutting the blackness were sufficiently awesome without the crack and rumble of thunder. All I could see of the cattle was the dark, moving mass, though at times a white face would loom up more clearly, and Gus's big, lightgrey horse was distinguishable when he dropped back to tell us, "Keep the drags closed right up with the main herd, boys. Don't let any of 'em get away from you. If you should need any help sing out 'Gus!' as loud as you can. Kimmons and Swanson are on point and they know the best way to get to the yards, so we'll make it all right."

I had every confidence in all four of the men. But time seemed to stand still, and although the herd kept moving steadily I was sure we'd never cross those plains. At last I realized we had turned to the left off the main road and were following a lane bordered by barbed wire fences. We came to a right angle turn and then to another, going on I knew not where. A passenger train, its windows showing light, streaked down from the north, beautiful to see, but frightening, too. Its piercing whistle was both mournful and startling.

Had the herd been closer to it, I'm sure the sight and sound of that train would surely have touched it off. Gosh! what if another train thunders along when we get close to the stockyards?

Stories I'd read and tales I'd heard about stampedes were in my mind. Suppose a bolt of lightning hit right in the midst of our cattle. They'd break out every which way, running blind and like crazy. And these double-darned wire fences! My horse'd ram into a wire fence, the cattle would ram into him, Wringtail would be cut to pieces and go down, and hundreds of hoofs would pound me into the mud.

I vowed I'd never tell anybody, but, although I'd always wanted to be a cowboy and had welcomed this adventure, I now wished I was anywhere but where I was!

In spite of my forebodings, slowly, surely, on and on moved the herd, as if neither rain, darkness, lightning and thunder, nor trains could stop them. At last, more by sound than by sight, I realized we were fording the Laramie River, and now the herd was no longer strung out. It had become a compact mass.

We crossed railroad tracks, and, by sound and feel and by the way my horse was acting, I knew we were in the midst of a big junk yard. Finally it fell away behind us, and we skirted a huge, dark building, the old abandoned glassworks.

All at once Gus and Bill Kerr were on the flanks of the herd, close to us boys, Gus calling, "Snap your ropes, kids. Don't hit 'em, but crowd 'em, shove 'em along. We're going into the yards."

My horse brushed against something I realized was the "wing" of the stockyards. Dark shapes of cattle were crowding through a gate, and at last both Kimmons and Swanson became visible as they kept the cattle from "hitting the gate too hard."

A freight train went roaring along the tracks, and thunder blended into its noise, but the cattle went on—on into the stock-yards big corral. The gate clanged shut behind the last of them and voices exploded around me:

"That's it! Pahlow's got the hay scattered, so everything's all right."

"Find baling wire and wire that gate shut, top and bottom, Andy."

"I'm wiring it right now."

Suddenly John Kimmons was close to me. "How'd you like your initiation, John?" he asked with his jolly laugh.

I doubt that my voice was strong, but I replied stoutly, "Just fine, Mr. Kimmons."

"Ha, I'll bet you kids were scared half out of your boots," thus Bill Kerr.

"Aw, bosh! We sure weren't."

"Well, I admit I was," he said. "And I'm taking my hat off to Andy and John and Gus as cowhands."

"WHEELS UNDER 'EM"

With the herd safely yarded at eleven o'clock of that dark, storm-ridden night, a new adventure began. From somewhere the stockyards manager materialized and the men talked briefly with him, whereupon he said, "I'll call the U.P. freight office and let them know you are here and ready to load out."

"How will you get in touch with the freight office?" Gus inquired.

The man replied matter-of-factly, "Telephone."

This means of communication, now common in Laramie, was soon to invade even remote North Park.

The stockyards were one mile north of town, and although one could not have found a more conservative group than the four cowmen with whom Art and I were riding, it seemed that even they must zip into town in traditional cowboy manner at full speed.

Dad was at the livery stable with the wagon, and after we spent a few minutes drying out by the office stove, I was happy to hear Kimmons say, "There's an all-night restaurant at the Kuster Hotel. Let's eat, men."

All I recall of that wonderful midnight supper is that everybody ordered beefsteaks (being cowmen, of course, we never got beefsteak!) and that we provoked the waitress by gobbling all the bread on the table and demanding more while waiting for the steaks.

Supper over, it was back to the stable, where we spread our beds down in empty stalls. The next thing I knew Dad was shaking me awake and saying, "Come on, boys. We've got to load the cattle."

However, we had breakfast first, at the Kuster again, with the cowmen worrying about where they could buy prod poles since no stores were open.

To a man shipping cattle prod poles, I learned, were as important as spurs to a cowboy. First, to prod the cattle up the loading chutes into the stock cars; then, to carry along to use if, when the train stopped, one or more cattle in a carload were found to be "down." A prod pole was the size and shape of a pitchfork handle, but some twelve feet long. If necessary, the men could push them through the cracks in the slatted cars, to "prod" cattle off the fallen animal and then "prod" it up onto its feet.

Gus solved the dilemma by calling up on the telephone a merchant whom he knew and requesting him to come and open his store to supply us with prod poles. Thus, when we were mounted—Dad riding double behind Art—all of us carried prod poles. It didn't take much imagination on my part to think of mine as a lance and imagine that I was now a knight in armor, as in Ivanhoe, ready to charge another knight "in full career."

Dawn was approaching, the small mountains to eastward all cloud-hazy, and at last I saw what I had not seen last night, the stockyards with cattle safe inside. A noisy, smoking switch engine was pushing a long string of empty stock cars onto the stockyards side track, and at the gate a railroad man said to us, "We'll spot the cars as fast as you can fill 'em."

"Cars been sanded?" Kimmons asked sharply.

"Sure thing," and the man shrugged.

" 'Sanded?' What's that mean?" I asked, and Mr. Kimmons explained, "Before you load a stock car, someone must shovel sand or cinders or plain dirt into it and spread a thin layer over its floor. It's to stop cattle from slipping as badly as they would otherwise. Naturally," he added, "the cars get sloppy and filthy, so at the place where you stop to unload your cattle for feed, water and rest, railroad mean clean 'em out and sand 'em again before they are reloaded."

Swanson said, "Men, we haven't time to sort the herd now according to brands and owners. But we can do that when we stop to feed."

" 'Stop to feed'?" I said to Dad. "What's that mean?"

228

"You'll see. I've been holding it for a surprise so I hadn't told you kids before, but you're going along with us to Omaha."

"Going to Omaha! Boy!"

Two mounted men began cutting whole carloads of cattle from the main herd, thirty-odd to each load, to fill the "close pens" of the two loading chutes. The rest of us, including three railroad men, worked on foot, and I found myself making a hand with the loading; "putting wheels under 'em," cowboys called it.

First, our men made sure the door on the far side of the car was closed and its "bull board" in place. (The purpose of a bull board— a stout piece of plank—is to protect the door and relieve it from strain when the animals crowd against it.) Next, the men lifted the small bridge which fitted between the car's open door and the loading plaform and put it in place, then closed the gates on either side of this front end of the loading chute so they came right up to the door jambs of the car. Finally, we prodded the bewildered and reluctant cattle out of the chute's close pen, into the chute and up it into the car.

The secret of success was to keep the cattle moving without a chance to turn and charge back down the chute. The instant the last animal was inside the car, the two gates I've mentioned were opened, thus allowing men to get at the car's door. While one man grabbed the "bull board," and set it in place, others lifted the little bridge out of the way and then slammed shut the sliding door.

The same thing had been going on at the second chute, and now the brakeman standing atop the string of cars signalled the engineer to pull ahead. Another arm signal told him when to stop, with the car doors in line with the chutes. This is "spotting cars."

Meanwhile, those of our crew who were mounted were filling the close pens again, so the loading job went off as if it had all been rehearsed. Eventually, I wiped sweat from my eyes and face and looked around, seeing none of our cattle left in the yards.

"Any of you men want to ride up town?" the brakeman called.

Dad said he did, and he climbed up a ladder to perch on top of a car.

The rest of us dashed back to the stable in Laramie where the horses were to be boarded until our return. The men, including Dad, got suitcases out of the wagon and changed to suits, clean shirts, neckties and shoes. Art and I had no change of clothing. Neverthe-less, along with the men we walked to the freight office, where we signed contracts with the U.P. railroad and received copies of these to show freight conductors along the line.

The shipper, not necessarily the owner, of one carload of cattle was entitled to accompany his shipment to market via freight train. He'd ride in the caboose. Two carloads entitled him to return transportation by passenger train. We had fourteen carloads and seven men, so this worked out evenly, two cars to each man.

There was a lot of fine print on those contracts, but the gist of it was that the railroad undertook to deliver the stock to such-and-such destination, with charges for freight, yardage and feed while enroute to be deducted from the gross amount of sale of said stock before the shipper received any money.

"Now they're on the cars, we have mighty little to say or do," John Kimmons told me. "It's up to the railroad."

"And nothing to say about your own cattle after they get to market," Dad remarked. "Then the commission men take over."

This entire shipment was consigned by its various owners to several different commission firms on the Omaha livestock market, these firms acting as agents or go-betweens between the sellers and buyers. I learned that although a stockman could consign his cattle to himself and then try to dispose of them on the market, he was badly handicapped. He wasn't "on to the ropes." But commission men knew all the angles. They were in touch with "feeder" buyers from the Corn Belt states and were always in close contact with buyers for the big packing houses, Swift and Company, Armour, Cudahy, and so on.

The commission firm's fee was fifty cents per head, and, as was the case with the railroad, all commissions, yardage (the cost to the shipper for his use of the stockyards), feed and anything else which might possibly be required, were deducted from the total amount of the sale before the shipper received his money.

Presently I was for the first time aboard a caboose. This one stood alone on a side track in the railroad yards while our train was being "made up," which meant that many other freight cars in addition to our loads of cattle were being switched and coupled together to form a full train.

I smelled the acrid coal smoke and heard the clank of wheels and the intermittent blasts of whistles while I looked critically at the interior of my first "crummy," as cowmen called a caboose. At the rear end, with toilet on one side and clothes closet and food cabinet on the other, was a narrow aisle. A short stairway led to the cupola, a fascinating place above the caboose proper and thus higher than the tops of the cars. It was, I learned, the rear brakeman's lookout post from which he could see along the full length of the train.

The main part of the caboose had padded seats extending lengthwise along either side with bunkers underneath them for coal and other items. The conductor's desk occupied one front corner and a big stove stood in the center of the caboose. It was securely anchored by iron straps to the floor; stove pipe and hot water can were also anchored. There was sufficient room to lay our many prod poles on the floor close against one of the side seats.

Mr. Kimmons had noticed my curiosity and now asked, "How do you like it?" He went right on, "A freight train crew is five men, engineer, fireman, head brakie, rear brakie and conductor. The con and the brakies live on their cabooses while on duty, cook meals while they are rolling along, and if the caboose is merely standing in the yards at the end of their run, they often sleep in it."

"End of their run?" I asked. "Doesn't the same crew go all the way to Omaha?"

"Oh, no. Only as far as the next division point, which is Cheyenne, where we get another engine, another caboose and another crew of men. Our present crew, after a rest period, will return to Laramie, using the same engine and same caboose on a westbound freight train."

"Oh, now I see how a certain caboose is a certain crew's temporary home. Railroad home."

"That's right, and although these cons and brakies have to put up with cowmen, sheepmen and hog men riding in their cabooses, they don't like it a little bit." Mr. Kimmons chuckled. "I wouldn't either if I was in their boots. Men track dirt into their quarters, spill tobacco ashes and spit all over the place, to say nothing of getting drunk.

"None of us are carrying bottles," he continued. "But your average cowman stays sober only until his cattle are loaded; then, once he's safe aboard the caboose, he thinks it's time to cut loose. Some say that's the only way a man can stand such a hard trip.

"A standing joke among trainmen goes like this: the conductor of a cattle train stepped off when it pulled into a station and another conductor came up to him and asked, 'What you got this time,

Ed?' 'Fifty loads of cattle,' said Ed. 'One load of hogs,' pointing at the caboose."

Up to this point we'd had the caboose to ourselves, but now, thrilling me, a switch engine hitched onto it, shoved it up behind a long string of cars and a brakeman coupled it to the last car. As the switch engine backed away, a dozen stockmen, led by a conductor, approached the caboose and began to clamber aboard. Some carried suitcases and packages, some carried prod poles and some carried quart bottles. Three of the men couldn't walk under their own power and were being supported and helped along by others.

The conductor went at once to his desk, threw a heavy sheaf of papers onto it, and settled down to work. The men took over the caboose as if it belonged to them. One of the drunks wanted to sing, another talked incessantly without really saying anything, but others made intelligent talk with our party.

"Who are they?" I asked Mr. Kimmons.

"Stockmen from farther west—Utah, Idaho, Nevada, Oregon. Their train pulled in while we were loading, and now our cars have been hooked onto it."

Several of the men lighted cigars, one uncorked and passed his bottle around. When Gus, Swanson, Kimmons and Dad all refused it, the generous donor snorted, "Huh! What kind of cattlemen are you birds? A new breed?"

I climbed up into the cupola and looked out of its front window along the train and wondered where'd we eat and how soon? Eating seemed a hit-and-miss proposition; sleeping too was going to be difficult unless a fellow could sleep sitting up. On the car ahead of our caboose stood a brakeman facing the engine and signalling with both arms, and far up ahead the engineer whistled a reply. Then, into the continul bawling of imprisoned cattle came a new sound, a great clanking as couplings tightened and the train wheels began to turn. The long journey to Omaha had begun!

I saw the brakeman slip down from the car ahead, and I lost sight of him until he appeared in the cupola.

"Kid," scowling at me, "this is reserved for trainmen. You ain't supposed to ride up here."

"I'm not? Well, there's no place down there for me. Would you mind awful much if . . . ?"

He'd been sizing me up and suddenly a grin replaced his angry expression. "All right, son. You're such a sort of lost-looking little shaver that..." His voice trailed.

So I was "a lost-looking little shaver!" He sat down and looked ahead, and following his gaze I saw black smoke belching from not one, but two, engines. Apparently the man anticipated my question. "Double-header to pull us up Sherman Hill. On top the lead engine will uncouple and deadhead back to Laramie."

"Deadhead back?"

"It won't be pulling anything, you see."

"Thanks, Mister. What you looking for the most up along the train?"

"Hot boxes, and to see nothing goes wrong, like a loose or broken coupling and the train breaking apart. Then I'd have to hustle and set hand brakes—fast."

"What's a hot box?"

My friend swore disgustedly. "The curse of a brakeman's life! You probably know how a wagon wheels turns on a spindle?... Well, so do car wheels, but we have what we call 'packing' to feed oil to the spindles and boxes. When something goes screwy they get red-hot; even get on fire. Then we have to stop the train and cool and repack a hot box."

"Am I learning new things!" I began, when my brother's head appeared as he started to come up ino the cupola. My brakeman friend waved him back. "Stay out!" curtly.

"All right, mister," Art said. "But I got to tell John—three of those men are sheepmen!"

"Sheepmen! Riding a caboose with cattlemen! Do they stink bad?"

The brakeman laughed uproariously. "You kids are cattlemen, huh? And you b'lieve all sheepmen smell like sheep. Well, they don't, and, of course, sheep cars and cattle cars make up a stock train. Stock includes hogs, too." He made a face as a kid might have done. "Thank God, no hog man is aboard today. You'll know it when just one gets into the caboose with you. How *they* stink!"

"So I've heard," Art said and withdrew. But I asked my friendly brakeman, "Just why does a hog man sti... smell worse than any other stockman?"

"Unless the weather is darned cold, hogs get hot when they're crowded into a car. So at a stopping point the man in charge'll get a hose, climb into the car and squirt cold water over his hogs. Now, he's sure to get muck smeared a-plenty, 'specially his feet, and that smell . . . Phew! It's worse than skunk!"

I was glad I wasn't a hog man! But it was good to be a cattle shipper, and I'd never admit I was hungry and tired, fighting to stay awake and enjoy . . .

I woke up suddenly with Dad shaking me. "Wake up, son. This is Cheyenne. We've been told we'll have time to get a bite to eat while they're changing cabooses and engines."

Cheyenne! How I wanted to see this city which had been only a few short years ago the cattle capital of the West, about which men told fascinating tales of its glory and its wildness. But a fellow couldn't see much from the railroad yards, nor from the fly-infested beanery where we North Parkers stoked ourselves.

Some of the men took their possesssions and climbed to the top of cattle cars, there to wait until a new caboose was attached; others with prod poles walked along either side of our train, peering into the cars to make sure all the cattle were standing up.

"Are many apt to 'get down'?" I asked Mr. Kimmons.

"No," he answered and smiled at my worry. "Strong, fat cattle seldom 'get down.' It's in the spring when stock are thin and weak you have to watch out for trouble. Notice the small doors high up at each of a stock car? You can get into a car through one of those if you are obliged to 'tail up' a critter."

"Get inside a car among all those cattle? Gosh, a fellow'd get killed," I said.

He laughed at me. "I've done it a good many times and haven't been hurt yet."

When our train was moving once again, I tried to get into the cupola. But the new brakeman ordered me out gruffly. On the UP.'s double track line a westbound passenger train whizzed past so close I felt I could touch it, and I saw people looking out of the windows. People! People! So many of them, and back on the ranch so few.

Somewhere east of Cheyenne, we had two hot boxes, the heavy train pulled onto a siding and the trainmen worked at the hot boxes, cursing them, delaying us for a couple of hours. Later our train was sidetracked to let an eastbound passenger train go past it. Other delays followed, some of the cowmen fretting and complaining because valuable time was being lost. Cattle, I learned, were permitted to stay on the cars only twenty-six hours continuously. Therefore, the conductor in charge must see that the stock was unloaded before the expiration of this time limit, unless either the owners or the shippers would sign a release which allowed the railroad ten additional hours in which to reach a "feeding point."

Later on our men did sign such releases and this permitted us to reach Grand Island barely within thirty-six hours after the stock had been loaded at Laramie.

The air in our caboose was close and hot, foul with tobacco smoke, smells of sweat and corral dust and the stench of unwashed humans. Our men sat stiffly, as if this was an ordeal to be endured, but I was enjoying it all.

At Sidney, Nebraska, we had a chance to eat while waiting for another train crew to take over. Bill Kerr and Swanson and some other men walked up alongside the standing train with their prod poles. They had not returned when a new caboose was coupled onto the last stock car and the train pulled out.

Deeply concerned, I asked Gus, "What'll happen to Bill and Andy if they're left behind?"

He laughed. "Nothing bad," he said. "If a shipper loses his train, he can get permission to ride a passenger train to a point where he'll be sure of overtaking the stock train. Oh, the railroad company doesn't like it, suspecting he is trying to slip something over and get a comfortable ride. But they'll give him a pass."

"I'm glad they won't have to walk to Omaha," I said, and then I saw Bill, Andy and others coming in at the front door of the caboose—and by this time the train was traveling fast.

"How'd you get here, Mr. Kerr?" I demanded.

"When the train began to roll, we just climbed up the ladder at the rear end of a stock car," he replied. "Then we walked along the top of the cars back to this caboose."

"Say, I'd like to do that."

"Well, don't try it yet. Not until you're older."

(I did not get permission to walk on top of a train on this trip. But in the years that followed I became an experienced cattle shipper and was obliged to walk along the top of a moving train many times, and I found it too dangerous to be enjoyable.)

We were now rolling across the seemingly endless plains of Nebraska, and I saw good houses and enormous barns on small farms, herds of the best dairy cattle and beef cattle I'd ever seen, thousands of tiny haystacks, cornfields — and pigs. Great droves of them, yellow pigs, white pigs, black and white pigs and plain black pigs. When some of the men were able to identify all the different breeds, I thought, "Always something new for me to learn."

Art and I went out to the small rear platform and sat with our legs dangling down the steps of either side of this cramped space and listened to the musical song of the wheels against the rails: "Click-click. Click-click." We were happy until the brakeman stepped out, glared at us and snapped, "Get back inside, you fool kids. If this train gave a sudden lurch, off you'd tumble and likely be killed."

So we went inside. Night came, and, wedged in between two big men and nearly smothered, I fell asleep — so soundly that when we reached North Platte and Dad carried me into yet another caboose, I didn't even know it. Thus the night passed, and late that evening we arrived at Grand Island where the cattle must be unloaded and fed.

All of the men were impatient to leave the caboose before we actually got into the railroad yards, and while we were waiting, a big, rough-looking man from Idaho and a wizened old fellow, whom everyone called "Dad from Utah," got involved in a "tall tale" contest.

Idaho finished his story and winked at the audience, convinced he had Dad from Utah stopped.

Dad, however, looked around in the flickering lantern light, finger-combed his fringe of grey hair, and began:

"One day last summer I was riding in my big pasture when I saw a dust cloud puffing up by the gate. I rode over there to see what was making it and I saw a big snake with his tail in his mouth, whirling 'round and 'round.

"As I set there on my hoss, watching him, his tail went further and further into his mouth with every whirl he made, and presently, b'jingo, the tail disappeared completely. There wasn't nothing left but a little hole in the ground. That snake had swallered himself!"

At this moment, the train shuddered to a stop. The conductor shouted, "Grand Island! All out!" and the man from Idaho laughed and clapped Dad from Utah on the back. "Your story stopped the train, Dad. I give up!"

With prod poles and baggage, all of us trooped to a hotel and registered for rooms, washed, and had supper. I'd believed we ourselves must go to the stockyards, unload the cars, feed the cattle baled hay, and turn water into the troughs. But now I learned all of this work was taken care of by yardmen, who would also reload the cars at the proper time.

After breakfast the following morning, however, the men cut the herd according to brands and owners, something we had been unable to do in Laramie. I helped by handling a gate, and I saw a demonstration of sorting or cutting as it is done in stockyards.

The work went along smoothly and quickly, so presently all of Dad's cattle were separated from the others' and put into small pens, each holding one carload; the same for those belonging to Kimmons, Kerr, Swanson and Dwinell.

Our stopover at Grand Island was memorable for another reason. There was a bath room in the hotel, and, for twenty-five cents in addition to room rent, the management would supply soap and towels for a bath. I paid the required sum out of my own money for my very first introduction to a real bath in a real bath tub! Was that something!

Late that afternoon we boarded a caboose for the last lap of the trip, Grand Island to South Omaha.

Long before the conductor announced "South Omaha! All out, men!" a most peculiar aroma invaded the crummy.

"This is a horrible smell!" I told John Kimmons. "What makes it?"

"Horrible?" and he laughed. "That's a good smell to a cowman; the combined odors from packing houses and stockyards."

As the heavy train ground to a stop, I stepped out onto the small rear platform in the murky, smelly first light of a Monday morning and saw our brakeman with a lantern standing nearby. A switchman, also with a lantern, came up to him and said, "How're you, Joe? What you got this time?"

"Sixty-two cars of cattle and sheep," answered the brakeman, "And," pointing his lantern at the caboose, "one load of hogs."

SOUTH OMAHA

"The hogs" (men) poured out of the caboose, and Art and I, stumbling along in the darkness, trailed them across countless railroad tracks to a street where we bunched up, waiting until a noisy streetcar came along. We clambered aboard and I had my first streetcar ride. Eventually we got off near the Livestock Exchange Building, where all stockyard business was transacted in dozens and scores of commission firms' offices. I also saw a bank, a wash room and a huge restaurant on the ground floor.

Here our party separated. Kimmons, Swanson and Bill Kerr were not patronizing the same firm as Gus and Dad. Early as it was, our commission men were on hand, and I was mightily impressed, for it was apparent that these men were keen and sharp, glib-tongued and clever. They had the faculty of making their customers feel confident and at ease, and they welcomed us boys as if we were as important as our father.

Yes, they'd had word that our cattle were in; soon they'd be unloaded and moved to their block of pens. How was the market? Off a bit last week, due to heavy runs, but sure to pick up this Monday, beginning a new week.

Dad and the other men had carefully planned to reach the market on Monday because cattle bring more the early part of the week than the latter part. This seems unfair, for the prices should be stabilized, or so it seems. But marketing cattle is an uncertain, tricky and hazardous business, and sharp cattlemen and commission men take into account that the identical herd may sell on Thursday or Friday for fifty cents less per hundred pounds than on Monday or Tuesday.

The commission men told us to make ourselves at home for an hour or so, then to come out to the yards, and, carrying buggy whips, they left us alone except for the bookkeeper at work in a small office behind a window.

We washed up and had breakfast in the big restaurant which was buzzing with humanity. Then out to the yards where noises clashed on my ears: cattle bawling, horses' hoofs clattering on brick paving, banging of street cars, distant sounds of a train and engine, and human voices yelling, "Yoho! Yo-yo-yo! Hip!"

These were the stockyard punchers working on foot with whips and prod poles, bringing cattle up the alleys and into the various commission firms' pens from the chutes.

Those yards seemed at least a mile square, the fences made of planks nailed to posts, with other planks laid flat atop the posts so men could walk on the fences. Pens, pens, small and large, cut and cross-cut by alleys, with here and there the roof of a building showing above the fences. These were the "scales houses" where all livestock was weighed immediately after being sold. On the ranches we bought or sold stock by the head; here every type of animal was brought or sold at so much per pound, live weight.

Away yonder were sheds and a big sign, "Sheep Market." Another was marked "Hog Market." Still another section was the "Horse Market." All the rest of this area was the cattle market, cut into blocks, each bearing a sign telling it was for the exclusive use of such-and-such a commission firm, or, in a few cases, of such-and-such a livestock trader — a speculator.

Huge packing houses bordered the area, and long ramps led up from certain alleys into the second story of these plants. Later in the day I was to see carload after carload of beef steers and beef cows, canners and old bulls, driven by punchers, climb those ramps and vanish into the maws of those packing houses.

As we tagged along after Gus and Dad, who were walking a fence, I began to see the cattle in the yards; thousands of them, already penned, and more coming up the alleys . . . "Yo-yoho! Ho! Hip!" . . . and I began to realize what a tremendous business was the marketing of livestock.

Omaha drew its cattle from all the vast norhwestern area of the

United States. Yet it was only one of the big markets. Chicago, "Hog Butcher for the World," was — and still is — the largest and best market. Kansas City, Missouri, rated second in volume of business, drawing its cattle from all of the great Southwest — but getting, on an average, lower quality stock than either Chicago or Omaha. St. Joseph, Sioux City, Iowa, Sioux Falls, South Dakota, and Denver, just emerging as a livestock market, were others.

Refrigerated cars made it possible to ship fresh beef, pork and mutton to any point in the United States, and the demand and consumption of these products created the demand for our range cattle, so packing houses served a most important function. They had become indispensable to the national economy, and the packers had soon learned to salvage each and every part of a cow brute — even to the horns and hoofs. Nothing was wasted, nothing was lost.

In this connection it was said that the only part of a hog not utilized was its squeal. John Kimmons said, "Soon they'll catch and save even the squeals and sell them to the Indians for war-whoops!"

It was truthfully said that here on the Omaha market there was a buyer for any animal in the livestock line, cripples, hopelessly sick, even the "skinniest old pelters" and those which had died in cars. Sharp traders made money dealing exclusively in this "trash," a great deal of which would reappear in the form of fertilizer.

At once I began to understand what tiny frogs stock raisers such as Dad and Gus were in this immense puddle. Yet, when multiplied by thousands of other little cowmen scattered all across the great West, even they were important because each made his small contribution toward feeding beef to the nation.

But, of course, to a boy of fourteen, the magnitude and scope of this great business did not emerge full-grown on my initial trip to the Omaha livestock market. This came later and was a matter of gradually comprehending how major factors interlocked to make this enormous business tick — the range producer, the Corn Belt feeder, the packing house. Each was dependent upon the other; without the other, none could function.

We from the ranges sold our fats cows and heifers, our mature grass-beef steers, canner cows, veal calves and old bulls to the packers. But we sold our stockers and "feeders" — calves, yearlings, or two-year-old steers — to the Corn Belt feeders. These were farmers scattered far and wide throughout the Midwest, Illinois, Iowa, Indiana, Missouri and Ohio, the heart of the "feeder" district, though not entirely confined to these areas.

By means of *The Breeders' Gazette*, and through contacts with men who had come West from the Corn Belt states, I had learned that these farmers produced purebred cattle, including both beef and dairy breeds; also horses, hogs and sheep, all of the finest quality. From this area came the purebred Shorthorn, Angus and Hereford bulls which were improving beef stock on the Western ranges.

These same farmers, both those raising cattle and those who were not, purchased young range-grown steers to fill their feed lots, used their surplus feed to put weight and fat on them, then shipped them back to market as "corn-fed beef."

But still another movement of cattle must be mentioned to get a clear picture of the business. The northward march of cattle from Texas did not stop with the end of the trail drive era. It continued by means of the railroads, and every spring countless thousands of young Texas cattle, mostly steers, poured northward.

Such steers were now called stockers because they were used "to stock" either a range or a farm. But the bulk of them were purchased by range men and scattered across the Western and Northern ranges to be "grown out," or matured, on grass and hay.

Commission houses were beginning to finance the purchase of such cattle for Northern stockmen. In this way a ranchman who had no money could, if he had the feed, obtain cattle and run them in the hope that, come time to market, the stock would pay the debts against them and return a profit for his feed and work.

To return now to my initial adventure at the South Omaha Stockyards. Art and I kept close to Dad and Gus as we walked the fences looking for our commission firm's pens. I took notice that, in addition to hay, the yards used countless tons of baled straw, with which all of the cattle pens were bedded, and men with one-horse wagons were much in evidence hauling hay and straw and cleaning pens.

When we came to our firm's block, I saw we were not the only ones patronizing this firm, for hundreds of cattle filled the pens. Ours were there, standing knee-deep in fresh straw, eating hay piled in mangers, and drinking at troughs. This was "giving 'em a good fill," something very important, making them weigh more than when they came off the cars empty.

One man handled the sales of steers, another those of cows, heifers, canners, veal calves and old bulls. In addition to these "salesmen," each commission house had its corps of helpers who worked on foot. The salesmen, however, rode fine horses, and whips to them seemed as necessary as ropes to cowboys.

Four men came along an alley and stopped to look at Gus's and Dad's steers and to make talk with them. They were farmers eager to buy feeder steers. As the shop talk ran along, I became interested in two men riding Western saddles, carrying heavy ropes and clippers, who now entered one of the pens holding our cattle. They were the brand inspectors, and every animal on our commission firm's block of pens was scrutinized before they went on to look at more cattle.

They had not found any strays. (A good definition of a stray is "either a horse or a cow carrying a different brand than the brand on all other cattle or horses in the same bunch.")

I asked Gus what these inspectors did when they found a stray or a number of strays.

"First of all," he said, "they ask the shipper if he has a bill of sale for it, or can in any other manner prove his ownership. If not, they make a note to the firm handling the stock, permitting this firm to sell it, because there is nothing else to be done with a stray once it gets to market, but directing it to send the money the stray brings to the rightful owner—that is, to the man who owns the brand on this stray."

"Fair enough," I said and then took notice of two rather portly men who had reined in their fine horses near us. They were riding English saddles and had small, light-weight English spurs on their flat-heeled boots. They wore full suits of clothes and derby hats. Each carried a long buggy whip.

"Now, who are those dudes?" Art inquired of Dad and Gus, and both of us snickered. "Gosh, if they were out on the range how the cowboys'd hoorah 'em!"

" 'Dudes?' " said Gus with a smile. "Those men are neither dudes nor tenderfeet. They're packing house buyers."

" 'Packing house buyers!' " Instantly Art and I were deflated and felt foolish. We'd already been told those fellows knew their business. They could look at a cow brute and tell within three pounds how much it would weigh alive or as dressed beef.

Our cow salesman greeted these buyers by their first names and invited them into a pen filled with fat cows. Then, while the salesman talked, the buyers flicked the cows lightly with their whips, turning them around and critically looking them over. Yet it was only a few minutes before they were riding out of this pen and into another and another until they had seen all the fat cattle our salesman had to offer, whereupon, they clattered away to another firms' block of pens.

Now our salesman reported briefly to other stockmen whose cattle he was handling, then came back to Gus and Dad, saying he had been bid so and so much per hundred pounds for Gus's cows, so and so much for Dad's. (Unfortunately, I do not remember the figures, but they were pitifully small compared with the prices of today.) He might have to accept these bids but would hold off until Armour's buyer had a look.

Meanwhile, our steer salesman had been showing our feeders to the farmers with whom Gus and Dad had talked. They wandered away, and he reported that he'd been bid so-and-so much with, in the case of Dad's cattle, seven head out at less money.

The business of buying and selling stock was moving along so swiftly that already cattle were moving toward the scales houses, so Art and I went to one of these to see what we could see. The scales platform or weighing pen, plank-floored and strongly walled with gates on two sides, would accommodate just one animal, to be weighed separately, or a couple of carloads. The commission houses had to wait their turn to get use of the scales, and herds were backed up all along the alleys, held apart by gates or merely by men.

The man in charge of a bunch would shove his herd into the scales pen and give the weigh master and his clerk all required information. But another man representing the stockyards company, but not connected with any commission firm, counted all cattle on the scales. For each animal, or dozen, or carload, the clerk made out a ticket giving the commission house, the owner of the cattle, the person to whom the sale was made, the kind, for example: one canner cow, fourteen two-year-old feeder steers, four bulls, seven vealers, twenty grass fat cows, and so on; the price per pound or per hundred pounds, the date, of course, and the weight.

These tickets were picked up by representatives of the various commission firms and dispatched to the firms' offices so the bookkeepers could be making out the proper sales sheets.

We saw some of the stock after it was weighed go on its own power up the ramps and into the packing houses.

Bunches of feeders went to other pens than those from which they had come, pens reserved for cattle to be shipped out. We learned they'd be weighing cattle all day and perhaps half the night. But the yards, except for a few bunches held over for one reason or another, would be cleared before another day to make room for another influx of cattle.

How true it was that the producer had nothing at all to do with his stock after they were loaded on the railroad until they were sold! Nothing except look and listen and wait. Art and I tired of waiting and went out to one of the business streets of South Omaha. We found dozens of stores where sharp salesmen practically dragged customers into their establishments.

My brother wanted to buy some clothing and thought he could do better in Omaha than in Laramie. That was a mistake. Art bought a fine shirt whose initial wearing was its last!

He also bought a winter coat made of canvas with a rubberized lining between the canvas and the blanket lining, which later proved about the coldest garment he'd ever tried to wear. The price was three dollars. Art had only two-fifty, so he tried to talk the salesman down, and finally turned to me.

"You can let me have fifty cents, John."

"I can. But I don't want to," I said. Turning to the salesman I said pleadingly, "Can't you just let him have it for two-fifty?"

Oh, how distressed the man looked. Almost heartbroken. "My boy, I'd do it in a minute if I could, but I can't."

He made me feel even sorrier for him than for Art, and when I forked over the fifty cents I was sure I'd done a good deed.

Back at the commission house's office we found Gus and Dad waiting for their sales sheets.

A "sales sheet" is an itemized statement of the entire transaction. The buyer or buyers who have purchased the stock pay the commission firm authorized to handle this sale. Then, after deducting all expenses, the firm pays the seller. In the majority of cases, however, the seller draws only a small amount of cash for current needs and stipulates that the commission firm send the balance to his bank, either to be credited to his account or to be applied on the mortgage against the stock.

"We're all sold out and ready to go up town as soon as our business is finished here," Gus reported. "I want to show you fellows the real Omaha. How about it, Jack?"

Dad looked at us, and what he saw—two ragged, unbarbered kids, who looked as if they belonged in some hinterland rather than on any city street—must have registered with him, for he said, "Not this trip, Gus. But the three of us will get our contracts converted into passenger tickets and meet you at the depot at eleven tonight."

I'd secretly hoped we could stay over one night and take in a show, for I'd heard there were wonderful theaters in Omaha. No such luck. Swanson did not return to Laramie with us, but Gus, Dad, Bill Kerr, Kimmons, Art and I left Omaha the same day we had arrived; and riding a swift passenger train, so unlike the slow, ponderous freights, was another wonderful experience.

Laramie now looked strangely small and only half-grown in height, but it was "good ol' Laramie" and mighty like home after having been " 'way outside."

THE LONELY WINTERS

For several years following Dad's purchase of the Mendenhall Ranch, he made no new deals either for land or cattle, just sort of rocking along on an even keel, our herd increasing in a normal manner. He did, however, take renewed interest in our horses and began to improve their breeding, something long dismissed with a disgusted, "What's the use? Loco'll get 'em."

Then, quite abruptly, one of my very earliest heroes, though I'd never seen him, Dillon H. Cross, reappeared in North Park.

Here was a big-framed, iron-muscled man; stubby fingers, powerful hands, square-cut face, grey mustache and heavy thatch of black hair streaked with grey. He was also a dusty man, for it never seemed to occur to him to brush his old black Stetson or his suit of clothes. No longer the bronc buster and horse tamer of old, he was still all horseman. He had come from "down the valley"—meaning from near Fort Collins—where he now had his home, and he had brought with him not one, but a half-dozen stallions to sell to North Parkers.

For many years following this initial venture, Dill Cross would reappear each spring (like Skinner, our vegetable peddler) with a new string of stallions, thus getting for himself the nickname of "Stud Horse" Cross.

As a matter of course, he put up overnight with Dad, and what an outfit this stud horse man had! First of all, a spring wagon, loaded with grain and horse blankets and other items necessary to horses. He and his helper rode the seat of this wagon and drove a team of rollicky stallions. To hold their heads apart and thus stop them from fighting, Dill made use of a "jockey stick," a small rod of hardwood or iron about two and a half feet long, equipped with a snap at both ends with which to fasten it to the bridle bits of each horse.

Behind the vehicle, wired crosswise to its tail end, was a pole projecting out three feet on either side, a sleek stallion tied to each end of it.

Wired to its center (D. H. Cross was a master in the use of baling wire) a long tongue ran back to an old hay rake, minus teeth and seat and everything else except framework and high wheels. This rattle-and-bang contraption was to keep Dill's stud horses separated, and behind it were tied two more stallions.

One explosive stallion is all an ordinary man cares to handle, but Dill Cross managed six of them as calmly as if they were kittens!

A few years later, when some North Parkers had shown interest in raising mules, Dill brought in a half-dozen jacks. Now jacks are three times more troublesome to handle than stallions, and when one starts to bray, every other jack will add its voice. So the jack outfit's approach was always heralded by a terrific racket.

On this first trip Dill had a pair of Standardbred trotting horses, one fine Thoroughbred, a Percheron, a Clyde, and an English Coach horse or Cleveland Bay, a beautifully proportioned dark bay animal weighing about twelve hundred pounds. Even before he had gotten his charges stalled, he said to Dad, "Old Coach'll be just the hoss for you, Jack."

Now most ranchers wanted to raise either heavy work horses such as Percheron, Clydesdale or Shire sires would produce, or the light, trim, quick saddle horses. There was still a big interest at this time in fancy trotting teams for light rigs, too. But after talking the matter over with Dill, Dad agreed that Old Coach would sire all-purpose horses and this stallion proved the best investment in horseflesh Dad could have made. We raised some splendid horses full of vigor, fire and stamina. What those broken to work lacked in size and weight they more than made up in agility and pep. And as either driving or saddle horses, they were tops.

After stopping overnight with Dad, Cross would move on to Walden and put up at Loucks' Livery Stable, where Loucks, a true horseman himself, helped him make sales.

Dave Hendrickson was with us that spring, and I remember Dave and Dad and Dill sitting around the bunkhouse stove, rehashing early days, recalling old timers.

"Wonder what became of Clyde Folsom?" Thus Dave.

Dad shook his head. "I don't even remember him."

Then Dill spoke in his slow easy drawl, "I don't know what became of him, Dave, but I remember that rooster, for I had a kinda funny introduction to him. I was riding along a draw leading to La Porte when I saw an old, white-bearded fella up on the hillside, digging a prospect hole. Just as I was abreast of him, I met another man on horseback who, as he passed me, made some remark about me.

"Can't now remember what it was, but it made me mad. I hipped around in my saddle and said, 'If you'll stop a minute, you such-and-so, I'll knock the whey outa you.'

"He stopped all right and we went at it. I had downed him before I saw this old fellow from up on the hillside had joined us, brandishing a long knife.

" 'That trouble maker's Clyde Folsom,' he told me. 'I come to help you if you need any help.'

" 'No I didn't need any help,' I said. 'But thanks, Mister.'

"Folsom got up and managed to climb on his horse. I climbed on mine and each of us went our way."

Dill was so silent a man that after I became acquainted with his splendid wife and family, I often wondered how he ever managed to propose to her. It was a rare treat when he'd loosen his tongue to tell one of his stories, another one of which runs:

"I was sitting in the store at Pinkhamton one night when there was quite a crowd there, doing a lot of drinking, and this big rooster, Jake Something-or-other, was abusing an old man who couldn't even talk back to Jake, let alone defend himself.

"I stood it as long as I could; then I walked over to them and said, 'You've bullied that old man enough. Talk to me a while.'

"Jake sorta reared back and growled, 'Lookin' for a fight, you meddlin' such-and-so?'

"I nodded and hit him. He hit the floor, got up slow and felt of himself and said, 'You couldn't do that if I'd a-been lookin'.'

"I said, 'Are you looking now?'

"He said, 'Yes,' and I hit him again. He didn't get up for quite a while. When he did at last, he went out and got on his horse and we never saw him again."

I have now written of several men who at one time or another were more or less my heroes. But I have scarcely mentioned either women or girls.

In my younger years girls played very little part. In their presence I was embarrassed and tongue-tied. With older women, too, I was shy and uneasy. Yet, although it was "sissy stuff" for a regular feller, I liked many of our schoolteachers and admired them a great deal. With very few exceptions, those teachers were splendid women in every resepct, and one among them comes clearly back to mind for special mention.

As secretary of the school board, Dad received the applications for the position of schoolteacher in our district, and it was astonishing how many letters came to him, this because in those days so few positions were open to young women who must make their own way. How this situation has changed!

During my boyhood, to become a teacher was far more desirable to a high class young woman than to become a waitress, for waitresses were dubbed "hashers" and "biscuit shooters." They had a long, hard fight to win the respect they hold nowadays.

Sometimes Dad would allow us boys to read these applications, and he'd have his own choice pretty well in mind before he met with the other members of the board when they selected the next teacher. They had already done this one spring when Dad received a late-arriving letter from a lady who said candidly that if she did not get this position she did not know what she would do. She must have work for the summer.

Something about the appeal got under Dad's skin, and suddenly he gave voice to a wild idea:

"Boys, I'm going to ask her if she'll cook and keep house for us. What do you think about it?" He laughed. "Of course, she'll turn me down."

" 'Course," we agreed. "But, golly, we'd sure like to have a cook."

Forthwith Dad wrote to the lady, outlining the setup, offered her twenty dollars per month plus board and room.

Lo! She accepted the offer—and then Dad was suddenly regretful, mighty uneasy, no doubt remembering past unhappy experiences with cooks, particularly with the first two we'd had after Mother's death. We had had better luck with man-and-wife couples since that time, but even so there had been one such team, which had a boy of seven, and they had given Dad some trouble.

Through the haying season we'd made out all right with this pair.

But the evening Dad paid them off, the man got his wagon loaded and when Dad got up the following morning, the fellow was gone. He was gone with his wagon and team, but wife and boy were still very much on the Payne ranch.

"What's the meaning of this, Mrs. E?" Dad asked grimly.

She replied, "He's tried to run out on me before. This time he's managed to do it . . . I suppose he figured this was a good place to leave me because you'd keep me on as your cook," she added resignedly.

She was a nice woman and a pretty good cook, so maybe Dad would have agreed if it hadn't been for the kid. Art and I couldn't stand this boy, nor could Dad.

Dad now hunched his shoulders and shoved out his jaw, and that certain flash of determination we knew well filled his eyes. Not stopping for breakfast, he got a horse, loped to the Scott place and borrowed a shotgun. Shells for it, too. Then he hit out after the deserting husband.

It wasn't difficult to trail Mr. E, and late that evening the wagon pulled back to the ranch, Dad riding alongside it with the shotgun across his saddle fork. Mr. E. called to his wife and kid; they climbed up to the seat, and he drove away with them.

"Gosh, Dad, you sure brought him back," Art said, awed. "He give you any trouble?"

"Would have if I hadn't taken along this shotgun," Dad replied, and began to grin as he relaxed. "I doubt that I could have licked that big bloke in a fist fight, but if I hadn't had the gun, I'd have had to do it."

Dad's uneasiness about what he might have let us in for by his proposition to this applicant for schoolteacher vanished, however, when, several days later, he met the stage and escorted Miss Carrie E. Disharoon to our home. Even we boys recognized at first sight that she was a well-educated, cultured woman of first-class family and background. She was not merely a lady; she was what the *neighbors* would call a lady.

She had a hobby of reading human character by one means and another, and I gradually learned that hands, particularly the lines in them, could tell a lot about a person; the shape of ears, nose and mouth something else. Especially you could tell a lot about a person by his mouth. Later, Miss D. told Dad she would not have ventured to come had she not been able to read his character from his hand-writing.

From the first we hit it off fine. All three of us liked Miss Disharoon. She'd come originally from Maryland and she introduced us to Southern cornbread, the best I have ever tasted, Southern fried chicken, naturally, and Maryland biscuits. Ranch life and cooking over a wood stove were at first mysteries to her, yet quite soon she caught on and became the best cook we had ever had.

But she stayed with us only the one summer, for that autumn she got the job of teaching the winter school at Cowdrey. I do not know how this came about, whether the teacher who had obtained the position resigned, or what happened. Anyway, Miss Disharoon moved to Cowdrey. To save money she rented two rooms in one of the buildings at Cowdrey and did her own cooking and housekeeping, setting herself up as a "bachelor girl."

That same autumn Arthur went East to visit our sisters and uncles and aunts, and I was left alone with Dad and Dave Hendrickson.

We boys had tried to keep up our "pard" relationship with the Blevins boys, but it hadn't worked out. They were now twelve miles away, had other important interests, and we seldom saw them any more. Nor did I have any particular pal among the new kids of our school, and, since I had already taken the eighth grade, I was not attending school this winter under Miss Disharoon.

Now, with Art gone, I believe I was the lonliest kid in America. Dad and Dave had no sympathy for me, nor could they have filled the gap left by my brother's absence if they had wanted to. The busy days weren't so bad, but, although I was a great reader, the evenings were almost unendurable. So pretty soon I saddled my horse, took off for Cowdrey, and tied the horse to the clothesline pole in front of Miss Disharoon's quarters. I found her glad to see me, for she too was lonely.

After this first visit, these pleasant evenings became a regular event two or three times a week. It was not "puppy love," a kid's infatuation for an older woman; rather, it was a very lonely small boy's seeking refuge and understanding he'd have found in a mother. This lady was good for me and good to me.

I wasn't tongue-tied or shy with her. We'd have great long talks, and she'd try to answer some of my perplexing problems, often, however, with one of the old aphorisms. For example, I said once, "I'd like to do something big and noble and great. But how can I when I don't ever have a chance?"

Miss D. answered, quoting, " 'Whatsoever the hand findeth to do, do it with all your might.' "

My other release from loneliness was in writing volumninous letters to Art. Too bad he did not stow away some of them, for how strange and funny they would sound now!

My good friend went away during the summer, but was back to teach school again the next winter. However, Art was home again and my visiting with Miss D. stopped. During this period all of the neighborhood rather expected we were going to acquire a stepmother. Dad was certainly romantically inclined and hopeful, but it didn't work out that way. However, he never did confide to us the inside story.

There came a winter when our father too went East to visit his daughters and our relatives, leaving Art and me all alone in full charge of ranch and cattle. What he thought about leaving two kids to shoulder this heavy responsibility, he never said. But we boys took it as a matter of course.

This ranch was our home, and that we'd be batching and fighting the intense cold and storms of winter did not dismay us. But to conserve firewood—we would think of that!—Art and I moved our beds into the living room and agreed to take turns at being first to get up; agreed, too, on which one would do what in the way of chores.

We estimated how many tons of hay we had in stacks on the home ranch, at the lower field three miles away, at the Mendenhall place, and on a neighboring ranch where Dad had bought hay from the Barnes boys. All told, there was barely enough to carry Dad's three hundred and fifty cattle through the winter, even if we could hold off feeding the main herd until after Jaunary first.

The horses, with the exception of one team and our two saddle ponies, were on pasture in the lower field. Pawing holes in the snow to get at the grass, these horses usually "rustled" all winter. We'd not worry about them. Regular chores and looking after and feeding the cattle were our big responsibility.

Although light snow had fallen, the main herd, on the home ranch, could still get plenty of grass, and live springs in big sloughs provided it with water. Every few days, however, we would ride around through this herd, and if we found weak or sick animals or springers (cows about to have calves), we'd take them to the corral where we already had established a "hospital herd." The big calves had been vaccinated earlier, yet fear of blackleg was always present, the vaccine of that day being no sure preventive of that dreaded scourge.

On these rides we'd take time to look at our traps, which we set at old carcasses, hoping to find a trapped coyote. Its pelt would bring money, something we rarely saw. But magpies, jackdaws and crows were always springing our traps. Too bad for them—and for us.

The day's work began with the alarm clock's imperative summons at six A.M. When it was my turn to roll out, I'd slowly realize that Dad wasn't there to start the fires, and I'd think: "Pitch dark, and cold! Oh, just to snuggle deeper into the blankets and . . ."

"Hi, kid! Your turn," would come Art's voice.

I now suppose that Art, being older, felt the responsibility far more than I. But, to his credit, he never tried to make me do more than my part, and I honestly tried to hold up my end. So, flinching, shivering as bare feet touched the cold floor, I'd scratch sulphur matches and light shavings and kindling readied before bedtime for fireplace and cook stove. Then to dress in front of the fireplace. It smoked and ate wood faster than a hungry cow ate hay, but oh! how welcome its comforting warmth!

Bundled in sweaters, heavy coats, overshoes, caps and mittens until we looked like midget Eskimos, we'd take lighted lantern and milk pails and force ourselves out into the below-zero darkness. But the little old cow barn was warm, and here the ranch cats would be loudly demanding their panful of fresh milk. Dad would have stripped the four cows in less time than it took us to milk two apiece —and we'd have been happy to let him do it!

Art usually cooked breakfast. Necessity had made him a good cook, and I liked his delicious pancakes with butter and corn syrup, oatmeal with real cream, slices of fried beef or pork—until the chickens began laying more eggs—and stewed dried fruit. Dried apples were the stand-by of those days, and the coffee was Arbuckle's, glazed but unground, at fifteen cents per pound-bag.

While big brother was preparing this meal, I'd clean cow and horse barns and turn the milk cows out into the big yard with our saddle horses. The team which was stabled I'd water and feed and harness. Although I knew the use of currycomb and brush, I never used them!

Breakfast over, one of us swept the house, believe it or not! The other skimmed pans of milk, often partly frozen, the cream going into a big crock and the pans of milk going atop the stove to warm for skim-milk calves and our two pigs. One washed the dishes and scalded milk pans and pails; the other dried them.

Dreading the outdoor cold—I was always stamping feet and pounding hands to keep warm—I'd want to dawdle over these house jobs, but it was time to feed pigs, chickens and skimmers, open water holes on the ice-bound creek, and shake down hay in the feed crib for the "hospital herd."

Art had built a set of corrals on the Scott place where we now lived, and adjoining the large main corral was another of his improvements, a tight shed into which we drove this herd every night during cold weather. With the big doors cloosed, the cattle themselves kept the shed warm enough for a newborn calf to survive.

Saving calves was most important, and if there was any doubt that a calf wasn't going to get up on its feet, we'd carry it into the house, put it on a gunnysack by the fireplace, rub it with another sack, feed it warmed milk, and eventually get it ready to go back to its mother.

At eight o'clock the outbound Walden-Laramie stage would be passing our mail box a quarter mile from the buildings, the tires of the heavy spring wagon howling as they bit into the thin coat of cold, dry snow. At this time we had rural mail delivery, and during the day one of us would contrive to get our mail and put outgoing letters in the sack for the stage driver to pick up that evening.

Chores finished, we hitched the team to the hayrack sled and hauled hay for the stock in the corral and for the hay barn. Then we went out to bring in firewood. Not yet had our winter woodpile been built up, and although many ranchmen provided good logs from the mountain forests, we burned old fence poles and bucks which had been replaced with new.

Our noon dinner we prepared as quickly as possible, and, leaving dishes unwashed we hurried back to work, for rustling plenty of firewood was a must. Although work was not yet driving us hard and we could knock off early, visit a neighbor, or even take in some event like a dance or a "social," somehow we did not feel justified in neglecting our job.

At approximately four-thirty the inbound stage would come in sight, and perhaps a six-horse, two-wagon freight outfit would rumble along the road. Ranchmen hauled their winter supplies home from Laramie early in the fall, but regular freighters who supplied the stores in Walden worked the year round.

Evening chores included cutting firewood. The dull, crosscut saw and beaten-out old axe seemed to return our hatred for the job. The fireplace, with its insatiable appetite, had reason to gloat. It not only devoured the wood we stuffed into it, but delighted in smoking us out of the house as well.

Lamps and lanterns, too, made slaves of us; kerosene containers always empty, wicks out of kilter, chimneys sooty and oh! so easy to break!

Supper by lamplight did not end the day's work. We loved to read and had plenty of books, papers and magazines, including *The Youth's Companion*. But with Dad gone, could we sit down to read and aggravate our chilblains by toasting our feet? No! Next day's dinner and supper required planning and cooking at night.

In a cellar—another improvement my brother had built—protected from freezing were potatoes and onions, other vegetables and canned tomatoes. The storeroom held staple foods unaffected by freezing and the carcasses of a hog and a beef, frozen flint-hard. But hungry, growing boys managed to saw or hack chunks and steaks from quarters of both beef and pork.

Supper over, we boiled meat, beans, spuds, dried fruit and so on, made cornmeal mush, and occasionally baked light bread. Usually we found it impossible to keep the dough warm enough for good results, and the bread's rock-like consistency defied human teeth. But the pigs went for it, and Art's biscuits, corn bread and pancakes were always "lickin' good," so we made out satisfactorily.

When the cream crock was full we would churn and work and mold the butter. Before this, we had disliked any job which seemed dairy-farmerish. But now we found ourselves wishing the cream crock would fill up faster. Why? Because, by sending all surplus butter by stage to the Laramie Grocery Company we got back its value in trade—"goodies" not included in our regular line of grub!

Saturday night was bath night, a traditional rite I had always supposed. We used the laundry tub, took turns at being first to scrub, and then in the same water washed out shirts, underwear, towels, socks.

We were bone-weary kids before we could at last fall into bed, not forgetting to put the screen in front of the fireplace, least a spark fly out and set the house on fire, yet once in awhile neglecting to fix shavings and kindling, which the first one up was sure to regret bitterly.

The novelty of being entirely on our own carried us through December's clear, biting-cold days, and being busy kept us from feeling too lonely. Then January ushered in a real storm with eight or ten inches of fresh snow covering the grass. Grazing the cattle was at an end; we must begin to feed them hay.

First of all we corralled the main herd and weaned all big calves, holding these in the corral, and turning out of it the mother cows and other stock. Some one in Cowdrey, three miles away, said the racket of cows bawling to calves and calves bawling to cows kept him from sleeping. We were much closer, but it didn't interfere with our sleep!

The next morning we were up an hour earlier than usual and moving the main herd to the Barnes ranch. I drove the hayrack, on which was a small jag of hay to induce the cattle to follow me. Art, on horseback, rope-whipped the stock away from the corral and out on the trail. Finally we got the herd into Barnes' field, opened a haystack and hauled out and scattered three loads of hay and then took another load home.

By dark, however, the cattle, having broken the fence, were back home, bawling and crowding around the corral. We'd had no dinner that day, and I was so dragged out and disgusted I was ready to quit.

"Art, we just can't go on this way. We've got to get help."

"Ask for help? Admit we're licked? Not much!"

"We'd feel queer about it, but ... "

"You going to let Dad down?"

"I hadn't thought of it like that. No. Sure not."

Wearily, but doggedly, we moved those cattle to the Barnes ranch again and fixed the fence so this time they didn't come home. Now the job demanded everything we had, every day, with no letup. Bright day, stormy day, punishing cold day, this inexorable amount of work had to be done even if it took us far into the night!

Once we broke our routine to go to a neighborhood all-night dance. Daybreak found us stupid, numb, dead on our feet, but the cattle must be fed, and we fed them.

Relentless winter, the sameness of our meals, and the job, which had become a monotonous grind, were getting us down when our morale got an unexpected boost. Four men with team, sled and camp outfit came past the ranch and asked if they might camp at the Mendenhall place and get hay for their horses.

We knew what they were after. Deer, driven out of the mountains by winter's snow, were always plentiful along the foothills and hogbacks at this ranch. So we told them, "Sure, that's okay."

When the men returned three days later, they gave us the carcass of a two-prong buck. What a welcome change in the bill of fare was that venison.

We tried to tan this deer's hide, but with most disappointing results. Our buckskin was useful only as a rawhide bottom for a chair.

We had marked off twenty-two days of January when we experienced the most ruthless ordeal of the winter. We were at a haystack a full mile from the buildings when all at once we heard the distant roar of wind and saw, marching down from the north, a white wall of storm. It was as terrifying as the cyclones of which we had often heard. Art yelled, "Get in the hayrack. Quick! If that hits us before we get home, we'll be lost!"

"Lost?" I gulped. "That means frozen to death?"

Art was whipping the team to a lope when the wind hit us. It swept the hay out of the rack, and would have taken us with it if we hadn't been hanging onto the rack. Another moment and the flying snow was so thick we could see nothing.

I thought numbly, "This is the end. Winter wins the fight." But Art got down on the doubletrees directly behind the team to try to see the trail and to keep the horses on it, and it was the wise old team that eventually saved us, taking themselves and us home!

Except for doing the most necessary chores and rustling firewood, which proved a savage ordeal, we stayed indoors for three full days. We had the assurance that the main herd of cattle were safe in a big shed, and the corral stock also were sheltered. The horses in the lower field were exposed to the storm, but they would mrely hump up, rumps to wind, and take it.

When at last the wind died and the clouds lifted, "we looked upon a world unknown, or nothing we could call our own." Even the stage had been stopped.

But now it came right past the ranch buildings with a six-horse team ahead of it to break trail. "Sure glad to see you kids made out all right," the driver called. "Say, we'll break trail past the Barnes ranch. Get your team and come along, so you can feed your cattle."

By working until midnight we got hay out to all of our hollow-flanked cattle. None had perished in the storm!

A week later the snow had settled, and our routine was back to normal when Dad got off the inbound stage. "Hello, boys! Glad I'm home?"

"Oh, we're making out all right," Art replied. But, of course, we were glad he had come home.

And later, after he had had a chance to see the stock, it was heart-warming to hear him say, "You've done a good job. I've reason to be mighty proud of you kids!"

FEATHERBED COWBOYS

In the process of growing up and becoming more useful, at last I made a trip to Laramie with a two-horse team and wagon, trailing along in the dust behind Art's four-horse outfit. We were, by this time, using a more direct road from Mountain Home to Wood's Landing. This ran through miles of magnificent lodgepole pines, and so narrow was the right-of-way that wheel hubs often scraped these pines.

It was perhaps nothing short of providential that, while crossing the railroad tracks in Laramie, I did not have a bangup runaway. But I didn't. I got home safely too—a long step toward a goal yet to be reached. To make the grade as a real teamster, or "skinner," I must successfully handle a four or a six-horse team.

One event of that first trip stands out in memory. I'd sent to a mail order house for a wide-brimmed, flat-crowned "Never Flop" cowboy hat. It was a dinger, but I was scared to wear it in Dad's presence. He might do more than snort and make barbed remarks; he might grab "Never Flop" and poke it into the stove.

So, as we left the ranch, I hid it in the wagon and wore my regular hat. Then, safely away, out came Never Flop and onto my head. Up along the neck of the Park, we drew near to where Bob Coe, who often took a job as one of the country road overseers, was working on the road. His son, Lindsey, had returned to the Park, and Art and I had met this likeable young man, an expert cowpuncher, bronc

259

buster and teamster. More than all this, Lindsey was a keen-witted humorist and natural-born story teller. But, doggone him, he surely could razz a fellow!

"Ockoo!" I thought. "If Lindsey sees this hat, I'll be in for it. He'll have everybody laughing at me."

So off came Never Flop, to be hidden again, and back on my ragged hair went the old lid until after we were safely past Bob and Lindsey Coe and their road crew. But in Laramie I was the most conspicuous kid in town—wearing Never Flop.

It was inevitable that Dad should at last catch me wearing it, but, to my relief, he let the matter drop with a disgusted, "How crazy can kids get!"

Yes, how crazy can kids get?

Following my initial trip to Laramie with a beef herd, I made a hand on this job every autumn. In fact, as time went on, I'd make two, three or even four such trips between September first and December. Sometimes these herds were made up by many owners; again just Gus and I, or Dad and I, would take the herd through. On one occasion Norm McDonald threw in with Gus and Dad, Norm, Gus and myself being the cowpunchers on this drive. Then Gus and Norm went on with the cattle to Omaha and I brought home the saddle horses. The men would get home by stage.

As was always the case, I didn't have much money, but I'd spent all I had, forgetting to save out enough to buy breakfast at the Kuster Hotel on the morning I was to leave for home.

I tried to get an early start, but it must have been eight o'clock before I got out of Laramie. My mount was the afore-mentioned Charlie. Gus had ridden George, one of his best horses, and Norm's mount was a stumble-footed old black plug. I led these two horses out of Laramie, then tied up the bridle reins to the saddles and drove them ahead of me.

The wiggling of empty saddles always causes the blankets to creep and crawl backwards, so before long the saddle blankets on the two loose horses worked free and hit the ground. I caught the nags, put the blankets back in place, and took the road again. Half an hour later I was doing the same thing all over and losing a lot of time.

Eventually I solved the problem by cinching the empty saddles on the horses, minus blankets, and tying the blankets to the saddles. Then—jiggle-jig- jigglety! at the cow pony's jog trot we went on and on across the endless Laramie Plains, this young cowboy growing emptier and hungrier every mile. But he was determined to ride home —fifty-six miles—in just one day, for the simple reason that many cowmen and punchers did make this ride—Laramie to Clark's road ranch or to Pinkhamton or to Jack Payne's or farther in one day.

(Let me hasten to say that this ride was not considered as unusual. Far from it. Quite often John Kimmons, when returning from Omaha, took his horse from the stable in Laramie and rode to Fort Collins in one day to see his wife and family who made their home in Collins because the children must be sent to school. This was about a seventy-mile ride. All my life I had heard how the Cross boys would either ride or drive from their North Park ranch to Fort Collins, one hundred and ten miles, from "sun to sun." These stories were true, and to my certain knowledge Victor Hanson on one occasion rode one horse from Fort Collins to his Park ranch in one day, plus half the night. Even so, for the average cow horse and the average rider fifty miles in ten or twelve hours is an ordeal.

I might have stopped at Lund's or at Wood's Landing for dinner and had it charged, but this did not occur to me. I had no money, road ranches demanded money, so, although Norm's plug was determined to stop at every ranch we passed and I had to beat his tail off with a doubled rope to get him on the trail again, I passed up Wood's Landing.

No other stopping place now short of Clark's and it was three o'clock in the afternoon. On and on and on through the endless timber, with Charlie, to my disappointment, showing weariness, but not nearly as great as that of one breakfastless, dinnerless boy.

It was long past dark and snowing when at last I reached Mountain Home. No one was living at this place, but across from the house stood a big barn, its door open. I led the horses into it, and I would have fed them and buried myself in a manger, just too darned tired to go on, if there had been any hay in the barn.

The situation being what it was, I let the horses rest for a half hour or so and hit the road again. Snowing steadily, no travel on the dark road. I saw the lights of Clark's ranch where I could have stopped. But I'd started to make this ride in one day, and I'd do it. Then when other people bragged about their long rides, I could tell what I'd done!

Norm's plug was now so completely fagged I had to slow down, and those last nine miles must have taken three hours. At last, in the snowstorm, home, the house all dark, Dad and Art in bed. I turned Gus's and Norm's horses out to pasture, but I stalled Charlie, and fed him a mangerful of hay before I wobbled to the house, stumbling and staggering. I thought, "Gosh, I'm hungry! Ought to get something to eat, but I'm too awful tired to fix anything . . . Just bed, bed, bed. But oh, boy! I rode from Laramie in one day!"

How crazy can kids get?

Mention of Norm McDonald brings to mind a much more interesting character than Norm himself, namely Gene McDonald, who always spoke of Norm as, "My brother No'h McDonald."

These brothers were as Eastern as the Barnes boys and Dwinell, but they had come from Maine and spoke with a different accent from the Massachusetts men. Both Norm's and Gene's pet expletive was, "By Jawge." They owned a small ranch on the Michigan just above Cowdrey's old place and grazed their range cattle in the Sand Hills. They also ran a small dairy herd and made butter.

Norm, a married man, made all decisions, attended to all business matters, and these heavy duties, plus apparently the necessity of going to town often and of visiting the neighbors, kept Norm fully occupied. His hands were completely uncalloused. Gene's were the opposite, for they were an excellent example of a willing team—Gene willing to work and Norm willing to let him.

In fact, so willing was Norm to let Gene do the work that, when Gene went to town one winter day and left brother Norm to feed their cattle, Norm decided:

"By Jawge, those cattle were well fed yesterday, so I'll give 'em a chance to rest their stomachs and pick the foxtail out of their teeth today."

Roundups conducted by the big outfits no longer bothered with the Sand Hills, but every summer all the people who grazed stock in this area would hold what Art and I called, "A granger roundup."

While Art and I were riding on one of these, we fell in with Norm, and we were pushing a herd along toward the bunch ground when a calf broke back right past Norm. He should have turned it; instead, he called to me, "Get that calf, boy! My horse can't run."

I glared, thinking, "Probably the reason you ride such a no-good plug is to get out of doing any hard work."

Gene, however, never complained about doing the work. Norm was his hero, and he almost reverenced his brother's wife, often saying, "By Jawge, M's a mighty fine woman."

Once in a while Gene would get hold of enough money to go to

Walden and stage a moderate spree, his only diversion. Once when he was three seas over, a bully began picking on him. Gene "rared up" and told the bully, "By Jawge, if my broth' No'h was here, he'd hit you and he'd hit you ha'd."

This so amused the bully he burst out laughing, and for years thereafter North Parkers were quoting, "If my broth' No'h was here, he'd do so-and-so."

After my first camping experience with Mr. Hadden, I was sold on pack horse trips. While hunting for cattle and exploring our Beaver Creek range I made many such trips, with Dad and sometimes with both Dad and Gus.

This exploring helped us to find more range for the Payne and Dwinell cattle, and since cowmen seldom have enough grass, we immediately moved cattle to these new areas to take possession before someone else did. One such area lay east of the Platte River at Six Mile, a great, rough, as yet ungrazed, basin which Mr. Hadden had also discovered. He and Dad and Gus believed we could graze cattle there late in the autumn, thereby saving grass at home which would be invaluable in the spring. So we organized a cattle-moving expedition, and realizing darned well that our stock would hike out for home as the first snowstorm hit them, plans were made for me and another rider to camp somewhere in the area and ride herd.

I entertained the hope that Gus would hire a real cowhand to be my companion. That hope died when he announced that his right-at-this-time cowboy, Fred Endeman, would help me.

Fred, a tenderfoot, came of a good family, his father being a prominent physician in New York City who had given Freddy a good education and other advantages, including a liberal allowance with which the young man attempted to make the grade as a real playboy. In other words, Freddy was going to the dogs when his desperate father asked Gus, whom he knew, to give the youth work on his ranch and to try to reform him.

This was the same situation as that which took place with worthless sons of prominent English families. They'd be dispatched to the far West in an attempt to reform them, or perhaps to get rid of them. Wyoming was alive with such young Englishmen, and one enterprising fellow, who must have been a Yankee to think of such a thing, opened his ranch near Laramie as a school to teach them ranching.

He merely put the tenderfoot to work and not only got all of his ranch work—fencing, manure hauling, ditching, irrigating, building, haying, etc.—done, but was also paid by those who did the work!

Anyway, it was not strange that Gus should assume the responsibility of Freddy, because Gus's idea of thrift sometimes reached ridiculous extremes. He would not pay top wages for hired help, so he often employed strange characters.

Freddy at his best was less than half a man. But Gus got him for twenty bucks a month and had initiated him as a cowboy.

Gus also tried to make a cook of Freddy, having him drive a wagon on a trip to Laramie with a herd. One incident of this trip sticks in my mind: Gus, Art and I were bringing the herd up the neck of the Park, intending to put up for the first night at Clark's Road Ranch. Freddy had gone ahead with the wagon and snow had started falling, so Gus told me to go and help him get supper.

Freddy had pulled the wagon up close to Clark's bunkhouse, had stalled the team, and had somehow managed to start a sickly fire. I found him standing idle while "Splut! Splut!" the snow hit the fire, almost putting it out.

He looked up, saw me, pulled a long face and said dolefully, "Gus was sure we had everything we'd need, but we haven't got a water bucket or a dishpan. Worse still, we *forgot the most important thing.*"

"What's that, Fred?"

"A *can opener* . . . How can I get supper when I can't open any of these cans?"

"The most important thing" a can opener! I doubled up and roared with laughter. He had never opened a can with an axe, a hatchet, a butcher knife or his jackknife! But he soon learned how it was done.

While Freddy must at times have irritated Gus a great deal, he was also a constant source of amusement to both Dad and Gus. To Freddy every little mishap was pathetically tragic; to Gus it was uproariously funny as happening to Freddy the greenhorn, the misfit with whom I was to camp and herd cattle on Six Mile.

Our cattle-moving project got off to a bad start simply because we were hampered by too many bosses. Mr. Hadden had strongly promoted the idea, and since any area bordering the Platte was definitely his territory, he elected himself as boss. In such matters Dad usually bowed out in Gus's favor, but this time he didn't, nor was Gus willing to have his authority usurped by either Dad or the Britisher.

The result of this smouldering conflict was that we attempted to do too much the first day.

Dad loaded a wagon with rock salt, a liberal supply of grub, including many items which Mr. Hadden would not have considered "the necessities of life," cooking utensils and camp equipment, two tents—Mr. Hadden's small A-shaped tent and a good wall tent supplied by Gus—and bedding.

He selected for his team a pair of horses which could be ridden or packed as well as driven, because all supplies and equipment must be transferred to pack horses to make the final four or five miles into the Six Mile Basin from the Beaver Creek side.

Early in the morning the entire outfit—Dad's wagon and cowboys Gus, Freddy, Mr. Hadden and I got away from the Payne ranch, where I'm sure Arthur was quite happy that he'd been elected to stay at home. Dad made it to the North Fork of the Elkhorn, the end of the wagon trail, by four o'clock in the afternoon.

Meanwhile we four cowpunchers had rounded up all the cattle we could find on Beaver Creek, about two hundred head, and had driven them to this same North Fork of the Elkhorn on the way to Six Mile Basin. This took time, a great deal of yelling and pounding and hard riding, for the cattle were all set to go home; consequently, attempts to drive them in the opposite direction met with stubborn opposition. And a cow brute can be every bit as ornery and stubborn as either a mule or a burro. When we reached the place where Dad had stopped, the critters simply balked and told us in cow language where we could go.

Mr. Hadden, who'd been tearing around like a wild man, trying to whoop the "stupid beasts" along, either bawled out or cussed out Freddy, who then told me in a great huff, "Your Englishman insulted me."

I laughed and said, "Aw, forget it." But he was really burning, and Gus was also in a bad humor.

I asked him, "What'll we do? Night herd these dogies?"

"Perhaps when Jack and Hadden string out on the trail ahead of 'em with the pack horses, we can get the herd going again," he replied.

So, Gus and Freddy and I held the cattle in a bunch while Dad and Mr. Hadden, who had volunteered to do this job, packed our equipment on three horses, the team and Hadden's saddle horse, Tom.

Now, Mr. Hadden had his own bed, Freddy and I one each, all

three small rolls. But Gus and Dad decided they were going to sleep in comfort and had brought along a full size mattress. Mattress, plus quilts, blankets, pillows and tarpaulin, made a roll almost three feet in dameter and the width of the mattress, four and a half feet, in length.

This is the sort of bedroll that an old-time roundup cook would refuse to load on his chuck wagon, and Mr. Hadden's opinion of it, as expressed at the ranch, was equally scornful and contempuous, "Aw, you chaps must be featherbed cowboys!" he had snorted.

I was not close enough to overhear the argument when Dad and Mr. Hadden tried to put this bed on a horse, but both men lost their tempers.

Even so, they got started along the trail, leading three packed horses on foot, the controversial bed thrown crosswise over a saddle and lashed down, but sticking out two or three feet on either side of the horse—a hazard going through narrow places along the timber-bordered trail.

Darkness was coming on fast, but Gus, Freddy and I managed to string the cattle out behind the pack outfit, Gus taking the point.

Immediately after we got into the pines, a fellow could not see much of anything except the mass of cattle, but fortunately, it was open, standing timber reasonably free of dead stuff and undergrowth. Freddy and I kept whacking the cattle along, going on and on until I began to get worried. I'd been over this trail and knew we had about three miles of forest, then we should come out to an open ridge, a gulch at the right with a big mountain beyond it, another gulch at the left which quite soon widened out to more open country.

"Fred," I called. "I can't see any sign of a trail. Can you?"

He was still grumpy. "Why ask me? I'm not supposed to know a trail if I saw one. Are we lost?"

"W-e-ll, if we are it's Gus's fault. I've heard him holler every once in a while. So he is still pointing 'em."

"Where were that—that Englishman—and your father going to camp?"

"I don't know."

"Ha, you don't even know where they'll be!" Freddy's laugh was hollow and mirthless. "So now we're lost somewhere in the Wyoming mountains and we haven't got a firearm to protect ourselves from wild animals."

"Cheer up. I ain't admitted we're lost."

"But we are. Breakfast at six o'clock. In the saddle all day. No lunch, and now this. I'm so tired I don't give a d--- what happens, though."

"Humph! I'm more bothered about worn-out horses than tired men. Keep qnockin'. Surely we'll be out of this timber soon."

And we did come to open country. But I at once realized something was wrong. Here we were on a big sagebrush side hill with a stream deep in a gulch at our left.

Gus materialized and called, "John, where can Hadden and your dad be? Is this the right place? I'm completely turned around."

"Ha ha, you're not the only one!" said Freddy. "This'd be funny," he added, "if I was the only one lost. You'd get a big laugh, Gus. But now ... "

"Are you as turned around as I am?" Gus asked me.

"No," I said. "When was the last time you either saw or heard the pack horses?"

"I lost all sight and sound of them soon after we started through the timber. Why?"

"Well, what's happened is the cattle swung off to the left, and we have come through timber until we are now away down toward the Plate—on the North Fork of the Elkhorn."

"What?" said Gus, then, "Gorry! Are you sure of that, John?"

"Dead sure," I asserted. "And now, with our horses 'most all in, I see no sense in fighting these cattle anymore. We can pick 'em up toworrow. Either we lie out the rest of the night or try to find the new camp. Which'll it be, Gus?"

"Gorry, I still can't believe ... " Gus began, then, "I don't want to lie out or herd cattle the rest of the night. If you really believe you can find the right place and the camp Hadden and Jack will have made, lead out."

I led out, not through the timber, but up the creek valley. Gus and Freddy followed Indian file and neither was a very jaunty figure on horseback. Probably I wasn't either. I was mad that we'd been thwarted; and I was so hungry and tired I was one big ache. But back I led the men to the place where Dad's wagon stood all alone and then through the dark forest, but on the right trail, to the Six Mile Basin.

Just as we reached an open ridge we met Dad. "Where're the cattle? What happened to you fellows?"

267

Freddy laughed and spoke up, "Mr Payne, Gus got lost, and the next time he starts making fun of me I'll remind him of it!"

"That so, Fred? Well, Hadden said if you were lost it would serve you right to stay out all night. But I thought I should try to find you . . . Come on to camp. Gus, in spite of Hadden, we've got a good bed to sleep in."

As we rode along, I learned from Dad that since we had last been in this area Charlie Porter had built a cabin for a "trapper's shanty" on this same ridge we were following, and he had been as surprised to see Hadden and Dad as they'd been to see him. Porter had suggested they make camp in the gulch just north of his cabin at the foot of a jackpine-covered hillside. Since this spot would be "behind the cattle" once we did get them onto the new range, they had followed his suggestion.

And were Gus, Freddy and I happy to see a campfire, and, after we had unsaddled and picketed our weary horses, to fill up on hot coffee, fresh bread brought from the ranch, fried beefsteak and a variety of canned items!

Porter was there with Mr. Hadden. They had heard us coming and hurried up a meal for us. Then, perhaps due to the magic of the campfire, to the fact that we had company present, and to the good feeling of well-filled stomachs, all tensions relaxed. We began laughing and joking about the day's ordeal.

When Freddy suddenly asked, "Where's the privy?" and Mr. Hadden replied, "Privy, man? You've got the whole state of Wyoming!" everybody howled and all hard feelings were forgotten.

THE MAN WHO KNEW ANIMALS

The following day we picked up the cattle we had dropped in the night and succeeded in driving this herd to its new range. We put in four more days rounding up sections of our original range each day, bringing more and more cattle into Six Mile Basin. Then Dad and Gus helped to pack in the rock salt from the wagon and establish salt licks. (Salting cattle always helps to hold them on an area which is new to them.) This done, they went home, taking the wagon and—to be sure—their mattress bed with them.

Mr. Hadden stayed on with Freddy and me another week to do some hunting and fishing. Although he failed to kill a deer, he provided us with more grouse, snowshoe and cottontail rabbits than we could eat.

Meanwhile Freddy and I were busy and exasperated cowboys. We'd thought we had the cattle blocked from getting out the same way they came, the way they would try to escape. But they outsmarted us by working their way through dense timber, often cluttered with windfalls, to get back to the Elkhorn and Beaver Creeks. They were real sneaky about it, doing it at night.

Day after day we'd go out to Beaver Creek where we'd overtake a homeward-bound herd and bring it back. This was the same method John Schultz and I had used on the theory that after a time the brutes would decide to settle down in their new environment. But although we did hold those cattle for a full six weeks on Six

Mile, they never stopped giving us plenty to do and were never contented.

One reason for this restless discontent was the time of year, winter coming and instinct telling the dumb brutes it was time to go home. Every few days we'd get a light snow storm, a mere two or three inches, but sufficient to stir up the cattle and start them moving — homeward. If we had had a stem-winder of a storm, two or three feet of the white stuff, our job would have ended abruptly with rounding up all animals that did not have enough sense to hike out of heir own accord and driving them home.

Another major reason the cattle were so uneasy in this big, rough area where there was plenty of water, grass and shelter, was that this was bear country. Neither cattle nor horses like bears as close neighbors.

I never actually saw even one bear, but at chokecherry patches which they trampled down to get the berries, I'd see their tracks and smoking hot bear sign, and also find old rotten logs they had ripped apart to get ants. Like hogs, bears will eat almost anything, but they are not naturally cattle killers and we lost no cattle to them.

When I had first ridden range with Schultz, we'd had a cabin, stove, bunk, cupboard, table and makshift chairs. Freddy and I had none of these — merely a couple of tents, and our beds laid on the ground. We sat on the ground, when it wasn't covered with snow or sopping wet, and our table was Mother Earth.

All cooking was done out-of-doors, sunshine or storm, over an open wood fire, and to eat we squatted on our bootheels or sat by the fire, plates on laps or on the ground. We had a granite-ware kettle for cooking dried fruit, a black iron pot for boiling vegetables, frying pans, coffeepot, water pail, wash basin, dishpan and two good Dutch ovens. One of these I used for the bread oven, the other for frying and roasting meat and all other needs.

I seldom made frying-pan bread, but did become quite expert at making Dutch-oven biscuits; a tricky art, but through trial and error, I learned to put exactly the right amount of coals and ashes under the oven to cook and brown the biscuits quickly on the underside without burning them; also to sense when the lid was hot enough and slap it on the oven and shovel the right amout of live coals atop it for best results. To heat the lid it was placed right in the fire. I even made pies in the Dutch oven, and also used it for a bean pot, burying the oven in ashes and dirt and live coals so the beans would slowly simmer all night long.

Freddy and I got along together well enough. But he had no real interest in punching cows or in anything Western, his sole ambition being to get back to New York City and take up his old life again. This interlude was something to be endured, and, by enduring it, he thought of himself as a martyr. He was here and suffering only because his father had ordered it and because the old tyrant refused to send him money to come home.

As for me, my great ambition was to become a real cowhand, so, when I'd get tired and fed up with the job, I'd tell myself this wasn't the right attitude. B'gosh, I was punching cows, learning something about the ornery critters all the time and learning to cook out-of-doors!

I was also getting acquainted with a wonderful man and acquiring a new friend, Charlie Porter. How strangely these things come about. I'd known the man slightly, knew that he had a wife and two small sons, one home near Mountain Home Park and another house at a mine down along the crest of the Medicine Bow Range, and I'd heard a stage driver say, "That Porter must be part Indian. Goes off hunting and fishing, trapping, prospecting all by himself. Leaves his family alone, but does make a good living for them."

By coincidence, we had found Porter here in the Six Mile country, and we now had for a close neighbor this lone wolf prospector, hunter and trapper. A stocky man, not tall, but powerfully built, all muscle and bone, with big, square-cut hands and square-cut face, of a reddish complexion, spotted with freckles.

The man's eyes might give a stranger the creeps, for he had casts in both, making them appear to be crossed. But there was nothing wrong with his vision, particularly when he trained his right eye along the sights of his high power rifle with which he was the kind of marksman who never wastes a bullet.

He owned no horses, got around on his own feet, and, although he wore high-laced heavy boots studded with hobnails, he could glide through the woods as silently as a fox, and how he could cover the miles, rough going or smooth!

From his home, Charlie and his wife and boys had brought his outfit — food, equipment, bedding, traps — to this spot on a small, very narrow, homemade wagon, the family staying on a few days while he threw up the cabin. This was a tiny affair, only about nine feet by twelve, built of fallen logs he sawed off in the windfall on the jackpine-studdend ridge. The dirt to cover its pole roof he had dug from the earth on either side of this shanty, and daubed the cracks with a wooden trowel. No window, only a hole in the door, covered with a gunny sack. To get the lumber for this door he had walked three or four miles to the Platte and salvaged planks and boards flood waters had left strewn along its banks.

His bunk extended full width across the back of the cabin, with room under it to pile a lot of articles. His table and bench, also made of boards salvaged from the Platte, took up the east wall, and in the southwest corner he'd built of rocks an inside fireplace. This smoked badly, but he cooked over it, and it gave his only light at night.

Why was he here, and why had he built this shanty? Because he had cleaned out the fur-bearing animals near his home but had found that this Six Mile area had so far been untouched by trappers. As I've mentioned, he certainly got around on foot. As if it were his own front yard, he knew every niche and corner, valley, park, stream, hill and mountain of our cattle range, as well as far more territory than this alone.

With pack horse outfit Dad and I had explored a certain nameless little stream, finding along it fresh beaver work, new beaver dams and houses by the dozen, whereas along other streams of our range all beaver work was old and abandoned. We'd supposed no one else knew about this beaver colony. But Charlie Porter did, and his early fall project was to trap those beavers. Then, as winter came, he'd go after mink and weasels, foxes, martin, bobcats, lynx and coyotes.

He told me there were no grizzlies in this area and that the small black bears, which were plentiful, were not worth the bother of trapping them. A bear trap must be enclosed in a stout log pen with an entrance so small that deer, horses or cattle could not get inside it. Notices must be posted to warn people so no foolish greenhorn or his dog would get caught, for a bear trap is a wicked thing. Its jaws are spiked, it weighs at least fifty pounds, and clamps must be used to press down its springs to set it. Such a trap will break a man's ankle, and, if caught it it, he is powerless to free himself.

In Porter, Mr. Hadden found another man like himself, who loved to get alone, far from civilization, and in hunting, fishing, exploring, find something priceless—relaxation, enjoyment and strange contentment. This love of the outdoors and of adventure formed the basis for a mutual interest, and from the first they cottoned to one anther as if they were old cronies.

I see them now, those two men so unlike in background, early training and education, for although Charlie was not illiterate, he boasted mighty little "book learning." Sitting by the fire at night,

Hadden so intensely interested in Porter's stories, told in a soft and whispery voice, that he even put aside the *London Times*.

"That man," Mr. Hadden told me later, "knows more about wild animals than anyone I've ever met. Animals of the Rocky Mountains," he amplified. "Most of these peculiar chaps are so secretive they won't tell you anything. But he will."

Yes, Porter knew animals far better than men whose books I had read. His tracking skill was a source of amazement to me, and merely by reading "trail sign" he could tell a fellow what a lynx, for example, had been doing; even what he'd been thinking. Rightly or wrongly, Porter gave all wild animals credit for thought processes, even for ability to reason, or as he phrased it, "Figure things out." His was a kinship with the wild life and with Nature which Mr. Hadden had never attained.

But Charlie Porter was much more than a mere trapper and hunter. He was familiar with every angle of prospecting and mining; yet, like so many others, he had failed to make the "big strike." He was also an expert blacksmith and tool sharpener—one who sharpens and tempers the drills for hard rock mining, a trade in itself.

As a lumberjack he was the equal of any Swede at swinging an axe, and a first class carpenter to boot. The house at his mine was in an area where the snowfall was heavy, and above its roof, dirt-covered for warmth, he had built another, more sharply-pitched shingle roof so the snow would slide off it. These shingles, split with an axe from selected blocks of wood, were so smooth, so perfect they were actually better than the manufactured product.

Making skis was one of his specialties, for as Porter himself said, "I kin do anything," and if that "anything" was work with his hands he surely could.

But what gripped my interest and held my admiration, as an impressionable kid who had read *The Leather Stocking Tales* and stories about Daniel Boone and other great American adventurers, was that here in the flesh was a survivor of an era already past and gone, the true frontiersman.

Every morning he was up and gone at daybreak, or before, a small packsack on his shoulders containing his lunch, and maybe a trap or two, and other items: sheath knife and hatchet at his belt, rifle across a shoulder. As days and weeks passed, beaver and other pelts began to pile up at his cabin. Evenings, I'd be in his shanty visiting him, or he'd be at our fire visiting Freddy and me.

I'd sent Freddy to the home ranch to bring back winter clothing and a pack-horse load of grub. Mr. Hadden had gone by this time, so one horse Freddy brought back to our camp was old Tom. This gave me a second mount, but, when Porter ran short of meat and shot a big buck some three or four miles from his cabin, I let him have Tom to pack the buck to camp.

Somehow I was uneasy about this. Did Porter know anything about a horse or how to handle one? I warned him, "Tom's never had a deer packed on him. He may raise thunder and run away."

Porter rubbed the horse behind the ears with his strong fingers. "We won't have any trouble, will we, Tom?"

Tom sniffed at him and they looked at each other, and I could clearly see in Tom's eyes his understanding of this man and his perfect trust in him. Not only was Porter akin to the wild animals, he was akin to horses as well!

Late that autumn, after we had moved out and had taken the cattle home, we had a heavy snowstorm. As soon as it stopped, I rode by the west side route to the Platte to ford the river at Six Mile and hunt for cattle we might have missed. The country was now snow covered, and all of the rough brakes along the river on both sides were alive with deer. They had been driven out of the higher country and the timber, and showed very little fear of a lone rider. I did not try to tally them, but I must have seen and actually ridden among at least five hundred; more deer than I'd ever seen before or have since.

The following spring, I rode again to Six Mile to see how the grass was coming along and if it would be feasible to move a herd to this area in the spring before grass on the Beaver was advanced enough for grazing. Again, I came in from the west side, fording the Platte, which was high and dangerous, at Six Mile.

I knew Porter was not at his trapping cabin, but I also knew he had left some bedding there, suspended by a wire from a ridge pole so the rats and mice wouldn't get at it. I'd brought along enough lunch for three meals, so I could stop at the cabin overnight and make use of that bedding.

I slept fairly well. Then, riding out by way of Beaver Creek the following day I began to feel as if all of my skin was crawling. Had I picked up lice somewhere? Most men did get 'em once in a while. But I didn't know how they'd feel for I'd never had "seam squirrels."

It was a bright sunny day and warm for the time of year, so

when I reached Beaver Creek I decided I'd take a bath. I peeled off my clothes and then—Wow! Off of my body and my clothes as I shook them and beat them and went over them inch by inch, I picked thirty-two woodticks!

We had not yet heard anything about spotted fever, but those ticks could not have been "fever" ticks, for I suffered no ill effects from the transfer from their cabin incubator to my person.

PROFILES AND PROGRESS

Up until my brother was eighteen, neither he nor I received any wages from our father. Once in a great while he did give each of us a calf or another horse. (As was the prevailing custom, however, these calves generally grew up to become Dad's cows!) Art raked in a few dollars by selling chaps and other leather articles. My only income was the small sum Gus gave me for summer range riding, and I had earned a forty dollar saddle which he paid for!

I galled Art that all—all of the kids we knew—were being paid by their parents for their work. "We'll put it up to Dad," he said, and we did, Art pointing out that we were both doing a man's work, and that since we owned no part of the outfit we figured he should pay us going wages.

Dad was grumpy about it, probably due to the British idea that boys should work for their fathers until they were at least twenty-one, fathers being heads of the families and the absolute bosses.

"Humphy! You kids get some queer notions. Don't begin to appreciate what I've done for you. But ... " A tension-building pause. "All right, Art, I'll pay you thirty dollars a month. What are you waiting for, John?"

I clenched my hands and wet my lips as I said in what was intended for a strong, man-like voice, "I won't stay unless you pay me, too."

Followed a few moments of grim silence. Then, "Don't forget you're still a little kid. Will twenty dollars a month suit you?"

I did not try to crowd my luck!

Dad took an active interest in local, state, national and foreign affairs, but to me changes and events taking place in my own small world were more important. Changes which older folks spoke of as advances and progress, toward improved living conditions and prosperity.

Already I had both seen and heard a most amazing invention which reproduced the human voice—a talking machine. One man in our land now owned an automobile. Almost everyone still maintained that, "Them horseless buggies'll never be practical." But Jack McKee, the Walden barber, was making use of his new toy.

"We-ll, Jack can afford to amuse himself," people conceded. "He's got more ready cash'n anybody else."

This was because Jack demanded cash for his services. I once heard Hubert Chedsey complaining to Dad, "You know that Jack McKee wouldn't trust me for the price of a haircut. I'd sat down in his chair before I told him, 'I haven't any money with me. You'll charge this, Jack?' But, by George, he made me go and get the cash before he'd cut my hair!"

"Well, you might have forgotten it," Dad tried to soothe Mr. Chedsey's hurt feelings. "You know you are a bit absentminded."

"Nonsense!" said Mr. Chedsey. "You've been listening to that confounded Jim Marr."

Although they were good friends, Jim Marr delighted in hoorahing Chedsey, a learned and dignified man, known to be the best lawyer in North Park.

Jim Marr's favorite story on Mr. Chedsey was: "One spring Hubert hitched up his team and took along his wife to Walden to bring back a jag of grub. That same evening he pulled into his ranch, and the family came out to welcome home Mother and Dad.

" 'Where's Ma, Dad?' the oldest boy asked.

"Hubert looked all around thoughtfully. Then remarked ruefully, 'By George, I thought I had forgotten something.' "

Of more importance than either the talking machine or the automobile was the telephone line which ran from Laramie to Walden. Other lines were branching out to tap ranches. Many of these were strung on barbed wire fences for this devilish material had invaded the Park and was replacing poles.

We now had a Stock Growers Association also! I believe Jap Monroe was the first president; Dad was the first secretary-treasurer, and he became almost a permanent fixture in this capacity.

The association authorized inspection of brands and appointed Victor Hanson as brand inspector. This was a long step toward eliminating the shipping of strays to market, for all cattlemen (and horsemen) whether or not association members, were notified they must have their herds inspected before trailing them out to the railroad.

Later, when the State Board of Livestock Inspection Commissioners was established in Denver, about 1905, Victor Hanson was duly authorized as a State Stock Inspector for our district. No better choice could have been made, for this sharp-eyed Swede could "spot a stray" when a dozen other good brand readers had missed it.

Vic was one of the many young fellows whom Andrew Norell sponsored and brought to our country, and about whom our natives would say, " 'Nother young Swede has come to work for ol' Andy. That means 'nother cowman and rancher here in the Park in less than two years."

How true! The Scottish and English and others already established also brought new blood to the Park, and some of these greenhorns, particularly the Scots, made good. But every youth, "yoost over from Sweden" who worked for Andrew Norell got the hang of the cattle business along with his naturalization papers, took up land, acquired a few cows and branched out on his own.

Victor Hanson had arrived in 1889. In 1900 or 1901 he had established his own outfit on the Platte due west of the old Moore and Blevins ranch. Most Swedes are ultra-conservative, inclined to go slow and never gamble. Vic was an exception to this pattern—a live-wire, tireless individual with the physical stamina of a mustang, who thought cattle, lived cattle, probably dreamed cattle. He loved to take long chances, make deals for whole herds, small or large— the larger the better—and the more stolid, "build-up-slow" Swedes were mightily proud of him.

They'd say, "Yoost watch dat Wic go! But sometime he sure to bite off more dan he can chew."

Until his oldest son, Carl, got big enough to sit a saddle, Vic did pracically all of his riding single-handed, including the stock inspection which kept him hustling every autumn.

He carried a pair of horse clippers and when, as sometimes happened, he could not "figure out a brand," he'd ask a couple of punchers to rope and throw the critter; then he would clip off all the hair directly over and around the brand or brands. With the hide thus bared, the brand generally shows up plainly. This is called "clipping out a brand."

If, after clipping, the brand still baffled even Vic, he would take charge of the animal, advertise it in several papers as a stray, then, if no rightful owner climed it, he was authorized to sell it and all strays at public auction. I believe money thus obtained went into the school fund. On three or four occasions Dad bought such strays.

Mavericks were also taken charge of by the brand inspector. But with mavericks—cattle or horses carrying no brands—there were always plenty of fellows eager to beat the inspector to them, out-fox him and get away with them if possible.

Another wonderful new neighbor was Archie Hunter, youngest of Jeff Hunter's many sons. In 1895, as a boy of seventeen, Archie had come West from Illinois to work for Uncle Jack Hunter. He also worked on the Big Creek Ranch, owned at the time by his father and his Uncle Barney Hunter.

Now, as has already been mentioned, when Moore and Blevins dissolved their partnership, Moore retained the original home ranch. He then hired Charlie Baker to irrigate the ranch and harvest the hay crop, and he made a deal with Barney Hunter of Big Creek, who agreed to buy both the pasture and the hay with the privilege of running cattle on the property.

Thus in 1900 it came about that Barney Hunter moved a big herd of cattle to the old Moore and Blevins ranch and put his nephew Archie in full charge of these cattle.

Soon thereafter the Hunters spayed approximately fifteen hundred cows and heifers at this old ranch, and naturally Art and I were greatly interested. We took time out from our jobs to go and watch the ropers head and heel these critters—Archie was one roper, Charlie Baker another, and white-haired Tommy Hunter still another—and to watch the veterinarian at work, all of it fascinating to ranch-raised boys. We learned Barney Hunter was spaying these heifers because spayed heifers and cows would command almost as much money live weight on the market as steers.

But this experiment did not turn out well. Something went wrong and about ten percent of the spayed heifers died from the effects of the operation.

Eventually Barney Hunter sold all of his cattle, and then Archie bought the Moore and Blevins ranch. He also bought a herd of dairy cattle, milked cows and manufactured cheese. I do not know how well the business paid, but in 1903 Archie sold one-half of the ranch to his brother Hugh, a transaction which marked the establishment of a new cow outfit in the Park and our acquiring Hugh Hunter and his splendid family for close neighbors.

In 1905 Archie sold the balance of his ranch and followed this by a strange move—for a cowman—accepting a position in the North Park Bank at Walden. Several years later, however, the cowman cropped out strongly once again and, purchasing a ranch close to Walden, Archie started raising purebred Herefords and high class saddle horses!

Along about 1903 interest in mining had taken a sharp upturn. Earlier there had been extensive placer work on the west side of Independence Mountain. That had petered out, but down the Platte Valley in Wyoming several mining camps were booming, and from the chief of these camps, Encampment, the flame of miners' hopes leaped on to Pearl in North Park.

This tiny settlement began to boom, and our local freighters, plus some impressively big outfits from "outside," prospered briefly. How exciting to a boy to see these great teams snaking along the road, hauling in the building material, machinery and other equipment for a smelter.

The smelter and also a fine hotel were built. But, as had been the case in Teller City rich ore simply wasn't there. Pearl became a ghost town with Cook Rhea and his wife the chief inhabitants. Encampment held out longer before it too folded as a mining camp.

Meanwhile coal, of which we had an unlimited quantity, was replacing wood as fuel in Walden and on ranches. But we Paynes still cut wood.

New settlers were at work, the areas of unfenced and open range land becoming less and less, and early established ranchers increasing and improving their herds. Swift and Company had been unable to close out their many scattered ranches, so the Two Bar Two and the Bighorn (Two Bar M) were the two remaining big outfits.

Montie Blevins had not expanded his ranch, but he was dealing in cattle all of the time and he had begun to experiment in fattening steers on hay (winter feeding). Apparently, this worked out profitably, for as the years ran along, Montie brought to the Park more and more steers—three-year-olds mostly, which were already carrying weight and flesh—fed them all the hay they could eat for six months or so, and then marketed them.

To feed these cattle, Montie bought hay and pasture from any number of ranchmen, which enabled them to become firmly established. I venture to say that he contributed more toward the general prosperity of North Park than any other one man, and my early bronc-busting hero, Wash Alderdice, had become Montie's foreman.

In addition to hay sellers and small stockmen, a goodly number of our ranchers were running a thousand head of cattle or more. Al Marr of course; and the Mallons, with Elmer Mallon manager; the Petersons, Eli and Andrew, in separate outfits; old-timer Fletcher Campbell; the Murphys; newcomer Alfred E. Hills, Easterner and tenderfoot who was astonishing the oldtimers by making good in a big way in the Rand neighborhood; Andrew Norell and others.

I recall asking old Andy, "What's your brand, Mr. Norell?"

"N Yah, yug handle."

You're stumped? . . . This brand was N J, and "yug handle" correctly pronounced was "jug handle." Still baffled? Well, a jug handle's relationship to a brand is similar to that of an ear mark, a wattle or a dewlap—a distinctive mark, merely a slit cut low down in a cow brute's pendulous brisket. After this gash heels, a hole or small loop remains which looks not unlike a jug's handle. Occasionally this slit is too big, permitting an animal accidentally to run a front foot through it, creating a situation which calls for cowboy help.

North Parkers made use of every conceivable ear mark, some men going so far in butchering a calf's ears as to point them, or cut all manner of notches, or even bob them. Jack Frost often performed this "bobbing" operation on winter calves and for good measure would "bob" the tail as well, frozen tails and ears usually dropping off.

Sometimes Jack Frost would work on a newborn colt. Thereupon, regardless of its sex, the colt's name would be either "Crop-Ear" or "Croppie."

A wattle is made by cutting loose a bit of skin, generally on an animal's jaw or neck, but leaving it attached at one end. Blood will continue to flow into this partially detached bit of skin and as the wound heals the loosened skin will form a hairy ball or knob, or a *do-jiggie* shaped like a tassel or bell.

Gus Dwinell's mark (not that he had need of one for his three letter S X F brand was always readable) was a small wattle on the left jaw. I've been with Gus in Omaha when feeder buyers would look at his stock and say, "What on earth is that little ball on the jaws of your cattle? How'd it ever get there?"

Proud of his mark, Gus was always happy to explain the matter. Wattles on either the left or right side of the neck were common, and the Two Bar Two marked its calves with a small wattle underneath the neck at the point where lower jaws and neck meet. But of all the marks I've seen, Fletcher Campbell used the most noticeable—and most hideous. He sliced loose two big hunks of the pendulous lower brisket.

One such mark is a "dewlap." So Fletch's was called a "double dewlap." They flopped and bounced when a critter broke into a trot or a run, and their bell-like shape prompted Wash Alderdice to remark, "If only a man could fit 'em with clappers, every cow in Fletch's herd'd play a tune."

I began quite early to hate all such marks, seeing no real need for such mutilation, particularly of a critter's ears, if cattle were properly branded.

Speaking of branding, Salem M. Hardy, one of the first men to run cattle in the Park, once tried other means than branding to identify a big herd of steers. He ran them through a chute and painted their horns with green paint. (I've always taken this story with a handful of salt, and yet old-timers who knew Mr. Hardy claim it is true and add, "He sure made it easy for rustlers to grab them steers!")

To return for a moment to Fletch Campbell, shrewd old Fletch, while squinting thoughtfully at a tenderfoot wearing high-laced boots and a straw hat, confided to me: "Don't ever hire a man wearing high lace boots or a straw hat, if you expect to get any work out of him. When he ain't busy lacin' up his boots, he'll be chasin' his hat."

In the line of progress, our near neighbor, Cap Fox, after four or five years of seeking by every means at his command to find a wife in North Park, went to Missouri where one of his brothers lived. He returned with a radiant bride and reported, "Back there, b'jabbers, I had my pick of thirty, maybe forty girls."

Cap was so happy he didn't protest when his new wife made him build a house, not connected to his stable. More than this, he added to his small outfit by buying the Barnes boys' ranch, and, a few years later, John Coe's place. Mother Coe and John then loaded their wagon and pulled out for some spot in Canada.

Irving Swinks, who worked for Dwinell for many years, was another who was crazy to get married. A big husky fellow, but past middle age, he was the slowest, most deliberate individual I've ever known. Once, when on a bitter cold night I was bedded down in Dwinell's bunkhouse, lamplight awakened me, and I saw Swinks putting on his clothes, overshoes, mittens, sweater, heavy coat and cap.

"What's up, Swinks?" I asked anxiously. "Where you going?"

He told me where he was going and then lighted a lantern. Anyone else, moved by a similar call, would merely have jumped into his overshoes and thrown a coat over his shoulders. But Swinks had taken a half hour to dress completely. Lantern in mittened hand, he turned at the door and remarked solemnly,

"When I get married and get me a home of my own, I'm goin' to get me a pot, I am."

Although several men advised Swinks to do as Cap Fox had done —go to Missouri and get a wife—he didn't seem to believe it would work out.

"Back there," he said, "it'd be just like it is here! Same trouble: the gals I'd want wouldn't have me, and gals that'd have me the *devil wouldn't have!*"

Poor Swinks! I'm afraid he never did get a pot.

Deer were still plentiful, but the elk seemed to have mysteriously vanished and the great bands of antelope, which had, in earlier days, come each spring from the vicinity of Rawlins and Fort Steele, had stopped coming to the Park. As far as I recall, only one lone antelope was still making out as best he could in our little world.

He had joined a bunch of horses and ran with them on the flats between the Michigan and Canadian. Apparently this canny pronghorn knew that as long as he stayed with the horses he was safe from coyotes.

Most men respected the horse adopted antelope and cheered his fight for survival. Others were not so chivalrous. Yet, when these fellows went gunning for Mr. Antelope, they came home emptyhanded to report, "That ol' buck sure sticks right in with them horses. Couldn't line my sights on him without takin' the chance of killin' a horse."

Many years passed before someone found our antelope's carcass. He died a natural death from old age.

As early as 1904, North Parkers became excited over the building of the Moffat Railroad, this to come from Denver over the Continental Divide into Middle Park, on to Steamboat Springs and, presumably, to Salt Lake City. Our cattlemen welcomed it as a new outlet for shipping cattle, affording a short haul directly into Denver.

Denver was coming up as a stock market, yet if a cattleman did not wish to sell there, he could go on East with his herd.

Looking back quietly now, I do not see why our men got "all fevered-up" about shipping by the Moffat Road. After all, the established drive to Laramie was no great hardship on herds, or men, and the mighty U.P. was sure to get shipments through to their destination.

In 1905 the Moffat had built as far as a station it called Arrowhead, on the east side of Middle Park, and Victor Hanson was one of the first stockmen to load cattle at this station.

Said Vic, " 'Twas a nightmare of a drive, and did we get into a mess after we got there! Got a load of cattle in the chute pen and started to load a car. Now the boys hadn't looked to make sure the door on the far side was shut, and it was wide open. The steers had started up the chute, and every one of them jumped out on the far side of the car and took to the timber ... Thought for a while we never would get 'em rounded up and into the corral again."

As far as I recall, Vic never again tried to ship his cattle by the Moffat Road, even though it eventually was built on across Middle Park and as far as Craig in Route County.

Dad and Gus had seriously considered trailing a herd to the Moffat, but after hearing Vic's report, they changed their minds in a hurry. Many ranchers in the south end of the Park, much closer to the new railroad than we, as well as men who were summer-grazing herds in Middle Park, began making use of it, however, and continued to do so.

Several years later, 1909, in fact, North Parkers and particularly Waldenites had something new and wonderful to cheer them. This came about when North Park split off from Larimer County and became a brand new county. Jackson County, with Walden the county seat.

This objective had been in the making for several years, the strongest argument in its favor being that Fort Collins, the county seat of Larimer County, was one hundred and twenty-one miles from Walden, and this distance worked a hardship on men who had business to transact at the county seat. The "all-for-a-new-county" people had other good arguments, too.

But both my father and Andrew Norell were outspokenly against the change. Why, they asked, should North Park take upon itself the full expense of operating a new county? Moreover, very few people had business at the county seat which could not be taken care of by mail.

Many ranchmen, dreading higher taxes, sided with Norell and Dad, yet Norell was the only one who "worked himself up into a big lather" over it. When he heard that the opposition was circulating petitions, Andy got out and visited the ranchmen to tell them not to sign those petitions.

Charlie Baker, circulating a petition for the new county, was at Dad's ranch when Nndrew Norell arrived, and I heard their arguments—good as a circus for me.

Both men lost their tempers and finally Baker snorted, "You blankety-blanked foreigners believe you can come over here and run our country. But I'm tellin' you . . . "

"Foreigner yourself!" Norell exploded. "You come from Missouri and dot ain't in the United States!"

But the new county was merely in the "talk about it" and "talk it up" stage when Dad invested in more land, the Charlie Barnes ranch, the Sam McIntosh place and another homestead, a total of four hundred and eighty acres, all of which adjoined the original Cross ranch. This acreage provided additional pasture and hay and prompted him to buy more cattle.

I do not know how it came about—probably through Granny Bill Hunter who so often stopped at our ranch—but he made a deal with the Big Creek outfit for one hundred weaner calves, and he took me with him to go and get the calves.

This was a trip I'd long been eager to take, a new and great adventure to widen my range horizon!

SAGA OF BIG CREEK

To me as an impressionable kid who loved tales of frontier adventures, the story of the founding of Big Creek Ranch held glamour, excitement, fascination—all to a greater degree than any other event which had taken place in my own homeland.

This saga begins with the "older" Hunters, as Dad spoke of those four brothers, Barney and Jeff, Tom and Jack (our North Park's "Uncle Jack"). Of these four, cowmen all, Barney and Jeff made cattle history in those long-gone days of the Texas trail herds. Quite soon after the end of the Civil War, they left their home state, Illinois, went to Texas and became pioneers in this great movement of bringing herds north.

Then, in 1874, Barney and Jeff embarked upon another enterprise, one which so far as I know has not been recorded in cattle histories of the West. The two went to Montana in the early spring, and there bought thousands of steers. Three, four, five and even six-year-old steers, matured and grown-out on Montana grass, which they then trailed down across Wyoming, eventually to strike the Union Pacific Railroad at Hanna, Wyoming.

We do not know what trail they followed, and there is no one left to tell us. Granny Bill Hunter was one of the "hands" on these drives, but he has long since crossed the Big Divide, and of the hired punchers there certainly cannot be even one still living. But they must have held as closely as possible to running water as they crossed this immense land, a land populated only by roving Indians and natural wild life, a land of sky and earth and grass. Grass; house-less, unsettled and unfenced.

This stirred my boyish imagination and stirs it even today. I see the Hunters' chuck wagon and their cavvy moving slowly southward across the limitless open spaces of Wyoming. I see the cattle, too, those enormous, wide-horned steers, fourteen, fifteen, sixteen hundred pounds of beef on four cloven hoofs; two thousand-odd, a herd to stir a cowman's pulses and spark his eyes.

They are not strung out on the trail as pictures of Texas trail drives usually show such a herd. They are loosely bunched, held to-gether by the punchers just enough so the big mass is under control. Jeff and Barney Hunter did not "drive" as we North Parkers would "drive a herd" to Laramie. They "grazed" the animals, taking all summer to cross Wyoming and reach Hanna in the autumn. By grazing the steers, the Hunters put even more growth on them, fattened them on the trail.

In my mind's eye I see these big steers bedded down at night by quiet-spoken, slow-riding men. They lie, chewing their cuds con-tentedly unless, of course, the weather's bad or something makes them uneasy. As dawn breaks, they begin to move, getting up, stretching, and then slowly, unprompted and unhurried by the men, they leave the bed ground, pointed in the right direction you may be sure. On fresh grass ahead, they fill up as they meander along. They drink and lick their coats with their rough tongues, lie down and sun themselves. Then toward evening they begin to graze again, filling up for the long night. Slowly, oh, so carefully the men work the big fellows into a compact unit and circle around it as the steers bed down, and soft music from tinkling cavvy bells, sounding from where the extra horses are held by a lone night wrangler, plus the songs of the men on night herd, help to soothe the cattle to sleep.

"Grazing a herd" is the ideal way of moving cattle. An old range axiom runs: "Never let 'em know they're being driven, but never let 'em take one step back." Hard driving always produces both sore-footed and badly lamed animals. But the slow, slow move-ment of a grazing herd practically eliminates this hazard as it also eliminates loss of weight.

Of course, there was another angle to it, the rough and tough and frightening aspects of it: gnats, mosquitoes, flies, thunderstorms, danger from Indians and, quite possibly, from rustlers, bog holes, mean places to negotiate, mountains, badlands, heavily wooded areas;

and at times the drovers must have been obliged to make forced drives between far apart streams.

Yet, day by day on this summer long trek, each new bed ground found the cattle nearer their objective, and Barney and Jeff always got their herds through to the railroad shipping point. Their market was Chicago, where the huge steers were sold for export as prime grass beef.

But there was a tremendous financial risk involved in handling these steers, and in the autumn of 1877, when the Hunters reached Hanna, they learned that cattle prices had fallen so low that marketing their big herd was sure to bankrupt them. Faced with this disaster, Jeff and Barney decided to hold the cattle over until the next fall, and they made a deal with a man who owned a ranch near Hanna to look after the stock; then, looking toward the future if they should get caught in a like predicament again, Barney and Jeff set out to explore the country.

Far south of Hanna these two cowmen discovered the valley where Big Creek tumbles down from Big Creek Lake in the mountains surrounding Pearl, Colorado, to cross an open area and join the North Platte. So taken with this setup were Barney and Jeff Hunter that in 1878 they filed on homesteads, named this spot the Big Creek Ranch, and stocked it with cattle. Thus, these two great cowmen wrote their names large both in the cattle business and the early settlement of the West.

In 1880 another brother of this same family, Tom Hunter, took up land on the Platte at the far northern end of North Park proper, and raised cattle until 1887 when he sold both his ranch and cattle to Uncle Jack, the fourth brother of this family.

Although Uncle Jack also bought a great deal more land and established his home some three miles up the Platte River, Tom Hunter left his mark upon our North Park, for his original homestead is still known as the Tom Hunter Ranch.

As an old-timer Dad knew all four of these great cowmen brothers, of whom I knew only Uncle Jack. However, there were the "young Hunters" as Dad called Jeff's sons and also Tom's boys, and it became my privilege to meet them. Tom's sons whom I knew were Hank and Tommy, expert cowpunchers.

White-haired Tommy I can see now, a straight-up rider, white Angora chaps and small hat with brim pulled low over his eyes, a pleasant man who'd treat a kid as if he were an equal and tell him stories of the old days. Wonderful stories, for he had known the

Cross boys, the Scott boys, the Mendenhalls and the Benbows, bronc buster Billy Weaver, and all other early day men of the Park.

But for some reason, neither Hank nor white-haired Tommy built up names for themselves in the cattle business as did Jeff's boys, Will, Ben, Harry, Hugh and Archie. "Beaver Creek Will" lived on Beaver Creek, some fifteen miles north of Big Creek. (Not to be confused with the Beaver Creek of the Payne-Dwinell cattle range. I suppose there are at least a thousand Beaver Creeks. This one originates in the Sierra Madre Mountains and flows eastward to the North Platte.) Will was married, was a cowman, of course, and also a successful farmer.

Will often stopped overnight at Dad's ranch, and once Dad made a trip with team and wagon to Beaver Creek Will's place to bring back a load of potatoes and onions, barley and oats. Men who lived in this great Platte Valley—an area bordered on the west by the Sierra Madre Range and by the Platte and the Medicine Bow Mountains on the east and extending north from North Park to Saratoga—raised first class oats, barley and alfalfa as well as hay. Long before my initial visit to Big Creek, some North Parkers—Arthur Allard for one—were freighting oats and spuds grown in this area to the Park.

To return to the Big Creek Ranch, through the years I had heard such glowing reports about its inception and steady upward growth to where it was now a "real cow spread" that I was a-tingle with anticipation that autumn day when, riding with my father, I at last had my first look at it. And I wasn't disappointed.

At this time the road ran through the ranch, and a sign nailed on the gate at the south end read, "Please close gate." I was to learn that the distance from this gate to the northern boundary fence was nine miles!

Dad and I rode across a thousand-acre meadow dotted by haystacks, with other meadows ahead and to our left. Much of this area had been sagebrush land, and grubbing out the sagebrush was just one of the big jobs of making a great ranch. Ditching and fencing were two more. Slowly over the years this work had been accomplished. In one huge block, here was the greatest ranch I'd ever seen. To north and south, splendid open range; to the west, enormous pastures running back to the mountains.

We saw a thousand-odd beef steers in one of the big meadow fields, and a big herd of two-year-old feeder steers in another. My eyes fairly popped.

"Dad," I said, "this is something like we ought to have. I guess Barney and Jeff Hunter knew what they were about."

Dad's eyes sparkled. "They did," he said briefly.

"Was building up this outfit a slow, hard pull for them?" I asked. "Like it's been for you?"

"They had their ups and downs, you can bet. Great men that these older fellows were, however, one of Jeff's sons, Harry Hunter, deserves a lot of credit for this outfit."

"I've heard a lot about Harry, but tell me more, Dad."

"Well, in 1884—same year I came to the Park—Harry, a mere kid, came here from Illinois, worked a few years as a cowhand and was promoted to manager. From that point on, he worked his way up so successfully that in 1900 he and Granny Bill organized a company—Hunter, Castile and Hunter—and bought this ranch.

"Jeff Hunter, Harry's father, seems to have dropped out of the picture even before that. But as you know, Barney Hunter, after selling out to this new company, moved part of his cattle to North Park."

"Uh-huh! Archie took care of 'em," I said and Dad resumed:

"Of all the young Hunters, Harry is the cowman genius. He'll probably make a bigger name for himself than his own father, Jeff, or his Uncle Barney."

I thought excitedly, "Wonder if I'll ever make a name for myself? Shucks, no! All I want to be right now is range foreman for a real outfit like this one. Golly! What more could a fellow want?"

Dad went on to say, "These three men, Harry Hunter, Ira Castile and Granny Bill, have now built up and expanded this outfit, and are running about five thousand cattle. Mostly steers. They buy 'em young, grow 'em out and market 'em, some as feeders, some as beef. Harry is the spark, the driving force, the real manager, but you can bet that Granny Bill is consulted about every purchase of stock they make. Granny Bill is also the shipper, the man who accompanies each and every shipment of cattle to markets."

"What's Ira Castile's part?" I asked.

"He's the bookkeeper and secretary."

"Bookkeeper? You never keep any books, Dad."

"I might be better off if I did. A bookkeeper and secretary are necessary on any big outfit. Castile also runs the ranch. Not that he does any of the hard work himself, for they hire a ranch foreman, 'straw boss,' and the hired men work under him."

"They hire a range foreman, too," I said. "And other cowboys work under him."

Arrived at the ranch headquarters, I saw a good frame house, but the rest of the buildings were not at all pretentious. The old original log house was now the bunkhouse, where I wanted to stay. But Castile gave Dad a room in the main house and I had to bunk with him. Harry Hunter rode in before dark, and at last I met the great man and found him a regular sort of fellow, as unpretentious as any cowhand.

The calves Dad was to buy, we learned, had not been gathered. "They're still on the range," Harry told us, "and must be brought in and weaned. The cowpunchers will get at it first thing in the morning."

I asked for my old friend, Granny Bill, and was told that Bill was shipping cattle so we'd not see him this trip.

For the next three days Dad put in some of his time fishing while I was riding with the Big Creek cowboys! Charlie McVail was foreman. Scarcely more than a kid, he was a straight up rider and a good hand. He was so blond that his hair was almost white and everyone called him "Cotton."

He supplied me with a string of saddle horses, and I got a big kick out of riding with him and two other men. We did not have a chuck wagon nor run a real roundup, but rode out from the ranch to a certain area of the range and "picked up" J Bar cows with calves old enough to wean. J Bar on the left hip was the outfit's main brand, although they also used a half dozen other brands.

In this "picking up" method of gathering cattle, we did not disturb cattle on the range; we merely rode among them, and when we found an animal we wanted, we drove it toward the next bunch of cattle. Soon we "picked up" several. One man hazed the herd along; the others rode far and wide, getting a cow and calf here, another there, and driving them to the "catch bunch."

Apparently the outfit did not at this time own a great many stock cattle, for it took us three days to gather a mere hundred cows with calves old enough to be weaned. Each of those days, we went without dinner, rode one horse the entire time, trailed our day's gather to the ranch corrals after dark.

There was a hired woman at the main house who cooked for the bosses, guests, ranch hands and cowboys. She must have been delighted to have this puncher crew troop in for supper after eight o'clock each day!

291

One of the ranch hands hauled in hay for the calves, and each evening we cut the cows out, leaving the calves alone in the corrals. Early on the morning of the fourth day, Dad and Harry Hunter counted the hundred calves. Dad accepted them and paid for them; then Cotton and his two punchers gave us a hand to whoop the calves out on the trail.

We lashed them into a run and chased them for three or four miles, getting 'em "plumb away from their mothers and travellin' good" before we let up and permitted a normal pace. After Cotton and the boys turned back, Dad and I drove the bunch all the way home, twenty-odd miles, that same day and later vaccinated and branded the calves. This deal turned out well for Dad.

At last I had been to the Big Creek Ranch, for me another step upward on the ladder of experience. While there, I'd taken keen interest in everything I saw, noting how the bosses and the men did things and whether there was any improvement in their methods over those we used.

They had a blacksmith shop, and the punchers shod their own strings of saddle ponies, something we should do, for we often rode sore-footed horses. I liked their system of two bells in the morning. One, rung by the cook, sounded at about 5:45 to tell late sleepers to get ready for breakfast. The second bell promptly at six meant "Breakfast's on the table. Come and get it!" Cotton wrangled the cavvy of work horses and saddle stock before breakfast, and the chore man would also be at work early.

The horses I was given to ride were pretty much old jugheads. But Harry Hunter had purchased a black Thoroughbred stallion, a trim, fiery animal with which the outfit won a lot of local races, and he was crossing this Thoroughbred on broncho mares to raise saddle horses.

The colts were beautifully proportioned and trim and quick, but hard to break — plumb ornery — because it seemed they inherited all the meanness of the broncho and all the fire and spunk and cussedness of the Thoroughbred. Also, many of them were light boned and not heavy enough for the hard work. But Harry Hunter liked them, so that was that.

We had found that on their she-stock herd, Big Creek was using the best purebred Hereford bulls they could buy, and you can bet Granny Bill always had some fine bulls for sale. Dad and Gus too had by this time switched over entirely to Hereford sires.

The outfit preferred to handle top quality cattle and Harry Hunter purchased hundreds of yearling steers from individual ranchmen who lived farther down the Platte Valley. These steers were called "Natives." Shipped-in steers, if they came from Texas or other Southern states, were either "Southerns" or "Dogies."

In range parlance, all cattle are sometimes called "dogies." If you pronounce it "*dog*'-ies" you're a tenderfoot. It's "*do*'-gies." Poor quality Southern cattle of both sexes are definitely "dogies," and an orphaned calf (one whose mother has died and whose papa has gone off with another cow) is always a "dogie."

Shipped-in steers from the West, Oregon and Idaho for example, were either "Westerns" or just "dogies."

But, Natives, Dogies or Westerns, Big Creek handled all three classifications. When shipped in by rail, they unloaded these steers a Walcott on the Union Pacific, and they shipped a great many cattle "out" from this same station. But they also trailed herds "out" by way of North Park, to strike the same Walden to Laramie road which we used in driving to Laramie.

During April, May and June the outfit would be busy bringing in dogies and Westerns and locating them in pastures and on the range. Shipping out began in July and continued clear into January, for this outfit seldom marketed a big herd at one time. Granny Bill, who understood marketing as well as, if not better than any cowman, would string out the shipments — two hundred head this week to Omaha, two or three hundred next week (or next month) quite likely to another market.

I was intrigued by the business of buying young steers in the spring, holding them for eighteen months or longer, and shipping them out as feeders or as grass beef. But I couldn't sell Dad on the idea of going into it.

"Humph," he said. "Let me tell you this, young fellow: ninety per cent of these big deals in steers are made entirely on borrowed money. I couldn't get that sort of financial backing even if I wanted to risk taking it. Besides, steer men go broke; cowmen never do!"

This was a tragedy he had already seen happen many times, and he was merely quoting an old, time-tried range axiom.

I liked the system whereby the owners had a ranch boss who, with other hired hands, did the hard work, although I realized that it was not practical for any small outfit where the owner himself must do most of his work. Best of all, I liked the idea of a range foreman, who, doing no ranch work, rode and handled cattle all year long. Maybe someday I'd reach that goal!

In the years that followed my initial trip to Big Creek, I became so familiar with the outfit that I felt quite at home on the ranch. The Payne and Dwinell cattle learned that they could cross the Platte, although, as the range rider, I tried to hold them on their own range. I'd find a lot of them every fall on the flats adjacent to Big Creek Ranch.

To gather these stragglers, I began riding Big Creek's fall round-up, eating for free of course at their chuck wagon. I'd work with the roundup for a week or ten days, or until it moved on farther to the north where none of our cattle would be found.

Hugh Hunter and his oldest son, red-headed Ernest, and Uncle Jack's youngest boy, Ed., and at least one rep from the Big Horn outfit also rode these roundups.

Hugh Hunter was grazing most of his cattle on the open range south of Big Creek, so I did a lot of riding with him. Hugh was a pleasant, breezy fellow who loved to punch cows. Harry Hunter, on the contrary, seldom made a hand on roundup, or with a herd. Occasionally Harry'd ride out from the ranch to "cut" a bunched herd, but that was all.

Soon after he made his home in North Park, Hugh had hired two of the McCasland boys to help him, and, to hear him tell it, "By dogies, I sure made good cowhands out of Harry and Viv . . . I got hold of Ed (Uncle Jack's Ed) in time to make a bronc buster and cowpuncher of him, too."

"How'd Uncle Jack like that?" I asked.

"Oh, Uncle Jack's not so set in his ways as he used to be. You'll notice, Ed's carriyng a rope on his saddle, using a curb bit for his bridle. By dogies, I make good hands out of all the boys who work with me."

We worked hard on those roundups, but we surely had a lot of genuine enjoyment as well. One autumn I found a lanky cowhand, with a long, weather-seamed face, riding for Big Creek and soon learned that he was John R. Hunter. (There were actually so many Hunters all related that a new one I'd not met before was always showing up.) John was a bit down on his luck at this time and had taken a job with Big Creek Harry.

Like Hugh, he was an agreeable man to know, and soon proved himself a top cowhand. One afternoon when John R. and young

Ernest and I were dangling along with the "day herd" toward their next bed ground, John told us young fellows:

"I've never found anything on earth quite so nice as making a hand on roundup, living in the open, eating your meals at the chuck wagon. . . . Boys, if I thought this'd be the last time this outfit'd run a chuck wagon, I'd sit right down here in the sagebrush and cry."

"And I'd join you," I said.

But actually we weren't much worried, for during those good years Harry Hunter was building Big Creek up and ever up. He further expanded and improved the original ranch, bought hay and pasture at other ranches all down the Platte Valley as far as Saratoga, shipped in more and more cattle and finally began purchasing ranches.

In its heyday, about 1915 to 1921, Big Creek was running upward of ten thousand cattle, and Harry Hunter bought out his partners. He also became the individual owner of at least four other big Wyoming ranches, plus the Jack Hunter ranch in North Park. Perhaps the ghosts of those outstanding, pioneer cattlemen, Barney and Jeff, witnessed this achievement, nodded at each other and said, "We really started something when we established Big Creek Ranch!"

FIELD ROUNDUP

In addition to the summer calf roundup and the fall beef round-up, Norther Parkers quite early organized a "field roundup" to take place in November after all cattle had been gathered off the ranges. It was authorized and was managed by our Stockgrowers' Association. Usually, either the Two Bar Two or the Big Horn outfit was asked to supply a chuck wagon and four-horse team, the wagon to be loaded with grub in Walden at the Association's expense. The Association also hired a cook, a horse wrangler and a roundup foreman. The rest of the crew — the roundup riders — was composed of one or more reps (cowboys) from each big outfit, individual cattle owners or their reps and men and boys who would help for a few days while the roundup was working in their particular neighborhoods.

From its inception and for many years thereafter Joe Graham always bossed this roundup. A high class fellow who "savvied" both men and cattle, Joe was gifted with such a pleasing personality that although I never heard him spoken of as "Gentleman Joe," the nickname would have fitted him well.

Joe took pride in personal neatness, dressed far better than the average ranchman, and was one of a very few North Park cowboys of the old order, a hold-out who would do no work other than cowpunching and jobs directly connected to it. He'd not blister his hands on a pitchfork handle! As a consequence, Joe'd often be out of a job during the winter, but spring and summer he rode range for a pool of ranchmen who grazed herds in Middle Park, ran their calf roundup, fall roundup and, finally, the Association's field roundup.

The purpose of a field roundup is to pick up all strays and get them to their rightful owners. Because cattle wander a great deal on the ranges and those of many different owners get badly mixed, nearly every ranchman is sure to have strays in his herd. Generally he is as eager to get rid of such strays before winter feeding sets in as the owners are to get them.

But occasionally a ranchman is happy to have strays in his fields — provided no one else knows they are there. First of all, he'll get free beef for his table. Next, if he has a cow with a big unbranded calf, he'll wean the calf and slap his own brand on it. In fact, he can well afford to winter a cow if said cow will calve in the spring. He will then range the cow in some out of the way spot and, come fall, wean and brand the calf along with his own and thus add a calf to his herd for the mere cost of feeding a cow all winter.

Although this type of petty stealing was rare in the Park, the Association hoped by means of the field roundup to stamp it out entirely.

Early in November all our cattlemen would be notified that the roundup was to meet at Walden on a specified day.

Typically, as soon as the chuck wagon is loaded with grub, the assembling riders pile their beds atop this load and the wagon pulls out, bound for — let us say — Hugh Hunter's ranch to pitch camp for the first night. The cowboys turn their extra ponies — each has a "string" of from two to five horses — in with the cavvy which, hazed along by the wrangler, follows the wagon. Hay for this cavvy and a corral or feed lot in which to put the horses for the night is provided by the cattleman at whose ranch the roundup makes camp.

The cowboys, six or a dozen or even twenty strong, leaving Walden, sweep northward down the Michigan River. The riders fan out, some dashing to the far corners of the first field they enter, and whoop the cattle into a bunched herd. Most of the men now merely circle around this herd, holding it, but the foreman, who is always one of the "bunch" or "cut" men, and one or two other cowboys who are qualified by experience as "brand readers" and as "cut" men, ride slowly through the bunch looking for animals carrying brands other than the brand or brands belonging to the owner of this particular herd.

They may not find a single stray, or they may find one, two, a dozen or more. All of these are cut out and held by one or more punchers in a bunch by themselves. Then the main herd is strung out (as if the cattle were filing through a gate) in such a manner that every animal can be scrutinized by two or more expert brand readers to make sure there are no strays left in this field.

Immediately after one herd has been worked, the cowboys spur on to the next adjoining ranch and do the same sort of job all over again. Meanwhile, the men who have been ordered to hold the strays drive this small herd up close to the new bunch of cattle so that more strays may be added to it.

So it goes, the cattle in each field on down the river being bunched and cut until night puts a stop to the work. The bunch of strays — called either the "jack pot" or "the cavvy," not to be confused with a horse cavvy, however — is thrown into a strongly fenced pasture for the night.

All the cowboys head for the chuck wagon, turn their mounts in with the horse cavvy, and then scramble to appropriate good places for their beds, such as the ranch haymow or bunkhouse, and the un-written rule is: first man to find a choice spot gets it and holds it.

The cook shouts, "Come and get it!" and most of the men wash — after a fashion at least — then rustle utensils from the cook's chuck box and load plates and coffee cups from Dutch ovens and other pots banked near the cook's fire, and they either squat on their boot heels or find places to sit down and eat. If the weather is stormy or very cold, they'll simply take possession of the bunkhouse.

Supper over, the riders have a few hours in which to amuse them-selves, and the "full-of-the-dickens" young hands who love to play pranks and "put up jobs" on tenderfeet get busy. But no one is safe from this horseplay.

I vividly recall one prankster who'd bide his time until the cook and horse wrangler had finished their work at the campfire. (For as long as the cook needs the fire it is his and his only; prominent ranchers and cowpunchers alike are asking to be "cussed out" if they sprawl around the fire and get in cookie's way. The same holds true for his wagon and chuck box. "You blankety-blanked knot-heads, keep out. Somethin' you got to have out my wagon, ask me, an' I'll get it for you. Mebbe!")

This joker would also wait until sober cowmen'd be comfortably seated, and until the gamblers would have poker or dice games going

298

full tilt close by the fire; then Mr. Prankster would suddenly whip a handful of six-shooter cartridges out of a pocket, yell, "Look out!" and toss them into the fire.

The immediate stampede by everyone in the vicinity was most amusing—to all the jokers.

Another delightful amusement was "stuffing" or "loading" a green hand. Neither a rattlesnake nor a hydrophobic skunk had ever been seen in North Park. But according to the "stuffers" (tellers of tall tales) a fella was liable to have a rattler or, still more terrifying, "one of them pizen skunks crawl right into his bed to keep warm 'most any night.' " A small piece of fur of any kind, carefully planted in the green hand's bed where his bare foot was sure to touch it, often produced most hilarious results. (This is "putting up a job" on some victim.)

In case you have not heard of the "rackaboar," also known as the "side-hill growler," he is a savage little beast that lives only on steep hills and mountains and can travel in only one direction because his two legs on the upper side are shorter than those on the lower side. This enables the rackaboar or side-hill growler to hold his body upright as he dashes around hill or mountain, savagely attacking anything he meets. His bite is deadly. Should your horse throw you in the path of a rackaboar, you're a gone goose, unless you bear in mind that he can't turn around and thus throw his two long legs to the upper side of the hill or over he'd fall!

If a victim could possibly be found, snipe hunting was a mirth provoker, and, of course, the most common practice of all, one which never, never fails to amuse a bunch of cowhands, that of putting a tenderfoot, green hand or anyone for that matter astride a "plumb gentle horse." Not very funny to the victim but for the audience—as an old range song expresses it:

> That time when Bob got throwed
> I thought I shore would bust.
> I like to died a-laffin'
> To see him chewin' dust!

Invariably, and this holds true with any crew of men, in addition to pranksters there are always gamblers. One or several fellows "jus' a-rarin' " to get up a game of chance. If the cowboys have neither cards nor dice, they'll match pennies or pitch coins at a crack, or, if someone will make a top, they'll play "Put and Take."

This game requires a crude top, usually made from an empty thread spool. One wide end of the spool is cut off; the other is flattened on four sides. A stick is then whittled to fit tightly into the hole in the spool, lower end pointed, upper end projecting far enough for a man to grasp it with a finger and thumb. Each of the squared sides is marked with a letter and the top is complete.

Any number can play, so the players crowd around a saddle blanket spread on dirt, each puts a dime in the pot and the first player spins the top. If it falls with the letter "P" up, he relinquishes the top to the next man and he must "put" another coin into the pot. But if the top falls with "T" up, the player grabs all of the money and a new pot is made at which he gets first chance. When "N" comes up, he gets nothing, contributes nothing and the play goes on to the next man. A simple little game, but fascinating!

Not often, however, are cowboys caught without either dice or cards, and a fellow could count on lively poker games and livelier crap-shooting each night.

Our field roundup worked practically every ranch in the Park where cattle were to be found, the wagon moving its camp each day, the stray herd (jack-pot) being driven from place to place. But every few days this jack-pot would be cut, big outfits and small owners alike cutting their cattle out of it and taking them home. Cattle bearing brands which none of the ranchmen could legitimately claim were carried along until the end of the roundup when, if owners still had not been found, they were turned over to the State Stock Inspector.

While Arthur and I were still little kids, we'd have the big thrill of riding field roundup for one day or possibly two when the work was in our neighborhood, and we came to know Joe Graham and many other expert cowboys. Three of those that come to mind were certainly top hands, and also men willing and eager to shoulder heavy responsibilities. Irving Brands got his training working for Bill Marr's Big Horn, then hired out to Big Creek with the definite goal of range foreman in mind. Irv had a long, tough pull to convince Harry Hunter he was the man for that job, but he did it! Bun Quigley, the Mallon outfit's top hand, was a fun-loving, rip-tootin' cowhand and a plumb good one. The third was Billy McGowan. Billy had several years of cowpunching experience in the Bear (Yampa) River country before he came to the Park and hired out to

Bill Marr. Shrewd old Bill soon recognized Billly's worth and promoted him to range foreman or "cow boss of the Big Horn."

Finally came a year when I rode field roundup for a full week; a week of out-of-this-world adventure when a fellow'd love to live forever! By this time I had broken seven or eight horses to ride and "sorta figgered" I was a tolerable good buster. To be sure, there had been incidents which I thought best left unmentioned, incidents which I dreaded to have a josher like Lindsey Coe bring up. Such as a bronc unloading me in a patch of sandburs and leaving me to hobble five miles home in my too-tight boots; such as another horse wheeling sharp away from me when I dismounted to open a gate, kicking me galley west with both heels and then taking off for the open range.

I also reckoned I was a good trader and a real poker player. Oh yeah? My first evening out on this field roundup I took part in one of those exciting poker games. My enjoyment was brief. My two dollar stake lasted for three hands, then I was out of the game.

Looking on can be fun but not so much as playing. So when one of the boys hit me for a trade of chaps, I was tempted by an offer of five dollars to boot. At this time I owned a first-class pair of white Angora chaps. But I'd get a tolerable good pair in exchange for them—plus a poker stake! I made the swap.

Came a game next evening. I sat in, and after he had taken my five bucks a real player sneered, "Small contributions thankfully received!" Nobody wanted my IOU, nor did I want to go in debt, so I was broke and out of the game again.

But—aha!—another cowboy suddenly wanted to trade chaps with me. The pair he had were badly shot, but if I could get enough boot to even up the deal . . . I got it. Four bucks!

I'd heard miraculous stories how Lady Luck'd hit a fellow, and he'd run two bits up to twenty or thirty dollars. That's what I would do. Lady Luck was riding with my opponents. Or could it be that I didn't know how to play poker? Oh, *no!* I was a bang-up good poker player, a bang-up good trader, too!

I made two more chap trades, getting boot each time, each time enjoying a few losing poker hands. Then I went home, flat broke, wearing the worst pair of ragged old chaps a fellow ever tried to fasten together with string and rivets. How big brother hoorahed me!

But I did learn something. The next time I acquired a pair of good chaps, nobody could talk me into swapping them off. Did I also learn that I wasn't cut out to play winning poker? We-ll, how about gettin' up a li'l penny ante game? I'm feelin' lucky.

FIFTY-SIX BELOW ZERO

Sometimes on those roundups a fellow couldn't ask for more pleasant days, chilly at night, right nippy before sunrise, but not a cloud in the sky, very little wind and brilliant sunshine. Possibly there was even more brilliant starlight, the starlight which seems to be reserved for high, mountain country.

On the other hand, Old Man Weather could be, and often was, rough in November as in midwinter, but, regardless of storm or wind or cold snap, the work went right on. To be sure, the majority of "set-in-their-ways" cowmen wouldn't attempt to brand stock during a heavy storm. Otherwise, "the job's got to be done. Get at it, and to heck with what kind of a day it is."

Even so, I don't think Arthur and I would have made a seventeen-mile ride on a certain December day had we known how savagely and unbelievably cold it really was.

In the autumn of that year, Dad had bought three hundred tons of hay on the Dave Sudduth ranch. It lay just above what had been called the Lower Hardy Ranch on the Canadian, but had now become the Two Bar Two's home ranch. Harry Green was the foreman in full charge of both ranch and cattle. Next up the river was this Suddith place, bordered on the east by Bill Kerr's foothills ranch, which snuggled against Medicine Bow Range. On upstream Al Marr's big Cross LX adjoined Sudduth's land.

In September we moved three hundred odd cattle to the Sudduth ranch to eat the meadow grass and, because no one was living there, we left this herd unattended.

All went well until mid-December when, following a heavy snowstorm, Al Marr sent Dad word by the stage driver, "Your catle have broken into my lower field. Tomorrow I'll be working my herd there, so come and put them back where they belong."

That evening Dad came to the bunkhouse and told Art and me we must meet Al Marr and his cowboys not later than eight o'clock of the following morning.

Then he turned to our current hired man, Frank Payson. "Frank, the boys and I will help you get ready tonight to take a saddle horse, team and hayrack loaded with everything you'll need, including a cook stove, to the Sudduth ranch tomorrow. You're to batch there and feed the cattle."

I've never seen anyone so completely flabbergasted. Frank was only twenty-two, still so kiddish in many ways that I was much more mature than he, and this was the first inkling he'd had that he might have to batch alone on a remote ranch all winter long. I could easily see he had a big notion quitting.

But Frank had been raised on a farm in faraway Maine where cold winters are not unknown, and as a kid he had learned to hunt as well as to do all manner of farm work. Although he was an unusually small-bodied man, only five feet five, he was a good ranch hand, tough, wiry and quick. He'd turn off more work than two ponderous men, and how he loved a gun!

He had arrived at the Payne ranch broke, but the first wages he drew from Dad he sent to Montgomery Ward for the best single shot .22 rifle, fondling it as a woman'd fondle a baby. "Crackies! Ain't that a lovely thing, boys?"

Later he also got a .30-.30 Winchester, and in September Frank and I went deer hunting up on top of the Medicine Bow Range. We might have taken a pack horse and full camp outfit along, but, kidlike, we wanted to rough it for the experience, lie out by a fire the same as the first settler, old man Pinkham, had done. We rode up atop the mountains, found a place to picket our horses and build a fire and, with no bedding except our saddle blankets, we "roughed it."

I've done the same sort of thing many times while moving cattle; night herd them until the animals are bedded down and reasonably quiet, then ride back a little ways from the herd, make a fire and snatch a short nap. But this hunting was an experience I do not care to repeat, for during the night three inches of snow fell.

"Just the thing for tracking deer," Frank said as we plunged out at crack of day.

He skulked off on foot in one direction while I took another. He was an experienced hunter, which I was not. I never told him, but I got lost in the timber and only by good luck managed to find the camp once again—so "plumb wore out" I didn't think I could walk another hundred feet. Was I ever glad to see my horse!

Frank got a four-point buck. I got the experience.

His second hobby, which he loved not quite so much as his guns, was playing a mouth organ. "School Days" and "Down By The Old Mill Stream" were two popular songs which he sang as well as played. But Frank wasn't doing any singing after Dad told him to go to the Sudduth ranch, nor did he do any harmonica tooting or singing the next evening when he got there!

Dad had breakfast ready for Frank, Art and me soon after four o'clock. Dark and cold. Cold.

Dad said, "Our thermometer has frozen at forty below. But it can't be much colder than that."

Later, when we had a report from Walden, we learned that this day was colder than forty below, colder than forty-five below, colder than fifty below. It was fifty-six degrees below zero!

By lantern light, Frank and Dad began loading Frank's hayrack sled. Art and I saddled our shivering horses, but we used hackamores in place of bridles. (A merciful man either warms a bridle bit by a fire in cold weather or dips it into water to pull out the frost before bridling a horse. Even so we hated to put those cold steel bits into our horses' mouths.)

There were only five inches of snow, but how it squeaked and screamed under our horses' hoofs as we started out in darkness so chilly that even the stars looked as if frozen.

We had not travelled a half a mile before our horses' coats were rimmed with frost; our coats, mittens, chaps were white with it; our breath and our horses' breath were streams of white fog, like smoke but not warm smoke.

Icicles formed in the horses' nostrils and they'd jerk their heads down to rub noses against sagebrush or earth. I have heard that these

305

icicles get so bad they will clog a horse's nostrils and shut off his breathing. But I have never seen it happen.

We'd walk a hundred yards, beating ourselves and stamping our feet to keep from freezing, then ride a half mile and walk again, but with no thought of turning back.

Daylight had come before we reached the Two Bar Two, ten miles from home. The men had already gone out to work, but we knew Mrs. Harry Green, who'd once been Bessie Langhoff, was there, and pushing our horses into the barn we made a beeline for the main house. Bessie welcomed us and immediately made fresh coffee, while Art yanked off his overshoes and put his feet up against the big heating stove. He was wearing light-weight, one-buckle riding overshoes over boots. I had big and roomy four-buckle overshoes and had put one layer of newspaper between my socks and shoes, another between shoes and overshoes.

My feet were cold, but not frozen. Art's were—and he thawed them out by the hot stove! By the time we hit our saddles again, he fully realized something was terribly wrong, for he could not stand the pain of putting his feet in his stirrups.

The sun was now up, but it was the coldest sun I ever looked at. On we went, for another five miles to the deserted Sudduth ranch then up along its meadow to Al Marr's lower field. Here we found Al himself and three cowpunchers rounding up about a thousand cattle. Old Al's nose was fire red and long tobacco juice icicles dangled from each side of his mustache.

"You're late," he said gruffly. "It's after nine o'clock. What kept you so long?"

Both Al and Bill Marr were gruff-spoken men. Both had a habit of pulling down their heavy eyebrows and glowering at a fellow so he'd naturally think they were cranky as balky mules. Actually, however, they were kindly, humorous, warm-hearted men, loyal friends.

"Stopped at the Two Bar to get warm," Art answered. "Thawed out my feet, and now I know they were frozen."

"Lad," said Al Marr, "ye'd better go 'long to my house. We've a telephone and ye can call the doctor. I'll cut out your cattle."

"Thanks, but I'm here and I'll cut 'em out," Art said.

Tight-jawed with pain, riding with feet hanging free of stirrups, he put his good horse, Mac, to work popping Payne cattle out of Marr's herd, often a dozen or twenty at a time. The two bunches of cattle had not been together long enough to get acquainted with each other and thoroughly mixed up, so my brother was able to slash small bunches free of the big herd.

I held the cut, and, the job finished, Al drove his herd up the river, while we put our cattle back into the Sudduth field and patched up the fence. Then we pushed the cattle on down to where the buildings stood lifeless, unoccupied and cold. So cold! But here with sled runners howling against the dry snow came Frank Payson, looking awfully unhappy, but not frozen.

Art gave us a hand to lift the cook stove off the hayrack and set it up in the house; then he said, "I can't stay here to help you two. I've got to do something about my feet."

"We'll make out," I told him. "Get to the Two Bar fast as you can and get those boots off. Maybe Bessie'll know what's best to do. Maybe you better phone for a doctor."

Art stayed with Harry and Bessie Green that night and rode home the next day. Although he did not loose his feet, all of his toenails came off, and dead skin kept peeling off for several months thereafter.

Frank and I had to make camp in the empty house. We unloaded all the equipment he'd brought, then drove to the nearest haystack, hauled out one load of hay to the cattle to keep them quiet, and also a jag for the stable. The river ran close to the buildings, and we opened up a water hole, watered the horses, including Frank's mount which he had led behind the hayrack, stalled and fed them all.

It was full dark by this time. We hacked up some firewood by lantern light, closed all connecting doors to one room of the old house where we had put up the stove, and made a fire. Now to get supper. I had coffee at the Two Bar but neither of us had eaten since four-thirty that morning, and all of the food, except a sack of potatoes which Frank had rolled inside his bed, was frozen solid.

We didn't bother with potatoes, but soon had a loaf of bread thawing out in the oven, a can of corn thawing atop the red-hot stove and the coffeepot boiling. Then with an axe we chopped slivers of ice-like beef from the quarter of beef—and fried the slivers. Few meals have ever tasted better.

The only furniture was a couple of old tables, some wrecked chairs and a cupboard, so we spread out the bed on the floor—oh! but that floor was cold!—pulled off our footwear only, bundled our feet up in whatever came to hand, and crawled in with all the rest of our clothes on, including our caps. We kept the sack of potatoes as our bedfellow to keep those precious spuds from freezing.

The next day dawned bright and after sunrise became a great deal warmer. Even so, Frank was still "tromping all over his lower lip." The previous evening I had tried to cheer him with light talk, but he had acted as if he'd never, never smile again.

I still had the fear he'd quit, just say, "To H - - - with it," get on his horse and ride out—which would put me on the spot. I'd have to stay on the job until Dad got another man and no telling how long that might be. But although Frank hated this job, something in him—perhaps the way he'd been brought up—wouldn't let him quit. If he did, he could not face up to the stigma of being called a quitter and he'd despise himself.

We fed the cattle and opened a water hole for them, and I showed Frank everything about the job, told him exactly what would be expected of him. He still wasn't talking. All I got were nods indicating that he understood. Finally, when I was ready to leave the place, I said, "Well, so-long, Frank. I know you'll make out just dandy."

"Yeah, I'll make out. But not just dandy!"

A week later I returned to the Sudduth place with a pack-horse-load of grub and other items for Frank, dreading the reception I might get. But lo! Frank welcomed me with a big grin and a "Glad to see you," followed by a cheerful laugh.

He was once again his old boyish, optimistic and enthusiastic self. Marvelling over this change I asked, "What happened to . . . well, to . . .?"

"Oh, this is not a bad spot after all. I met a nice fellow on the Kerr ranch and we've been visiting back and forth. But," and his eyes sparkled, "better still, Dr. Henry Fisher, the dentist, and two other men from Walden came and stayed with me a couple of nights.

"They knew what I didn't know. Those foothills . . . " He waved a hand toward the hills bordering the mountains—"*are full of deer!* I went hunting with Doc Henry and got a buck. It's hanging up in one room of the house. Like venison for supper?"

I liked venison for supper! Afterwards Frank showed me how he had built a bunk in one of the rooms adjoining the kitchen. By leaving the door open, he now had a fairly warm bedroom. Then he showed me his guns as if I'd never seen them before. Finally, he produced his harmonica and filled the warm kitchen of a house no longer unhomelike with music!

RATTLESNAKE JACK

The winter of 1909 and 1910 when Dad had cattle on the Sudduth ranch will forever be remembered in North Park for the very coldest day on record and also as the "Winter of the Wolves."

For all of my life, I had listened to the coyotes' "yip-yip-yip—yoow-ie" but had never heard a wolf, to say nothing of having seen one. We simply did not have the big grey timber wolves in North Park. We didn't have them until . . .

On the home ranch, late in December, Dad, Art and I rode out into the field to corral cows and calves in order to wean the calves. The cattle were grazing on rank grass along a big slough. Suddenly I saw the carcass of a big calf, almost completely devoured, and all around it coyote tracks by the score.

Had this calf died of blackleg? How had the coyotes found it so quickly? And why so darned many coyotes?

Farther up the slough Art and Dad found the remains of another animal—and coyote tracks. Then all of us noticed a dejected looking lame calf, lame because a big piece of flesh had been torn out of its hip just above the hock joint.

Wolves bring down their prey by "hamstringing" it. Deer, horses, cattle or what have you, the wolf attacks from behind, leaping in and biting its victim just above the hock joint. If this bite is successful it either rips loose or severs the great tendon, corresponding in a human to the tendon of Achilles. Instantly the power of the injured leg is gone, the attacked critter falls, and, having hamstrung its victim, the wolf, or the pack, move in for the kill and for the feast.

Somehow, possibly by scent, coyotes always know when wolves are about. Certainly not by sound, for wolves make no noise where they are hunting.

(There may be exceptions, for I have read stories which contradict the above flat statement—stories, written by reliable men, in which the wolves howled before starting out to hunt and howled as they killed their victims. Yet, to my certain knowledge, the wolf pack which invaded North Park did its savage work always silently and always at night. Nor did we at any time hear one or more of them howl.)

We Paynes were worried but didn't think the matter too serious until a few days later when Harry Green came to the ranch and said: "Wolves hit our cattle last night, killed both a fat two-year-old heifer and a fat three-year-old."

"Wolves? Sure it was wolves?"

"Yes. Couldn't have been anything else, though we couldn't find their tracks for the coyote tracks."

The very next night, near Spicer in the south end of the Park, wolves stampeded a herd of cattle, killed three and left a heifer with its tail completely skinned. Doubtless the wolf missed his grab at the tendon, and his jaws closed on the tail.

No one yet had actually seen the wolves, but here was ample proof that a pack of them had come to the Park. A hurry-up meeting of the Stock Growers' Association was called at which the members voted a bounty of seventy-five dollars for each wolf killed and also sent for the famous Wyoming wolfer, Rattlesnake Jack.

Rattlesnake Jack had accomplished wonders in certain areas in Wyoming, ridding ranges of wolves where ordinary trappers had failed utterly. Such was this man's reputation that North Park stockmen pinned their hopes on him. But he was very slow in responding to their urgent summons. Meanwhile the wolf pack continued its ruthless slaughter.

Following the initial cold snap we were now blessed with a milder than average winter. Consequently, the stage, freighters and other teamsters were still using the road along the lane north of the Payne ranch.

One January day a rider came dashing into the ranch and reported breathlessly: "Last night, wolves killed a deer in the lane within a quarter mile of your buildings. Did you hear 'em?"

We had heard nothing! I saddled a horse and rode out to the lane where the snow was trampled down by coyotes. The trails came in from every direction to this one spot where all that could now be found of the deer were the skull, antlers and some of its leg bones.

By circling far to the north, I found tracks showing clearly how wolves—at least four of them—had chased this deer down from Sentinel Peak, leaving trails like horses in the soft snow. How that deer had been running! But they had overtaken it at the lane. On this foray, however, the wolves killed none of our cattle, and we heard nothing more of their activities for three weeks.

Then they made their presence known again. Striking at Uncle Jack Hunter's, they killed and ate a colt, swept on along to the Payne ranch where they feasted upon two prime fat heifers, and the following night struck at the Sudduth ranch, fifteen miles away. Again they picked two choice fat heifers. Two days later the killers were in the Spicer neighborhood, thirty-odd miles from the Sudduth ranch, and had themselves yet another feast.

Came then reports of their killings on the west side of the Park, but all too soon they were back again to favor Jack Payne with a visit. By this time we had moved our main herd from the home ranch to the Mendenhall place, and there the wolves destroyed two more of our choice heifers; then at the Two Bar Two they slaughtered three cattle, and, after lying low for several days, they struck again at the Sudduth ranch.

Lindsey Coe, who was at home this winter with his father, Bob Coe, got another man to help him, and they tried to track these wolves on horseback, armed, you may be sure, with high power rifles. Lindsey tracked the pack from our ranch up behind the lower Sand Hills. Here the wolves took to jackpine timber on the mountain sides, going through windfalls, down into gulches and out of them again, places where it was impossible for a horse to travel. Nor could a man on skis or snowshoes have followed their trail.

Lindsey had to admit failure, and desperate ranchers and others set out traps. But nobody caught even one wolf, and nobody ever saw them or could predict when and where they'd strike next.

Then, at last, came Rattlesnake Jack and his son, known as "Little

Rattle." They appeared at our ranch with a team and a rig, loaded with all their equipment, and three mongrel dogs.

I had the job of feeding our cattle at the Mendenhall place. To do this, I left a hayrack there and drove a team hitched to a light sleigh back and forth each day. On the day that Rattlesnake Jack showed up, I was coming home when, still a quarter mile of the house, I knew some stranger was there. For any normal human could smell Rattlesnake Jack a full quarter mile away!

He was a heavy-set man past middle age, with a meaty face and strange, bloodshot wild-animal eyes, always affected by the dope he could not live without. He used fifty cents worth of morphine each day, which our doctor P. W. Fisher at Walden let him have or the man would have gone nuts.

He had sort of scattered whiskers of a nondescript color, neither grey nor brown nor white. Layers of dirt caked on his skin gave his face an odd color and probably influenced the color of his beard and mustache.

I actually know very little of his past, but we heard that he enjoyed rattlesnakes as food and that a fellow who'd gotten storm-bound and was obliged to stop with Jack overnight swore he was offered a choice of fried rattlesnake or fried skunk. He pleaded sudden loss of appetite.

Once upon a time Rattlesnake had worked in a circus side show with a rattlesnake act. He, himself, when I got to know him, boasted, "I'm the only man livin' can handle rattlesnakes with their fangs in. All other rattlesnake charmers pull their fangs 'fore they touch 'em."

Some folks said Jack was so full of dope (morphine) that a snake bite had no effect on him.

I do know first hand that one of his favorite dishes was fried or stewed muskrat. No doubt, he had a real last name, but I never heard it mentioned. He was just Jack or Rattlesnake Jack, and his son was "Little Rattle."

Not that Little Rattle was undersized. He was a husky six-footer, in his late twenties, not so unwashed and loud smelling as his father, yet I can't imagine anyone enjoying being cooped up in the same room with him either.

Jack and Little Rattle had come to Dad, as Secretary of the Stock Association, to make sure they'd get paid the bounty on any wolves they killed and to find a place to camp. Although it was late in the evening, Dad did not ask them to supper nor invite them into the house, and later I heard that Rattlesnake Jack bitterly complained, "That Jack Payne's an awful tightwad. Won't ask a man to a meal."

Probably it never occurred to Rattlesnake that no one except his son could have eaten at the same table with him, or even stayed in the same room. You had to meet Jack outdoors where there was plenty of real fresh air!

Dad suggested the wolfers go to the Mendenhall place where they could make use of the cabin and stable and get hay for their horses. They agreed that this ranch, close against the mountains, was probably as good as any in the Park for their purpose and moved to it that same night.

Soon thereafter the two men were setting out trap lines and poisoned bait, and, since I was feeding cattle at the Mendenhall, I saw them quite often. All three of the mongrel dogs had been trained the hard way to avoid both traps and poisoned bait, so Jack never had to worry about their being caught. They used their team for saddle horses, and, this being a mild winter, the trappers could move around in the open country, even on foot, without difficulty.

Jack said it was useless to set traps at a fresh kill, that the wolves would never return to it. But if you used scent, you could sometimes trap a wolf at an old, dried-out carcass.

All trappers are most secretive about the "scent" which they use to lure coyotes, wolves or other wild creatures, and Jack was noncommunicative as to what he put in his "wolf scent." But a man could smell the vile stuff for four miles, so a wolf could probably smell it for forty. A whiff close to would floor you, yet something in that mixture would attract a wolf.

In this connection, stories and rumors about Rattlesnake Jack which floated down from Wyoming said that when he trapped a female wolf, he kept her alive for several weeks and picked up and saved all droppings. So perhaps the secret ingredient of his scent would not have been too difficult to name. It was also rumored that, in some areas where he had operated, Jack deliberately turned shewolves loose so he would have an increase in the wolf crop and thus have future work.

I was driving to the Mendenhall one day when I found Rattlesnake setting some traps on the bank of Sand Creek and stopped to chinwag with him.

"Aw, you got to be smarter'n a coyote or a wolf to catch him," said he. "Now, here's a coyote trail leadin' up this bank from the crick, and I set a trap right here. Buried, of course. But Mr. Coyote sees that a man has been here, so he backs up and then he goes around by jumping up on this bank.

"That's where I fool him. Three traps he don't see are set right where he'll jump . . . And he won't smell 'em, cause I don't never use no soap and water. A coyote'll smell soap quicker'n he'll smell scent." A snort. "Them fools as use soap'll never catch nothin'."

Maybe one reason why my brother and I were such poor trappers! But, on the other hand, Charlie Porter, the best trapper I had known prior to meeting Rattlesnake, used soap and water freely. Naturally, Dad had thought of getting Porter to help with this wolf problem. Other members of the Stock Association had declared, however, that the best bet was to rope in a professional wolfer, which Porter admitted he was not. It seemed a trapper must have a specific knowledge of wolves—wolf savvy—in order to qualify as a wolfer and this was something Rattlesnake Jack certainly had.

The wolves' depredations were still going on full force but soon Rattlesnake and Little Rattle appeared at the Payne ranch with one wolf they'd trapped. This was the first grey wolf I ever saw, and it wasn't alive but very dead. Except in captivity, I have never seen a live grey wolf, and no one seeing a real grey wolf would ever mistake a coyote for one.

To collect the bounty, the wolf killer had to show Dad all four feet and the scalp and also obtain a written statement from two Stock Association members to the effect that they had seen the evidence and knew this man was entitled to the bounty.

Even though Rattlesnake Jack had brought in the whole wolf for Dad to see, Dad made him get such a statement from a couple of other ranchmen before he paid out the bounty money of seventy-five dollars.

Now, in our home ranch field only a half mile from the house lay an old carcass at which the wolfers had set traps and put out scent. It so happened that I saw Little Rattle riding up to look at that "set" on the same day when two men we knew came to see Dad, armed with a written statement from Sam Brownlee and Norm McDonald to prove they had killed a grey wolf.

"We've come for the bounty, Mr. Payne."

Feet and scalp? They didn't know the wolf killer must show the feet, but the scalp was still part of the hide for they had skinned the wolf's head. All four feet were still on the carcass of the wolf, which they had shot, out on the ridge east of Sam Brownlee's ranch. But sure thing, they'd get those feet, they'd bring them to Dad, first thing tomorrow morning. However, they were awfully short of money so wouldn't Dad let them have the cash right now?

Dad said, "Well, Sam and Norm signed this paper for you, and I believe you fellows are all right. Here's the money."

They had not yet gone away, when flying across the field came Little Rattle, so excited and burned up that his lips and even his grimy face were white.

According to him, a wolf had been trapped, by one toe only, at the trap set in the Payne field. Apparently it had pulled free and escaped. But Little Rattle asserted flatfootedly, "Looks more'n s'picious. Looks like that trap was robbed."

The two fellows expressed concern and sympathy. But when Dad told Little Rattle he had just paid them the bounty for a wolf although they had not yet produced the feet, the trapper, scarcely able to talk he was so mad, said, "Now I'm sure that wolf didn't get out of the trap all by himself!"

Dad said to the two men, "Get those feet tonight and bring them here. If there is any sign that this wolf you say you shot was caught in a trap, you'll return the bounty money."

Sure, they'd get the feet. It was ridiculous to think they'd rob anybody's trap. They shot the wolf and they'd prove it.

Still fuming, Little Rattle went and told his dad about it. Rattlesnake Jack flogged to Walden, no doubt to get some morphine, and there spread word he'd shoot those two trap robbers at sight. He'd probably have done it except that by next morning he couldn't find them. Both men had left the Park, nor did they return.

Two wolves had now been gotten rid of and the pack's activities quieted down noticeably, although they still killed occasionally. Jack and Little Rattle trapped a score of coyotes but no more wolves. Then one day late in April, here came the wolfers in their rig, accompanied by their dogs. They drew up in the yard, jumped out of the rig and dramatically pulled from the back of it the carcasses of four big wolf pups.

That was an eyeful! Four grey wolf pups, as large as big coyotes, and even in death the wickedest, most savage beasts I ever saw.

It seemed those mongrel dogs were really of some use, for it was the dogs which had helped Rattlesnake and Little Rattle to locate a wolf den in rough country behind the lower Sand Hills. The parent wolves had eluded the hunters, who had cleaned out the den however!

And none too soon, for North Parkers had chalked up a total loss of three horses and forty-eight cattle to the wolves. They had killed only one deer to our certain knowledge, yet no telling how many they actually had slaughtered. But this pack seemed to prefer eating beef, and Jack Payne's beef in particular.

Due to the setup whereby we had cattle both on the home ranch and on the Sudduth ranch, the wolves on their forays almost invariably hit us at both places. We had no answer as to why this was so, but, excepting the Two Bar Two where this pack did kill three or four cattle, the wolves passed up Dwinell's, Bill Kerr's and Al Marr's all in the same general vicinity as the Sudduth ranch to pick on our cattle there.

After suffering a loss of twenty cattle, mostly prime fat heifers, Dad and we boys were mightily relieved when Rattlesnake Jack showed us those four dead pups and said positively, "Our tough luck that both the old dog and old she was a mite too smart for us. But killin' their pups'll spook 'em outa this part of the country, pronto. You can bet on it."

He was right, for although one or two lone wolves did show up a few years later, our wolf menace was definitely ended. Ended, too, was my brief association with a most unforgettable, soap-hating character who made good at his profession, Rattlesnake Jack, wolfer!

NEW VENTURES

I suppose inhabitants of remote and lonely places always look forward with pleasurable excitement and keen anticipation to the coming of a railroad, and in an earlier chapter I have mentioned how the building of the Moffat Road into Middle Park stimulated North Parkers. But this stimulation and morale boost was overshadowed when, in 1907, we were assured that yet another railroad, not the Moffat, but the Laramie, Hahns Peak and Pacific, would enter North Park itself!

This major project had been started at Laramie, Wyoming, in the year 1901. But at that time tapping North Park was not contemplated by its promoters. According to their plans, the road, a feeder for the Union Pacific, was to begin at Laramie, follow the Little Laramie River to the small mining town of Centennial, cross the Medicine Bow Range and the North Platte, then strike Encampment, lead through the Sierra Madre Mountains and dip into Colorado striking Hahns Peak and Steamboat Springs, thence on to Vernal, Utah, and Salt Lake. Thus, according to the promoters, the new line would open a vast, potentially rich, undeveloped empire.

North Parkers had reason to be sceptical about the project as merely an Empire builder's dream, for six full years passed before a train actually reached Centennial, which nestles close under Wyoming's famous Snowy Range, part of the Medicine Bow chain. Then came an abrupt change of route for the new railroad. Swinging left at Centennial, it was now to cross the wide valley of the Little Laramie, climb to the top of Medicine Bow Range behind (west of) Sheep Mountain, and, by way of the neck of the Park, lead into the Park. Here at a station named Northgate, a branch line would take off for Walden and Coalmont where immense coal deposits were waiting for a market. The main line was to cross the Continental Divide near Pearl, swing down past Hahns Peak to Steamboat Springs, thence on through Salt Lake to the Pacific Ocean.

This was the promoters' dream, never fulfilled. But the road into North Park, ending at Coalmont, was eventually completed.

Naturally, all North Parkers welcomed this railroad as a major asset, a progressive step upward and onward. It would open a real market for the vast storehouse of timber on Medicine Bow Range, also for North Park coal and baled hay.

It would put an end to horse and mule freight outfits, and no one except George Post, Jerome Decker and Jake Hartzell, those doughty, time-tried freighters, worried about what they might then do to make a living. The railroad would also put an end to the old reliable Laramie-to-Walden stage line, and travellers would ride in the comfort of a passenger coach no longer exposed to rough weather and other hardships of stage travel. Ranchmen would be spared the work and hardships of hauling their supplies from Laramie, and—this the greatest of all benefits the railroad would give us—it would now handle all incoming or outgoing shipments of cattle!

No more trailing of herds to Laramie. Think of the saving in both time and money. Load the cattle on the L.H.P. and P., whisk them to Laramie and there turn the loaded cars over to the mighty Union Pacific!

Perhaps best of all, and certainly a comforting idea, no longer would North Park be shut off from the outside world during a hard winter! But let us look ahead a few short years to when the Park became completely dependent upon the L.H.P. and P. No freight outfits, no stage line, no ranchers hauling their supplies, no trail herds moving out, in fact no winter road open—and the railroad snowbound.

This happened all too often during a merely average winter. No train in or out for two weeks, four weeks, six weeks. Not that the railroad wasn't trying to keep the line open. It was. It put its snowplow ahead of a train, but if the plow got a bit too far ahead, blowing snow or a blizzard would fill the cuts behind the plow, between it and the train. Moreover, either plow or engine was sure to get "off the tracks." Ice would do it, and this was always happening, taking hours of labor to get plow or engine back on the tracks.

With a train snowed in behind the plow, the plow must run ahead to a station where it could be turned around. If this could be done, it plowed out the stalled train or trains. By this time snow would have filled the cuts behind it, so again it must be turned around to plow a path for itself and the train.

Quite often the L.H.P. and P. had to call on the Union Pacific to send a snowplow to rescue its own plow. Then, after untold grief, hard work and loss of time, once again a plow and train would come to North Park. Once again after two weeks, four weeks, six weeks of isolation we would get mail, and passengers would get home.

How did the passengers fare? They signed slips releasing the railroad of responsibility for their welfare before boarding a train at Laramie, or at any point in the Park, and took their chances. Once aboard the one sorry and aging coach, coupled behind a string of freight cars, they were without bedding, and often without food, until the train got through to North Park. Actually, North Parkers, and others along the line, endured far greater hardships than did anyone ever have with teams and saddle horses for their transportation.

Riding the Hahns Peak in winter was an adventure to be dreaded, even by the stouthearted. If a North Parker was counting on the railroad to ship his cattle at a certain time, he could bite his fingernails and grow a beard—and wait until at last the L.H.P. and P. got cars for his shipment and was able to roll his cattle out.

As early as the fall of 1907, when the rails reached Centennial, North Parkers began shipping cattle from this point. The new trail through the timber which they must follow was not plainly marked and a half-dozen outfits became thoroughly lost and ended up, in some cases, fully twenty-five miles from their objective. Owners of cattle and their cowboys were compelled to stay out all night without food or shelter and guard their herds. But even those misadventures did not stop the hardy North Parkers from making use of the new railroad.

They continued to do this as the rails were pushed farther toward the Park; loading cattle at new stations along the line. Then at last came the great day when the first train reached Walden on October

10, 1911. On this occasion Walden staged a rip-roaring celebration, and in a mock ceremony buried freighters George Post, Jerome Decker and Jake Hartzell.

A new era had dawned!

In 1906, my own adventure of growing up took an entirely different turn from anything which had gone before. Both Art and Dad had been East and now my aunts and uncles in Springfield, Massachusetts, invited me to visit them. I strongly suspect those good relatives believed I was a young barbarian and it was time they were taking me in hand to civilize me and knock off some of the rough edges.

I didn't want to go East, but Dad said, "I want you to take advantage of a wonderful opportunity to get a new outlook on life. This is your chance to get more schooling, religious training and to join our family's church."

All of these ends were accomplished and although I could write an interesting chapter on the experiences of a homesick country rube transplanted to a big city, my Eastern adventures do not belong in this story.

From Springfield in April, 1907, my oldest sister, Olive Mary, returned with me to Dad's ranch. Seventeen, going on eighteen, she took over the far-from-easy job of cook and housekeeper. Just a matter of course, something to be taken for granted, I thought at the time, but now I know how greatly this was to her credit. She was crazy to ride horseback, yet she couldn't feature herself riding astride as Mamie Leek and most of the girls were doing by this time. She must have a side-saddle.

Fortunately, the Scott boys had left an old sidesaddle on the ranch—the same saddle which, as recorded earlier in this narrative, Miss Hussey had briefly used. I resurrected it, cinched it on one noble old plug, the gentlest horse we owned, and ... Well, it's quite a trick to get a lady in long, full skirts seated on a sidesaddle. But eventually Olive "got set." I led the horse for a time, then gave her the reins, and this was my sister's first ride. Very soon afterward she forgot about the sidesaddle idea, fixed up a divided skirt, and appropriated Dad's saddle when he wasn't using it. She made a right good horsewoman and so did my younger sister, Elizabeth Emily, who joined us the spring of 1908.

One winter, far later than 1908, however, those two girls, with their toothbrushes and other necessities for overnight stopping tied in flour sacks behind their saddles, would start out on their ponies to make visits ten, fifteen, twenty miles away, thinking nothing of such a trip. Wash Alderdice, who was foreman on the Blevins ranch when my sisters visited Mrs. Blevins and her daughters, immediately dubbed them, "The flour sack cow gals."

I am reminded that the only equipment a man—any man— carried when he made a trip or a mere visit was his own pocket comb. Certainly no nightgown or pajamas. Once in a while some fellow would have a razor and a toothbrush. Gosh, he was a dude—and a heap of trouble to himself!

Toward December of 1907, entirely on my own initiative, I decided I was going to the State Agricultural College in Ft. Collins, which was offering a "Short Course in Agriculture." The tuition was free, except for a few books which must be purchased, and I could get board and room with a private family for twenty dollars a month.

(You readers may find it hard to believe that it did not, all told, cost me over thirty dollars a month to go to college. When I went back again the next winter, I got board and room for sixteen dollars a month!)

Perhaps the best part of this experience was meeting the college professors, splendid, learned, understanding men; also meeting boys and girls of my own age from all over our state, and other places. One young Englishman was from far-off Patagonia.

Early in the summer of 1908, our neighbor, J. S. King, who, as I have related earlier, had gone in for purebred Hereford cattle, came to Dad and said, "If you want to be the big man of this end of the Park, Jack—and I know you do—I'll give you the chance. Ill lease my ranch to you and sell you my cattle."

I doubt that Dad really wanted to be a big cattleman, yet he had leanings that way and Art and I—this was, of course, shooting at the moon—wanted the Payne outfit to be as great and important as the Big Creek.

Whether or not Dad really wanted to plunge, he was sharp enough to know that those registered Herefords were the best investment he could make, and he wasn't passing up the opportunity to get this herd. So, after considerable dickering, he closed a deal with

Mr. King. This gave him four hundred head of new cattle which we branded with a new brand, Lazy S. Triangle, on the left hip.

King kept his horses and retained some of the upstairs rooms in his big block house for the use of himself and his wife. My sisters were both at home, and Olive was delighted that she'd live in that grand house with plumbing and a bathroom.

We now had the hay crop on the King ranch to put up as well as our own, and for the first time we ran a full hay crew. Before this, our mowing machine men would cut down a patch of grass and then switch over to run the sweeps. But this year we ran two mowers, two rakes, two sweeps and the stacker outfit. I was a mowing machine man, Art was the hay stacker, Dad drove the pusher. Olive and Emily cooked for this eight-man hay crew, and we ripped into the job, taking first the home ranch, then the Mendenhall and finally the King ranch.

At the Mendenhall we always batched while putting up the hay, and we always found the cabin occupied by mountain rats. We'd either humorously or grimly go about exterminating the rats; yet no matter how many were killed one summer, there'd be a new crop the next year.

One summer when Art and Dave Hendrickson and I were camped in this cabin, we set a "figure four" trap to catch one bold rat who would not let us sleep. We should have made this trap a "dead-fall"; instead, we used an empty wooden box which would trap the rat alive. Soon after lights were out and the three of us were bedded, came a crash. The rat had sprung the trap.

"Let the stinkin' such-and-so stay there till morning," Dave advised.

But Mr. Rat made such a racket shoving the box around on the floor that he made us get up. I held the lantern while three grotesque figures in their underwear made weird shadows by its light. Dave got the axe.

"You lift the box, Art," he ordered. "I'll chop the blank-blank's head off as he comes out. Hold that light steady, John."

I still see old Dave with his axe gripped in both hands. Art lifted the box just a few inches and out rushed the rat, a gray-brown streak as he scooted for his hole. Wham! The axe fell, ripped into the floor, and how Dave cussed! But I burst into a howl of laughter.

We set the trap again and went to bed. The rat came back and got caught again. In spite of his racket we didn't get up, and, believe this or not, Mr. Rat chewed a hole in that box large enough to make his escape.

We lived on the King Ranch while we put up that hay, but neither Dad nor the girls liked anything about the "big, wonderful house" even if it did have running water and a bathroom.

Nevertheless, because the King ranch had a good bunkhouse and a big stable in which to shelter the Herefords, Dad decided to make it his headquarters. He and the two girls were still holding it down— Art on the home ranch—when I hiked off again to the Agricultural College. Within a month I got word that Mr. King had agreed to take back his ranch and the Paynes were back home—all of them delighted to be on the old place once again.

I also got word that it looked as if North Park was in for "a stem-windin' old winter." October snow had not melted and new storms had compelled feeding hay to cattle a full month to six weeks earlier than was customary. For the first time, Dad was "loaded" with cattle, having over eight hundred to winter. But in addition to the King hay, Art had bought hay for the outfit at a ranch up above the Boswell ranch on the Laramie River.

Shouldering what had been my work as well as his own, Art had moved a herd of cattle to this place, and the hay seller was to feed them.

While both Dad and Art were snowed under with work, I was having a grand good time in Fort Collins. My first winter I had taken the Short Course in Agriculture. But upon my return I found that the college had established a course in "farriery," the art of shoeing horses, and had imported a Scottish blacksmith to teach the students.

I'd liked the parts of the course I had already taken which had to do with livestock but had never cared about learning to be a farmer. So, I decided, "That horseshoeing course is my meat."

This decision, made entirely on my own initiative, won Dad's approval and worked out satisfactorily for me. Not that I learned the blacksmith trade in four short months, but I did get enough "book learning" and enough practical work to enable me—through practice—to become a first class horseshoer and a fair-to-middling all round blacksmith.

When back on the old ranch once again, I built for myself a shop, with Art's snorting contempt of my carpentry. I put four posts in the sandy ground, boarded up three sides of the structure, leaving the front side open. I left a big hole in one corner of the roof to allow smoke to escape, and then found I must make a gate for the front end to keep out milk cows and other animals.

In the northwest corner of this cubbyhole, I placed a forge fitted with an old squeaky and leaky bellows. Whenever I'd start a fire, black smoke poured out of the building as if a haystack were burning. Along the east wall I made a work bench. I managed to buy a good vise, good anvil (always in earlier days we used a piece of railroad rail about two feet long for an anvil), a drill press, hammers and tongs. Then I ordered a sack of blacksmith coal and a small supply of horseshoes and nails from Laramie and was all set for business. But it took me all of one long day to shoe my first horse without the help of our college smith's guiding hand, and it was not a good job. I showed, however, that I too possessed some of the dogged persistence which so strongly came out in my brother. I stuck to it and made good.

The gate did not keep the ranch chickens out of my shop and, to my disgust, the forge was irrestible to a setting hen. I'd violently route one from what she considered an ideal nest, only to have her return as soon as the forge had cooled and get settled to set once again.

But the ranch had grown to where there was a great deal of blacksmith work to be done, all year long, so eventually my brother built a good and roomy blacksmith shop and my original eyesore went into the wood pile.

Eleven other boys also enrolled for the horseshoeing course at the college. Where the regular four-year students had dubbed the Short Course boys and girls "Short-horns," they now tagged us farriers as "The Dirty Dozen."

Both winters I was at college I contrived to save enough money to get to Denver for the National Western Stock Show in January. It was often said that if a North Parker had his choice between going to Heaven or to Denver, he'd choose Denver!

As a livestock market, this Queen City of the Plains had forged ahead steadily and rapidly, and ranchmen who had earlier scorned it were now shipping to Denver, especially at Stock Show time. In 1906 our Andrew Norell won first prize for a carload of two-year-old feeder steers which sold for the astonishing price of five dollars and ninety-five cents per hundred pounds! (In 1957 descendants of Andrew Norell cattle were exhibited by a descendant of one of the Carlstrom boys whom Norell sponsored as a green Swede and brought to North Park. These cattle once again copped first prize as champion feeders—and sold for forty dollars per hundred pounds. Forty dollars per hundred! And we thought Norell was getting a wonder price when he received five dollars and ninety-five cents.)

Ah yes, Denver was the magnet, and for me the Stock Show was ... For real superlatives, I would have to call on our modern teenagers!

When I saw it in January of 1909 both Gus Dwinell and Dad were showing carload lots of feeder cattle, as were Andy Norell, Harry Hunter from Big Creek, and scores of stockmen from other areas.

At this early date there was no rodeo. In fact that word, adopted as the name for a Wild West show featuring bucking horses, roping, racing, bulldogging, trick riding, was not used then. But the afternoon and evening shows—events put on in the arena—were plenty good. And the cattle in the show barns and in the yards—I could have spent a week looking at them!

BACKS TO THE WALL

The horseshoeing course ended March the fifteenth, and I was eager to get home. The previous year I had wrangled a ride with John Kimmons, who had spent most of the winter with his family in Fort Collins. He had a team and a buggy, and a fellow couldn't ask for a better or jollier companion. Right at this time he'd just had a freakish cowhide tanned for use as a lap robe. It came off a black cow with a wide white stripe all along the back. We had this robe spread over our knees as Mr. Kimmons drove out of Fort Collins and a puzzled man signaled us to stop.

"Excuse me, but what sort of a skin is that, Mister?"

Without cracking a smile John Kimmons said, "That, sir, is a Rocky Mountain skunk's hide."

For a moment longer the man stared, then gasped, "Gosh, but he was a whopper!"

This spring of 1909, however, Kimmons was at his North Park ranch and I had to take one train to Cheyenne, another to Laramie, and then ride the stage as far as Boswell's where Art was to meet me with a saddle horse.

I had one lone dollar left, not enough to pay stage fare. But I knew Sid Lawrence, "Old Sid," veteran stage driver, with more bushy mustache than any two men should have had, so shriveled, wizened and dried-out that he looked as if a puff of wind would blow him off the stage seat. But Wyoming's gales at their worst had so far failed to do that. Sid was sure to appreciate it if I invested my last dollar in a pint of whiskey.

In the darkness of a cold morning, Sid's ancient spring wagon rattled across the bleak Laramie Plains, from which the snow was always blown away. But advancing daylight revealed the mountains ahead to be rimmed and loaded with the white stuff.

In the seat behind Sid and me, a woman began to complain. She was cold. Her feet were freezing.

"Ain't you got overshoes?" Sid asked, and to me, "She's a cook going to work at the hotel in Walden. These tenderfeet don't know nothin'."

"Overshoes?" She had supposed spring came in March and she would not need winter clothes.

"Lady, a shot of this'll warm you," I said, and produced the bottle.

Sid's mittened hands moved fast. He shifted the lines to his right, and grabbed the bottle with his left. "What you think you're playing, Johnnie? She wouldn't touch it nohow . . . Well, here's lookin' at you!"

With this Sid warmed up two ways, but the lady was still cold when we stopped at the first stage station to change teams. "Get warm in the house," I told her. "I'll fix up your feet in just a minute."

In the barn I found a couple of gunny sacks and carried them into the house where the lady was sitting by a hot stove. "Wrap up your feet in these sacks," I said. "Warmest overshoes you can wear."

"If I have to wear such dirty rags, you'll have to fix them," she said.

Flustered and embarrassed, I was still at the job when she asked abruptly, "Anything left in your bottle?"

"Wh-- wh-- yes. I'll get a cup and . . . "

"Won't be needed, young man. Give me the bottle."

Sid had already lowered the contents by half. The lady sampled the fiery liquid, made a face, and pushed my bottle into a pocket of her overcoat!

I stared a question at her. "A boy your age shouldn't have whiskey," she told me grimly. "And I certainly don't want a drunken stage driver. So I'll keep this."

327

Soon after we were rolling again, Sid reached out his left hand in a significant gesture. "Time for a nip, Johnnie?"

"No more, Sid," I said firmly.

"Have it your way," he replied in a peeved tone, and I saw my strategic plan to work the old stage driver out of my stage fare swept away on the Wyoming breeze.

The only road open into North Park was by way of Boswell's ranch. So from Wood's Landing we followed the Laramie River to Boswell's where I found Art waiting to meet me—and got another shock. My brother was growing a beard. His nose and spots on his cheeks unhidden by whiskers were burned fiery red, his eyes were rimmed by white circles where snow glasses had protected eyes and flesh.

"Hello, Art! What's the idea?" and I rubbed a hand across my face.

"You'll soon find out." He grinned. "And better hope you can grow 'em, too. If you didn't bring dark glasses with you, I've got an extra pair. Wear 'em or you'll sure get snowblind."

I caught on then. Snowburn is far worse than mere sunburn, and whiskers did help protect a man's face from searing glare of sunlight upon snow.

The outbound stage from Walden met Sid's stage here, and Sid would return to Laramie this same day. Of this he reminded me, saying, "The ride'll be two-fifty, Johnnie."

"Well, uh," I stammered, "I'm broke, Sid. Art, you got . . .?"

"Not a slim dime." Art hunched a shoulder.

"The company gets nasty and insists that . . . " Sid began, when the woman spoke unexpectedly,

"Here you are, driver. Two dollars and a half. I didn't find you doing anything to keep my feet warm, but that boy did."

"Shucks," I began. "It's not right you should . . . "

"Forget it, kid."

Charlie Oviatt put his head out of the house to shout, "Dinner!"

This gangling, loose-jointed man was N. K. Boswell's son-in-law, and at this time he was managing the old ranch for Boswell. Mrs. Oviatt was living in Laramie to send their children to school. So Charlie was batching but had two hired men to help with the work. In addition to getting Boswell's cattle safely through the winter, Oviatt had to feed the stage horses and accommodate freighters and other overnight stoppers, and like most everyone else he was desperately short of hay.

Because the Paynes were wintering three hundred-odd cattle up the river a short distance above Boswell's, my brother was able to meet me here. Art was keeping a close eye on those cattle, and on his frequent trips to the Laramie River, Art always put up with Oviatt, a sharp, well-educated, and clever man with a keen sense of humor.

Dinner over, we boys took a ride up the river. There was deep snow in the valley, but on the hills westward the sage showed through in a salt-and-pepper pattern. Beyond those foothills all was white except for the green of pines.

"You sure had it soft all winter," Art said. "But there's plenty of time yet for you to get a real workout."

"Just what do you mean?"

"We're facing the toughest fight we've ever had, kid. If we don't get our cattle through this winter—alive—we're broke."

"Broke?" I said, not liking the sound of the word and realizing I had been out of touch with what was actually going on.

"Yes," Art growled. "As you should know, Dad plunged when he bought the King cattle. He paid for 'em with borrowed money, every cent of it. He was expecting to cut four hundred tons of hay on the King ranch. The crop measured two hundred and twenty tons. How's that for a socker? Then, he had to pay King I don't know how much to get him to break the lease and take back his ranch.

"Next, this rip-snorting winter had to hit us, forcing everybody in the Park to start feeding hay a full month to six weeks earlier than usual. That's what makes our situation tough and grim.

"Now, buying the King purebreds is certainly the biggest and best deal Dad has ever made because, at weaning age, practically all the bull calves will bring fifty dollars apiece, where the average high grade calf will bring only from fifteen to twenty dollars. So now you can see that if—and it's a big if—we get through this winter without a heavy loss, Dad'll practically have it made. He'll be solidly on the upgrade. But if we take a heavy loss, we're sunk, brother, sunk."

"Why are we sunk?" I thought I knew, but wanted my brother's answer. "No winter can kill a ranch. Dad's still have his land."

"Ha! All of the ranch is still mortgaged. It'd take what equity Dad has in the land to pay off the debt against the cattle. A debt against dead cattle in this case. Savvy what we're up against?"

"Savvy plenty," I told Art. He was still wound up and went on:

"Everybody is up against it for hay, and not a spot of bare ground in North Park. I'm trying to get—I've got to get our herd here on the Laramie through to green grass, and yesterday I bought the last stack of hay to be found anywhere near our cattle. Five tons, one hundred dollars."

I stared, open-mouthed. "Twenty dollars a ton for hay?"

"Yep. That's how grim it is, brother. Not that we're as bad off as the Big Horn and Jack Hunter."

"Um? The Big Horn always runs out of hay in March," I said. "I remember Bill Marr telling Dad that he got the wrong slant on North Park when he first came. A couple of light winters, early springs, and Bill said he believed it would always be that way and never could get through his head that to be safe a man must have feed until the first of May."

"Bill knows what he's up against," Art said. "In February he managed to lease a big pasture somewhere on the Little Laramie. No hay, but plenty of old grass, and he moved fifteen hundred young steers there. Young Montie is riding herd on those steers and, at last report, was going to bring 'em through all right."

"Young Montie" was our early day partner, Montie Blevins, Jr., who had left home and was working for the Big Horn as a cow-puncher.

"But that move hasn't saved the Big Horn," Art resumed. "They are close to being plumb out of hay. A lot of the ranchers are talking of moving herds out to the Laramie Plains, same as in 1884. But in those days the Plains were wide open and well grassed. Now all the land is owned and fenced, and the people who own it are short of feed themselves. There's no place to put cattle if they were trailed out, no feed for 'em. None."

"You mentioned Uncle Jack Hunter," I said. "What's bothering him so bad?"

"I guess nothing's bothering Uncle Jack much. He's in Texas where it's warm, his wife and some of the boys with him. But on the old ranch, Joe and Ed, with eleven hundred cattle on their hands, are almost out of hay. Are they worried!"

We rode into the field where the Payne cattle were being fed. The hay was of first quality and thick willows along the river provided good shelter. At once my own interest in those cattle, which

I had helped to raise, returned, and it was good to see they were in first-class condition, strong, fleshy and healthy.

Art talked to the man who was doing the feeding; then we headed for home, twenty-four miles from the Boswell Ranch. For the first five or six miles there was very little snow, but all the rest of the distance, across the mountains through scattered timber, past Howell's Road Ranch, through Mountain Home Park, and then past Clark's Road Ranch and on down the neck of the Park, the snow was on an average at least six feet deep. Only the roofs of Clark's buildings peeped out of the snowbanks.

A snow trail goes over the top of the snow. Sled runners and hoofs pack the snow down so there are two parallel hard, firm paths. When cattle have crowded along a snow trail, the snow between these paths is also well packed. Wind and storms fill the paths with fresh snow, and this in turn gets packed down. The firm trail thus built up actually becomes higher in many places than the soft loose snow on either side.

All such high-packed trails are somewhat dangerous, aptly described by the expressions very common in North Park, "Falling off the trail," or "He fell off the trail." When a loaded sled slips to one side and the runners on that side hit into soft snow, the sled is then "off the trail" and may tip over and be bogged down unless the teamster can get it back on the trail. A horse or a cow may make a few missteps and "fall off the trail" into deep snow, or a man on foot steps off the hard-packed path and finds himself in snow halfway to his neck. He has "fallen off the trail."

Art and I rode home quite easily on that March day along the twin line of snow-packed paths which tied North Park to the Laramie River and the world beyond. Other snow trails within the Park led mostly along the valleys and through the ranches, to take advantage of cattle feeding operations and to avoid as much wind as possible.

But there was no road open across the range to Middle Park or to Steamboat Springs; no road open down the Platte Valley to Big Creek and beyond, nor was there a trail open to the newest terminal of the L.H.P. and P. Railway. Quite early in the winter ranchmen had stopped attempting to ship cattle from either Albany or Centennial on this railroad, and winter had halted its construction work while it was still, this spring of 1909, far from North Park. Except for the one and only snow trail to Boswell's on the Big Laramie, the Park was snowbound, cut off, isolated.

331

Both of my sisters were at home that spring. With Dad, they were holding down the old home ranch and he was fortunate to have for his hired man Dave Hendrickson. Dave, old Teller man, who had survived more hard winters than Dad himself, could, when a trail was invisible under a fresh fall of snow, simply "smell it out." Dave's rugged face was pitted from a bout with smallpox, much dreaded then as were also pneumonia, diphtheria, typhoid and scarlet fever, but he had the type of skin which does not blister and peel and was the only man I knew who refused to wear snow glasses. He said he narrowed his eyes to tiny slits and even closed one, then changed off and closed the other—and somehow he withstood the merciless glare of sun on snow.

All of North Park was white, except for the green pines on the foothills and mountains, the snow deeper than it had been that first hard winter of my experience as a small boy. Our close neighbors were not bad off, but none could spare even one ton of hay.

But Dad was optimistic, saying, "A few warm days and a chinook wind, and this snow'll melt faster than you'd believe possible. We'll make out all right."

Instead, came a new storm, a stem-winder, and when at last it stopped, twenty inches of fresh snow on top of the three feet of old snow blanketed our world. Of the road there was no sign except for the line of willow sticks—"trail markers"—thrust in the snow. No traffic had opened it, not even the stage, when Art started for the Laramie River.

His mount followed the trail, which neither horse nor rider could see, but Art turned back. "I can't make it without playing out my horse," he told Dad. "I can wait to get to Boswell's until somebody else breaks out the trail."

The new snow was settling fast, but all hope of an early, April spring was gone. Something must be done to save our five hundred cattle on the home ranch. But what? Then Gus Dwinell came to the ranch. Because his family was in Cowdrey, the boys attending winter school, Gus had kept a trail open along the Canadian from Cowdrey to his ranch. This was the route he had followed to get to Cowdrey and then by stage trail to our place.

"Jack," he said, "I've got to move two hundred cattle in order to save the rest. How are you fixed?"

Dad and Art had already talked over the situation, so Dad replied, "If we can get rid of two hundred and fifty, Gus, I believe we can bring the rest through to green grass. But can you tell me where either of us can buy any hay?"

"Didn't you know that Owen Case has from fifteen hundred to two thousand tons of hay on his Alkali Flats ranch? He's holding it at ten dollars a ton, the buyer to accept the old measurement."

"Ten dollars a ton? Robbery!" Dad snorted. "Foxtail! All that hay is foxtail. Cattle'll starve to death on it."

"Several men have already bought this foxtail and are feeding it to their cattle," Gus said. "Any kind of feed is better than none, and I believe our cattle, well-fed and strong as they are now, will pull through on the stuff."

There was further talk and I learned that Owen Case had a good ranch on the Illinois River six miles above Walden, and that he also owned at least three sections of barbed-wire fenced land, including several small alkali lakes on the Alkali Flats. This area lay west of Case's good riverbottom ranch and between the Illinois and Big Grizzly Rivers. Case, a comparative newcomer, had been for the past three summers harvesting the hay crop on this Alkali Flats ranch. No one had bought his hay simply because the flats were a terribly bleak place to feed cattle and the hay was practically all foxtail.

Foxtail is a pretty grass with a bright red or golden head, but, like bearded barley, this head is all sharp barbs which stick into anything they touch and keep working in. Foxtail is not of itself poisonous, but it might almost as well be. Neither cattle nor horses will eat it unless they are starving.

Now, in desperation Gus suggested that he and Dad buy some of this hay, throw their cattle into one herd and move it to Case's Alkali Flats. They would have to provide a team, hayrack and a man to feed the cattle. Case would board this man. Gus was short of help, so could Dad spare Hendrickson to do this job for both outfits?

Dad said he could, and, since some of our neighbors now had telephones, I was dispatched to the closest phone to call Owen Case and tell him what Jack Payne and Gus Dwinell wanted and ask if he could "fix 'em up."

Gus waited until I returned and reported briefly, "All set."

The next day Dave did all of the feeding while Art and Dad and I cut our herd of cattle, selecting dry cows, young heifers and young steers to take to the Case Flats, thus leaving the "calfy" cows at home. We had, however, a total of seventy bulls, approximately fifty of them the male increase of the King purebred Herefords, calves, yearlings, two-year-olds and some three-year-olds. Dad had managed to sell many of last year's calves, and these were mostly leftovers—culls—King had had on hand, a sorry lot. But selling the male increase of a purebred herd as bulls is what makes money and eventually Dad disposed of all of them.

We had to get this big herd of bulls off the home ranch to save enough hay for the cows heavy with calf. So we threw them in with the other stock to be moved and were all set to hit the trail the next day.

So far there'd been no teams over the road, but when we got up the next morning there was a good, wide, packed-down trail ripped out through the fresh snow on the line of the sled road, and standing woozily, hopelessly in the shelter of a shed wall were three forlorn stray cows. But the moment we read the brand on these cows we knew what had taken place in the night. The brand was Two Bars M. The Big Horn outfit had trailed out!

Only people who have been faced with similar tragic situations and have lived through such trying days can really understand what this meant. Bill Marr, staunch old Scotsman, had made the decision to do the only thing left to save the cattle still left on his ranches, possibly also to save this big herd he took to the Laramie River. It was a tremendous feat, a last ditch fight for survival.

Later we heard all about it, but the men who did this work didn't think they had done anything out of the ordinary, to say nothing of being heroic. Bill Marr gave range foreman Billy McGowan a job to do, and Billy did it with the help of Irving Brands and Tex Jurgis, old Bill himself and another man.

Starting from the Boettcher ranch those punchers put fifteen hundred cows on the snow trail with no place to stop and rest short of the foothills above the Laramie River. They strung 'em out, kept 'em moving slowly, but moving, moving all day long and all night long, weak and worn-out critters dropping out every mile, but the main herd going on and ever on. Hungry, tired cattle and horses; hungry, weary men. Deathly weary men.

At last in the sun of a new day they came to the foothills west of the valley of the Laramie River, and there, where sage stuck its stems above the snow, they let the herd stop and begin to scatter across the hills. Bill Marr had been out on the Plains, but had been unable to buy pasture or hay anywhere. Stopping the herd here was his last resort.

Charlie Oviatt on the Boswell ranch could do nothing to help Bill, nor could other ranchers in the vicinity, and for as long as I live I shall not forget the tragedy of this last-ditch, heroic fight. Here along the foothills there was no new grass, no old grass, nothing for cattle to eat except sage and quaking aspens and willows. Willows! The cattle broke into the Boswell ranch and got to the willows along the river, grubbed out the small ones and ate willows as thick through as a man's wrist. But this feed did not save their lives.

Tex Jurgis, left to watch this herd, rode around among the animals with a tweny-two rifle and shot all new-born calves, with the forlorn hope that the mother cows, which had no milk anyhow, might live. He gave away all the calves he possibly could to ranchmen who had milk cows, so they might feed the calves. But he had only a few takers and most of the calves they accepted died. Fifteen hundred cows the Bog Horn trailed out. I do not know how many they eventually took home, but the outfit had been branding twelve hundred calves annually. That year they branded less than four hundred!

SNOW CORRALS

Bill Marr's dramatic move created a great deal of comment within North Park. What, people asked, oh, what would have happened to other cattlemen equally as hard pressed as the Big Horn if Bill Marr had bought all of the Owen Case hay? He could have done so, for businessman Case was following a policy of first-come first-served.

Some men said, "We-ll, the Big Horn is owned by Boettcher and other wealthy men, who can stand a terrific loss and still not go broke. Fully realizing this, Bill passed up the Case hay so that other North Parkers, not so well-to-do, would have a chance of survival."

Bill himself scornfully disclaimed any such noble idea. "Hell! I wasn't trying to help anybody but the Big Horn. Never occurred to me to buy that domned foxtail on Alkali Flats. I believed I could save my cattle by moving them out, and that I did. That I did."

Be that as it may, at least a score of ranchmen were thanking their lucky stars that the Case hay—nigh two thousand tons of it—was available. On his Alkali Flats ranch Owen Case played host to more than five thousand cattle that savage spring, Jack Payne and Gus Dwinell being only two of the many cattlemen who took advantage of this one and only opportunity to save their stock.

I was destined to be on the firing line in the thick of that last ditch fight. This adventure began at dawn on a clear March day, for which we were thankful, as the Payne outfit made ready to trail cattle to the Case ranch. Dave Hendrickson loaded on his hayrack sled a bedroll, extra pitchforks and extra handles, two shovels, an axe, crowbar, pick, hay knife, hammer, nails, staples and a spool of barbed wire. Without asking Dad's consent he added a couple of sacks of oats for the team.

Dad tied a saddle horse for Dave's use behind the sled and told him to get Case's men to load their hayrack as well as his and then have two loads of hay ready to feed our herd that night at the ranch on the Illinois.

Art and I forced our herd onto the trail and, as had been planned, Gus Dwinnell, helped by one hired man, brought his cattle down the Canadian River bottom to meet us near Cowdrey. Here Gus turned back, Art took the "point," Dwinell's man the swing and I brought up the drags.

The winter trail led past Cowdrey to the valley of the Michigan at the old Moore and Blevins ranch, now owned by Hugh Hunter. Here we learned, to our dismay, that Uncle Jack Hunter's entire herd of cattle, eleven hundred head, bound for Case's Alkali Flats ranch, was on the trail. Fortunately, Dave had managed to get ahead of this slow moving outfit.

As has been said earlier, Uncle Jack was in Texas. His sons, Joe and Ed—still a mere kid not over sixteen—were in charge of his North Park ranch and cattle. Before March first, Joe had realized they would soon be out of hay and had sent for "Pa." Apparently Pa didn't believe the situation was desperate for he had not come home.

Joe, who simply wasn't up to shouldering such heavy responsibility, had, nevertheless, done the best he knew how. He had cut down, down on the feed, hoping, as had so many ranchers, that winter would end by April first. Now, at the eleventh hour, Joe had been forced to move the cattle to the only hay available. Cutting down on the feed earlier had already done inestimable harm.

Harm? "In what way?" one might ask. With the exception of the strongest animals, those which always manage to get more than their share of hay, starvation rations had taken the flesh off the cattle and pitifully weakened them. Here was a herd already tottery on its feet, hollow-flanked and hollow-eyed, moving to one of the bleakest, least sheltered spots in all North Park to bed down in a snowbank and feed on foxtail hay.

Strung out for three miles on the double file snow trail ahead of us, this herd crept slowly up along the valley of the Michigan. The ranchmen who lived along this route had posted themselves to guard their individual trails leading off this main one to their feed grounds or buildings and thus to stop any part of the big Hunter herd from swinging off on these side trails to mix with their own cattle. Had they not done so, the Hunter crew and my brother and I, too, would have had no end of trouble in keeping our respective herds on the main route.

Now that we were following the big herd, we came upon cattle wearing Uncle Jack's brand, Sixty-Six Bar, singly, in pairs and in small bunches which had "fallen off the trail" and of necessity had been abandoned.

Such brutes always fight a man who tries to help them, so I, bringing up the drags, made no attempt to get any of these stragglers into our herd. Joe and Ed went back the next day to try to save these animals, but most of them had died during the night. This was a desperation drive. This was a death drive.

All of our cattle were strong, eager to walk much faster than the weak herd ahead of us. But there was no possibility of getting around the Hunter cattle, so Art stopped our herd just west of Walden on the Illinois, and let them rest on an area where the snow was packed down. Eventually I brought the drags to this spot and was close enough to Art to speak with him for the first time since we left home.

"Think that outfit'll ever clear the trail ahead of us?" I asked anxiously.

"Don't know. We'll wait a couple of hours and hope for the best."

Something about our own cattle caught my full attention. "Art," I yelped, "thirty, forty, maybe fifty of our herd are snow-blind!"

He shrugged. "I know it. More'll be snow-blind before we get there. This sun on the snow is something awful. We'd be snow-blind too without glasses. Already your face is plumb blistered, kid."

"Think I don't know it? Sure making me miserable."

However, I didn't yet realize the agony of a snow-blistered face; cheeks burned and peeling, lips sore and swollen until a fellow could scarcely eat, nose so tender it was torture to blow it. Ed Hunter actually bawled with his painful snowburn, and he and I and some others put vaseline on our faces. That was an awful mistake! The grease sort of fried, and we'd peel off great patches of gooey, fried vaseline. Men tried sticking cigarette papers on their lips, which seemed to afford some relief to their lips. This was the spring when every man who could, grew a beard.

It was impossible to do anything to relieve the snow-blind cattle. Eventually they recovered with no serious after effects. In this connection, I have never seen a horse go snow-blind, however.

At long last we again took the trail. Late afternoon now, and sun glare against dead white snow hit us like a blast from a red-hot furnace. Again I was on the drag, Dwinell's man in the swing, Art on point. How well I recall passing Henry Boston's ranch, where old Henry himself was out in the yard guarding his stable and corral with a pitchfork. A red cow and an old white cow of Uncle Jack's defied him to drive them into our herd.

"Take 'em along with you!" Henry yelled at me. "Take 'em along with you! I don't want 'em here."

"Not our cattle," I said.

"Take 'em with you! I don't give a - - - - whose they are. Take 'em off my ranch!"

But I shook my head stubbornly and went on.

Far up ahead I saw two riders, bound towards Walden, meet our herd and wondered dubiously, "Will they try to force cattle off the trail, coming this way?"

A minute later I breathed easier as I saw the men jump their horses off into the deep snow. When eventually I came abreast of them, I saw them sitting their mounts in snow up to the horses' breasts, waiting, no doubt impatiently, until all the cattle had passed them.

Calling out cheerfully, "Hello!" and "Good luck, fella!" they jumped their mounts back onto the trail and hit a lope for Walden.

Incidentally, it was unwritten law that on the snow trails cattle had the right of way. Even the stage—the U. S. Mail—if it met a herd, had no recourse except to pull off into the snow and permit it to pass.

On and on up the snow-locked valley of the Illinois, the afternoon sun canting far to the west. To me it seemed this day would never end. Then at last, I saw the tail end of the Hunter herd go over a low hill westward and vanish, moving straight to its new feed ground on the Alkali Flats. They were out of our way!

Soon thereafter, against the light of the setting sun I saw two big loads of hay drawn up and waiting for us. Dave was on the job, and he had had Case's men load their hayrack as well as his for our cattle.

As the men started up their teams and rolled hay—bright green hay, life-saving hay—off their racks, it struck me somehow as one of the best things I'd ever seen, altogether wonderful.

This was hay grown on Case's river bottom ranch, the last good hay our cattle had that spring. He could not spare us any more, not even for our work team and saddle horses.

The south side and one corner of Case's main house and the stove pipe stood out above the drifted snow. But, oddly, the tiny bunk-house was almost clear of snow. The big stable was buried, and a fence had been built along its west side to stop stock from getting onto its roof; the entrance was through a door on the east side along a canyon-like passage cut through snowbanks. A long shed which hooked onto its south end was also buried, but these two buildings had protected the corrals and big feed lot on the river which provided a good water hole.

Owen Case, his youngest brother, Carl, and their father, two hired men and two women, one of whom I believe was Mrs. Case, were holding down the ranch. The women treated us exceptionally well, giving us splendid food and plenty of it.

But our first night in the bunkhouse was something to remember. Counting Dwinell's man, there were four of us. Dave had only the one bed, for which he managed to get a place on a bunk. Case's two hired hands had one bed, and there were six of Jack Hunter's crew with only two beds. Twelve men in a bunkhouse where there was room for only three double beds, a stove and a wash bench. But somehow we all slept, and I thought, "I can take it one night. I'll be back home tomorrow night!"

Joe Hunter had sent two men with hayracks and teams ahead of the herd to get out hay for the cattle. One of these was an old-timer and good hand, John Brien; the other was a practically worthless kid, whom I'll call "Fuzzy." Joe had hired two other fellows to help drive the cattle, but they pulled out first thing next morning, leaving Joe very short-handed for feeding the big herd. They wanted no part of that job!

Breakfast over and snow burns doctored, Carl Case gave Dave the information about which stacks of hay were for Payne and Dwinell and where to break out a feed ground for the cattle; then Dave drove away to get at the job.

Art, Dwinell's man and I, with the help of Carl Case, cut our herd and shoved all of the bulls and the weak animals into the feed

340

lot. This done, we took the rest of the cattle over the snow trail to the Alkali Flats ranch, a distance of toward three miles with snow about three feet deep all the way.

Once in sight of the Case fields, I saw something the like of which I've never seen before or since. Except for the tips of taller than average posts, no signs of fences were visible. Here lay a vast, snow-blanketed area which gave the illusion of extending, unbroken, to the far mountains against the western horizon and also for as far as eye could reach to north and south. This white desert was spotted by dozens of mounds. Actually each mound was a haystack. Wind had drifted snow around and over them until stacks and fences were completely buried. Several stacks had been opened, however, as attested by the dark green of hay against the universal whiteness.

In the foreground was the dark colored, closely packed mass of Jack Hunter cattle. They had been shoved to the right of the main trail which led on across the ranch to Big Grizzly Creek and to Hebron post office.

But it was neither the haystack mounds nor the Hunter cattle which so amazed me. It was other bunches of cattle, spotted here, there, everywhere, like dark colored islands in an all white ocean.

To be sure, I had heard that thousands of cattle had been trailed to these Alkali Flats before we made the same move. But I hadn't known how—how in the world—the individual owners were keeping their herds apart from one another, something which seemed to be impossible without fences. But someone had found a solution for this problem in the depth of the snow itself and in cattle's unwillingness to wallow trails through deep snow of their own initiative.

Each of these spots which I have likened to an island was a feed ground for a bunch of stock, impounded in a snow-walled corral! For example, at my left, a trail led off from the main snow trail to the first of these snow corrals four or five hundred yards away. This trail was the only inlet or exit to the snow corral or feed ground where the snow was trampled down hard and firm, while three-foot deep snowbanks all around it remained unbroken.

The man who fed this herd turned off the trail which led to his snow corral to go to a nearby haystack. From this stack, he hauled hay back to the trail leading into his feed ground or snow corral, and, when he finished his job, he merely stuck up in the center of the sled trail, near the feed ground, a rag on a stick. These flags were the gates which stopped the cattle from leaving their snow corrals!

It was hard to believe that flags would serve this purpose. But they did; at least twelve different bunches of cattle were held on their individual feed grounds—held in their snow corrals—in this manner.

With the exception of Uncle Jack's crew and of the Payne-Dwinell crew, the men who fed these cattle did not put up with Owen Case but came each day to do the work. They came from the Grizzly, the upper Illinois, the Rand neighborhood, the Spicer area and other places. Most of them left their sleds and teams at the hay-stacks and rode back and forth on horseback.

We, with the Payne-Dwinell herd, pushed our cattle right through the Hunter bunch and went on to another field, as marked by a wire gate hung on posts stuck in the snow, to the place where we were to feed the critters. This was the second field and there was still another beyond it, three in all, each with a full quota of snow-corral feed grounds. Bunches of cattle dotted all over three sections of land—where no land could be seen. None of the cattle were getting any water except as snow melted and afforded them a supply. Other-wise, all were licking snow. None had shelter of any kind. But here, here was the life-saving hay!

Beyond the wire gate, Dave had driven off of the main trail and made a small circle to establish a feed ground. This, with his team wading through breast-deep snow, had taken so much time he hadn't yet tried to open up our first haystack, as identified by a long mound.

Art was busy on the point, forcing our cattle to take the trail which Dave had plowed out and I was closing the gate behind them, when Dwinell's man worked his way back through the herd and said to me, "That's that. My part of the job's done, and I'm pulling out for home."

Oddly, although that fellow made a strong and unfavorabl impression on me, I have forgotten his name. But he was a husky young buck and we badly needed his help to get hay to the stock.

"Hold up," I said. "I heard Gus tell you to stay and give us a hand until we got organized."

"No, no! Gus said for me to come home right off."

The fellow now realized how tough the job of digging out that buried stack was going to be and wanted no part of it.

Burning up, I snapped, "All right. Ride out. You're worse than a low-down quitter. You're a plumb stinker!"

Dave would have told him off in far stronger language. But at least I was letting the fellow know what we thought of him. And he merely grunted, hunched his big shoulders and took the back trail.

I helped Art push our herd onto the new feed ground; then we rode to help Dave and found the crust near the haystack would support horses' weight. Dave drove over the invisible fence to the stack, then on to make a turn and come back in order to be facing right to strike his trail to the feed ground. He stopped with the hay-rack standing on hard drifted snow level with the top of the stack, and the three of us went to work with shovels, crowbar, pick and axe digging and chopping snow and ice off the hay and heaving it to the far side away from the team.

Dad and Gus had bought one hundred and twenty tons of this hay, and we would get another stack in addition to the one we were opening. It was made up of six benches, each measuring approximately ten tons. Each "setting" of a slide stacker makes what is called a bench. If there is to be more than one bench in a full stack, the stacker is moved and "re-set" and a new bench adjoining the one already finished is added to it. This low and squatty six-bench long stack was wedge-shaped, wide on the ground and rising to a peak like an A-shaped tent. At every point where the benches came to-gether were great deep holes which fall rains and melting snow had filled with water, rotting the hay which was now a mixture of frozen hay and ice.

Snow, wind-packed against either side of the entire stack, walled in and bound the hay so it was almost impossible to tear a forkful loose with a pitchfork. We had to cut it with a hay knife, pick it and chop it and pry it loose, and the big holes yielded blocks of ice mixed with black and rotten hay.

While resting for a few moments, old Teller man Dave said, "By jocks, I've done a lot of mining of all known kinds, but I never before mined for hay!"

But our hay mining problem was no worse than that of all other men feeding cattle here!

Eventually we hauled out half a load—the team could not pull more until we really had a snow trail—and dumped it off among the cattle. They swarmed on it like flies on a small spot of honey and beat most of it into the snow with their hoofs. But this would help to pack down a feed ground, which we would enlarge day by day.

Another small load and another and another followed our first and by sundown of that evening Art, Dave and I, all working as hard and as fast as we could, got the cattle fed. We had dared to hope we might find some good hay. That hope soon died. All of it was rank foxtail, dead ripe, which makes it worse than if it is not mature, and full bearded, horrible stuff.

We still had to bring a load of hay to the Illinois ranch for the corralled bulls and our team and saddle horses. Art and I helped Dave to load it, then left him to bring it in and hit out on horseback. Late though it was, Art said, "I'm bad worried about the stock on the Laramie River, so I'm going home tonight and will get out there tomorrow." After a moment's thought he added, "It'll be a full-time job, and I won't be back until we bring the cattle home in May."

"Gosh, I'm plumb beat out," I said. "But I'll ride home with you yet tonight."

"Oh no, you won't! Dave's as good a man as we could have, but the shape those stacks are in even he can't possibly feed the cattle alone. You'll stay and help him until he doesn't need your help."

There are few jobs I've been given in my life I have welcomed with less enthusiasm.

NIGHT DRIVE

Thus it came about that for all of April the Payne family was split up, Dad and the girls on the home ranch, Art at the Laramie River where, so far as he and the welfare of our cattle were concerned, conditions were far better than they were inside the Park. But on the Alkali Flats, where I was now posted, worse conditions for feeding and saving cattle can scarcely be imagined.

King Winter had been kind in giving us and Uncle Jack's outfit two bright days in which to get the stock moved and settled. But when Nature goes on a rampage with tornado, flood, fire, hail, storm, drought, or hard winter, little man is helpless.

And once again, as if determined to wipe out North Park herds, Winter cracked the whip. Twenty-below-zero days, unprecedented cold weather for April, were followed by merciless blizzards howling across the bleak, bleak flats. Oh, the torture of that wind and snow when it hit a fellow's blistered, peeling face.

But Dave's team, as we drove to our work, ducked their heads and stuck to the trail when a man could scarcely see the horses through the swirling storm. We led a saddle horse behind the hayrack in case we'd have need of a mount, and we also took along a lunch and a jug of water.

For the first four days we stopped as we drove past the Hunter cattle and tailed up critters who were "down." Dave was a master at this and I learned fast. With the hayrack close by, we jumped up into it as soon as we got a cow on her feet and avoided being hooked or butted. But this difficult and dangerous work was utterly wasted. The same animels would be down again the next day—some of them dead—so we stopped tailing up Hunter cattle.

I was eager to get water for our herd, and Carl Case showed us where a lake was supposed to be, ice-locked and snow-buried. Dave and I broke a trail to the lake, dug a hole in the snow until we struck ice, then chopped and picked through the ice until at last we had a water hole. The water, rank with alkali, looked positively black, and it stank like a trapper's coyote scent. But we put hay along the trail and thus got the cattle to the water hole. One sniff was plenty for most of the animals; other thirstier ones took two sniffs. None sampled the water. They'd rather lick snow than drink the vile stuff.

The work of digging, chopping, cutting, prying out the hay, and getting it to the herd, kept both of us busy all day long. Often Dave became disgusted and I feared he'd walk off the job; simply quit. Then where would I be? What could I, alone, do?

After one of his particularly violent outbursts, I ventured to ask Dave, "A real man won't quit a job in a pinch like this, will he?"

Dave stopped talking to himself and stared at me for a few minutes. Then he said, "No. What the - - - - made you ask a - - - - fool question like that?"

At once I felt any amount better. Of course, I'd always known that no real cowboy ever deserts a herd, and Dave, though cursing and hating this job, measured up!

Any normal youth looks forward to his twenty-first birthday as marking a significant turning point in his life, and had I been at home, Dad and my sisters would have done something nice in recognition of my change of status. As it was, I secretly hoped that old-timer Dave, who had helped to raise both the Payne boys, would remember and mention this great day. But he did not, so April the fourth, 1909, came and passed like any other day, including Sundays. I celebrated the major event by digging hay out of a snowbank in a twenty-below-zero blizzard.

Nights spent in Case's overcrowded bunkhouse were nights to remember forever. Young Ed Hunter had soon gone home to look after Uncle Jack's horses. But Joe Hunter, John Breen and Fuzzy . . . the Hunter crew . . . occupied one bunk, Dave and I another, and

346

the two Case men the third. Our quarters were either terrifically overheated or freezing cold.

After supper we'd try to relax tension and be a little bit gay, play cards or checkers or study catalogs. But Joe, Fuzzy, Breen, Dave and I were usually so plumb beat out we hit the hay early. Often John Breen, who was of a philosophical nature, would make light of our troubles. Most cowboys have this same characteristic. No matter how trying and grim the situation, they'll find some humor in it.

John Breen's favorite song never failed to give me a smile or a chuckle. It was a parody on a well-known old favorite and exactly fitted one of our major irritations:

> Scratch, scratch, scratch, the crumbs are biting.
> Cheer up comrades, they will come,
> And beneath the starry flag,
> I have got him by the tag,
> And he'll never bite the hobo any more!

But it was not lice that were preying on us. I doubt that lice could have been as persistently irritating as foxtail beards. Seemed as if the darned stickers worked their way even through overshoes and heavy coats and britches. Our underwear and socks were filled with the tiny barbs—and fingers simply could not pick them out. Either a sweater or a wolly cap looked as if it were growing a coat of some coarse fur.

Scratch! Scratch! Foxtail was worse than the itch. I'd wake up in bed and feel Dave scratching, then I'd begin again, and in the next bunk, Joe, Breen and Fuzzy would also be wiggling, squirming and scratching.

In a different way foxtail made our horses suffer, too. Dave and I did our best to clean their teeth and gums, digging out foxtail wadded into each small pocket. Fortunately, cattle have much tougher mouths than horses, but later that spring, after we had the cattle back home, my brother and I roped and threw at least forty of them and Dad lanced foxtail lumps on their jaws and throats.

Although we lost a few newborn calves, none of the Payne and Dwinell cattle died. The same could not be said for the Sixty-Six Bar herd. One day Dave and I, driving out to work, came past a long haystack into which the Hunter cattle had broken. The men had opened this one and had gotten one bench down about halfway.

Now the entire top of the stack was as alive with cattle as an anthill with ants. Joe, Breen, and Fuzzy were yelling and using pitchforks to try to chase the cattle away.

Ordinarily, range cattle are afraid of a man on foot and will run from him. But those starving brutes paid no attention to prodding pitchforks wielded by Joe, Breen and Fuzzy. Finally the hay pitchers gave up, pulled one sled to the open part of the stack and, surrounded by cattle, started to load the rack. When they pulled out with a small jag of hay, three cattle were riding on the hay rack!

The flag-on-the-trail method hadn't stopped the Hunter cattle from getting to their haystack, but it did stop our herd. Nevertheless, some of them did wander along the main trail and broke through a wire gate to get into Fletcher Campbell's herd. I learned of this the next day when I saw a rider on a white horse cutting out these strays and starting them back along the trail.

I rode at once to see what was going on, and met a fellow who was an old friend, Carl D. Johnson. He was a young, husky, black-haired Swede, whose face had neither burned nor peeled like mine, and it looked as dark as an Arab's.

"Hello, John? How you making out?" with his heart-warming grin.

"Makin' out, Carl? Don't b'lieve I got it made yet. Have you?
"No, but I'm working at it."

As I helped him to patch up the gate, we chin-wagged at length, this being one of the few enjoyable events while I was a "hay miner" on Alkali Flats.

I'd first met Carl about 1900. Art and I were visiting the Blevins boys at the J R ranch and there found another visitor, a black-haired Swedish boy who couldn't speak English. He was not one of those who had been brought to our country by Andrew Norell, but was staying with an aunt of his on the nearby Tibbets ranch. All four of us pards thought he was the "funniest kid" we'd ever seen, but we liked him.

Soon thereafter Carl got a job doing chores for John Riggen near Walden and went to school there. Then, even before he was able to do a man's work, he hired out to Fletcher Campbell.

Campbell had a reputation as being a good cowman who was both shrewd and tight. Real tight. Eventually there came a day on his home ranch when a man who was helping Carl feed the cattle quit abruptly. Fletch said to Carl, "If you can make out to feed 'em to-day, I'll go to Walden and bring out another man."

Carl and his helper had been putting out a total of seven tons of hay per day, but Carl now answered his boss, "You don't need to find another man. I can do this work."

This so pleased Fletcher Campbell that he raised Carl's wages to fifty dollars a month.

Park Blevins, who told me this story, added, "And if a man's worth fifty dollars a month to Fletch, he's worth a hundred to anybody else."

Of the young men who made good in North Park many were helped and prodded by their pioneer fathers and mothers. Others who merit special mention received no such aid. Two of Dad Allard's boys for example, Arthur and Ovid, starting from scratch, for Allard's ranch was worthless and he could give his sons no help, became prominent ranch owners and cowmen.

Two more, standing out above all others who worked and fought their way up from hired hands to top-ranking cattlemen, are Victor Hanson and Carl D. Johnson. Vic's story has already been roughly sketched, and the saga of Carl Johnson would make a book; how this black-haired Swedish boy, by thrift, horse sense and hard, hard work, built up in North Park a million-dollar cow outfit!

But this spring of 1909 when I chin-wagged with Carl on Alkali Flats, he was still working for wages, while Vic Hanson, like the majority of our ranchmen, was struggling day and night to save his own cattle. I learned this firsthand during a howling blizzard when, through the swirl of snow, I saw a small herd of cattle approaching along the trail from the Grizzly. I climbed on my horse and rode out to help the riders get their cattle past ours, and recognized the tall fellow, pointing the herd, Victor Hanson—frostbitten nose, swollen lips, wind and sun and snow-chapped face.

But his teeth gleamed in a cheery grin. "Hello, John. Pretty rough, isn't it?"

"Why, Vic! Hello. Rough? You should have been here yesterday. Couldn't have seen your horse's ears yesterday! Has this mean spring caught you, too?"

"I'll say! I'm taking this bunch home, hoping bare ground will show up soon."

Naturally, there was more talk as I helped drive his cattle past our herd and then went on to help Vic and his man get through the

Jack Hunter cattle. When I returned to the haystack and Dave, I was feeling warm inside for having seen a friend.

On another day which happened to be clear, Fletcher Campbell came riding to our haystack.

"Hello, Dave?"

"Hello, Fletch?"

The two real old-timers peeled off their mittens to shake hands, greeting each other as if they were long lost brothers, and although I'd known Fletch practically all my life as one of the ranchmen who so often stopped overnight with Dad, I was ignored and forgotten as they "chewed the fat."

"By jocks," said Dave, "I always thought we'd never see anything to equal that spring of 'eighty-four, but this . . . "

"'Eighty-four wasn't a patchin' to this," stated Fletch. "If it had been, we never could have trailed cattle out of the Park."

He was one of the pioneers who had saved a herd by trailing them out, and Dave was one of those who had helped do this big job. So they rehashed those grim days.

After Fletch had gone, Dave was cheerful for all the rest of that day, and I felt pleased to know for sure that this was the worst winter yet; worse than 'eighty-four about which the old-timers boasted. When I got to be an old-timer I'd proudly boast about living through the spring of 1909!

The days ran into weeks, and finally came clear, warm days with the snow settling and melting and I asked Dave if he could make out for one day while I went home. Not intending to stay on this job, I had brought no change of underwear, shirts or socks, and was feeling both filthy and itchy.

Yes, Dave'd get 'em fed all right. But I helped him give the cattle an extra load of hay to help out with tomorrow's feeding and did not start home until after supper.

It was eleven o'clock when at last my faithful Bob carried me into the home ranch where buildings were all dark, Dad and my sisters asleep. I did not waken them. First I looked to see if there was wood in the bunkhouse. There was, so I built a fire, got two buckets of water and the laundry tub, heated water atop the box stove, and then . . .

Well, I doubt that a World War I soldier fresh out of the tranches more needed a bath or enjoyed one so much! And for a short time I was rid of foxtail stickers.

Knowing that Dad had his work cut out for him, I'd worried about him. April was the peak of the calving season and the long end of the "calfy" cows were here at home. Of necessity, Dad had three different jobs, chore man, cattle feeder and calf boy. Yet, as a matter of course, the girls helped with outdoor jobs as well as indoor work as much as they could.

He did have good help, I'd assure myself, and I now found him both cheerful and optimistic. Among the old-timers, and greatly to their credit, there was no whining and cursing their bad luck when they were "up against it." They took it in stride.

Dad said the girls had given him a big lift. They were saving the newborn calves. Had lost only one. There was some bare ground on the south slopes of Independence Mountain and Sentinel Peak. Dad had pushed all our extra horses out onto Sentinel Peak. They'd pull through, and he believed the hay on the home ranch was sufficient for the cattle he was feeding. Here in the north end of the Park, the snow always "went off" earlier than in any other part of it. Soon, there'd be bare ground—and the girls had seen and heard a meadow lark!

Art's report from the Laramie River, as relayed to Dad by the stage driver, was good, as far as the Payne cattle were concerned; very bad for the Big Horn, however. How were Dave and I making out? Why hadn't I come home sooner? Was it still impossible for Dave, alone, to haul out a mere four big loads of hay each day?

I said, "I'm not staying home, now I'm here. Dave and the cattle still need me on the job. We're feeding them all they'll eat, and all other men who have herds there, except only Joe Hunter, are doing the same. The cattle are still strong, but they are losing flesh. Every day a fellow can see 'em going down a little bit. Don't worry though, Dad, we are going to save 'em."

"All right, son, stay on the job and do the best you can."

I rode back to the Case ranch, and just a few days later several of the herds in the snow corrals moved out. As long as the hard-packed feed grounds inside those strange corrals remained frozen, conditions were not bad. But with the advent of warm weather, the feed grounds became a filthy, slimy muck. Dave and I unloaded the hay on the clean snow surrounding our feed ground and thus prevented some of it from being trampled into the muck.

Now at last the deep snow was turning to water; water hugging the ground, snow on top of it. Soon, too, ice would be breaking up on all the streams and they'd be running out of their banks. There was also grave danger that the snow trails, especially the one down the Illinois and on down the Michigan, would "go out" any day, and this hurried the Hunter boys' decision to take their cattle home.

Joe's older brother, Harry (not to be confused with Big Creek Harry Hunter), had come to give Joe a hand. Soon after his arrival, Joe confided to me:

"I sent for Pa. Pa didn't come. Sent Harry instead. Harry! He don't know any more'n I do. Pa should have come himself. I could sit down and bawl."

The strain had told on Joe; he was near the breaking point. But I gathered that his confidence in Pa (Uncle Jack) was unlimited. Pa was equal to and master of any situation. Had Pa responded to Joe's appeal, Pa could have produced a magic wand and solved this knotty problem.

Joe Hunter was not unlike many other boys. All his life he had leaned on Pa, depended on Pa to make decisions. Suddenly expected to stand on his own feet and make his own decisions, he was lost— lost and fearful, with no self-confidence.

Actually, after the situation got so completely out of control on Jack Hunter's ranch, neither Pa himself nor anyone else could have done much more than Joe had done. He was not to blame for the tragic mistake of using all of the hay they had on the home ranch. The decision to buy feed much earlier in the winter and to move part of the herd to this feed should have come from Pa. Finally, with all hay at home gone, Joe was forced to buy Case hay and move the entire Sixty-Six Bar herd to this hay. He could not leave at home the thin, the weak and the lame, and the heavy springers.

Unable to get more help, Joe had hoped that with two hayracks and three men he could feed this herd; difficult enough under the best of conditions, on snow-locked Alkali Flats where every haystack was buried, it was impossible.

Impossible because, first of all, there were twice too many cattle in one bunch, a setup which always permits the strong and agressive cattle to get more than their share of the feed, the weak ones getting very little. In this case, the three hay pitchers would load one of their two small hayracks, carrying not more than a ton of hay; then one man would pull out to the feed ground and scatter this load while others were loading the second hayrack.

Under such conditions, the strong cattle, as wild as starving house cats to get feed, knock the weak ones out of their way and even butt them down to follow the hayrack and gobble up the hay, often "catching the last forkful on the fly." Therefore, the laggards and famished critters get no part of this first load, and this same thing is repeated with the second load of hay, the third and the fourth. Not until, let us say roughly, seventy percent of the big herd have filled up will the other thirty percent get more than a few mouthfuls.

Joe, Breen and Fuzzy, working until exhausted, could not begin to feed this herd properly. Consequently, the feed ground was littered with carcasses. Day after day this awful toll continued and all newborn calves also died. Everybody in the Park suffered losses that spring, but this tragedy to the Hunter herd was the most drastic and horrifying thing I have ever seen. Dave and I were unable to help Joe because we had all we could do to feed our own herd; other men, doing the same sort of job, were in the same fix.

Harry and Joe decided they'd start the herd in the evening and "go through in the night." "Going through in the night" was the accepted move in the late spring when the snow trail softens during warm days and becomes easy for teams, sleds or cattle to slip off of it, or sink into it. But when frozen at night, a snow trail is still reasonably safe.

On the twenty-second of April, I was on hand in the afternoon to help "get 'em rolling." Harry, Joe and Ed, who came to help, and John Breen were the punchers. Fuzzy was to drive a hayrack ahead of the herd, so he started out toward the Case's Illinois ranch, and the rest of us pushed the big herd onto the trail. "Feeding them onto the trail" it is called, a very slow process, for the entire bunch must thin out to only a double file.

Someone should have taken the point at once, but no one did— and it was not for me to tell Harry and Joe how to drive cattle. We had a half-mile-long string of cattle on the trail when the hayrack up ahead came to full stop, halting the cattle.

"What's the matter with that idiot? Why don't he go on?" Harry wanted to know.

It was melting rapidly, turning the snow on either side of the trail to slush, a mess to try to put a horse through. However, I said, "I'll go see what's wrong up there."

By forcing my good mount through the slush, sometimes stumbling into holes saddle-skirt deep as we paralleled the snow trail, I finally reached the stalled hayrack. One of the team, a brown horse they called Jumbo, which I'd noticed had been wobbly for several days, had fallen down.

He was flat on his side in the water and slush and Fuzzy the kid was standing up in the hayrack calling, "Get up, Jumbo! Come on. You can get up."

"Unhitch him," I ordered.

Fuzzy stared at me. "And get soaking wet? I will not ... What's the matter with Jumbo anyhow?"

"Starved to death on foxtail," I growled, thinking what a good thing it was for the Payne team that Dave had brought along oats. "He can't ever get up unless you get him loose from the singletree and neckyoke. Going to unhitch him?"

"Not me!"

I tried to loosen the tugs by bending from the saddle, but couldn't do it. So I stepped down into the slush and water and managed to unhook the tugs and to free breast strap and lines. Then I took Jumbo's halter rope and pulled on it. Nothing happened, so I belted him with a strap. Jumbo merely floundered helplessly, unable to get up on his feet.

Soaked now to the waist, I took my own rope, put its loop on the horse's front legs, climbed back to my saddle, and used my horse to pull Jumbo onto a small hummock, bare and out of the water. Here I saw a colony of prairie dogs which had been flooded out of their holes. With no place to go, they were most unhappy.

Harry appeared. He'd decided if I could ride through the slush he could, too. After I'd told him what was the matter he said, "You're wet anyhow. Bring some hay off the rack and pile around Jumbo. We'll leave him here. He'll be all right by morning."

"What about the hayrack?"

"Leave it, too. Fuzzy can ride the other horse."

I told the kid to step out on the tongue of the sled and climb on the other horse, which he did, but I had to unhitch it for him. I also carried hay to Jumbo. Then, fearing my wet feet might freeze, I headed for the Case ranch.

It was now almost dark, and Harry decided to let the cattle move go until another day. He signalled to Joe and Breen to join him and they left the half-mile string of cattle packed double file on the snow trail. Naturally, nearly all of the animals turned and drifted back to the feed ground.

But the temperature dropped way down that night, and the next

morning when Dave and I drove out to feed our herd Jumbo was
dead, and, standing upright on the snow trail, feet and legs bogged
down in the frozen slush, we counted ten dead cattle frozen into the
trail.

This same day Harry and Joe moved the cattle by taking them
out toward the Grizzly and turning north to strike the road from
Habron to Walden. Joe had left the Hunter ranch with approximately eleven hundred cattle; he took home less than eight hundred.

We, too, took this trail out when, about the first of May, Gus
came to help Dave and me move our herd back home.

There was now bare ground in the north end of the Park, and
elsewhere the snow was melting, all streams out of their banks. Green
grass was showing its lovely shoots on the Payne ranch and Dad had
sent word to Art he could bring home the Laramie River herd.

He had replied, "Send John to help me. Two of us can do it."

So I rode to the Boswell ranch on the Laramie, and, at first hand,
I both saw and heard what had happened, and was happening, to the
Big Horn cattle.

Charlie Oviatt greeted me in his jovial manner, took a long look
at my face and chuckled, "I thought I had here under my roof the
toughest, meanest looking bunch of men who ever came out of the
mountains, but you top anything I've seen yet!"

Art was making his quarters with Oviatt and riding to the field
where our cattle were being held. Bare ground there, bare ground
on all the hills both east and west of the Laramie's valley, but deep
snow still held across the top of the range and down the neck of the
Park. The freighters had temporarily stopped trying to negotiate
this trail, and the stage was traveling it only at night.

Knowing this, I said, "We'd best try to go through in the night,
Art."

He gave me a sharp look. "You seem a mite jittery about this.
Heck, we'll get through, daytime or at night."

"Uneasy is the right word," I said and told him what I'd seen
happen to Sixty-Six Bar cattle on a soft snow trail on Alkali Flats.
"Ten cows were bogged in the soft snow and slush, then frozen into
it standing up, dead on their feet. The most starkly terrible thing
I've ever seen. Now I know a snow trail's as treacherous as quick-
sand."

He was silent for a time, then, "Glad I didn't have to see that
... We'll try to go home in the night."

There were over three hundred cattle in this Laramie River herd, not counting calves. We looked them over carefully and decided to attempt to take all of them home. None so weak we reckoned that they could not survive the long hard trip.

On the afternoon of the fourth day of May, Art told the stage driver, who was starting back to Walden, not in the daytime but late that evening, "If you see anyone coming out of the Park, tell 'em to keep off the trail tonight. Cattle'll be on it."

He promised he would and added, "East Beaver Creek was out of its banks and the bridge washed out near Howell's ranch when I came through last night." Another hazard for me to think about.

Late that afternoon the two of us trailed our herd down the Laramie, past Boswell's buildings where Oviatt waved to us, across the river on the bridge, then through mud and water, barely creeping along until about six miles from Boswell's we came to the snow.

Here Art, who was the point man, held the herd up, waiting impatiently for the afternoon to wane. The day was fair and warm, the snow trail soft—too soft. Toward five o'clock, the stage driver came with a spring wagon, transferred his load to a sled and went on. We held off until after sundown, then Art put ten cows onto the trail and followed them.

All I had to do was to turn back a foolish calf now and then, and hold my horse and wait. The cattle knew they were going home and they were eager to go—something which makes a whale of a difference in handling stock. Had the herd been leaving home, I'd have had to fight them onto the trail and keep them moving. Having learned through range-riding experience to be patient, I let the animals believe nobody was attempting to drive them.

Slowly, so very slowly, like a ball of yarn unwinding, the cattle moseyed after the leaders, and a big problem I'd feared solved itself. This was that the young calves would pile up at the drag end, all bawling for their mothers and all determined to run back. But wasn't I happy to see that mother cows had their calves right with them as they took the trail.

Stars were shining and night's chill had replaced sun's warmth before the last straggler of our herd was on the trail and moving. That long string of cattle, single file in many places, broken in others, stretched that night from Howell's road ranch to Clark's more than five miles.

I had feared that at East Beaver Creek, near Howell's, the cattle

356

would stop. But the old cows knew they were going home. They took the high water at the ice-rimmed ford as if they wanted a bath, and the younger cattle plunged in after the matrons.

That was good, but quite soon I found I had a dozen-odd weak and faltering critters to nurse along. If I crowded them, they'd either go on the fight or fall off the trail, so I gave them plenty of time. Quite often they would stop altogether. Then I'd let them rest until they felt strong enough to mosey along of their own accord. This nursing them paid off, for not one fell off the trail and had to be abandoned.

Slowly, slowly on and on through the timber in the starlight, and my thoughts went back twenty-five years. On the fourth day of May of 1884, Dad had walked along this very same trail, driving ahead of him his initial start in the cow business, eighteen head of mixed yearlings.

Twenty-five years ago he had homesteaded in North Park. That homestead had now expanded to a three-thousand acre ranch. From eighteen cattle his herd had grown to eight hundred, not counting calves. He owned a high grade herd and also a purebred herd and controlled ample summer range to handle both.

His sons were now bringing home, on this same trail Dad had trodden twenty-five years ago, a big herd of his cattle. Once those cattle were safely in his fields, the gravest crisis we had faced would be over. There'd be others, for we still had loco and poison weed and various diseases to combat. But surely we had reached a turning point toward a brighter future. Dad had succeeded!

Thus, thinking, but with no remote idea of what the future might hold in store for me, I kept my weak-kneed critters moving on the frozen snow trail down the seemingly endless neck of the Park. Eventually however we passed sleeping Pinkhamton and reached the sandy hill lying between Cap Fox's ranch and the Barnes' place. Here we were out of the snow. Here was bare ground!

The stars were fading out of a cloudless sky as, following the course of the old Teller road, I nursed the drag end of the herd along for yet another mile, across Big Government Creek to open range on the east side of Jack Payne's fenced ranch.

In the advancing light of day I now saw Art, the point rider, whom I'd not seen all night long. He had turned the bulk of the herd into the east field of the Payne ranch, where there was bare ground and new grass to please the tired and hungry cattle, and was waiting for me to show up.

"Got all of 'em ahead of you, cowboy?" I heard his voice.

"Yes. All of 'em ahead of me. *All of 'em!*"

Far down the valley we saw the lights come on at Dad's buildings, and the morning sun, as it topped the Medicine Bow Range, shone on the glistening peaks of the Continental Divide. Then moved slowly down their white shoulders until suddenly the high range was indescribably beautiful.

"Look yonder, Art," I called. "I've made a discovery. Those mountains are riding herd on North Park, on us and on all of its people!"

Date Due

MAR 13 1967					
NOV 11 '71					

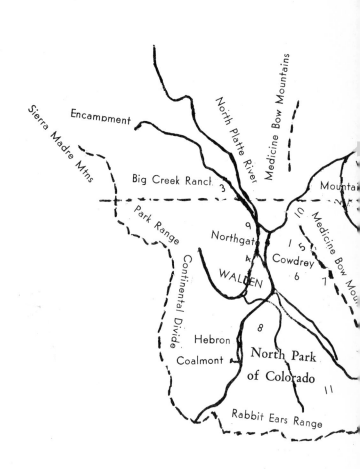